THE WORLDS OF LUCY LARCOM,

1824 – 1893

SHIRLEY MARCHALONIS

THE WORLDS OF

Lucy Larcom

1 8 2 4 – 1 8 9 3

The University of Georgia Press / Athens & London

© 1989 by the University of Georgia Press
Athens, Georgia 30602

All rights reserved
Designed by Richard Hendel
Set in Trump Mediaeval

The paper in this book meets the guidelines for permanence and
durability of the Committee on Production Guidelines for Book Longevity
of the Council on Library Resources.

Printed in the United States of America

93 92 91 90 89 5 4 3 2 1

Library of Congress Cataloging in Publication Data
Marchalonis, Shirley.
The worlds of Lucy Larcom, 1824–1893 / Shirley Marchalonis.
p. cm.
Bibliography: p.
Includes index.
ISBN 0-8203-1113-8 (alk. paper)
1. Larcom, Lucy. 1824–1893—Biography. 2. Poets, American—19th
century—Biography. 3. Women and literature—United States—
History—19th century. I. Title.
PS2223.M37 1989
811'.4—dc19
[B]   88-28660
CIP

British Library Cataloging in Publication Data available

Earlier versions of portions of this book appeared in chapter 4 of *Patrons and
Protégées*, Shirley Marchalonis, editor. Copyright © 1988 by Rutgers, The State
University. Used by permission of the author and Rugters University Press.

This book is affectionately dedicated

to old friends in Beverly

CONTENTS

ACKNOWLEDGMENTS

Writing this biography has been a long task but a rewarding one. So many people helped in so many ways that I cannot mention all of them. Several stand out and must be noted.

Elaine Showalter gave me encouragement at a crucial time and helped me find the center of this book. It was my good fortune to be part of her National Endowment for the Humanities Summer Seminar at Rutgers (1984), and I found it an unforgettable experience. Let me thank, as well, Cheryl and Jack Torsney, Mary DeJong, Joanne Karpinski, and Elizabeth Keyser for hours of talk and good company.

Friends have been patient and kind. To Cheryl Oreovicz I am grateful for steady, comfortable friendship since graduate school days, and for advice on specific questions in this book. My friends and colleagues Josie Prescott Campbell, David R. Johnson, Linda Patterson Miller, James D. Boyer, Carol Farley Kessler, and William C. Pencak all were kind enough to read or listen. Gwen and Jim Nagel gave good advice and encouragement. Carol Coyle and Phyllis Palson of Beverly provided the exile with places of rest. My cousin, Nancy Parry Blampied, helped me follow Larcom's New Hampshire travels one gorgeous week in October.

I have been fortunate, too, with libraries. The Essex Institute became almost a home; I do not think I ever had a question that its excellent staff was not able to answer. The Houghton Library, the Massachusetts Historical Society, and the Congregational Library were equally helpful. I have special thanks for Robert Perron of the Beverly Historical Society and Zephorene Stickney of the Wheaton College Library, both of whom showed me much kindness and helped a great deal. Deena Morganti, research librarian at Penn State Berks Campus performed interlibrary loan miracles. I think I must thank Harvard's Widener Library simply for existing.

Time and money came to me from several sources. The National Endowment for the Humanities gave me a Summer Stipend in 1983 and a chance to participate in Elaine Showalter's Summer Seminar in

1984. The Institute of the Arts and Humanistic Studies of Penn State University provided me with time to begin the writing of the book. Also from Penn State, the Research Development Fund, the College of Liberal Arts, and the Berks Campus Fund all gave me time and money for research. I am very grateful for this help.

    Above all, I thank Judy Donahue, who typed the many visions and revisions and somehow managed to stay calm, good-humored, and smiling through it all.

Introduction

*When I look back upon my life, I think I see it divided
into epochs, similar to geological ages; when, by slow or
sudden upheavings, I have found myself the possessor of a
new life in a new world.*

Lucy Larcom to Philena Fobes,
10 January 1855

Lucy Larcom wrote these words two months before her thirty-first
birthday. Although she was young to have assumed so retrospective
a stance, she was quite right about the pattern of her life, for she did
indeed move from one world into another. Each offered a widening of
her horizons, and, given the limitations imposed by nineteenth-
century attitudes about women and her own physical and psychological problems, this remarkable woman expanded to fill each new
world she entered.

Geography, occupation, and time define these worlds: Beverly,
Massachusetts, where she spent her free and happy childhood
(1824–35); Lowell, where she was confined and developed by the
mills (1835–46); the Illinois prairies, where she was teacher and student (1846–52); Wheaton Seminary in Norton, Massachusetts,
where she taught and endured (1854–63); Boston, where she edited a
magazine and became part of the literary world (1864–73); and fi-

nally Boston and Beverly, her bases as a free-lance writer and lecturer (1873–93).

Nineteenth-century American literature is so dominated by Olympians that it often seems as if only a few people wrote. It is easy to forget or ignore the fact that Boston (and New York and Philadelphia) teemed with writers—essayists, poets, journalists—whose reputations in their own time were very different from what they are today. From about 1858 until her death in 1893, Lucy Larcom was a nationally known writer. Her verses and articles appeared in the popular magazines and newspapers of the day, and she received quantities of fan mail that clearly indicated how well she suited her times. The twentieth-century attitudes that swept away the high reputations of male poets of the nineteenth century devastated the women, so that it is hard to realize that Larcom, Harriet Beecher Stowe, Adeline Whitney, Harriet Prescott Spofford, and others were indeed familiar names. The successful efforts of later critics to restrict American literature to what Nina Baym has called "melodramas of beset manhood"[1] have all but annihilated the men and women who wrote based on belief in a personal God, a sympathetic nature, and a clear definition of right and wrong. The nineteenth-century literary establishment valued form and message but felt the latter was more important.

I do not wish to suggest that one view is correct and the other is not; my point is that it is hard for us today to realize how thoroughly these writers, male and female, belonged to their age and represented it. It was an age that valued poetry as ours does not, that demanded the message of inspiration rather than analysis. Larcom, like her contemporaries Whittier, Longfellow, Lowell, Bryant, and Holmes, was part of her times; what she believed and said was what her readers wanted to hear, and they were grateful for her work.

It is not my purpose in this study to claim that a great poet's work has been overlooked. Rather, I am interested in the complex and often contradictory life of a talented, intelligent woman who developed her own strategies for survival and a degree of success in her own world. Earning a living and being autonomous were not easy, especially if one was to avoid being thought "unwomanly." Larcom, although she never achieved financial success to match her fame, did manage to provide herself with the kind of life she wanted.

Larcom's poems are topical, occasional, and autobiographical, growing directly out of events in her own life and in the world around her. She herself seldom called her work poetry, but spoke with habitual modesty of her verses or her rhymes. She began writing verse as a child, winning the approval of her proud family by doing so, and the impulse was fostered by her sister Emeline and confirmed by the editors of the *Lowell Offering;* by the time she was twenty the habit of expressing herself in rhyme was ingrained.

As literary works, the poems vary. Some, particularly those written while she was caught up in the emotionalism of the Civil War, are overstrained and sentimental. Poems based on local legends and history, many of which were written in the mid-1850s and collected and published years later as *Wild Roses of Cape Ann* (1880), are narratives that pleasantly tell Essex County stories; one of them brought her almost overnight fame. Her best poems can be classed as contemplative nature poems; they are informed by the widely held concept that nature reveals God to man. They are richly textured—she loved the outdoors and was a close observer (and a painter), so her descriptive details are precise and colorful, and there is a joyousness about these poems that is attractive. At her best she is certainly as good a poet as her friend and mentor John Greenleaf Whittier, and she appealed to the same audience. Technically, she was a precise craftsman who liked to experiment with verse forms, but who had an unfortunate fondness for fourteeners and occasional lapses of taste. She was never guilty, however, of Whittier's attempts to make his rhymes by New England pronunciation and other distortions. His "Little Eva" begins,

> Dry the tears for holy Eva,
> With the blessed angels leave her.[2]

Even at her worst Larcom was never that bad.

Larcom's fame persisted well after her death. She was frequently anthologized; in 1924 the *Boston Transcript* ran a half-page article celebrating her one hundredth anniversary; a newspaper from the 1930s on display at the Lowell Museum asks what Lucy Larcom would have thought about an impending strike. Although she never quite reached the top ranks, she came close; even at the end of her life, when her poetry had become almost wholly religious and was, like Whittier's, no longer quite in style, she was respected and widely read.

In spite of their numbers and Hawthorne's frequently quoted out-
burst about scribbling women, nineteenth-century women writers
had real problems. A talented woman was in a difficult position,
caught between her drive to use her gifts and the male-generated
standards of womanly behavior that, at their extremes, would have
made her invisible and inaudible. These ideas were in force when
Larcom was growing up during the early half of the century, and they
lingered.

All but a few women writers used pen names to protect themselves from the charge that they were unwomanly. Woman's sphere
was clearly delineated: a good woman ruled her home, provided a
safe haven for her husband after his day in the corrupting material
world, and brought up her children to be God-fearing, useful men
and good potential wives and mothers.

It was a religious age, with a strong concern for duty. The question, "What does God want me to do with my life?" was fairly easy
for men to answer, but for women, especially gifted women like Larcom, it was often hard to separate the voice of God from the voice of
society.[3] Why would God give talent, ability, and inclination if He
did not mean them to be used? The conflict lay not between duty
and pleasure, but in defining what duty was; it was a conflict that, at
one point in her life, brought Larcom perilously close to a nervous
collapse.

Larcom never expected to earn her living by her poetry, but, in
order to be free of the teaching she so disliked, eventually she did
support herself as a free-lance writer. Much of this kind of writing
was journalism: she wrote newsletters for papers, particularly the
widely read *Portland Transcript*; she put together calendars with inspirational readings; she compiled anthologies, including three with
Whittier, for which he took the credit—and most of the money.

She liked her prose better than her poetry, and worked harder at it.
Verse, which she wrote with much facility, took less time; once she
was established the poems could be sold quickly. They were a steady
source of income. She was right, however, in her judgment of her
own work, for she had a clear, graceful, undecorated prose style that
is pleasant to read. The closest thing to a novel that she wrote was
An Idyl of Work (1875); it did not sell, possibly because it is virtually
plotless and she chose to write it in blank verse.

In the literary world of Boston, she was a valued figure. If an occasional New York critic attacked her work, it was praised by the mighty: Whittier, Emerson, Longfellow, Holmes. She was personally popular as well; Whittier admired her serenity and William Dean Howells never forgot her hearty, infectious laughter.

It is not possible to tell the story of Larcom's life without talking a great deal about John Greenleaf Whittier. For talented women he was the best of the patriarchs; his support and encouragement was active and consistent. Biographers have treated Whittier's literary protégées with varying degrees of responsibility, ranging from the scholarly objectivity of John B. Pickard to the thesis-ridden sensationalism of Albert Mordell. Generally the women are two-dimensional objects. Perhaps a fair example of the treatment of Larcom appears in Robert Penn Warren's study of Whittier's poetry; after naming her as "a poetess of some small fame" he has a languid footnote: "Lucy Larcom was, apparently, also one of the ladies who were in love, to no avail, with the poet."[4] I have not challenged Whittier scholars point by point, although much of what I say contradicts them (see chapter 5, note 4).

In the case of Whittier and Larcom, the evidence of letters does not back up the romantic claim. Through their nearly fifty years of friendship, Whittier did help and inspire Larcom; in fact, in my opinion, he turned her into a professional writer. She owed him much, but their relationship was far more complex than biographers and literary historians, focusing on the male poet, have made it.

Nor was Whittier the only important influence in her life. Larcom was a child of her time, subject to the same currents and beliefs that affected others: the West, abolition, conflicting ideas about women, and new religious attitudes. The latter were especially important, given the belief she shared with the majority of her contemporaries that religion was the most important part of human life. Never a transcendentalist, she was strongly if not directly influenced by Ralph Waldo Emerson, whose ideas gave her permission to think outside conventional boundaries. While she could not accept all his teachings, his thought became catalyst and guide as she worked out both her beliefs and her behavior. From one point of view her life reflected Emersonian principles, always modified by her temperament, conditioning, and gender.

Immediately after Larcom's death, the Reverend Daniel Dulany Addison, rector of Saint Peter's Episcopal Church in Beverly, began collecting materials for a biography; *The Life, Letters, and Diary of Lucy Larcom* was published in 1894. It is a thesis biography: Lucy Larcom was an almost perfect being who needed only to slough off the traces of the Calvinism into which she was born to become an Episcopal saint. Summing up, he says, "Her life was one of thought, not of action. In their outward movement, her days flowed on very smoothly. She had no remarkable adventures; but she had a constant succession of mental vicissitudes, which are often more dramatic and real than the outward events of even a varied life."[5] Ann Douglas Wood uses this passage as an example of "the favorite tribute clerical biographers offered their feminine subjects . . . the standard obeisance to her insignificance."[6]

To make his point Addison suppressed and distorted his material. The passages he quoted from letters and journals were carefully selected—and sometimes edited without acknowledgment—to emphasize the religious being. He totally ignored the woman who should have been his most valuable informant, for Larcom's lifelong friend Harriet Hanson Robinson was, after all, that unwomanly creature, a women's rights activist. To show Larcom as a natural singer whose work was divinely sent, he says that she knew nothing of "verse-making" but had unconsciously caught the idea of "spirit and metre" from reading other poets; yet he must have read her own partial autobiography, in which she told how she learned prosody from the front matter of Johnson's *Dictionary* as a child.[7] But the "sweet singer" label, with its implication of an empty brain through which the breeze of inspiration might blow, fitted his concept of the lady poetess. The result of Addison's work is a simplistic account that centers on her religious development and all but ignores the less-than-idyllic elements of her life. The image he presents to the world is neither borne out by fact nor supported by the tone and content of her letters. It is excellent gentlemanly reticence, of course, but it is hardly excellent biography.

I certainly do not wish to discount the importance of religion in her life. It is true that she was preoccupied with spiritual matters, as were most of her contemporaries—a fact that twentieth-century biographers frequently ignore. The long and sometimes painful journey from the Calvinist dogma of her childhood to a kind of triumphant Christian transcendentalism that somehow found a home in the Episcopal church was vital. But Lucy Larcom was a "doer"—

indeed, she had to be, for her alternatives were total dependence on her family or starvation. To present her as a saintly, inhuman creature who did little but think about God is to give a partial view of a whole human being.

Since mine is the first modern biography of Lucy Larcom, I have tried to present a reasonably factual account of her life and to avoid being overly limited by a thesis. Accurate accounts of the lives of nineteenth-century American women writers are needed before other scholars can generalize and draw conclusions about them and about women's writing. There are themes in Larcom's story that are so consistent and important that any one of them could be called a thesis, but they all operated to direct her life.

Her need for autonomy seems to dominate many of her choices. In a draft of *A New England Girlhood* she contrasted the two Massachusetts towns she knew, sedate Beverly and bustling Lowell, summing up the two in the phrase "stillness and stir." She cut the passage from the final version, perhaps because it was too revealing, for it sums up both the pattern she tried to maintain in her life and her own definition of autonomy. She wanted both worlds and she wanted the control that would allow her to move in and out of them as she chose.

At various times other themes seem equally important. As a woman and a writer she had to solve the problem of a private person acting in a public sphere. There were questions of name, self, and identity involved in using her intellect and talent while remaining womanly. Independent though she thought herself, she consistently sought male mentors, probably because of her early relationship with her father. As a single woman she had to deal with her own sexuality, either repressed or channeled into her religious quest. Any of these issues might serve as a dominant point of view, but I have tried to balance the forces and complexities, using her letters as my guide.

Addison's biography is useful for dates and for parts of letters otherwise unavailable, but most of my information comes from nearly two thousand letters. These have been a joy and a frustration. Larcom and her contemporaries wrote letters as we today make telephone calls, and her letters are richly detailed accounts and observations of people, events, and ideas from a perceptive, intelligent, often humorous mind. My chief regret is that so much of interest had to be left out, for not only do the letters present the growth and development of a human being, they are fascinating documents of social history. Larcom's life spanned three quarters of a century, a period full of change and drama, and much of what happened is reflected in her correspondence. Reading them and discovering the person who wrote them has been a rare pleasure.

The letters are a source of frustration because so many were lost. Apparently she burned many in the last year of her life, and her niece, Lucy Larcom Spaulding Clark, destroyed the rest after her aunt's death. What remains are letters saved by her correspondents, but there are none to or from her closest sister, Emeline, or to Frank Spaulding, the young man to whom she was engaged and whom she finally did not marry. Notes for a proposed book about her years in the West were probably destroyed at the same time, as were some of her journals. I am aware, too, that batches of letters may lie forgotten in an attic, and that therefore some of my interpretations may deserve qualification. Frequently, my most helpful guides have been comments made in later years about earlier events.

Larcom's own partial autobiography, A New England Girlhood, which deals with the years 1824–46, is an obvious source of information, but it must be approached with caution. It is impressionistic rather than factual, and it goes lightly over the major traumas of her father's death and her first years in the mills. For modern readers the moral message to young girls is hardly appealing, but it is more than balanced by the charm of her evocation of a free, happy childhood.

Comments from contemporaries have been useful, especially Harriet Hanson Robinson's Loom and Spindle (1896) and her journals. The two women knew each other slightly as children in the mills and in school, although their real friendship and correspondence did not begin until 1854. Robinson provides, for example, the only available description of Larcom as a young woman.

After she was established as a poet, Larcom was often asked for biographical information, which she preferred not to give. Usually she said that her work was public but her life was private, but at one point she wrote that she would not give information about her life "because I have already done something like it—in my verses. I can read my own autobiography in them very well, and so can some of my friends who know me best. My impulse in writing them has been to set my life to music as best I could;—a life that has always had to be occupied with many things besides. In verse I have found the most natural and free expression of myself. I do not claim to have written much poetry; perhaps only some true rhymes. I cannot understand how anybody can take pleasure in writing insincere ones."[8] I have taken her statement as permission to use the poems to discover what she thought and felt.

Earlier I said that her life was contradictory; nowhere does contradiction show more clearly than in her attitudes about women. She affectionately but firmly rejected all Hattie Robinson's attempts to involve her in the struggle for women's rights. Indeed, her stated ideas about women are conventionally idealistic: woman was the guide to the spirit (like Agnes holding the lamp and pointing upward), the comforter and inspirer, and the keeper of the sacred home and family, yet she wrote some perceptive poems about women's lives, and she evaded marriage, living, by her own stated standards, an unconventional life as a single woman with a career.

Barbara Berg, in *The Remembered Gate: Origins of American Feminism*, differentiates between feminism and women's rights activism: "It [feminism] is the freedom to decide her own destiny; freedom from sex-determined roles; freedom from society's oppressive restrictions; freedom to express her thoughts fully and to convert them freely to actions. Feminism demands the acceptance of woman's right to individual conscience and judgment. It postulates that woman's essential worth stems from her common humanity and does not depend on the other relationships of her life."[9]

In this sense Larcom was a feminist. Never articulated and perhaps hidden from her own self-analysis, the dominant element in her life was her need to control it. Under the conventional womanliness that she presented to the world lay the drive to live as she pleased, to use her talents, to be the individual that she was. The need for autonomy opposed the standards of womanly behavior that were part of her upbringing and caused the conflict that troubled her for years, but, in the end, it was the force that shaped her life.

She praised marriage, home, and motherhood, but rejected them for herself. Her friends called her "motherly" as a tribute, and she accepted the term and extended it to her nieces and nephews—and her poems. She avoided confrontation but learned to get what she wanted by evasive strategies and tactics. She demanded privacy, yet her poems are amazingly public—a fact apparently unrealized by her audience. Her life seen today is at once a paradigm of nineteenth-century American women's lives and a contradiction. To live as she did, on her own terms, took a kind of courage that deserves to be known.

CHAPTER I

Free as a Child

In the spring of 1846 Lucy Larcom left her Massachusetts home to teach school on the frontier, at that time the Illinois prairie. Her departure was part of a pattern at least as old as she was: the movement of young people away from the settled East to the vastness of the unsettled West with its chances for freedom, independence, and useful work.

She was twenty-two when she left; behind her was a free and happy childhood followed by ten years of work in the Lowell mills. It was a family group that went west: her older sister Emeline with her husband, George Spaulding, their baby, and George's brother, Frank. Sarah Holbrook, a friend from the mills, came with them, for she, too, like so many of the Lowell girls, would teach and marry in the West. Frank Spaulding and Lucy shared strong, positive dreams of the future, and as their friendship deepened it seemed probable that they would share that future itself.

They were all young and strong, and the West seemed to offer them opportunity and purpose. George and Frank had talked about the West for months. Once the decision was made, it had not taken long to get rid of the little house outside of Lowell, pack up clothes and baby, and be ready to leave. Lucy and Sarah had only to give notice at the mill; living in a boardinghouse did not encourage accumulation, even if mill salaries had permitted it. Lucy regretted leaving some of her books and the ever-blooming red rosebush that had been her companion in the mill, but the worst part was saying goodbye to her family.

She made herself a journal, carefully stitching together seven pages of six-by-ten-inch white unlined paper, for by this time the habit of writing her thoughts and experiences was ingrained, and she had promised to send back letters and poems for the *Lowell Offering*, the magazine the mill girls published. Surely there would be plenty to write about in the new world and new life that lay before them.

For Lucy Larcom the future meant freedom from the twelve-hour day and six-day week at the mills. Teaching was a more "respectable" job that would give her the chance to use her learning, while her salary of forty dollars every three months, pitiful as it may sound today, was more than she earned at the mills and would bring her financial independence. There were importance and purpose in such useful work, and those were vital elements to anyone brought up so firmly in the Puritan tradition. Undoubtedly there was also that comfortable sense of bringing gifts felt by so many New Englanders who went to civilize the West.

Years later she wrote, "The exhilaration of starting off on one's first journey, young, ignorant, buoyant, expectant, is unlike anything else, unless it be youth itself, the real beginning of the real journey—life. Annoyances are overlooked. Everything seems romantic and dreamlike."[1]

In leaving the East, Lucy and Emeline were turning their backs on two hundred years of settled family history. The earliest Larcoms had come to Cape Ann Side in the Massachusetts Bay Colony with other English Puritans in 1630.[2] For a time they settled in Ipswich, but by 1684 they had begun to buy land on the coast east of Beverly village, in what became known as Beverly Farms. Like their neighbors—Obers, Haskells, and Woodberrys—they were hardworking, God-fearing Yankees. They turned the wooded land into gently rolling fields and pastures that sloped down to the rocky shores or occasional half-moon beach. Wood was a major crop, and small red cattle grazed the pastures.[3] The sea provided another means of livelihood, and most of the men were both farmers and seamen.

Beverly's economy was for many years a balance of land and sea, farming and sailing or fishing, with shops and small businesses in support, and a small cottage industry of shoemaking. Like Salem, but always more sedate than its bustling neighbor, the Larcoms' home village was cosmopolitan. Most of the men and many of the women had made long voyages and were familiar with foreign places and ways. They knew Hong Kong, Calcutta, and Gibralter; women wore silks and carried fans from China, Smyrna, and Turkey. Foreign money circulated along with local coinage. Ships were part of local legend; there were memories of the terrible wreck of the *Persia*, or stories about the more recent wreck of the *Margaret* and the horrible experience of the survivors that was gossiped about until Captain Henry Larcom's "true account" appeared in the *Salem Register* in 1810. Other tales, told in whispers lest the children should hear, went back to the dreadful days of witches, whose terror had been stopped by Beverly's own Reverend John Hale.

The town celebrated its two hundredth birthday in 1826. It was old, settled, and already traditional, lying along the base of Cape Ann facing south to Salem and east to the islands and the open sea. From the Beverly-Salem bridge one main road curved through the town and eventually went north to Newburyport. Most of the buildings clustered near the harbor and bridge, although as the town grew, more homes and shops and the town's churches began to move out along the road, encroaching on open fields and farms.

Lucy's grandfather, Jonathan Larcom, had been a sea captain and probably a privateer during the early years of the Revolution. He was lost at sea in 1777, and his widow, Abigail Ober Larcom, brought up her eight children on the farm. Her son Benjamin, born in 1776, went to sea early, and by 1804 was well established as a sea captain, usually sailing for the wealthy merchant and shipowner Israel Thorndike, of Beverly and Boston.[4] At twenty-eight Benjamin married Charlotte, daughter of Captain Samuel Ives. They had two daughters, Charlotte (1806) and Adeline (or Adelaide) (1810).

Captains of sailing vessels formed a kind of aristocracy. While they were not rich merchants with fleets of ships, like Thorndike, they were experienced men who had commanded other men, who bore the responsibility for ships, men, and cargoes, and whose authority accompanied them ashore. Part of the captain's duty was to sell his merchandise and buy again for the return trip; he received a percentage of the total profit of the voyage, so most captains retired with comfortable fortunes. Other men made a living from the sea as crews of coastal vessels or as fishermen, but although respectable, these seamen lacked the glamour and prestige of the deepwater mariners.

Charlotte Ives Larcom died in 1810, apparently in childbirth, and the Captain made arrangements to board his two children with a respectable woman until, in 1811, he married again. His second wife, Lois, had a different background; she was the daughter of Thomas Barrett of Newport, Rhode Island, who as a boy had been an apprentice blockmaker in Boston and had fought in the Revolution. After the war he married a Salem girl and moved to Beverly, where he became sexton of the First Parish Church, a position to which he was unanimously reelected each year for forty-nine years. A man of great piety and charm, he was particularly noted for his courtly, old-fashioned manners. He lived to be eighty-four (the year before he died the town voted him an assistant, as he was beginning to fail), and he married four times.[5] He was the only grandparent that Lucy Larcom knew.

Benjamin Larcom was still a sea captain when he married Lois Barrett, but life for New England seamen under the Embargo Acts and during the War of 1812 was difficult and dangerous, and sometime after August 1812 he retired from the sea. He opened a shop on the main road and sold the goods the great ships brought from all over the world.

The second Larcom marriage produced eight children: Benjamin (1814), Louisa (1815), Emeline (1817), Jonathan (1818), Abigail (1820), Lydia (1822), Lucy (1824), and Octavia (1827). Charlotte and Adeline were very much part of the family; Lucy always described herself as the ninth child in a family of ten. It was a long family, however; Lucy was only three when her oldest sister, the beautiful Charlotte, married Captain Robert Welch of Newburyport in 1827. In 1831 Adeline married another seaman, George Meacom of Beverly, who later became a shipowner.

Benjamin Larcom was traditionally called Captain, even after he left the sea. He was as completely in command at home as he had been on his ship; his brief words were final decisions. He was forty-nine when Lucy was born, a tall man, handsome in an austere way, but reserved and abstracted, often aloof and uncommunicative. To Lucy he was a godlike being, to be trusted, adored, and feared. None of the children ever forgot the solemn Sunday afternoons when he gathered them together and questioned them from the Bible, ending the session with a prayer. He taught his children piety, obedience, the concept of duty, and the importance of work.

Lois Barrett Larcom, in the years when she was the comfortable wife of the Captain, was a pretty woman with blue eyes, rosy cheeks, dimples, and soft dark hair, which she kept pinned up under white lace-edged caps because her husband preferred it that way. She liked talk and people. The fact that her two stepdaughters and her own eight children survived to adulthood suggests that she must have been a good and careful mother, although having eight children in thirteen years limited her care to their physical well-being.

Lucy came into a world of transition and excitement. The year she was born, 1824, Lafayette made a visit to the new country he had helped to create, and crowds lined the streets to cheer him. Captain Larcom held his infant daughter on his shoulders so that she could some day say she had seen the hero. In 1825 John Quincy Adams became president, in the direct line of the founders and the Constitution makers; the next year John Adams and Thomas Jefferson, those old friends and enemies and finally friends, died within hours of each other on the Fourth of July. But 1825 saw as well the opening of the Erie Canal, changing the direction and history of the United States as hordes of easterners began the movement toward the free, open lands of the West. Lucy and her contemporaries grew up aware of the beckoning West and the promise of limitless opportunity.

Children during these years breathed adventure in the air. There seemed to be no limit to the opportunities for people to move and grow. The young country was becoming politically stable and there was strong national pride; at the same time there was the apparently endless West, available and untouched, existing as both reality and symbol. Belief in a glorious destiny, in the self, and in the right to take these opportunities became part of everyone's thinking.

At the same time, however, the restrictive attitudes about women that have been identified as the Cult of True Womanhood were growing—those standards of purity, piety, domesticity, and submission that affected women's lives, put them firmly in their "sphere," and, at extremes, reduced them to invisible creatures with muted voices.[6] The incompatibility between the two sets of beliefs must have created conflicts for many women growing up at a time when the world expanded and women's options narrowed.

The first six years of Lucy Larcom's life were for the most part extremely happy ones. A very intelligent child whose precocity delighted her family, at age two she was learning her letters at "Aunt Hannah's" school, and according to family tradition was reading at two and a half, chiefly from the New Testament. After the dame school, she and her sisters went to a small private school nearby. She passed her time in church reading hymns and found that she could memorize them very quickly; reciting hymns became a delightful pastime in which her proud family encouraged her. Although she did not understand all of what she read, she fell in love with rhythm and meter and the sound of language. Her cleverness brought an approval that she enjoyed, especially since she was the least pretty of all the beautiful Larcom girls.

The skills that were taught to girl children were never those in which she took pride. All her sisters were clever with their fingers, but Lucy was too impatient to like needlework; she wanted to read or, even better, to be out-of-doors and to be there on her own terms. Either by principle or preoccupation, Lois Larcom gave her children a great deal of freedom. They asked permission for their ventures, but often the answer was "I don't care," which the children interpreted in its broadest sense.[7] Lucy's chief playmates were the two sisters closest to her in age, Lydia and Octavia, and her brother Jonathan, who found her a good companion. She also had a world of imaginary playmates.

During Lucy's childhood there were still no roads except the main one; houses stood in narrow lanes that led to the highway. The Larcom shop was at the corner of one of these lanes, looking across the road to the impressive white brick Thorndike mansion. Farther down the grassy lane was the Larcom house, and beyond it fields and meadows stretched down to the "river"—an arm of the sea that was a stream and mudflats at low tide, but a full and sparkling road to adventure at the high. For the young Larcoms and their neighbors the river was a favorite place to play, particularly on an old mudscow that lay abandoned against a disused wharf. There they could watch the river traffic and let their imaginations run free, so that the gundalow became a gondola, and the tidal river the canals of Venice. At low tide they explored the river bed, finding strange sea creatures to examine and collect. There were forbidden escapades: a neighbor boy rowed them in his boat down the river, under the bridge, and out into Beverly-Salem harbor. As soon as the land began to fall away on either side, they remembered cautionary tales of children whose boats drifted out beyond the light on Baker's Island and past the Miseries, never to return—and it was time to row back to the gundalow.

Lucy's lifelong joy in the natural world began early and brought moments of sheer delight that stayed with her always. She loved flowers, especially the wild ones, and since her family could tell her little about them, she was convinced that she was discovering flowers that no one had ever seen before. Coming home from school one warm day at noon she noticed the mass of tiny blossoms of the red sandwort, and she never forgot either the spread of pale lavender on the ground or the fragility of the individual blossoms in her hand. Years later this memory, like so many others from her childhood, became a poem.

She was still a child when the family moved away from the lane to a house on the other side of the main road. The yard bordered the town graveyard, which seemed to the children "merely the extension of our garden."[8] There was a wonderful garret with a view of the ocean through its small window; at dusk the lights of the bay were like jewels, and on rainy days the children had a perfect place to play.

Her closest sister, Lydia, was exactly two years older; they were both born on March fifth. The family made a pleasant occasion out of a birthday. There were special cakes under pillows in the morning, and always a visit from Grandfather Barrett, who sat by the fire and counted out the years on the child's hand. To share a birthday was even more exciting, and the bond between Lucy and Lydia was strong, even though Lydia was slim and pretty like the heroines in the books and had a particularly sweet and loving nature. She was also much more docile about those household duties that Lucy found ways to evade.

Naturally enough in such a long family, Lucy had different kinds of relationships with her siblings. She was three when Charlotte married and went to live in Newburyport and travel with her sea captain husband, but Lucy adored her. A surviving miniature shows her to have had an elfin kind of beauty, with delicate features, a cloud of dark brown hair, and a hint of laughter in her eyes.[9] After her marriage her visits to her family were necessarily few, but each was a joyful occasion. Adeline was fourteen years older than Lucy; her marriage kept her in Beverly, so her sisters saw her often.

Louisa, the oldest and most beautiful of Lois Larcom's own

daughters, was nine years older than Lucy, and her engagement to ambitious young Edward Harrington, who was working his way up to a youthful captaincy, was a romantic part of Lucy's childhood. Emeline, the next sister, became the most important person in Lucy's young life. Abigail, two years older than Lydia and four years older than Lucy, must have been their playmate, but perhaps associated herself with the older girls, for she is hardly mentioned in Lucy's childhood reminiscences. She seems to have been sharp-tongued and lively. Octavia, the baby, was the charge of the two younger girls and everyone's pet.

She admired her brother Benjamin, but Jonathan, six years older than she, was a closer companion in their younger days. With him she ranged the countryside. A favorite excursion was the three- or four-mile walk to the family homestead in Beverly Farms, a journey not considered too long for a healthy five year old. The way led through fields rich in wildflowers and bushes of barberry and wild roses, past the Cove Brook, past Mingo Beach with its sudden sight of the open sea, through woods and sunny clearings, and finally to the farm and the welcoming aunts, uncles, and cousins who lived there.

Mrs. Larcom was bustling and chatty, concerned with setting a good table, keeping her house in order, and having her children properly dressed, suitably taught, and in good health. She ran her home to suit the dominating figure of her husband; whether she lacked the ability to encourage the sensitive parts of her children's characters cannot be judged, but certainly she lacked the time. The imaginative, beauty-loving, "poetical" strain in Lucy was a gift, she always felt, of her sister Emeline, seven years older and strong, bright, and imaginative: "golden-haired and golden-hearted."[10] Emeline was a storyteller who knew folktales and fairy tales and wild legends. She toughened herself for whatever the future held by taking cold baths, sleeping on a hard wooden sea chest in the attic, or running early in the morning, barefoot and lightly clothed, in the nearby burying ground. All these acts were designed for the purpose of subduing the flesh to the demands of the spirit.

One morning that small Lucy never forgot, Emeline woke her before dawn for a walk. "The birds were singing, and the sun was just rising, and we were walking east, hand-in-hand, when suddenly there appeared before us what looked to me like an immense blue

wall, stretching right and left as far as I could see. . . . It was a wonderful illusion to my unaccustomed eyes, and I took in at that moment for the first time something of the real grandeur of the
ocean. . . . That morning's freshness, that vision of the sea, I know I
can never lose."[11] It was typical of Emeline's care of her little sister
to encourage her love of natural beauty as well as to satisfy her need
for emotional security.

Emeline was strong, courageous, and determined; later in her life
she spent time and money—never in large supply—helping the
needy. She was interested in world affairs and she had strong antislavery feelings. She was the leader and model, the storyteller and
enchanter, beautiful and loving; her younger sisters listened to her
adoringly and believed everything she said.

Certainly she eased Lucy through one of the darkest periods of her
childhood. The younger child's feeling for her remote, commanding
father was intense; she cherished the moments when this un-
demonstrative man showed her affection. Her awe of him, combined
with the desire for direct signs of his affection, was the basis for her
childish idea of God: a distant, powerful being whose love she could
believe but never quite feel. In fact, the need for closeness to and
approval from her father or Father was to affect her entire life, and
partly explains many of its relationships and inconsistencies. Apparently Benjamin Larcom was the kind of person who is delighted by
babies, and for her first three years Lucy had his attention. But when
Octavia was born, she became his "playmate and darling," almost to
the exclusion of the other children.[12] All the family doted on the
infant, including Lucy, but she often wished that she could still be
the baby so that her father would notice her. Years later she dreamed
of him; in the dreams she felt joy at his presence and then pain when
his words rejected her again.

Emeline tried to teach Lucy to endure pain by going beyond it to
find compensations. The things that hurt had to be accepted, but
they need not be dwelt on or magnified. Above all, one should not
inflict one's pain on others; it was a private thing, and one's obligation to others was to help them be happy, and in doing so one found
happiness for oneself. It was certainly a difficult doctrine for a child,
but Emeline herself was so loving and so altogether wonderful that
the younger children, especially Lucy, knew that whatever she said
must be the right thing to do. Emeline's stories, her understanding

of the things that troubled and frightened children, her enthusiasm, and her love gave Lucy security in the bad times of her young life. Years later she summed up all Emeline had done for her in a poem called "My Childhood's Enchantress."[13] It begins with the child lying in bed, while "fears, that childish fancy weaves / Of airy nothing, banished sleep" until her sister, her golden hair like "an aureole-ring . . . round her head" came and soothed her fears and told wonderful stories, opening up the world of the imagination, and more:

> She gave me what no queen could give:
> Keys to the secret, How to Live.
> Fancy is good, but Faith is better;
> I am to my enchantress debtor,
> Whose doors swung wide to both. And she—
> God sent her hither, long before
> I came; he taught sweet mother-lore
> To sister-lips. Oh, dear and fair,
> My sister with the shining hair.

Some of Lucy's night fears came from the workings of an overactive imagination; Emeline soothed her by telling stories or taking her outdoors at night to learn the stars. Other fears came from her childish perceptions of Calvinistic doctrine. When Captain Larcom found Beverly's Old South Meeting House growing too soft and Unitarian for his beliefs, he moved the family to the newer Third Congregational Society, later called Dane Street Church, which still kept the older orientation. Lucy liked the ceremoniousness of the strict Sabbath, with the house all cleaned, the family dressed in its best, the beans and brown bread and Indian pudding all prepared the day before, the order and quiet of the whole town, and even Meeting, with its long sermon through which good children sat still and unsmiling; she could appreciate the special quality of the day, no matter how glad she was when it was over. She remembered with some pride the day that Benjamin and Lois Larcom with their eight children, all dressed in their best and fully aware of the occasion, joined the new church. But what she understood of the doctrines of election, of punishment terrible and eternal, and of infant damnation came back in the darkness to terrify her. Again, it was Emeline who calmed her fears by insisting on a God who held sinners in loving, not angry, hands.

Her fears and what she sometimes dimly felt as the loss of her father's love were the only dark spots in Lucy's childhood. There was security; Captain Larcom was respected in the town as an upright citizen, a man of wisdom, and a good provider for his big family. There was a definite place in a settled community. There were brothers and sisters who teased and snubbed and loved each other, cousins and neighboring children, aunts and uncles who were different and interesting, and sensible parents who imposed few restrictions.

She was a cheerful child with a face "round, ruddy, and laughing with health," which she disliked because it was not "pale and pensive-looking" like the heroines of novels.[14] When she was about twenty, she summed herself up with third-person humor and objectivity as "a homely, healthy child, having a dumpling form, round white face, gray eyes, and brown bushy hair, which was usually kept 'shingled off,' as the saying was then; and in her general appearance she much resembled a well-kept, good-natured domestic animal. She was the youngest but one of a family of ten, and was remarkable for nothing in her juvenile days, save a love of idleness and of books."[15]

She was in many ways timid and never sure enough of herself to be aggressive; her family knew, however, that she could be obstinate. She never made fusses, but stubbornly held on until she got what she wanted, and she often employed her considerable intelligence to find ways of getting out of the household tasks she did so badly. This trait, modified by experience, was to be characteristic all her life. She could never confront or argue. In a situation that she did not like, she pulled back and waited as unobtrusively as possible for things to change or for a way to evade what she did not want. Her family described it as stubbornness, but it was also a form of self-protection.

Thrifty Captain Larcom had a vegetable garden at the end of the lane. His children were expected to help in it; frequently he would take all the younger ones with a basket of lunch and a bucket of molasses and water to the garden and pay them a penny for each carefully weeded patch. Lucy always started off as eagerly as the others, but within minutes became bored, then so tired or so thirsty that she drifted over to the "luncheon tree" and enjoyed her daydreams in its shade. She seldom earned more than a single penny, but never minded when her sisters jingled their coins and laughed at her laziness.[16] It was simply not what she enjoyed doing.

Most of the things she did enjoy had to do with words. "I was much taken with the sound of words, without any thought of their meaning—a habit not always outgrown with childhood," she wrote years later.[17] Her preoccupation with sound and rhythm and the music of words, long before she understood the sense, made memorization of hymns easy, and the admiration of her sisters reinforced the skill. As a reward for learning one hundred hymns, Emeline promised to teach her to write and stitched together a little copybook for her. Lucy ruined the book because she was too impatient to wait for instruction, but Emeline soon relented and taught her her letters.

Letter writing was an important skill, and she began learning it early. To help her sister Adeline write her seaman fiancé, four-year-old Lucy dashed off a letter that began, "Dear George, You must be a good boy"; she was pleased with her achievement and quite indignant when Adeline decided not to send it.[18]

When she was eight, she discovered that she could write "poetry." One rainy afternoon she and her brother Jonathan were in the garrett, their favorite indoor play place, when he suggested that they write poems. Her first effort celebrated the thunderstorm:

> One summer day, said little Jane,
> We were walking down a shady lane,
> When suddenly the wind blew high,
> And the red lightning flashed in the sky.
>
> The peals of thunder, how they rolled!
> And I felt myself a little cool'd,
> For I before had been quite warm,
> But now around me was a storm.

This somewhat "anti-climactic effusion" won her much approval and praise from family, teacher, and even the neighbors; she herself was enchanted at the fun of making rhymes. She wrote a little book of tales with rhymed morals and illustrated it with watercolor paintings, but in a "fit of modesty" stuffed it under a loose board in the eaves so that it was lost.[19]

Above all, she was a child who loved freedom—the freedom of her mind to wander through books and poetry and the country of the imagination, and the freedom of her body to run half-wild through the natural world in which she found so much beauty. Much of her adult life would be spent trying to find the same kind of delight she knew as a child.

It is not possible to know what Lucy Larcom might have become had the pattern of her first seven years continued. In January 1832 Benjamin Larcom died, and the secure, free, happy world of childhood ended.

Lois Larcom was a good housekeeper as long as she was second in command; without the Captain she was lost. Even though she owned her home and other property and the older children helped her, she could not manage. There had never been luxuries in the Larcom household, but there had always been plenty of good food on the table, nice clothing for the children, and, of course, books in the house. Since the Captain believed in the sanctity of work, all the older girls had been taught a trade so that they could be self-sufficient, although it was expected that they would eventually be mistresses of their own homes. Undoubtedly Benjamin Larcom, with two sons and eight daughters to bring up and provide for, concerned himself about money, but there had seemed to be no financial problem as long as the good provider was alive. His death, however, revealed that he had hidden some problems; he owed nearly five hundred dollars, a substantial sum for the time. Mrs. Larcom, advised by her friends, was able to sell the property on the lane and remove the debt. She took her children to live in her father's house.[20]

For Lucy, the time brought bewilderment added to the pain of losing her father. With a head full of hymns and New Testament ideas, she wondered why her mother worried when the lilies and ravens did not. To give the comfort that she could not speak, she followed her mother about the house, singing hymns to her. When the elders of the family conferred with grave faces, Lucy escaped outdoors. In later years she moved lightly, almost impersonally, over the subject of her father's death, using the metaphor of a ship and its untrained crew losing the captain. But thirty years later she still dreamed of him.

Family life as Lucy had known it simply collapsed. Young Benjamin, who had always intended to follow his father's calling, went to sea on the brig *Mexican*, whose master was another Larcom captain. It was his first and last voyage; the brig was captured by pirates who robbed it, locked the crew in the hold, and set fire to it. The captain discovered a small skylight that had been overlooked, and the crew managed to escape and put out the fire. By the time the wounded ship returned to Salem, Benjamin had had enough of the sea. To his mother's relief, he became an apprentice carpenter.[21]

The older girls found work. Thanks to their father's foresight they had been taught the respectable trade of tailoring, which was ladylike and could be done at home. The younger children had more housework to do, something Lucy disliked very much, but at least there was Emeline to love and comfort her. The family suffered again when Charlotte died while on a voyage with her husband and was buried at sea in 1835.

Mrs. Larcom tried for nearly three years to maintain her family, but she could not do it. Casting around for another solution, she remembered that her husband had been interested in the mills and settlement established in the new town of Lowell. Conservative as the Captain had been in religious matters, he seems to have had none of the attitudes about women that turned them into helpless dependents. He had taught his daughters to be self-sufficient and he found the idea of the new community of Lowell, with all its advanced ideas, a possible solution if the task of bringing up and educating his long family became too difficult.

Lowell was by now internationally famous. It offered respectable ways for women to earn a living, and Lois Larcom, experienced at running a large household, arranged to move there and manage a mill boardinghouse. Her family and friends approved; in fact, several of the Beverly Farms cousins decided to go along. They would not be far from home, and Lowell offered financial security and promise for the future.

CHAPTER 2

The World of Work

The phenomenon of the Lowell mills has been examined by labor historians and by scholars interested in women's history.[1] For a brief period there was nothing like it; it stood before the world as evidence that the grand American experiment could create working conditions without poverty, loss of dignity, and destruction of humanity. Lowell was new, clean, bright, and prosperous, and the respectable young women who came to work there remained respectable.

When Francis Cabot Lowell pirated the design of new textile machinery from his English hosts and brought his information home, a group of businessmen calling themselves the Lowell Associates found abundant water power in the Merrimack River and built their first mill in 1822. Convinced that Americans could avoid the festering cesspools that were European factory towns, the planners, combining dreams and practicality, created a model town and a controlled society based on what Benita Eisler calls "those ultimate Yankee virtues, doing good and doing well."[2] For workers they called in the respectable, energetic daughters of God-fearing New England families who made a living from the thin-soiled subsistence farms of Maine, New Hampshire, Vermont, and western Massachusetts. The planners attracted these young women by creating acceptable conditions and by offering the highest wages available to women anywhere, from $1.85 to $3.00 a week—generous wages for women, although less than men were paid.

With the chance for financial independence, the well-bred, churchgoing, respectable young women poured into Lowell. Families allowed their daughters to go because of a widely held belief that "idle young women were particularly prone to depravity." Keeping them occupied was a "contribution to public morality," and they were not going to strangers: "The shared class and religious origins of labor and management. . . . Both the Boston merchants and the yeoman fathers of the mill girls were descendants of the Puritan settlers . . . some mill owners were less than a generation removed from the same farmlands which now yielded daughters to their corporate paternalism."[3]

The system was, of course, exploitative, trading on the fact that women could be paid less and giving all management positions to men. But although the long day and the controlled lives seem outrageous today, firsthand accounts show that life in Lowell was very different from the sterile horror of Melville's "Tartarus of Maids," with its white, corpselike girls reduced to walking-dead servants of the dominant machinery; in contrast Lowell seems bustling and full of color. Part of the difference was that Lowell offered community and culture; a more important point is that the girls who flocked there saw the experience as temporary. They came with specific goals: to save money for marriage, to help their parents, to see a brother through college, to get or finance an education, or simply to be independent. Lowell, generally, was a step to something else; the average length of time that girls stayed there was three years. Harriet Hanson Robinson, whose account of mill life is less consistently rosy than Larcom's and shows more awareness of problems, wrote positively, especially of the later lives of young women she had known who made important contributions to their world. One became an artist, another an inventor, "several were among the pioneers" in Florida and Kansas, some had businesses, some went to college and entered professions. They "married into the best families" in Lowell, or, if they went home, "instead of being looked down upon as 'factory girls' by the squire's or the lawyer's family they were more often welcomed as coming from the metropolis, bringing new fashions, new books, and new ideas with them."[4] Many of the girls founded libraries in their small, remote towns; a great number went west as teachers, missionaries, or wives; many became writers, although only Larcom achieved national fame. Reading about these young women, one is struck by the way those who were bright, healthy, and capable, with talents that might otherwise have been wasted, found and used their opportunities, and as well by their independence and self-respect, especially at a time when social codes attempting to regulate the behavior of women seemed to point in the opposite direction.

Not that there was a great deal of personal freedom: the girls went from their paternal homes to paternalism of another sort. In order to control morality the planners established boardinghouses where the girls had to live. They were, in fact, watched over by mill managers, supervisors, the town clergy, and the respectable women who ran the boardinghouses. These women, usually widows with small children, were in charge of the moral and physical well-being of the girls. When young Harriet Hanson seemed to lead a group of striking workers, she lost her job and Mrs. Hanson lost her boardinghouse; if she could not control her child, she probably could not control the girls in her care. Managing a boardinghouse was a responsible position, and one that fit in with the overall scheme of the mill planners. Regulations and control extended into every part of the operatives' lives: they began work at five o'clock in the summer and daylight in winter, with half-hour meal breaks at seven and at noon. The mills closed at eight (seven on Saturdays) and the boardinghouse lights went out at ten. Between eight and ten the girls ate, visited, cared for their clothing, read, wrote, and attended classes and lectures. On Sundays the mills were closed, and the Fourth of July was a holiday. Regular church attendance was compulsory.

For Lois Barrett Larcom, as for so many other women in similar circumstances, the position of boardinghouse keeper offered the best chance of providing for her children without being a burden on her family. The children found the move exciting; for Lucy the considerable pain of leaving her family and her beloved garden, fields, and shore was somewhat eased by the excitement of exploring new territory. The old furniture made the new house feel like home, and it was not long before she fell in love with the Merrimack River.

The contrast between the two towns could not have been greater. Looking back on the Beverly of her childhood, Lucy wrote: "The town used to wear a delightful air of drowsiness, as if she had stretched herself out for an afternoon nap, with her head toward her old mother, Salem, and her whole length reclining toward the sea, till she felt at her feet, through her green robes, the dip of the deep water at the Farms. All her elder children recognised in her quiet, steady-going ways a maternal unity and strength of character, as of a town that understood her own plans, and had settled down to peaceful permanent habits."[5]

If Beverly was drowsy, Lowell was wide awake. Part of its liveliness came from its newness, part from its purpose—a whole town built around an industry—and part from the vitality of its inhabitants. A *Handbook for the Visiter* [sic] *to Lowell, 1848*, gives population figures that show its rapid growth: In 1820, before the mills came to what was then part of East Chelmsford, there were two hundred people; in 1836 there were 6,477; in 1840 there were 20,981; and in 1846 there were 28,891.[6] The Lawrence Corporation, where the Larcoms lived and worked, was one of the oldest, and its buildings lay along the Merrimack River. The huge brick rectangles were still fairly clean, and the nearby boardinghouse blocks were repaired and painted each spring. Since the town was planned, its streets were unusually wide and there were many shops, but one visitor, a young, intense abolitionist and poet named John Greenleaf Whittier, missed the old shade trees and disliked the bareness and the harsh light of the new city.

Lucy wrote, probably to Emeline, "We have got a sink in our front entry. We live in a three-story block with fourteen doors. There is a great large stone house on one side of it. There is a canal close by."[7] Newness and the chance to explore with the young cousins who went to Lowell and lived in Mrs. Larcom's boardinghouse proved exciting. Lucy was most fascinated by the mill girls: the breezy, sociable mountain girls who had come to Lowell for so many different reasons. Their independence, their pride in their ability to earn money and control their lives, impressed her far more deeply than she realized at the time.

In fact, Lucy found everything interesting—the surroundings, the river, the busy working girls. She helped with light tasks like making beds, trimming lamps, and washing dishes before and after school. School was the least pleasant of the new experiences; she was put into the top grade, where the fact that she had never learned much arithmetic kept her frightened. The worst, however, was the teacher, a savage, violent man who ruled his class through terror.[8] Most of the time she was too terrified to learn.

As boardinghouse keeper, Lois Larcom had an Irish girl to do the heavy work, while she was completely in charge of buying and cooking food. The girls paid $1.25 a week board, and the mills subsidized them to the amount of $.25 a week each. Thrifty managers fed the girls well, if somewhat starchily, although European visitors were amazed to find that the girls ate meat twice a day. Unfortunately Lois Larcom was not thrifty; she was accustomed to serving good food without worrying about the cost, and her boardinghouse table continued her pattern. In a short time, in spite of help from the older children, she was in financial trouble. One of the children would have to leave school and work in the mills.

Lydia was older, but Lucy was bigger, and so she was selected. She did not mind, for she was glad to get away from the terror of school, and at first she enjoyed the novelty of work and felt immense pride at earning money to help her family. She was a "doffer," which meant that she changed the bobbins on the spinning frames. The job was given to children because it was easy; there were periods of half to three quarters of an hour between tasks, and the children could play or talk or even run home. But the sound of the machinery, the "buzzing and hissing and whizzing of pulleys and rollers and spindles and flyers" grew annoying and finally exhausting.[9]

A child under thirteen working in the mills had to go to school for three months a year. When Lucy returned, the teachers had changed and she had a year of mill work behind her; at any rate, she found that studying and learning were absorbing and delightful. She learned quickly, eagerly, and with such success that at the end of the three months she was told that she was prepared now for high school, a great honor and achievement. The high school had been founded in 1831; although it still met over shops and the new building would not be completed until 1840, it was a good school. It prepared boys for college and gave girls an unusually academic education for the time.[10] Lucy wanted desperately to go, to continue in the world of formal learning for which she was so well suited. But her mother could not manage without the dollar a week plus board that the child could earn.

Lucy tried to accept the return to the mill as she had accepted her father's death and the move to Lowell. But the cheerful stoicism Emeline had taught her did not work; she longed to go back to school for a formal education. She began to worry about her future.

Once she had thought she might want to be a teacher, like old Aunt Hannah; later she wanted to be an artist, without quite knowing what an artist was. Although her "poems" had been prized by her family and neighbors, writing as a way of earning a living never occurred to her. Obviously, her only future lay in teaching—a respectable way of earning, enhanced by the fact that preparation for such a position involved the reading and study that she loved so well. But without an education there was only the mill.

As a child Lucy's confused view of the human race was that Adam and Eve were very tall people who dwindled after the fall, and every generation since was a little smaller. She longed to be tall, an anxiety that, as she said later, was entirely groundless. She looked like a woman at thirteen, and her sisters insisted that she lengthen her skirts and put up her hair. She did not want to, and the effect of forcing the outward symbols of womanhood on her while she was still a child was to make her morbidly self-critical and reserved, overserious and grave.[11] Fortunately there were some cousins her own age at home, and Emeline had come to join the family in Lowell; her influence prevented self-pity and complaining. In her attempts to keep up the spirits of her sisters, and particularly Lucy, condemned by her size and strength to the work of the mills, Emeline gathered the children in the boardinghouse together to produce a little paper called "The Diving Bell." On Saturday evenings they met in the garrett where the editor, Emeline, who had received and copied the anonymous contributions, read them aloud to the writers. Guessing who had written what was part of the fun. Lucy wrote verses, primarily, since rhyme was so easy for her, and an occasional "moral essay."

Emeline liked Lowell and quickly made friends. She was, according to a contemporary, "tall and stately, with curling hair, and . . . much prettier than Lucy; she had a face full of sunshine, and, like Lucy, the bluest of eyes. . . . She was an enthusiastic student, reading abstruse books in the intervals of mill-work, and so becoming familiar with mental and moral science; or she would study mathematical problems, of which she usually had one or two pinned up before her, to occupy her thoughts at her daily toil." Her minister thought her "the most intellectual woman in his church," as well as "faithful and self-sacrificing . . . giving herself unreservedly to all good works."[12]

Under the influence of Emeline and her minister, Lucy followed her sister into church membership. Her decision was wholly emotional and subjective; she was not yet ready to analyze and question the Articles of Faith. She simply did what Emeline thought was right.

In the mill itself Lucy had become a spinner. This was a woman's job and it paid more money, averaging $1.75 a week. Her spinning frames faced the window, and at slack periods she could turn her back on the roomful of girls and machines to look out at the Merrimack, or think, or tend her plants, or read the poems that she, like other girls, had cut out and pasted on her part of the wall—poems by Mrs. Hemans, Miss Landon, George Herbert, William Cullen Bryant, and others, all chosen to inspire the mind and spirit.

But always there was the noise of the machines. She remembered years later how in "sweet June weather [she] would lean far out of the window, and try not to hear the unceasing clash of sound inside."[13] The machines, or more particularly the noise of the machines, became intolerable, creating both a physical and psychological reaction that she would never lose. Poetry helped; her head was full of poems and stories that she could repeat to herself. Emeline and friends helped, too, but still she was a child of thirteen and fourteen, and a child who had always loved freedom and the outdoors. The changes in her body with the onset of puberty distressed her. She was self-conscious about her size and uncomfortable in women's clothes. She seemed to belong nowhere; as tall as a woman, and dressed like one, inside she was still a child. Her two favorite occupations were denied her: she could not run free outside, and at the end of the long workday she was too tired to read much. She withdrew into herself, dwelling on her own faults and seeing herself trapped by circumstances against which her usual tactics were useless. In retrospect she would say that these years had taught her the discipline that she badly needed, but at thirteen there was no comfort in thinking that she was learning a useful lesson for the future. She hated what was happening to her. For two years her unhappiness grew; by the time she was fifteen her mental state, combined with the conditions of the mill—the close, lint-filled air, the long working day, the confinement, and always the assault of noise—began to affect her formerly excellent health. She was tired and tense, had severe headaches, and lost her energy.

Fortunately, before she became seriously ill, a way of escape opened. Sister Louisa had married her sea captain, Edward Harrington, in 1837. It was a very happy marriage, marred only by the fact that his long trading voyages to the coast of Africa kept him away from home so much. Like many young couples they rented one floor of a house that stood on the main road, not far from Adeline and the church. They dreamed of a fine big house of their own, and, in fact, at the end of that voyage Edward Harrington was to buy a large piece of land from the Israel Thorndike estate.

The town had bought the estate after the rich merchant's death, and the mansion at the head of the lane became town offices, public library, and meeting hall. The land, stretching from the main road to the water, was sold for houses, with some zoning restrictions: owners might not use the land for forges, or for raising pigs, for example. Edward Harrington was ambitious; he now owned part of his ship, the *Oregon,* and he was determined to give his children a liberal education to fit them to be outstanding Christian citizens. The logbook he kept on his 1840 voyage is headed "My private journal, and Scrap Book. Dearly, tenderly, & devoutedly [*sic*], intended to meet only the eyes of Her! whose Bosom only, can elicit the interest from its pages.—"[14] It is full of his love for his wife, his dreams for the children, his loneliness, and accounts of his bouts with fever, which sometimes depressed him so much that "O Dearest Louisa, I believe I will never live to get home" is repeated several times. The logbook also includes poems, but the greater part describes his visits and experiences along the African coast.

It was particularly difficult for him to leave Louisa alone at this point, for their oldest son, Edward, now two, had never been strong, and their second son, Benjamin Larcom, called "Larky," was a lively three month old. Louisa badly needed someone to be with her, just at the time her worried family decided that Lucy needed to get away from the mills. She was sent home to Beverly.

She had some doubts. Nine years separated Louisa and Lucy, so there had been no closeness between them, although Lucy had always admired her older sister's beauty. Lucy knew nothing of child care; she was only three when the last child of her family was born. And she had always disliked and managed to get out of those "womanly" tasks at which she was so inept and which kept her indoors when she wanted to be out. She was not at all sure how it would work out, but anything was better than the exhausting noise and confinement of the mill.

In fact, the arrangement worked beautifully. She and Louisa got along so well that it became a clear understanding that wherever Louisa was would be Lucy's home. The quiet town and above all the salt air, the breath of life to those born to it, restored her strength and energy in a short time. Household tasks made more sense to her now, and she learned them easily, taking pride in her skill and even coming to like an afternoon of plain sewing, sitting by an open window with her fingers busy while she listened to the wind and the songs of birds. She discovered a real love of children, especially her charge, young Larcom Harrington, a vigorous, wide-awake, happy baby whose development was fascinating and whose affection rewarded her care. There were walks and there were books; she read *The Old Curiosity Shop*, then appearing in a Philadelphia paper, "with the baby playing at [her] feet, or lying across [her] lap, in an unfinished room given up to sea-chests and coffee-bags and spicy foreign odors."[15]

She was glad to get to know her older family again, too. Adeline and George Meacom grew more prosperous every day, and now had a daughter, Charlotte, and a baby son, George. Benjamin, who had never regretted leaving the sea, was well enough established as a carpenter and housewright to marry a Salem girl, Abigail Hansen, in 1839, and their first child, Mary Abbie, was born the following year. Lucy enjoyed her status as aunt.

But pleasant as it all was, life in Beverly was the kind that went on and on, easy but leading nowhere. More and more Lucy began to think of that other world of action and ideas, of growth and expansion and communication that Lowell seemed to be. Her dreams of education and preparation for the future were disappearing in the peace and quiet of Louisa's home in Beverly. She still felt that fascination with the mill girls and their independence: they did not sit home passively waiting for the future. They used Lowell just as it used them. In later years she described the two towns and two kinds of life as "stillness and stir," but at the time she was not aware that her need for both elements would establish a pattern for the rest of her life.[16] Hard though it was in many ways, Lucy returned to Lowell. The year away had restored her health, given her a better perspective on her life, and provided an alternative. This time entering the mills was her own choice, a decision that she made consciously for herself with the security that she was not trapped. If she chose to leave, she had a place to go.

Mrs. Larcom was spending more and more of her time in Beverly, where her friends and a growing number of grandchildren lived; soon she would give up the boardinghouse and go home. Lucy did not mind, for as long as she had Emeline she could never feel lonely or deserted. And her year in Beverly had renewed her own sense of family, so that it became a regular thing to go back and forth on the Lowell-Salem stage.

Even the noise of the mills, though still horrible, was different, for now it seemed to signify activity, and Lucy felt she was back in the world of thought and action and people. She would find in busy Lowell rather than in quiet Beverly the chance to learn what she wanted more than anything else.

While she was away, the mill girls had begun to distinguish themselves in a new way. They had formed "improvement circles," often church sponsored, and in several of these groups the girls read their own writings to each other, often as a basis for discussion. The Reverend Abel C. Thomas of the Universalist church made a collection of some of the writing and called it the *Lowell Offering;* at the same time the Congregational church issued the *Operatives Magazine.* By 1842 the two had merged, keeping the title of the former, and two mill girls, Harriet F. Farley and Harriot Curtis, were the editors. Like the mill girls themselves, their magazine became famous in America and Europe; in 1844 an anthology called *Mind among the Spindles* was published with a preface by Harriet Martineau. The magazine was encouraged and perhaps in some ways subsidized by the mill owners. Charges that the magazine was simply a mouthpiece for the owners were made later by "radical" young women like Sarah Bagley, who found the *Offering* too conservative for her tastes and eventually drifted away from it.[17] Benita Eisler denies the charge, pointing out that the "showcase" value of the magazine lay partly in the fact that it was not controlled: "The *Offering,* uncensored and independent, provided a fortuitous medium for those expressions of distinctly American genius: public relations and packaging."[18]

The magazine was, in fact, consciously literary rather than political. It was a miscellany of poems, short stories, essays, and letters, as the girls tried their hands at whatever interested them. Harriet Hanson Robinson, an occasional contributor, years later pointed out its derivatory nature: "There is a certain flavor in all *The Lowell Offering* writings, both in prose and verse, which reminds one of the books read by the authors, and the models they followed in their compositions. The poetry savors of Mrs. Sigourney, Mrs. Hemans, Miss Landon, Mrs. Barbauld, Milton, Pope, Cowper, and Hannah More. Byron's sardonic verse is copied by one or two of the most independent minds among them. The prose models of writing were *The Spectator*, the English classics, 'Miss Sedgwick's Letters,' 'The Vicar of Wakefield,' and Lydia Maria Child's works."[19]

Emeline Larcom was a friend of the two editors and a member of their improvement circle; she quickly drew her sister into the group. As the youngest member, Lucy was at first terrified of the young ladies and literally trembled when her poems were read aloud, but she relaxed finally because everyone seemed to like her and the things she wrote. Her earliest efforts reflected the adolescent's joy in melancholy; one poem begged, "Weave me a shroud in the month of June!" Later, most of her verses were about nature and the outdoor world she loved. One poem suggests an attitude; it remembers the natural spirits, Zephyr, fairies, dryads, naiads, all driven from their natural habitat by the smoke, wheels, and engines of the factories. This poem, like others in the magazine, reflected an awareness that many shared: Lowell, clinging to its vision of itself as a center of industry in a clean, idyllic, rural setting, was becoming urban and its pastoral setting was being destroyed.[20]

On her return Lucy went to work with Emeline as a dresser. This job was prized, for it called for a great deal of skill and therefore paid more; an expert dresser could earn between $2.50 and $3.50 a week. But Lucy, although she loved being with her sister, and loved their sunset-facing window, loathed the machine: "I felt as if the half-live creature, with its great groaning joints and whizzing fan, was aware of my incapacity to manage it, and had a fiendish spite against me."[21] She moved to the cloth room where the work was light; a few men and girls measured and baled the finished cloth and entered it into the account books. The cloth room worked an eight-hour day, and there were long spaces of time between busy spells in a room that was so bright and clean that the girls could wear light-colored muslins, even white, in the summer. It paid less than other mill work, but Lucy gladly exchanged money for time and the slower pace that suited her temperament.

Two letters exist from Lucy and Emeline in Lowell to their mother in Beverly. They are sending her a copy of "our magazine" and six dollars; "it ought to be a 6-1/4, but as Lucy is coming to B. we have not quite so much as usual." The other mentions sending money, comments on Adeline's new baby, sends love to the family, and ends, "We are in hopes to get a place, so that you can come and live with us by spring. I long to have a home once more, though I am very well contented here."[22]

With more time and lighter work, Lucy could read and write more; she also began to make close friends outside the family circle. In April 1843 Emeline, who had always declared her determination to be a useful, honorable old maid, married George Burley Spaulding, a young Lowell resident who was master of a grammar school. The marriage made drastic changes in all the Larcoms' lives. Mrs. Larcom thankfully gave up the hope of financial prosperity in Lowell and went home permanently to Beverly, taking Lydia and Octavia with her.[23] Lucy went to live in a strange boardinghouse, separated from all her family for the first time.

There were compensations for the loss of the home environment, such as it had been. Emeline and George lived in a small house in the open fields beyond the town, and Lucy was a frequent visitor, as was George's younger brother Frank. Having male friends was something new to Lucy. The partial separation from Emeline and the difference in their relationship brought home to her with something of a shock just how dependent she had been on her older sister's strength, imagination, and initiative. It was time to begin thinking for herself, although nothing ever could change the love and gratitude she felt for her sister.

It was interesting to watch Emeline in the new role of wife and mother (the Spauldings' first child was born in February 1844 and lived a little over a year), and to get to know George and Frank. The Spauldings were well-educated young men. George was a schoolmaster, but was headed for the ministry, and Frank was attending medical lectures at Harvard College. Emeline and George were both twenty-seven when they married; Frank and Lucy were seven years younger, and shared their birth month, March 1824, although Lucy was twenty-one days older. They seemed to make a logical family grouping. Neither of the brothers was entirely content to stay in old, settled New England; they were fascinated by the West, that vast land of opportunity and testing. Certainly in the 1840s they shared that feeling with many of their contemporaries, especially the mill girls, so many of whom saw the open lands and new settlements as a theater for their abilities and ambitions. Lucy was enchanted by Frank's intensity about the West and the future.

Besides the Spauldings, there were other new friends for Lucy. One of them was her first "girl-friend," Eliza Holbrook, with whom she "exchanged confidences, laughed and cried, read, wrote, walked, visited, and studied."[24] Eliza dressed well and advised Lucy on her clothes, while Lucy helped Eliza with her compositions, for the latter had not had much education in her childhood; her inability to spell was a shock and a revelation to word-loving Lucy. But Eliza carefully saved her money to take time off from the mills and educate herself. With her, Lucy began to study German and botany, two of the many classes or studies available to satisfy the mill girls' insatiable desire for learning.

Another close friend was one of her roommates, Sarah (probably Holbrook); she and Lucy read Carlyle's *Hero-Worship,* which was given to them by Sarah's brother, a student at Dartmouth. Carlyle's book and Lucy's longtime favorite *Pilgrim's Progress* established in her mind an image of her hero, her Mr. Greatheart, the ideal of what a man should be, although so far she had not met such a figure, except, perhaps, her father. They also read the "electrifying" *Festus,* which remained a favorite for years. This long, Faustian dramatic poem has a hero who is tempted, although the reader knows that the temptation will not succeed; its only analyst says, "As a drama, *Festus* collapses in its opening scene."[25] Nevertheless, people read on, and with each edition they had more to read, for the work grew longer (the 1845 edition, which Larcom probably read, had grown from eight to thirteen thousand lines; the final 1901 edition was forty thousand lines long), as Philip James Bailey incorporated his unsuccessful works into each new edition of his only success. The Byronic tale stressed experience and "rejected with scorn Original Sin and Free Will and with them all genuine humility and the need for discipline in life." It was, of course, daring, shocking, and romantic in its day, and had both a critical and popular success.

Besides reading everything they could, the girls went to the Lyceum lectures and heard John Quincy Adams, Emerson, Theodore Parker, Edward Everett, Daniel Webster, and any number of Harvard professors. There were always visitors from abroad, like Charles

Dickens and Harriet Martineau, come to look at the famous Lowell mill girls. There were classes in ethics and moral philosophy; Lucy attended one taught by the Reverend Mr. Blanchard. She found no one to teach her what she most wanted to learn—English literature—so she began to teach herself by going to the town library and reading and making extracts of Chaucer, Spenser, Shakespeare, Milton (whose poetry she had read since childhood), Pope, Wordsworth, Coleridge, Byron, Burns, Tennyson, along with a host of minor and popular writers of the day. The poet Bryant was a favorite whose work was eagerly awaited. All the girls read the current periodicals and talked about them; they knew about, and to varying degrees participated in, such enthusiasms as phrenology and mesmerism. They were fascinated by daguerrotypes and rushed to have the sun take their pictures. A few were Millerites, fearfully waiting for the Day of Judgment, originally scheduled for 1843. Generally, the mill girls were very much aware of their world.

In July of 1844 the *Middlesex Standard* brought to Lowell as its editor the thirty-seven-year-old antislavery activist and poet John Greenleaf Whittier. Although viewed by the establishment with considerable suspicion for his abolitionist activities, Whittier was known and cherished by the mill girls, who shared his antislavery feelings. They had far too often heard southern politicians declare that slaves were better off than mill workers; one of the girls, Clementine Averill, had replied in a national newspaper to the charge.[26] The fact that the mill owners, who depended on southern cotton, were totally conservative may in part explain the strong radical feelings of the mill girls. Whittier, especially in a poem like "The Yankee Girl," seemed to speak for them. The heroine of this poem, a northern farm girl, refused the marriage proposal of a rich southerner who offered her a life of luxury and ease, scorning the "haughty Southron" and a luxurious life based on the misery of slaves.[27]

Whittier's verse, which combined a moral issue with which good people had to agree, the ideals of the day, a spellbinding use of specific detail—especially place names—a romantic pride in the nation's history, and tremendous emotional intensity with a use of rhyme and meter that usually suggested marching hymns was immensely popular. His physical appearance matched his status: at thirty-five, said Thomas Wentworth Higginson, he was "a man of striking personal appearance; tall, slender, with an olive complexion, black hair, straight black eyebrows, brilliant eyes, and an Oriental, Semitic cast of countenance."[28] Portraits show his dark, deep-set eyes as the dominant feature in his austerely handsome face. He was a poet and a crusader—a completely romantic figure.

Whittier admired the mill girls, but he was not taken in by the paternalistic attitudes of the mill owners, and he was not really enchanted by the glaring new town of Lowell, as his essays, published a year later as *A Stranger in Lowell*, clearly show.[29]

One warm summer evening Harriet Farley, who knew the Whittier family from her home in Amesbury, brought the poet to a meeting of the Improvement Circle. For Lucy, dressed in her best white summer dress, it was an ordeal when her verses were read in front of him, and she could barely speak when he came and talked to her. He was a godlike figure, a hero, the Mr. Greatheart of her beloved *Pilgrim's Progress*, a man to be looked up to and followed, just as her father had been. He came often to the Improvement Circle meetings while he was in Lowell, and gradually Lucy came to know him better, although she still felt more awe than friendship; when Harriet took her to call at his home, she was much more comfortable with his mother and his sister Elizabeth.

Certainly the years from 1843 to 1845 were good ones for Lucy, full of books, conversation, ideas, and friends of all kinds. Her verses had gained some recognition; a Philadelphia newspaper copied one of her poems from the *Offering* and prophesied a fine future for her as a writer. But she was twenty-one years old, and the formal education she had dreamed of for so long was as far away as ever. Most girls came to the mill towns for three or four years; none of them considered their time there as an end, but as a means to something better. Lucy had been there for ten years. She was a tall, handsome, rather stately girl, not a beauty like her sisters, but attractive and with considerable presence. She had thick, wavy, light brown hair, smiling blue eyes, a radiant smile, and a laugh that her friends remembered with delight.[30] She had health, energy, talent, a gift for friendship, and a head full of knowledge, but there seemed to be nothing ahead of her but the mills. She might enjoy her life on a day-to-day basis, but when she looked to the future she saw nothing worthwhile.

Lowell in its inception had been visionary—Trollope called it an "industrial Utopia"—an American model for the Old World. For women, especially, Lowell delivered much of what it promised. The kind of community that came from working together under decent conditions and the kind of independence that came from earning a living wage were rare for them. The fact that there were actually young women who had bank accounts of their own shocked many outsiders while it increased the girls' pride in themselves.

At the moment, however, it was increasingly clear that the dream of Utopia had outlasted the reality; as competition increased, profits went down, and the mill owners chose profit over vision. They cut wages, increased the hours and the number of machines for each operative, and finally invited immigrant labor into the mills, paying them even lower wages than the mill girls earned, but still giving lip service to that ideal community they had originally established. As early as 1834 there had been a strike, and certainly by the mid-1840s it was clear that the bright experiment of the Lowell mills had dimmed and was on its way to extinction.

According to Philip Foner, "Many of the level-headed Yankee girls saw that the corporations were capitalizing on the favorable image of the factory girls created by the operatives' own efforts. It did not take them long to realize that a favorable image was no compensation for exploitation."[31] Girls left the mills and fewer of them came from the farms.

For Lucy and the friends she had made, it was time to try something else. She could, of course, always go home to Beverly. Her home was available and secure, even though there had been changes there as well. Grandfather Barrett was dead, and the whole family missed him. Louisa's third child had died, but her fourth one, given the same name, Charles, was healthy and flourishing. Tragically, however, dashing young Edward Harrington, with all his hopes and dreams, died of a fever off the coast of Africa in 1844 at the age of thirty-two. He left his twenty-nine-year-old widow and three sons well provided for; besides his valuable land, his personal estate was worth between seven and eight thousand dollars, a considerable amount of money that, carefully invested, would provide a comfortable life and security for his family. But the Harrington marriage had been a real love match, and Louisa was heartbroken. She dedicated herself to bringing up her boys to be the fine, useful citizens of her husband's dreams.

The same year, 1844, saw two more family marriages. In April

Lydia married Isaac Baker, a pleasant young man who was both seaman and businessman and came from a good Beverly family. In June
Abigail married a young blacksmith from Rowley named Luther
Haskell. Within a year Lydia had a daughter and Abby a son. Lucy
did not know either of her new brothers-in-law very well, but like
everyone she was particularly delighted with Isaac Baker's good
humor and warm, lively personality. Glad as she was at her sisters'
"good" marriages, Lucy felt a little out of things. According to social
usage, she was now, as the oldest unmarried daughter, properly addressed as Miss Larcom; the new dignity was not comfortable. It
emphasized her unmarried state and conflicted with a shapeless,
troubling wish to do something more significant with her life, even
though her dream of a good formal education now seemed unattain-
able.

She was not, however, the only restless one: the Spauldings were
going west. George, Frank, and Emeline were enthusiastic and their
arguments persuasive. The West was new and it needed what they
could bring to it. What could be more challenging and more valuable
than helping to create a new civilization, as their own ancestors had
done in coming to the New World? Surely that task was worth dedicating one's life and talents to? George would farm the Illinois prairie, and Frank would complete his medical studies at the University
of Missouri. Naturally Lucy would come; she could teach a district
school and help Emeline with the children. Sarah Holbrook might as
well travel with them, too, since she planned on teaching in the
West anyway.

Lucy, whose future looked blank and who had no dream of her
own, was caught up in theirs. It did not occur to her to wonder if a
young woman who loved books, libraries, learning, writing poetry,
and quiet but stimulating conversation would be happy as a pioneer;
any hesitations were lost in the drama of making such a change in
her life, or the more immediate excitement of planning the route,
anticipating the sight of places that were merely names on a map,
writing about positions, and finding out everything they could about
the West. They had read Mrs. Farnham's *Prairie Land*, but even better they liked a story of the West called *A New Home: Who'll Follow?*[32] They belonged to the modern generation that had grown up
hearing stories of the West and watching friends and relatives leaving the sedate old towns to make new lives. George and Frank talked

with eager enthusiasm about the land and cabin that awaited them on the Illinois prairie, a place that was the future, open and unexplored, untried and new, where work was challenging and accomplishment contributed to a new civilization. There could be no doubt of the value of their adventure, and in the spring of 1846, as soon as the roads were open, the little group left for the West.

CHAPTER 3

Living the Dream

Only the overflowing enthusiasm and belief in the future shared by the travelers made the complicated and uncomfortable trip west bearable.[1] Lucy made quick, pencilled jottings in her travel diary each day, recording, at least at the beginning, the route and the incidents. They left Boston on Monday, 13 April 1846, sailing to New York; Lucy, Sarah, Emeline, and George Francis, Emeline's nine-month-old son, were crowded into a tiny cabin, and Lucy disgraced the seafaring Larcoms by getting seasick. Sailing into New York at sunrise was beautiful. They had breakfast, then took a train across New Jersey—which she thought ugly—to Philadelphia. She enjoyed sailing down the Delaware River past that clean, pretty town, but the next train was hot and the boat across Chesapeake Bay had everyone but Lucy seasick. They arrived in Baltimore late at night; on the way to the hotel Sarah had her pocket picked. On the train ride the next day they saw slaves, a log cabin, wooden fences, and fields marked off with hedges, all for the first time, but it took all day to cross Maryland to Cumberland and the mountains.

The worst part of the trip came next. The stagecoach was overcrowded, with nine people and a baby. Lucy envied the baby, who cried most of the way, because he was the only one free to express his feelings. She herself, usually so cheerful, snapped when anyone spoke to her. The misery ended the next day at noon when they reached Brownsville and boarded a boat for Pittsburgh. They ignored the Monongahela River and slept. Pittsburgh was dirty, black, and smoky, but the river steamer down the Ohio was clean and beautifully furnished. Lucy could sit in her cabin with the door open and watch the spring beauty of the riverbanks—spring came so much earlier here—as she wrote in her journal, or she could talk with the other passengers and join them in singing, probably Joseph Philip Knight's popular song, "O, Fly to the Prairie," among others.

George's land and cabin were located about thirty miles east of St. Louis, in St. Clair County. They made the long trip by wagon, with eastern eyes vainly searching Looking Glass Prairie for trees; at the end was the cabin, virtually alone in the middle of nothing.

The flat, monotonous prairie was bad; the cabin was worse. It had four rooms, but they were small, low, and dark, and part of the house had not even been plastered. Emeline hung a curtain over the unfinished wall and they tried to pretend it was a medieval tapestry. One window had lost its glass, and twice a huge tomcat crept in during the night and terrified them with its howling. They thought they were prepared for what they would find, but Mrs. Kirkland's *New Home* dealt in a humorous way with backwoods characters and life; it said nothing of the day-to-day drudgery of keeping house and keeping clean where water was scarce, of cooking, caring for a baby, and living in tiny crowded rooms, only one of which—the kitchen— was immediately usable. Dust was everywhere. The baking heat was strange to the New Englanders, and there was no summer east wind to make the days bearable.

Since the clay soil did not quickly absorb water, the occasional rain stood in the furrows for days, providing a splendid breeding place for mosquitoes; Lucy, Sarah, and George all came down with malaria. It was pioneer experience far beyond what they had prepared for, reading books in their comfortable New England homes, and it took all of Lucy's cheerful, optimistic spirit and Emeline's stoic courage to keep from grumbling and complaints as the dream confronted reality.

Somehow they managed. They worked to accept the fact of prairie life and to go beyond its ugliness and crudity to find good. Lucy even liked the prairie after a while, "in a lukewarm way," eventually seeing a grandeur about it, especially when it blossomed with wildflowers in the spring.[2] George, a little shocked but still caught up in the pioneer dream, began to work the land; Emeline tried her best to turn the hideous little house into a proper home; Lucy took care of the baby;

Sarah helped everyone and set out a flower garden. Frank attended medical lectures in St. Louis but spent so much of his time on the prairie that later Lucy would say that they lived in the tiny house with the intimacy of brother and sister. Since she had grown up part of a big family and then lived in mill boardinghouses, crowded living conditions were nothing new and, although there were times when four or five adults and a baby or babies seemed about to burst the walls of the hut, life was warm and happy when they were all together.

She still had the people she loved best, and their presence compensated for a great deal. Furthermore, she knew that her sister needed her; Emeline's first child had lived only thirteen months, and baby George Francis was not as strong as they would like him to be. There was no doubt in Lucy's mind that her sister would soon be pregnant again. George and Frank, with their passionate ambitions, were still part of her world, and she was, at last, free of the mills. The future was not very clear at the moment, but that there was a future she never doubted.

She was eager to find a teaching position. Like most of her contemporaries, she viewed teaching as service; their ideals were summed up in lines from James Thomson's "The Seasons":

> Delightful task! to rear the tender thought,
> And teach the young idea how to shoot.

As many people did, she felt that the future of the country lay in the West; it was, therefore, a privilege and a tremendous responsibility to guide the young minds that would someday govern. Conscious of her lack of formal education and feeling humble and inadequate, she approached her job interview with the local school committee with dread.

The flat western lands had been surveyed into districts, and in each district a section was reserved for a schoolhouse.[3] Each one-room school was built, paid for, and controlled by the local farmers and was totally independent of all others. A term lasted three months, and the students might go for a term or two, stay home for a while if they were needed on the farm, and return when they chose. The farmers made up the teacher's salary of forty dollars a term out of their pockets.

Lucy emerged from her job interview a full-fledged district schoolteacher. The committee examined her handwriting, admired the way she made numbers, and agreed that she spoke correctly. She came away with the job and the comfortable conviction that however inadequate her own knowledge was, it was a hundred times better than that of her employers.

Her letters home were written in a tone of unquenchable good humor. She did not conceal the hardships but managed to laugh at them; she was able to distance herself: in the prairie world, but not of it. In a letter to Lydia she described the house with the room "we call our parlor, because the cooking-stove is not in it," dotting her letter with italicized westernisms like "the agey" to describe the fever they had all had, and giving in merry detail her life as a district schoolteacher. Her schoolhouse was "just the most literal specimen of a log-cabin" built of "unhewn logs, laid 'criss-cross,' as we used to say down the lane; the chinks filled up with mud, except those which are not filled up 'at all, at all,' . . . The floor lies as easy as it can on the ground." There had never been a school in the district before, and she was pleased that her "ideas" were beginning to "shoot," but the lack of knowledge was appalling. "I asked one new scholar yesterday how old she was. 'Don't know,' she said, 'never was inside of a schoolhouse before.' " Getting to school was frightening because she had to make her way through "cattlebrutes" turned out on the prairie by the local farmers.[4]

She had some comments on life, and especially woman's life, in the West. After describing George's livestock and her own flat refusal to learn to milk the cows, she went on: "Talk to me about getting married and settling down here in the West! I won't do that thing till I'm a greater goose than I am now, for love nor money. It is a common saying here, that 'this is a fine country for men and dogs, but women and oxen have to take it.' The secret of it is that farmer's wives have to do all their work in one room, without any help, and almost nothing to work with. If ever I had the mind to take the vestal vow, it has been since I 'emigrated.' You'll see me coming back one of these years, a 'right smart' old maid, my flat sides and cheeks shaking with 'the agey,' to the tune of 'Oh, take your time, Miss Lucy!' "

Forty dollars for three months was more money than Lucy had earned in the mill; the difficulty lay in collecting it. Often George had to find the school managers and demand his sister-in-law's money, for to some of the farmers that was a great deal to pay a woman. She could walk to the schoolhouse, which she did rather uneasily, never trusting cows and living in terror of meeting a snake—or, worse, having one come up through the carelessly laid boards of the schoolhouse floor. Most of her students did not aspire to much beyond the simplest reading, writing, and figuring. She could, and did, make amusing stories out of her experiences: the child put into the chimney corner as punishment who climbed up the chimney and disappeared, the child who knew what he was called but not what his name was, the attempts to teach penmanship with no writing surface, or the visits from sheep that looked in through the glassless windows. She laughed a great deal and carried her stories home to the family to make them laugh, but there was nothing in her teaching to inspire her, and she quickly came to loathe what she called "keeping school"—records, housekeeping, discipline, and interference from outsiders—as opposed to teaching.

The work of the farm and house, malaria, the unpleasant teaching conditions, and the intense heat and ever-present dust characterized the first summer; in October George Francis died. Winter, with its rain and mud instead of crisp, cold air and snow, was a dreadful time. The cabin could hardly hold them all. Lucy sent a poem back home to the *Salem Register* called "A Baby's Dirge" that began,

> Baby, 'neath the long grass sleeping,
> Thou hast found a lonely grave.

It ended on a slightly happier note, an affirmation that the pure and innocent child was now with God. Writing it eased the pain a little. She eased another kind of pain in a poem for the same newspaper called "Our Birthday" and addressed to "My Sister L——." For the first time she and Lydia were not celebrating their birthday together, and the poem is both loving and lonely.

Spring brought some improvement. There was beauty in the blossoming of the dull prairie, farming tasks were a little easier, and Emeline's third child, named Charlotte for the beloved older sister who had died at sea, was born; having a baby in the house made everyone a little happier. Frank had graduated from the college in St. Louis. It was still too soon to think definitely about marriage, for he was not sure whether he wanted to practice medicine or try some other field, but they were both young enough to wait until they knew what they wanted the future to be. George was finding farming far harder and less rewarding—spiritually or financially—than he had expected, and the hard life was not good for him, Emeline, or the children; besides, as he told his wife and sister-in-law, he had always really intended to be a minister, and ministers were scarce in the West. Sarah had left the prairie and was teaching in Belleville; she would be married the next year.

Unaware that she was making a decision that would affect her life, Lucy arranged to teach in a school near Alton, a sizable town just across the Mississippi River from St. Louis. It was certainly a drawback that she would have to board with strangers, for she was still shy and uncomfortable away from her family, but life in the cabin was confining and she had had more than enough of the prairie school. She began teaching in the Summerfield district, in a neat white schoolhouse with a solid floor, and almost immediately found friends. One of her pupils, Helen Spaulding, came from a family of New Englanders transplanted from Lawrence, just down the Merrimack from Lowell.[5] Their white clapboard, black-shuttered house with the lilac trees in the dooryard might have stood on any New England lane, and the brisk, cultured voices sounded familiar and right in Lucy's ears. They were a prosperous family; Don Alonzo Spaulding—the name was one that appeared in several generations of his branch of the Spaulding family—was the official surveyor for Madison County. He had a son, Henry, from a first marriage; his second wife was Ann Danforth Spaulding, and they had one child, Helen. Ann Spaulding's sister, Rebecca Danforth, lived with them, and with these two women Lucy felt an immediate kinship. She went to live in their house, and a long and close friendship began.

Vine Lodge, the name Lucy gave the house, was a gracious home. She never forgot the room where she sat and looked at the ailanthus trees, the garden, and the peaches that grew against the wall. Mrs. Spaulding and Miss Danforth became "Ma" and "Becky," and the entire family became her family. They knew George and Emeline—in fact, there was a distant relationship—but they were primarily Lucy's friends. The three women read aloud to each other, discussed issues and ideas, and talked intimately about their own feelings. They encouraged Lucy to write, admiring her work and suggesting some local papers that would appreciate it.

Like so many of the young women connected with the *Lowell Offering* who went away to build new lives, Lucy continued to write for the magazine. It had stopped publication in 1845, but was briefly reborn as the *New England Offering*. Harriet Farley, now the sole editor, was always glad to hear from its early contributors. Lucy sent a varied lot. As "Ruth Rover" she wrote short stories with western backgrounds, generally characterized by good description and almost no plot. "A Night of Suspense" (April 1848) tells of a lost child whose parents spend the night worrying about all the things that could happen to him until he is rather casually found the next morning. As "Angelina Abigail" she wrote amusing little verses making fun of her inadequacy at and dislike for the household tasks that living in the West forced her and other women to assume. She wrote translations of German poems, short moral essays called either "prose poems" or "similitudes," and some homesick-sounding poems with names like "New England Winter," "Farewell to New England," and "The Sea." Parts of her long letters to Harriet Farley were published as "Epistolary Extracts" and dealt with all facets of western life: election day, prairie fires, a plague of caterpillars, cholera in St. Louis. She wrote poems in her own name as well; one of them presents a theme that clearly concerned her: the wasted lives of women in the West. The first seven stanzas of "A Prairie Pastoral" (August 1849) describe Kate, just seventeen, fresh, young, and beautiful, full of joyful expectations as she is courted by young Will. The last stanza shows the result:

> But now for the belle of the prairie you'll seek
> In vain through the cornfields, or down by the creek.
> In the grove a new cabin has risen, and here
> Will has called her "old woman" for more than a year.

Now and then she sent verses home to the *Salem Register* or wrote for St. Louis papers. In the fall of 1847 the sight of the farmers burning off the tall prairie grass to enrich the soil inspired a poem called "The Burning Prairie." She compared the fire to the fires of freedom that would someday burn out the evil of slavery and enrich the free soil of America. There was one place where such a poem could be sure of a warm reception—she sent it to John Greenleaf Whittier, now corresponding editor of the Washington antislavery paper the *National Era*. It appeared in the spring of 1848, and with another poem, "Elisha and the Angels," was included in Rufus Griswold's anthology, *The Female Poets of America*, with a biographical sketch by Whittier. "Rumors of Peace," a lament for those who died in the Mexican War, appeared in June 1848, and later Whittier "noticed" the *New England Offering*, quoting in full Larcom's essay "A Schoolmistress' First Day" (July 1848).

All this encouragement, the renewed contact with Whittier, and the friendship of Ann Spaulding and Rebecca Danforth made this a much happier year than the preceding one. She was less worried about Emeline, for the family had left the prairie. George was ordained in May 1848, and they piled their belongings in three ox-drawn wagons and moved to the town of Woodburn, where George found a church. Their new home was still rough by eastern standards but much better than the cabin. They had neighbors and a garden, and the town itself had a common surrounded by locust trees and houses, just as New England towns did. Emeline, in her element as a minister's wife, immediately organized the ladies of the small brick church into the Woodburn Congregational Sewing Society, very like the improvement circles of Lowell.[6]

In spite of a faint dissatisfaction that she tried to ignore, Lucy was, on the whole, happy; she might have taught in the Summerfield district and lived at Vine Lodge for a longer time except for an incident that offended the local school committee. A young black boy came to school and she admitted him into her class. Major Long, one of the school committee members, appeared the next day to say that if she allowed the boy to remain the school would be closed. She did not fight them; instead she arranged to give the boy private lessons after school. Sometimes she went to his cabin and taught both the boy and his father. Both were extremely intelligent, and teaching them was a rewarding experience.[7] The school committeemen, however, were so angered that they refused to hire her again. She had, perhaps, misjudged her territory; not long before, in 1837, a rioting mob in Alton had murdered the abolitionist newspaper editor Owen Lovejoy.

She found a school near Woodburn easily and went to live with Emeline but was sorry to leave Ma and Becky, who gave her so much love and encouragement. In fact, they gave her something more: they revived her longing for a good formal education, that dream that had been nearly buried, first under the need to deal with reality and then under the temporary enchantment of the move west.

In Godfrey, a few miles from Alton, was Monticello Seminary, a school for young women reputed to be one of the best in the country and certainly the finest in the West. Its headmistress was the re-markable and formidable Miss Philena Fobes from Philadelphia, and under her guidance the seminary was in no sense a finishing school. It had been founded in 1837 by Captain Benjamin Godfrey, a former New England sea captain, so that his then-infant daughter and other young girls might be given a good education. Catherine Beecher helped establish its curriculum, and a young lawyer named Abra-ham Lincoln was an adviser. Its purpose was "the symmetrical train-ing of the whole being—physical, mental, and spiritual—applied to the education of women."[8] The reputation of the school and its prin-cipal was overwhelming. Here was what Lucy had always wanted—a good formal education; here was something new, an intellectual woman free to use her powers. And here was Lucy Larcom, former mill girl, district schoolteacher, with no formal education and no money to get one.

She had never even met a woman like Miss Fobes. Certainly Har-riet Farley and Harriot Curtis, even Emeline, were bright and cre-ative; her acquaintance Elizabeth Whittier was clever under all her Quaker gentleness, but none of these women were in positions of authority. Miss Fobes was about thirty-five, educated, intellectual, and commanding, and Lucy, diffident because of her admiration, made no effort to meet her. Ma and Becky, however, insisted that she should return to school; they knew Miss Fobes, and they finally per-suaded Lucy to go with them to make a formal call. Impressed by the young woman's "bright, intelligent face and sincere manner, with her good sense and enthusiasm," Miss Fobes was not just will-ing but eager to have her for a student.[9] Monticello was dedicated to educating young women of all financial levels, so there were ways to earn her tuition: Lucy would be a student, but she would also work. By November of 1848 arrangements had been made for her to enter Monticello the following March.

All her friends in Illinois and back home in Beverly were delighted at her good news. Through the late fall she was caught up in the future, in getting herself ready and looking ahead to the actual real-ization of the dream she had held for so long. She spent much of her time reading to prepare for her courses, and she wrote long letters to Vine Lodge. So preoccupied was she that she barely noticed the star-tling news of rivers of gold and fortunes to be gained for a day's work far away in California.

In November Lucy took full charge of Emeline's household; her sister was pregnant again, and the baby was due in a matter of weeks. Charlotte, called Lottie, was now a year and a half old, fat, healthy, and happy, running to her aunt instead of her mother for aid and comfort. It was a busy time, for Emeline came down with the "chills," and George was building a new house, smaller than the one they rented; George was finding that prairie ministers did not earn much money. Frank visited often, and at the end of the day there was conversation and laughter, just as there had been in the little house in Lowell. Lucy enjoyed them, but she was so busy and so wrapped up in dreams of her own future that she hardly noticed how Frank's eyes gleamed when he talked about California.

With his romantic and adventurous temperament, Frank was sure to be fascinated by all that California represented, especially since he was not particularly content in Illinois. He had decided against practicing medicine, at least for the moment, and had worked as a teacher and a store clerk; now he was learning surveying with D. A. Spaulding and was frequently away on short trips. So far none of these occupations satisfied his restless spirit. California was the ultimate quest: the journey, with its ordeals and tests, the confrontation, and finally the tangible and symbolic reward of gold. Frank found it irresistible and could not understand Lucy's lack of interest. If only to be practical, she should realize that a modest fortune would further their plans.

For Lucy there was no reality in the idea that fortunes came from anything but hard work. Her attitude toward money was formed early and never really changed. Experience taught her that money was a necessity; without it one could not live comfortably. However, obsession with money, or love of money for its own sake, was wrong—was, indeed, evil. Years later she was to say that looking down on rich people was "one of the temptations of the independent poor";[10] nevertheless, the belief that money acquired by any means other than hard work was shameful had grown in her in the Lowell years. She had, after all, seen the changes in the mills brought about by greed for excessive profits. She could hear the stories of California gold as interesting tales of adventure, but they seemed as unreal as the folktales Emeline used to tell the children, not anything that could affect her or her family.

Looking forward to Monticello kept her cheerful even when she was buried under household chores. Because the new house was not finished, she had to cook for workmen as well as for the family, nurse

Emeline, who had come down with fever, churn butter, make candles, and take care of her niece. After the baby, George Herbert, was born, Lucy was still in charge: "I am obliged to do the honours and drudgery for the minister and his daughter," she wrote Ma and Becky.

> There is plenty of the latter to do, and oh! how I don't like it! My experience for the last two months has given me a most incurable (I fear) dislike of housework in general, and of cooking in particular. I try to officiate with as good a grace as possible, but you know Sister Rebecca says my face will tell tales, and I more than half suspect that the minister begins to think I am not so amiable after all. I must rub up some old-fashioned smiles, or else he will refuse to give me a recommendation. Wouldn't that be dreadful?!!
>
> But, to tell the truth, I don't desire "domestic happiness" a bit, if it is to be earned only by working from morning to night to feed the "outer man." Only think, I have not found time to look at those books of Henry's yet; but I will begin to study them some of these evenings, if "the man" has to go without his supper.[11]

With rueful good humor she turned the housekeeping experience into an Angelina Abigail poem for the *Offering* (April 1849), using high-flown language to sharpen the contrast between romance and reality:

MOONWARD GUSHINGS

> O, virgin moon! O, queenly moon!
>   Turn, turn thy pensive glance from me.
> I'll scan thy circling glories soon;
>   But now, *I'm busy getting tea!*
>
> Fair Luna! thou'rt no partial queen:
>   Thou smil'st on lovers in a flutter;
> And just as tenderly, I ween,
>   On me, *When munching bread and butter.*
>
> O, say, within thy mystic bound,
>   Whose wonders unto man ne'er waked,
> Was e'er a doleful maiden found,
>   Who *burnt the cakes she should have baked?*

Hark! sphery music glads my soul:
Sure, from thy realm those numbers sweep.
Deep—louder—ah! too shrill they roll:
O, baby, *won't you go to sleep?*

Farewell! a weary weight of care
Now draws me earthward; no wild wishes
Or dark regrets my spirit tear,—
But O, *I haven't washed the dishes!*

Heavier than usual snowfalls made the winter pleasant to the New Englanders. As soon as Emeline recovered, Lucy went to visit at Vine Lodge. She returned to Woodburn at an unfortunate time, for as the deep snow melted, mud made the roads impassable. Frank tried everywhere to borrow a horse and carriage, but travel was at a standstill. Lucy was bitterly disappointed that she could not get to the seminary in time for the opening of the term. Accepting as cheerfully as possible what she could not control, she found a school and visited often at Vine Lodge. She had the excuse that Henry, Ann Spaulding's stepson, was helping her with mathematics. An excuse was necessary sometimes, for Emeline missed her sister and always needed her help.

The relationship between the sisters had changed, although Lucy often felt that only she perceived the difference. Nothing would ever affect the love and gratitude she felt for the older sister who had led the way for so long. Certainly, Lucy admitted to herself, she could never have come through the years in the mills without Emeline's care, encouragement, and imagination, or her determination to deal with life. "Does it make you warmer to complain of the cold?" summed up a large part of her philosophy. Emeline saw life as a place of pain and testing set up by a remote God who showed His love by chastising His people to temper them for the life to come. Duty to God demanded cheerful acceptance of whatever He sent. Pleasure came from loving and helping others and the consciousness of doing one's duty.

Lucy's intellect, her natural cheerfulness, and her practical streak all agreed with the first part of Emeline's belief. Of course one should accept whatever had to be, but weren't there things that could be changed? And if so, was life really so terrible and God so stern? Even the remote Benjamin Larcom had had tender moments when his children knew themselves loved. And what of the loving voice of the New Testament? The natural beauty that Lucy remembered from her childhood was matched by the beauty of the prairie in bloom in the spring. Was this worldliness a temptation? Might it not be God's gift?

At the time of Emeline's marriage, Lucy had been shocked when she recognized her dependence on her older sister; she decided then that she must learn to rely on herself. Now it seemed sometimes that Emeline could not let her go, or see her as anything other than little sister. But Lucy was learning to look with her own eyes, and one of the things she looked at was Emeline's marriage.

By contemporary standards Emeline was a perfect wife. As her husband went from schoolmaster to farmer to minister, she followed him without complaint, she handled the never-ending household tasks, she bore him children who died. Had all that Puritan strengthening of the spirit and mortification of the flesh been for this goal? Emeline had put aside everything else when she married; she no longer wrote, and the intelligence that had loved to deal with moral issues and complicated mathematical problems now was concentrated on the role of wife and mother. It seemed a terrible waste, and Lucy had begun to resent the assumption that big sister Emeline, as wife and mother, would lead little sister Lucy's feet along the same path. Perhaps that was not her path. Even for women there were different kinds of lives. Look at Miss Fobes.

Sometimes at Woodburn all Lucy's cheerful tact was needed to avoid hurting Emeline or offending George. Her feelings for him were ambivalent; he was her brother and he was a good man, but he could be exasperating. She viewed the sincerity of his "call" to the ministry with some cynicism, and there were times when she could not help resenting what he and marriage were doing to "golden-haired and golden-hearted" Emeline.[12] And the house at Woodburn was too small to contain three strong personalities, especially when one of them was just beginning to feel her strength. Vine Lodge was roomy and quiet and civilized; the inhabitants discussed life, ideas, books, and religion intensely, but in quiet voices.

Lucy finally entered Monticello Seminary in September 1849 and immediately found herself, as she had expected, part of a new world. From her room in the great gray limestone building she looked out over the parklike lawns to the woods that separated the seminary from the Mississippi; she could actually hear the steamboats as they passed up and down the river. Her courses included Latin, French, the hated mathematics, botany, geology, drawing, medieval history, and mental philosophy, a course which seems to have combined a study of major philosophers with an examination of the students' own thinking processes. She also studied English composition, finding, in spite of her writing experience, that there was much she could learn.

In the past her passion for learning had sent her to intense but undirected study of a few unrelated areas; now she was discovering the advantages of system and discipline. Years later she described the course of study at Monticello as "the broadest, the most college-like, that I have ever known. . . . The study of medieval and modern history, and of modern philosophy, especially, opened new vistas to me. . . . our Principal was also our teacher, and her method was to show us the tendencies of thought, to put our minds into the great current of human affairs, leaving us to collect details as we could, then or afterwards. We came thus to feel that these were life-long studies, as indeed they are . . . I learned what education really is; the penetrating deeper and rising higher into life, as well as making continually wider explorations; the rounding of the whole human being out of its nebulous elements into form."[13] The approach did more than open her mind; it changed her life.

To pay for her education Larcom did housework for a while, until she was asked to teach the primary classes, made up of girls preparing to enter the seminary. She was busy with teaching and her own studies, but when she had free time she spent it out-of-doors in the lovely grounds and the woods, often with her botany teacher, Sara C. Eaton, whose father, Amos Eaton, was a famous professor of geology and the author of several books on the natural sciences.

She was in a curious position, half student and half teacher, older than her fellow students. Monticello was prepared to be unconventional—it was odd enough to give women such an education, anyway—and neither her age nor the fact that she did not fit into either group caused any problems. She was liked for her warmth, her gentleness, and her "gleams of delicate humor," but she was reserved and seemed very dignified, perhaps partly because of her Junoesque stature.[14] She was an awesome figure to the younger western girls, too, for she had seen Boston, and the Bunker Hill Monument, and the Salem of the witches, and she knew the poet Whittier. Everyone admired, even loved Miss Larcom, but no one came very close to her.

She really did not need close friends at Monticello. She was engrossed in her studies, loving everything but mathematics. A friend remembered her plaintive summing up of her difficulties with geometry: "Oh, dear, I can see all the beauty, and feel all the poetry; but I cannot do the steps."[15] When she did need companionship, Vine Lodge was close by, with the family ready to hear about what she was doing and to encourage her in everything. In fact, with her mind being both stretched and disciplined, the satisfying environment of an excellent school, and the fulfilling of a treasured goal, with her friends near and Emeline close but not too close, Lucy was almost perfectly happy. Developing an identity separate from "sister Lucy," she was now Miss Larcom, not as the oldest unmarried daughter, but as an intelligent young woman with a responsible position.

In this satisfying existence there was only one flaw: Frank. He came frequently to Woodburn or to Vine Lodge, and gradually she was forced to realize the strength of his fascination with California. Young men from all over the East and Midwest, calling themselves "forty-niners," were heading for the goldfields. St. Louis was a stop on the road to Independence, the meeting and departure point; Frank constantly met the adventurers and listened to their dreams. He was really not much happier in Illinois than he had been in Lowell, for none of the work he did seemed to offer his restless spirit what it wanted. Why not go west?

Not, he assured Lucy, that he wanted gold, and not to stay—just to see what the real West was like, and to take part in the great national adventure. Perhaps California, not Illinois, was the future they had all been looking for back in Lowell—not exchanging one town for another, one school for another, but going to a world new, unformed, a testing place.

Lucy, beginning her own kind of adventure and worried a little by hints of restlessness in George and its effect on Emeline (baby George Herbert had died in September 1849; baby Edward was born in January 1850), thought the whole idea foolish. What kind of a useful life could anyone build in an uncivilized place like California? How could any sensible person ever expect a fortune for no work? It was one thing to go to the wilderness to build homes and towns and schools; it was something else entirely to go hunting for gold. She had no desire to leave the world she had just entered. About this time she wrote a story called "A Tale of California and Cholera" for the *Offering* (January 1850). The heroine, a lovely young girl from St. Louis, is caught up in the romance of California and decides to go with her father. To make the journey even more romantic, she and her fiancé will be married on the plains. Cholera strikes the company and the young girl dies the night before the wedding. The story contains revealing lines: "the fable of Midas has not yet convinced us that this bright delusion is not worth more than life itself," and, flatly, "El Dorado is no place for women."

The discussions within the family and between Frank and Lucy went on through the fall and the winter, sometimes calm, sometimes heated. At one point a furious Lucy declared that if Frank went to California, he was dead as far as she was concerned.

Frank was not the only one of their friends to be so affected. Letters from home told of the exodus of young men lured by gold and adventure. In fact, in the summer of 1849 a group of young men from Beverly and nearby towns bought the bark *San Francisco*, formed a company, wrote a constitution and by-laws, and agreed that they would not make the mistake other groups were making: they would stay together and share the profits and the hardships of the venture.

As master of the ship they had Captain Thomas Remmonds, with Andrew Larcom as second mate. The captain of the company and keeper of its journal was Lydia's husband, Isaac Baker.[16] Luther Haskell, Abigail's husband, was a passenger. The whole town turned out to see them off on the morning of 15 August 1849, as they sailed from Beverly harbor. The bark carried forty members, including a few passengers, sixty-three thousand feet of planed boards, ten thousand bricks, eight house frames, twenty pigs, a dog, a kitten, and a crow. There was even a ship's band, made up of drums, cymbals, accordion, tambourine, and bells.

The ship's log, kept by Joseph Carrico, records the events of the pleasant and fairly fast voyage; Isaac Baker's journal is less formal and more detailed. He had written the company song, to be sung to the tune of "Oh, Susannah!" and he also wrote a Thanksgiving proclamation for the company and crew. When the ship was running smoothly, the band played and the young men sang or talked politics or planned the future they would make with their California gold.

Baker's journal reveals a delightful personality as well as the events of the voyage. His entries are wise and good-natured, his descriptions are colorful, and he summed up or commented on situations in lighthearted verse. While lying off Monterey the ship encountered wind and rain and heavy seas. Baker wrote:

One never minds the water in such weather as this, when it's too plenty, both salt and fresh, so plenty, indeed, that we would like most any thing for a change and although we have not seen the sun of late and therefore not sure of our position, yet

> One thing we know, that we can show,
> And that too without boasting
> We've all enough of this 'ere stuff
> Called California coasting.

'Tis rather disagreeable at this season of the year, for although not cold, yet continual gales of wind and squalls of rain are anything but pleasant when close in to the land and so many vessels about, so we can't help saying

> And thus we talk and act, but then
> 'Tis useless so to hanker,
> These things we'll bear, 'til all is fair,
> And then run in and anchor.[17]

Although there had been some difficulty rounding the Horn, the voyage was a good one and on 11 January 1850, one hundred forty-nine days out of Beverly, they entered San Francisco harbor.

Of course news of the voyage came slowly. Passing ships brought information from the *San Francisco* to Beverly, and that news reached the prairie in letters from Lydia and Abigail through the fall, winter, and early spring. Lucy and Emeline were naturally interested in the fate of a cousin, two brothers-in-law, and a host of childhood friends, and everybody was relieved to hear of their safe arrival in California.

Lucy might not have shared Frank's dream, but she did care about the dreamer. She had promised to marry him, and she wanted to, although even then she was determined that her marriage should not be like Emeline's—all drudgery and duty and dead babies. She did not want to end the engagement, and the quarrels distressed her.

She was fighting for her idea of a future, just as Frank was fighting for his.

Eventually, with advice from everyone, they reached a compromise. Frank was to go for two years and get California out of his system while Lucy finished her education at Monticello. Then he would come back and they would marry. Perhaps, if California was worth seeing, Lucy might even make the trip west when she finished school, and they could marry, travel a little, then come back and make their permanent home.

Frank left St. Louis in the spring of 1850 with a group that included another Spaulding brother, Charles. Perhaps if he had waited for more news from the *San Francisco* he might have had second thoughts, for after the fair voyage the experience became far less pleasant but more typical. Isaac Baker's first happy impression of San Francisco vanished when he went ashore: "It's the most degraded, immoral, uncivilized and dirty city that can be imagined and the sooner we are away from here the better, were my afterthoughts five minutes after being landed on shore."[18] Furthermore, the price of lumber in the city was so low that they would not break even, so they decided to sail up the Sacramento River to the goldfields. Although the distance was only a few miles, it took them thirty-three days to get their heavily loaded oceangoing sailing ship up the river. Passage was hampered by tides, shallows, shoals, marshes, channels, and wind currents. Determined to manage on their own and not to abandon the cargo, they refused to hire a pilot for four hundred dollars. They spent more time grounded or becalmed than they did afloat, attacked by frustration and mosquitoes, and depressed when on trips ashore to hunt they saw piles of machinery and cargo dumped by other sailing ships that had attempted the same journey. The sight of the regular steamer traffic moving up and down the river did not help.

They reached Sacramento on 20 February, sold their cargo at a disappointingly small profit, and then, as usually happened with the companies, split up. (Baker summed it up in another set of verses.) With Luther Haskell and another friend, Baker set off to try his luck in the mines. From February to September they traveled around, making barely enough money to cover their expenses, although Baker's journal keeps its tone of interest and good humor. The trip home was long, dismal, and dangerous; his ship, the *Belgrade*, was nearly wrecked and it took five weeks to get as far as Acapulco. From there he took a steamer to Panama, crossed the Isthmus, and found another ship, arriving in New York on 8 November 1850. Andrew Larcom got back to Beverly about the same time, having made the long journey overland. By the time details came back, however, Frank was in California.

CHAPTER 4

A Separate Path

Larcom's first year at Monticello ended in early summer and she went back to Woodburn, where the small house was made even smaller by the presence of George's parents, who had come from Lowell to see their sons off to California and were remaining for a long visit. It was hard to find quiet and privacy, and with extra people there was more housework to do.[1] She escaped to Vine Lodge whenever possible, and her letters were an outlet for her exasperation, which had to be hidden so that it would not hurt Emeline.

It was a relief when school started in September. She was in charge of the preparatory school, which had its own building, so in a sense she had a school of her own. The girls were attractive and well-mannered. Larcom's generous spirit never resented her own loss of girlhood; the lack made her even more anxious that other girls should enjoy their youth. But her new position gave her less free time than she wanted. Even though the students were far superior to the district school children, she again found the mechanics of keeping school irksome and boring. She loved her studies and her reading, but it was harder to find time for writing. The *Offering* stopped publication with the March 1850 issue. On Harriet Farley's advice, Larcom sent a poem called "The Pioneer's Vision" to *Sartain's Magazine;* it was not only accepted, but to her amazement and delight she was paid the princely sum of five dollars for it—the first money she earned from her writing.

Monticello was widening her outlook and reviving her interest in national events. This was the year in which the overland mail service was established; it was also the year of the so-called Clay Compromise that attempted but failed to bring together different views on slavery. When Daniel Webster argued against restricting slavery in the new territories, abolitionists and his fellow New Englanders screamed at the betrayal. Whittier, in his widely read poem "Ichabod," lashed out at Webster, demanding that not scorn but contemptuous pity should be felt:

> All else is gone: from those great eyes
> The soul has fled:
> When faith is lost, when honor dies,
> The man is dead!

Larcom was thrilled and proud as she read the poem; she could picture the poet's dark eyes flashing in his austere face. She was grateful again for Ma and Becky, who shared her own antislavery feelings and to whom she could talk so freely. Neither George nor Frank felt very strongly about slavery, and it was seldom discussed at Woodburn. Then there was a second women's rights convention; Larcom was not sure how she felt on that matter, and at the moment nothing seemed so important as the antislavery fight. So many things were happening back East that fit in with the intellectual adventures that Monticello and Miss Fobes were giving her.

Though increasingly troubled, Larcom was not unhappy. Life was pleasant; winter brought sleigh rides, with the local minister driving the Monticello teachers through the snow as they rang tea bells and sang, enjoying the cold, brisk air that felt like New England. For Christmas gifts from her students she received copies of the poems of Burns, Coleridge, Moore, and Shelley, as well as *Rasselas* and *The Ettinck Shepherd*.

In the fall her friends moved from Vine Lodge to St. Louis when D. A. Spaulding became surveyor-general of Missouri. Larcom missed them and the comfort of their home dreadfully, but there were compensations: she was as welcome in the new home as she had been in the old, and she grew to like the advantages of a city. She and Henry Spaulding exchanged some flirtatious letters for a while.[2] Both of them wrote rather ponderous badinage, as if trying out a mode of behavior in which neither was comfortable. Henry's teasing is heavy-handed; Larcom's responses have slightly more wit and less archness. This phase of their friendship did not last long and did not affect her closeness to the family.

Of course there was news from the West, too. It was estimated that in the first six months of 1850 forty thousand people had passed through Fort Laramie on their way to the new state of California, and there were stories about the brave soldier Frémont, who had made sure that California would be a state rather than a part of Mexico. According to rumor, hundreds of ships lay deserted in San Francisco harbor, their crews gone to hunt for gold. Frank wrote whenever he could send a letter, and Larcom worried about him—but she felt both amazed and guilty that she did not miss him as much or as constantly as a young woman should miss the man she had promised to marry. Now that the intimacy of the "foursome" was broken, she was horrified to find that she increasingly often felt free and happy without him. (There were also times, usually following a stay with George and Emeline, when she questioned whether she was fit for marriage at all.)

Frank reached Fort Laramie in August and California early in the autumn; in the winter he was ill, and he wrote back gloomily to advise others not to come. By March, however, his feelings had changed. "At the last news," Larcom wrote her Vine Lodge friends, "he had recovered his health, and was *hoping* to accomplish something. He speaks of the climate as being very pleasant at San Francisco. He thinks Italian skies could not compare with theirs. I suppose it was sudden fit of enthusiasm, however. Have you heard that Dr. Goheen is dead? . . . It will be a joyful surprise to me if Frank lives to return."[3]

The same letter describes her own activity. "I am . . . 'over head and ears' in cares and studies. I have just finished a philosophical abstract thirty pages long—six grammars sit in the chair beside me, patiently waiting my attention—three empty canvases look anxiously at me from the window, &c, &c, &c—But it is all just as I like to have it, just as I make it; I would not stay here and be less busy, for anything. Not that everything is not as pleasant as things can be *at school*; but you know my tastes."

Larcom loved being a student, but chafed at the restrictions imposed by her obligations as a teacher. Several times her plans to go to St. Louis had to be canceled, and she hated having to ask for permission. There were lectures in the city that she wanted to attend, and she was determined to hear Jenny Lind when the great singer's sensational tour brought her there. She thought seriously of leaving Monticello, even though she needed another year before she could formally graduate. "What should you think I had better do?" she asked her friends. "If I could get into a good school as an assistant, I should like it; but I don't care about entering a public school—to go over the same old story that I've been telling these five years—Geography, Arithmetic, Grammar and Spelling, Spelling and Grammar, Arithmetic, and Geography. In truth and sincerity I am tired of it. If I come back here it will be for the sake of studying."

As a postscript to that long letter, she wrote, "I recollect you wrote to me once, about sending to a man up North who had some cure for the scrofula. Do you know anything about him now? I have decided that I will make an effort to cure mine. Do you know any physician in St. Louis that is skillful in humors?"

Scrofula is one form of the tuberculosis that affected half the world's population in the nineteenth century. Larcom and her contemporaries did not understand much about it, and most people believed it was hereditary. An 1859 newspaper advertisement for a cure (run along with one for Burnett's Cocaine to prevent hair falling off) gives an idea of the common perception of the disease: "Hall's Great Scrofula Remedy" is good for "impurities of the blood, removes all Vitiated Secretions, gives healthy action to the Liver and correct tone to the Stomach." It "causes the blood to flow . . . as pure and undefiled as it did in the primeval state of man, wherein the disease was unknown." Scrofula is classed with "erruptive ills" like eczema, bronchitis, tumors, ulcers, asthma, coughs, and boils, and the medicine promises to cure them all, "whether they have been inherited or acquired"—all for one dollar a bottle.[4]

Larcom might have developed scrofula in Lowell, since the crowded conditions there provided a likely place for the spread of contagious disease. So did life on a ship, and it is possible that her father had the disease. It was a painful and humiliating ailment; the glands in the neck became swollen, then broke into ugly running sores that itched and burned and frequently left scars. One outbreak might dry up, but another could come at any time. Medical treatment concentrated on healing the unsightly sores without any approach to the disease itself.

The disease had not been uncommon in Lowell, and Larcom

thought of it as something unpleasant that she would like to get rid of. Her references to her scrofula are often accompanied by comments about the doctor who was treating her. She seems to have had a mild flirtation with young Dr. Edwards, but her tone suggests that she regarded him with amusement, as if the flirtation were really a joke she shared with Ma and Becky.

She went to the Jenny Lind concert with a group from Monticello and the music echoed in her ears for weeks afterward, but she continued to resent her inability to go where and when she chose. Her dissatisfaction with that phase of her life is a theme that recurs throughout the letters of 1851 and into the spring of 1852.

The same letters faithfully report Frank's news and her own thoughts about him and the future. For a while he was in "the depths of azuredom,"[5] but his spirits soon improved. A few months later he sent her some gold, which she had made into a pin. By June he had been ill and apparently thought, or at least wrote, of returning. "Shall I be glad?" Larcom wrote her Vine Lodge friends. "Yes— to see him—of course—but certain other questions will be harder than ever to decide. . . . I am decided on one thing, and that is to do what will most increase my usefulness, so far as I can find that out."[6]

The term ended and Larcom went to Woodburn for the summer months. Her Vine Lodge friends were away, so until late August she had no escape; sometimes the noise and bustle in the small house made her feel as if she were back in the mill. Certainly the demands on her time kept her from studying and writing.

Emeline's son Edward died in August; twelve days later another son, Theodore, was born. For those whose religious faith was strong, grief at the death of a child was tempered by the conviction that the baptized child in its innocence was called to God, to be safe from temptation and far happier in heaven than it could be in earthly life. Larcom's questioning of her own traditional religious belief began during her years on the prairie, but there was never a time when she doubted the existence of a God and an afterlife. Nevertheless, she loved children and was very close to Emeline's. In the back of her mind must always have been the knowledge that Lois Larcom had raised ten healthy children to maturity—back in civilized Beverly.

Monticello, Woodburn, and St. Louis were the boundaries of her life. She thought about leaving the seminary and finding a position, preferably in the city, but common sense overruled that idea: of course she should stay and graduate. It was a relief, tinged with guilt, to get back to Monticello, where she had her quiet room, her books, and her writing and painting materials. Her preparatory class was bigger this year, but the girls seemed pleasant, and her neck troubled her "only a very, very little."[7]

There were two new teachers at the seminary that fall; one of them, Eliza Holmes, was from South Hadley, Massachusetts. Miss Holmes had arrived before classes started and had been bewildered, lonely, and homesick in the new environment, until she was introduced "to a large, fair-faced woman, and looked up to meet a pair of happy eyes smiling down upon me, so full of sweet human kindness that the dark clouds fell straight away."[8] Larcom was rather impressed by Miss Holmes's formal manners and precise way of speaking; she seemed a model of ladylike behavior. The friendship would influence the direction of her life, but at the moment merely seemed to make this year at Monticello much pleasanter than the preceding one.

Her letters through the autumn of 1851 and the following spring chronicle her life; books she was reading and some new experiences that she obviously enjoyed overlay a steady preoccupation with Frank and with scrofula, and her growing dissatisfaction with the confinement of her position as a teacher. She described a call from Dr. Edwards:

> I *saw* him just a few minutes in the *dark*, almost, and thought he looked quite sentimentally pale. He said he ought not to be out on such a damp evening, and I came pretty near giving him medical advice, instead of receiving it.—He tells me I must take that dirty medicine for a month yet; I have nearly used up what I bought. Shall I trouble you to send me a bottle full, three times as large as the one I have, by Mr Corey? The prescription is "Syr. Ferri Iodide." I would like it as soon as you can send it, as mine will not last longer than this week. . . .
>
> I send out *David[Copperfield]* and the *Midnight Sun*. If you don't like Agnes, we don't agree. I think "Doady" shows himself a little soft, sometimes; although he's a well-meaning chap in the main.[9]

In December she asked for "half an ounce of dichylon plaster and a very small vial of lunar caustic"; her neck was troublesome, "but I think I can doctor it myself as well as the physicians (sour grapes)—especially since they have left for parts unknown."[10] She described with great enthusiasm a debating society in which each member spoke as a senator: "I am preparing myself to be a member of Congress, when I get out there among the 'hombres.' . . . The honorable member from Massachusetts is highly successful in her forensic attempts—her argumentative powers are really overwhelming."[11] Formal debating was a challenge to her shyness, and she admitted that she became tongue-tied when Miss Fobes attended.

By now Frank's letters were cheerful and enthusiastic. He had settled in the town of Colusa, was practicing medicine there, and was beginning to enjoy the strange new life, but would have enjoyed it even more with his family there. Larcom vacillated: "I am getting *cool* about emigrating to the golden land," she wrote Ma and Becky. "But I must do something next year; do tell me what?"[12] She loved her studies, she had her dear friends in St. Louis, and life was pleasanter at the seminary with Miss Holmes there. On the other hand, what was her future? She hated the restrictions that being a teacher placed on her; she bitterly resented, for example, not being allowed to hear Kossuth, the great Hungarian patriot, when his American tour brought him to St. Louis. Although she was gratified when Miss Fobes asked her to consider staying there as a member of the staff, a life at Monticello might not be what she wanted. She really did not know.

Neither her friend Eliza nor her brother-in-law George had such doubts. Miss Holmes was enduring her year in the West and then going home to New England; she had already secured a position at Wheaton Seminary in Norton, Massachusetts. George, moved by his own restlessness and the new enthusiasm in Frank's letters, decided to move his family to California, the real land of opportunity, the future. Naturally Lucy would come with them.

Larcom did not commit herself. George, Emeline, and the children planned to leave at the beginning of May, and Larcom had to finish the term at the seminary. Then she and Eliza Holmes had been talking about a trip up the Mississippi River to the settlements around the Great Lakes and the Falls of Minnehaha. It would be a shame not to go, for if she went to California she might never see this part of the country again. And perhaps she might teach another year before going west; after all, Frank was not really established yet, not quite ready to marry and support a wife and family, so what would she do there while she waited? And shouldn't she see her family again before moving to California?

By early spring she was in a bad mental state—tense, nervous, and overly self-absorbed—as she grappled with decisions about the future. Emeline and George were getting ready to go to California, although Emeline did not want to leave her home in Woodburn. Larcom was still angry that she had not been allowed to go to Kossuth's lecture, and her anger was compounded when, at the Woodburn Fair, "somebody who is powerful here said she hoped it would never be necessary for teachers to leave in *school-days* again, because it always made trouble." Perhaps the depression her "real grumbler's letter" shows was triggered by her physical condition:

> Has Dr. Edwards returned? Mary said the "spirits" prophesied that he would be here last Wednesday. I don't know what to do with my neck; it troubles me now a great deal. I thought it was getting well; but it swelled again, and proud flesh appeared; I have applied caustic for more than a week,—it is the only thing I know of; but it almost sets me into the St. Vitus Dance every time I use it; the nerves there are so sensitive. It would have been wiser to let it alone in the first place, I suppose—but nobody is to blame, and I never should have been satisfied without an attempt at cure. If you should see "Dr." I wish you would ask him what is the best thing to do, and if he can send me something to heal this proud flesh which is, I *think*, the only trouble now. If he is not there, please send me another small vial of nitrate of silver, as mine is almost gone.—I have suffered a *little* more than is comfortable this winter; but we often have to pay dear for *experiments*—and then *after pain is over*, it is very easy to bear.[13]

Plans and discussions went on at Woodburn all through the winter and spring, and the normally cheerful Larcom said less and less. George and Emeline were taking it for granted that she would come with them to California, marry Frank, and continue the family unit. What else could she do? Women had to get married; all the Larcom girls except Octavia were married by now, and Lucy was twenty-eight in March. Of course it was fine that she had such a good education, for it meant that she would be able to manage her household and bring up her children better than most women.

She had the alternative of staying at Monticello. She would soon complete the good education she had dreamed of and worked for. Miss Fobes's offer of a position at Monticello was a clear statement of approval; coming from someone she admired so deeply, it gave Larcom confidence in her abilities and almost tempted her to remain in this attractive world of books and ideas, close to dear friends and a city whose advantages she enjoyed.

Each alternative, however, had its dark side. Teaching did not satisfy her. The details, responsibilities, and general business of "keeping school" had always been unpleasant. Although she had come to see beauty and grandeur in the prairie, she did not really like it. As for the people, she admired them, but the only close friends that she made were the Vine Lodge Spauldings and Miss Holmes—all transplanted New Englanders. California presented a more complex set of problems. Marriage was the conventional goal for women, and she had promised to be Frank's wife, but the life he was leading repelled her. Emeline, a perfect pioneer wife, felt that her little sister should follow her path.

Larcom had seen two marriages at close hand, her mother's and Emeline's. Certainly her mother's marriage had been a conventionally "good" one, but Lois Larcom, in her care of ten children and a household, had simply been carrying out the will of the benevolent despot who ruled the family. Her husband's death left her unable to function; perhaps twenty years of obeying his orders had killed whatever ability to think for herself that she had ever had. For seven-year-old Lucy, the death of her father had been a trauma that sent her searching all her life for a strong male friend to fill the emptiness, but it was her mother's incompetence, not her father's death, that sent her to the prison of the mills, and for a while at least, shattered the whole family structure. Everything of which Lucy's happy world had been constructed either disappeared or shifted its position, and the years just before she went to Louisa's house had been terrible ones for the sensitive, intelligent, freedom-loving child, no matter how she glided over them later. Lois Larcom's dependence on her strong husband made her whole family vulnerable.

In Emeline's marriage she saw her sister's beauty, intelligence, and force devoted to drudgery. There must have been times when she contrasted Emeline's half-finished houses with Louisa Harrington's and Lydia Baker's gracious homes in Beverly.

Larcom's conscious decision to become more independent of her sister had in no way reduced her love for and gratitude to Emeline, and now it hurt to see her sister's brilliance subdued and tiredness making shadows on that beautiful face. There were no more mathematical problems worked out for the pleasure of using her mind, no more essays and verses; all Emeline's intelligence, creativity, and energy were directed toward her husband and family. It seemed a terrible waste. As a perfect pioneer wife, building her home around her husband, giving up her own interests, and attempting to give George the kind of place her father had, Emeline was an object for admiration—but not for imitation.

Larcom was careful about George in her letters, as if he or Emeline might read over her shoulder as she was writing, but it is clear that her feelings about him were mixed. It is also clear that she had discussed him fairly thoroughly with the Vine Lodge people. Whenever George made a major change in his life, his announced reason for doing so was his health; his sister-in-law, for one, did not take his health very seriously. He seems to have been unable to make up his mind, or to keep to a decision when he did make it, and his life was full of new starts. There is a hint of exasperation in her tone when she mentions him, as if she felt he was not worth the dignity that Emeline gave him.

Then there was the problem of children. Of the twelve children Emeline bore, three survived her; at this point, the spring of 1852, four of her six children had died. Comfortable in her belief in an afterlife, Larcom worried more about her sister's frequent pregnancies and life of hard work than the premature deaths of the children. Every time Emeline bore a child, her life was in danger. Writing about Victorian women, Nina Baym sums up what is probably applicable here: "Childbirth was frequent and extremely hazardous . . . many [children] still died . . . the death rate for mothers, because of the primitive and unsanitary conditions at delivery, remained very high. . . . Thus every pregnancy meant a serious risk of the woman's life. Invariably, the marital situation produced a great deal of anxiety, which surfaced in that feminine distaste for sex misread by later generations as Victorian prudery."[14]

It was marriage rather than sex that was distasteful and frightening to Larcom. Although, with one possible exception, sex is never remotely a topic of her letters, she must have known a great deal. She grew up in a big, crowded family and certainly there could have been little privacy in the prairie hut where children were conceived as well as born and buried. She was a modest woman, but not particularly prudish; she believed, as she had written to Ma and Becky on another topic, "Women have been educated so delicately as not to be supposed to dream of things as they are, but I believe that the knowledge of God's handiwork cannot injure anyone."[15]

Of the hundreds of poems that she was to write in her life, very few can be interpreted as cynical or ironic; those that can all have to do with women and marriage. One of them, called "A Little Old Girl," came out of her western experience, although it was written years later. It describes the upbringing of Prudence, who is taught that the world of women is restricted to work and duty. At ten Prudence has learned to knit stockings, sweep, bake, make candles, milk cows, and tend the vegetable garden. She goes to school and to meeting. When the world of nature and beauty calls her, she is frightened,

> So she runs away from beauty,
> Tries its presence to forget.

The last stanza is so understated that the irony is almost lost (it was completely missed by the reviewers of *Childhood Songs* [1875], in which the poem was collected):

> Meanwhile at the romping children
> Their grave heads the gossips shake;
> Saying, with a smile for Prudence,
> "What a good wife she will make!"

She could and did admire the dedication that made Emeline a perfect wife, strong, hardworking, and submissive to her husband, but she did not find that dedication in herself. She did not want to submit to anyone; she hated the duties of a household and the restrictions that marriage imposed.

She had delighted in Frank's adventurous spirit and dreams of the future, but once he was gone and she was finding out so much more about herself—what made her happy and what did not—it seemed less possible that she should voluntarily accept more restriction and distasteful duties. She no longer shared Frank's dreams and she feared his restlessness; she could predict the kind of marriage she would have in California: like Emeline's, but worse.

Her solitary walks in the woods behind Monticello became longer and more frequent. Surrounded by natural beauty, she found herself praying, sometimes quite desperately, that God would direct her life. The ambition to matter, to accomplish something tangible, was growing; she could not believe that making a home and bringing up children was her vocation. More and more, as she took pleasure in the opening world and the opening of her own mind, she became less satisfied with the life that seemed to lie before her.

Years later, after the question of marriage was settled once and for all, she wrote a poem called "In Vision," addressed to Frank.[16] In it she says, "Although to me remains not one regret" at giving up the vision of the West that drew their hearts

> Where all our blending future seemed to swim
> In light unutterable,

the vision still remains,

> And I am glad I saw it, and with thee—
> Then near as my own spirit.

But, as she came to realize, his vision and hers were different:

> I gazed there at thy bidding: was it wrong?
> I knew a separate path awaited me,
> And I divined another quest for thee,
> Under strange skies, where I did not belong;
> But for one hour, letting Doubt stand aside,
> I saw Life pass, transfigured in Love's form.

Before that dream was fulfilled, a more important vision came to her, sent from heaven, and

> Though that apocalypse annulled thy claim,
> Thine eyes yet burn their question through its flame.

She could look back with affection and no regret at the life they might have shared, but

> Elsewhere our orbits meet, receding star,
> Lost in the dawn that floods me from afar!

The poem has to be approached with caution. It was written between 1868 and 1880, which means that she was looking back and seeing the event in the light of later knowledge; it was also shaped by its form as a poem. Nevertheless, it is true that she did have a significant religious experience that changed her during these years.

Although no existing letters describe the religious experience, references suggest that it was both mystical and intellectual: religious emotion combined with the opening mind that Monticello had developed. At Lowell and again at Woodburn she had simply followed Emeline into church membership, but what she perceived now had little to do with the rigid rules and harsh narrowness of Calvinism. Her vague vision was an awareness of all things, ideas, and people connected to each other, as part of a whole with God at the center.

She did not undergo any sudden road-to-Damascus conversion; in fact, the vision was so different from her narrow theological background that it was frightening at the same time that it was beautiful. Time had to pass before she had the courage and the support to make it the central belief of her life. Eventually her new feelings and ideas led her to a kind of Christian transcendentalism, to joy in a world of beauty that led without dogma to a loving, personal God. But during the years on the prairie and for some time beyond, the serenity and security that she would one day achieve were unimaginable. In fact, her feelings and her doubts frightened her, and for a long time she tried to reconcile her perceptions with some kind of established religion. Later she said that during this period she was trying harder to be a Calvinist than a Christian.

What the vision gave her immediately was the conviction that the God who had sent her this message had a purpose for her life that went beyond the ordinary. Believing so, it was harder than ever to accept the pattern that Emeline and society had laid out for her: marriage, children, oblivion. At the same time, she did not know what God's purpose for her was; all she could do was keep herself ready for it.

If fear of marriage as she had seen it led to the suppression and sublimation of sexual energy, it was hardly unusual for that energy to be channeled into religious ardor. To believe, however shakily, that God wanted a different kind of life for her, a different dedication, was in itself overwhelming; it also gave an acceptable reason for what might have been perceived as a selfish desire to stay out of a pioneer marriage, with its unending drudgery and unending childbirth, and even for evading marriage in general. However, if, as the poem suggests, she felt herself "called" to a different kind of life at this point, the call was not a very secure one. She vacillated about Frank for the next eight years and she felt a great deal of guilt over breaking her promise to him. The poem is a justification and at the same time a highly romanticized cover for a simple truth: the kind of life that marriage to Frank Spaulding made inevitable was not the kind of life that Lucy Larcom wanted. His dream was not her dream.

Her friends thought she was pulled in two directions by Illinois and California; she said little or nothing of the third pull. More and more she thought of Beverly's lanes of pleasant houses and old shade trees, the sound of the sea, the salt air, the crisp New England voices. She missed her big and loving family, all so proud of their highly educated sister. Circumstances had separated the Larcoms, but they were clannish; she longed to see them and the nieces and nephews she had never met.

Besides, with her Monticello education she would be able to support herself by teaching in a superior school; Miss Holmes, who was waiting eagerly for her own departure, certainly thought so. Then there were friends from the mills to look up, like Harriet Farley and Eliza Holbrook. And, of course, the Whittiers. She heard occasionally from Elizabeth, whose brother liked her impressions of Illinois and welcomed the occasional poems she sent. With encouragement from so important a person, it seemed intolerable to think of giving up writing, as Emeline had on her marriage. In fact, Larcom did not think she could give up writing, it was so much a part of her.

Still another influence was the association in her mind of freedom and happiness with her childhood home and the comfort and healing she had found there when she escaped from the mills. All the memories were good ones. In a letter written years later, in response to a former pupil who had congratulated her on *A New England Girlhood*, she said about herself in the early 1850s, "I had not got over a girl's feelings myself at that time, though I know I seemed very old—the consequence of early maturity, and of beginning a woman's work before I was fully grown."[17] Her childhood freedom had been cut off abruptly, not gradually directed to the acceptance of an adult role. If she could not have that forever-lost girlhood, she could at least avoid for a while putting control of her life into someone else's hands. Either a job at Monticello or marriage to Frank meant a loss of freedom and the inhibition of the still shapeless ambition to do something with her life.

Larcom's six years in the West had changed her, whether or not anyone else noticed how great the change was. While her duties at Monticello often vexed her, she loved her studies and felt a real and conscious joy in stretching her mind. It was the same kind of joy she had felt as a child, but it was now wider and even more delightful. There was so much to learn, and she so enjoyed the learning. She felt that there was nothing she wanted more than to read and think and write—to use the mind that God had given her for some purpose that mattered.

Equally important was her different perception of Emeline. In Lowell there had seemed to be no higher goal than to make herself like her sister. But marriage had dimmed or wasted Emeline's brilliance; to Larcom the pattern of her sister's life was not desirable at all. Blind adoration matured to a love that never faltered but was able to see flaws: Emeline was wrong about marriage and wrong about religion. At least, her way was not Larcom's way.

It would be oversimplifying to say that Larcom simply changed role models. Certainly Philena Fobes was a major influence in her life, but Larcom was never secure enough in herself to feel that she had authority—that was one of her problems with teaching—and she could not imagine herself in Miss Fobes's commanding position. What she saw in her headmistress was an independent woman in control of her own life, free to do what she wanted and to use her mind without apology or excuse or subterfuge. To a lesser degree, Eliza Holmes had the same advantages; the independence of these women appealed to the same potential in Larcom, and she found their self-confidence enviable.

Her decision was so difficult that it had physical effects: during the spring she snapped at everyone and frequently became red-faced and breathless. To avoid discussion she kept her thoughts secret, even from her closest friends. Letters to Ma and Becky dated 3 and 24 April still worried over going to California, but a letter to Elizabeth Whittier, dated 12 April, asked where Harriet Farley was and said, "I am coming home to New England soon."[18]

She evaded direct confrontation by leaving her options open; it was quite natural that she would want to see her family and Beverly again before making so complete a change. California was a long way. Her course was made easier when George Spaulding decided that he and Emeline should also go home for a farewell visit before moving west.

Larcom thought she was giving herself time and space and freedom from the advice of others; she had no idea that she was making (or evading) the most crucial decision of her life. By putting
off her commitment to Frank, she opened up for herself a different
kind of future. Though a writing "career" was never in her mind and
would not be achieved for several years, her journey east rather than
west moved her into position for such a future to develop—into the
orbit of a poet who delighted in helping women develop their
talents.

When Monticello closed for the summer, Larcom and Holmes began their travels. They went up the Mississippi River and explored
its headwaters and the famous Falls of Minnehaha, where they were
enchanted by the mist and the rainbow. They stopped at the bustling
settlement named Chicago and visited Monticello friends in another new village called Detroit. Boats took them through the Great
Lakes and they crossed New York State by the Erie Canal, then took
the train from Albany to Boston. By the end of the summer, Lucy
Larcom was again home in Beverly.

CHAPTER 5

Marking Time

In six years Beverly had grown beyond the harbor, as new houses and shops replaced much of the farmland. Many of the lanes now were named streets, but they still held tall old trees and graceful, upright frame houses, and were as lovely and peaceful as Larcom remembered them. The railroad had been extended from Salem to Portsmouth in 1840, and now the Gloucester Branch, breaking off eastward in Beverly and running through the Farms and Manchester, was well established. Larcom liked the convenience, but the tracks cut across the fields and meadows along the tidal "river" where she and her friends once played; as she traveled, her imagination peopled the area with little ghosts from her childhood.

The family had grown and changed, too. Brother Jonathan had married a Chelmsford girl and moved to that town to live; Benjamin had two children with a third on the way; Abby Haskell had two children and her husband was talking about moving to Newburyport where another blacksmith was needed; Adeline Meacom had four children and a "girl" to help in the house. Louisa's boys had grown, although the eldest, Edward, was a worry to the family, for he was a pale, saintly boy threatened by consumption. Lydia's daughter Lizzie was seven now, and her son, young Isaac, was an infant. Mrs. Larcom, still brisk in her sixties, made her home with various members of the family and was a great deal happier than she had been at Lowell. It was a large, prosperous family circle that welcomed sister

Lucy back lovingly, so that she found a security and sense of family that she had not known since early childhood.

She stayed at first with Lydia in the big, pleasant house at the far end of Cabot Street. Her brother-in-law Isaac Baker she soon recognized as an exceptional man: quiet and unpretentious, but full of affection, humor, and warmth. He liked to organize family picnics or expeditions by carriage or boat; he enjoyed life so much that everything somehow seemed better when he was about. Since he shared Larcom's love of painting, the two frequently set up their easels together. Later she called him her best friend among men, and, since she and Lydia had always had a rather special relationship, she was very happy staying with them; she left only because Louisa wanted her company.

As if to assert her independence and capability, Larcom started a little school of her own with ten local girls who, as she wrote Miss Fobes, were "advanced as far as the second class at the Seminary. . . . Some of them are reading Virgil and *Corinne.*"[1] An old schoolhouse just down the street from the Bakers became her working place. She held classes there, but more often used it as a quiet refuge where she could read, study, paint, and write in total freedom. She also had a favorite retreat on the beach, a spot in the angle of an old rail fence, sheltered by bushes, where she could dream for hours as she watched the sea.

On her return, Larcom quite properly made formal calls on family and personal friends, including the Whittiers. To her delight the poet and his sister were as interested in her as ever; she could hardly believe in the value Whittier placed on her writing.

Whittier had begun to move away from his role as a political activist. In the several years before 1852 his letters show that while he still had his abolitionist concerns (he worked very hard in Charles Sumner's campaign for the Senate), his directions were changing. In a letter to Grace Greenwood, the writer and editor, he wrote, "Overworked and tired by the long weary years of the anti-slavery struggle, I want rest."[2] Perhaps it was time now for younger men to take over, and for him to concentrate on his poetry. "Increasingly, Whittier wrote about a summer's day, a gift of a mayflower, or a walk in autumn. The incidents of his youth, the barefoot boy days, the nostalgic memories of a past social order or a lost love furnished the materials for his poems, rather than 'public wrongs.' Whittier had begun to tap the inner poetic wellsprings that produced his best ballads and genre poems."[3]

His relationships with his female protégées and his failure to marry have caused all kinds of speculation among his biographers; explanations vary widely according to theses.[4] Whatever his reasons and whatever psychological needs his behavior answered, the fact is that he did help women writers, going out of his way to do so. Had Larcom remained in Illinois or gone to California and continued her writing, Whittier would probably have "noticed" her work when it caught his attention. Her return, however, changed the situation; she was an attractive, gifted woman who did not know what to do with her gift. Whittier did know what she should do. He seems to have understood that what she needed most of all was confidence in the worth of her own writing and ideas. He gave her practical help, editing her poems ruthlessly and almost forcing her to publish, but his most important contribution was his encouragement and belief in her.

The friendship that was to last the rest of their lives began after Larcom's return and was initiated by Whittier. He called on her in Beverly, often inviting her to join him in afternoon drives to the homes of nearby friends and bringing warm invitations from his mother and sister to visit in Amesbury. Their roles were quickly established: he called her Lucy and she called him Mr. Whittier. He was the master and she the eager pupil.

For a long time Larcom's chief feeling for him was awe. She saw him as a poet, as an antislavery crusader, as an important older man taking a father's place, and as a dynamic and attractive male. Nowhere in her letters and journals is there the slightest suggestion that she expected more of him than the mentorial friendship that he offered. They were both complex people and undoubtedly there were layers of feelings; certainly on Larcom's part there was a romantic element in the early years of their friendship. But the dominant feelings were awe and hero worship. He was the glorious Mr. Greatheart of her youthful dreams, and in that sense she remained a little in love with him all her life. In the early years her role was clear: she became Elizabeth Whittier's close friend and the poet's pupil.

In 1859, after she knew him and his sister well and was established as a close friend of both, she described him in a letter: "He was never married; that perhaps is one reason why there is such a depth to his poetry, for if ever man was capable of love stronger than death, it must have been he. One cannot help feeling that he has been through the deep water, through the furnace-heat, and so is cleansed, purified. The calmness of some great self-conquest rests upon his life. Lizzie seems like a meek, timid bird that one would brood under motherly wings, and yet she has much mental and moral strength, and is a most lovely character."[5]

It is possible that the single-minded dedication to his work that Larcom saw in him affected her own choices, for as the only poet she knew, he was for a time not only mentor but role model. Certainly she was happy to follow his directions, and it was many years before she grew restive and uncomfortable with his guidance.

Immediately, however, there was the flattery of his interest, and there were other shared attitudes, the most important of which was their love of the natural world. They both saw the beauty of landscape, trees, flowers, water; this love of nature is reflected in all the letters Larcom wrote him. He encouraged her to use her good visual perception of the natural world in her poems. He did not share her love of painting and color so much, perhaps because of his red-green color blindness, but in other ways their similar backgrounds and important values matched.

Most important, Whittier's approval of her and her work, his attention and concern, satisfied something in her that had ached since her father first turned away from her to a younger child. That trauma, coupled with the uneasy position of women who pushed themselves forward, made her seek male approval all her life. Whether as mentors or surrogate fathers, men with some authority who approved her work were necessary to her. Whittier was not her only mentor, but he was certainly the most important.

There were other preoccupations than her writing and her growing friendship with Whittier and his sister. Emeline and George were in Lowell, making their long family visit before they went to California. Lottie, their oldest surviving child, was five, and the baby, Theodore, was just over a year old and healthy. In the late autumn George accepted a call from a church in Rochester, New Hampshire, and moved his family there. By September 1853 Larcom could tell Ma and Becky that Emeline had given birth to a daughter, and George was again thinking about moving west. "He has given up preaching, for the present, on account of his health. He is as well as he was at the West, however." Two months later they were back in Lowell, with Larcom there to help Emeline with housework and the children. In January George decided to move to Wisconsin although Emeline did not want to go: "I think they had better get a house on runners, with a good large nursery in it." By May the move to Wisconsin was completed. "He is preaching there in Genessee, has bought a house, and *I hope* will stay, for she has had a hard time moving about the world."[6]

It was easy to predict more pregnancies and more infant deaths in Emeline's life. Even though Louisa Harrington's son had recently died, there was a difference. Young Edward had been sickly and delicate from birth, yet had lived fourteen years. His death, as Larcom described it to Miss Fobes, sounds like something from a Dickens novel: "His great sorrow, as he went away into spiritland, was that he could no longer be a staff to his widowed mother; and he kept praying that he might be her guardian angel."[7]

Larcom's Vine Lodge letters are full of news and events. Shortly after her return she heard feminist Lucy Stone speak at the Beverly Lyceum, and wrote about her to Ma and Becky, and to Miss Fobes:

> Last night I heard Miss Lucy Stone discuss the "Rights of Woman" before our Lyceum with two men. She beat them both to nothing, and they had to acknowledge themselves beaten. The best of it was that she did not get in the least excited or angry, but just calmly argued into them what she believed the truth. I never heard a woman speak in a promiscuous lecture room before, and was prepared to be shocked, but she seemed so easy and at home that I couldn't be if I tried. One of our worthy citizens had the politeness to rise and speak of "crabbed old maids going around asserting their rights"—but she let that pass with dignified silence. I went rather prejudiced against her, if anything, but her arguments were so much clearer and she appeared so much better than the three men who opposed her, that it really seemed as though the men were making fools of themselves.[8]

One of the points that Stone stressed in her lectures was the need for women to keep their own names after marriage, as symbols of their identities. The extremes of true womanhood demanded something close to invisibility on the part of women, who lost legal and financial rights when they married. Larcom had already noted the loss of Christian name and therefore identity under the labels "wife" and "mother" (or the "old woman" of the prairie); the theme would recur in her life and writing.

For women who wrote, the problem of name and self was intensified. To sign one's own name to a poem, story, or novel was to put oneself forward against the standard that a lady's name should appear in print only when she was born, when she married, and when she died. Otherwise she stayed quietly and anonymously at home, presumably as a source of inspiration within her sphere. Hence all the alliterative pen names: Grace Greenwood, Fanny Fern, Mina Myrtle, and others. Many women novelists, too, hid behind pen names.[9] Even someone as outspoken and fearless as Mary Abigail Dodge wrote her provocative essays as Gail Hamilton.

Larcom's writing, even in the *Offering*, was unsigned or initialed, or she used a pen name like Angelina Abigail or Ruth Rover. For *Arthur's Home Magazine* she invented a rather ugly anagram, Culma Croly, but did not use it for long. Women writers of verse were less restricted than the novelist; newspaper verse, most of it of the Emeline Grangerford quality, was frequently signed. It was acceptable for a woman to be a "sweet singer"; it was not acceptable for her to be serious about her writing, to be good at it, or, above all, to earn a reasonable amount of money by it. That was male territory.

As time passed and the novelty of being home again wore off, Larcom became restless. Part of her unease was a reaction to the tension of the previous year, but it was inevitable that her return to Beverly should have elements of anticlimax. Home was lovely and safe, but Larcom was not the child who had been so free and happy there years before. Beverly was comfortable precisely because it was conservative, because little had changed—and Larcom herself had changed a great deal. The brisk freedom of Lowell and the widened horizons she had experienced at Monticello now seemed out of place.

Some new friends helped. She had written to Miss Fobes that she was able to borrow all the books she wanted; the lender was William S. Robinson, free-soil activist and editor of the *Lowell American*. On a visit to Emeline in Lowell, Larcom looked for her first friend from mill days, Eliza Holbrook. Eliza had married a young minister, John

Wesley Hanson, in 1846; John's sister was Harriet Jane Hanson, whom Lucy had known slightly as a tempestuous child who led a mill strike and was excommunicated from her Congregational church. In 1848 Harriet married William S. Robinson, a young man from Concord with a passionate abolitionist commitment who had worked on several newspapers; his refusal to temper his strong feelings meant that his jobs did not last long. In 1851 he had been elected to the Massachusetts House of Representatives, and he was editing the Lowell newspaper as well.

Harriet, perhaps because much of her energy was devoted to managing a household on very little money, seemed quieter than she had in the past. Larcom felt comfortable with her and appreciated Mr. Robinson's interest in her poems and his willingness to print them in his paper. With both Robinsons she could talk about books, ideas, and writers.

One writer in particular caught her imagination then and held it for years to follow. Among the reading material that William Robinson lent her were some of Emerson's essays. Larcom knew his reputation, of course, but whatever she knew of his ideas before had made no strong impression; now, however, they came to a mind ripe to receive them. Emerson became the catalyst that pulled together and gave form to her emerging but confused religious thought.

It hardly needs to be said that Ralph Waldo Emerson was the dominant figure of nineteenth-century American thought, that his ideas shaped his own time and much of the future. But not only those who were or who became transcendentalists were affected by his thinking. His ideas were "in the air" and people drew from them what they needed. Larcom found him compelling. Passages in letters, chiefly to the Robinsons but to other friends as well over several years, indicate that he remained an important presence in her mind. Her first response to Robinson was one that she would amplify: "I have read your books with much gratification; Emerson particularly. He's a great philosopher, but he seems to me very much like the old heathen philosophers. How such a head grew up among Yankee cabbages, I don't understand. Contrary to his precepts, I could reverence him, were it not for his heathenism. I shall never get over my Puritan *penchants*, and I don't want to."[10]

When she met him, after the Robinsons had moved to Concord and she was visiting them, she was so awed that she could hardly speak, but she reported, "One would know him to be a remarkable man just by *seeing* him speak. His face is full of wisdom and it talks all over." She did develop an acquaintance with him after she herself had become famous, but it was his ideas, not the man himself, that made an impact on her thinking and therefore on her life. She reiterated the contribution he made in many letters: "What I like best about Emerson is that he always sets you a-thinking. That shows him a prince of thinkers"; "I do enjoy reading what he has to say, always, because he gives you so much room to think in"; "there is the feeling of so much room to think in,—and wonders arising on every side," so that although he is "a heathen, to all intents and purposes," she wondered "whether something of this freedom of thought is not necessary to accompany spiritual growth, or develop it, rather."[11]

But there was a dark side, which in part explains why she could not follow him beyond a certain point; a few years later, when her internal conflicts had led her to the point of questioning her own sanity, she wrote, "He is a great thinker who does not imprison your thought in his. But he is cold, would lead us on forever and forever through endless spaces, without home or resting place."[12]

It is not surprising that Emerson's ideas should have so strong an effect on Larcom, for her education and her prairie experience had already brought her a vision of the unity of all things. That glimpse of a world in which all things are part of each other was fertile ground for Emerson's words and ideas. She, too, had sensed the transparent atmosphere that allowed one to see the "perpetual presence of the sublime," but she had not been able to define it.

Though Emerson pulled together and supported what was already in her mind, she still had enormous difficulties. Reared by a devout Puritan father in a devout Puritan world, she found pushing past dogma, as these ideas would compel her to do, terrifying. Eventually she would make her own modification: the vast, impersonal over-soul would become the vast, personal Christian God who knew the fall of a sparrow and could intervene to save his beloved children. God as Father was an absolute necessity to her; the absence of that concept in Emerson's thinking was what she translated as coldness and isolation. But her own Christian transcendentalism had to be thought through, for she was, she believed, dealing with the most important element of human life. Emerson made her think, but he also frightened her. She tried, she wrote later, "to build up a wall of difficult doctrines over my spring blossoms," first to ignore new beliefs and then to merge them with old ones.[13]

Only slightly less frightening and attractive were the ideas that expressed Emerson's individualism. The call to each separate being to be himself, develop his—or her—talents, use gifts, and live fully, subordinating social restrictions to the demands of talent, was another idea that fell on prepared ground. It fit in with Larcom's conviction that there was something she was to do with her life, vague though that conviction still was. Reading the essays today, one is conscious of the overwhelmingly masculine orientation; apparently Emerson's contemporaries were not.[14] Nevertheless, although men had social codes just as women did, they had far more room to move around. The extremes of individualism and those of true womanhood were simply incompatible. Larcom's courage was not and never would be the kind that could openly oppose cultural and social dictates. No matter how she wanted to believe and live, she was constrained by what she had been taught. Being different was sometimes attractive, but its penalties were severe.

The doors that Emerson's ideas opened were both enticing and formidable, and as yet Larcom had not worked out the ways to go through them without being noticed. Sent underground, the new ideas refused to disappear; they became part of the conflict that was to grow within her mind and last for nearly ten years, until she worked out how far she could live her beliefs without offending the standards of her time.

In the meantime, regardless of what she was thinking, her work went on. In the late spring she showed Whittier some of the little moral essays she had written over the years; many had been published in the *Offering*. He was enthusiastic about them and urged his own publishers, Ticknor and Fields, to make a book of them.[15] Larcom was horrified at the idea of submitting her work to the most prestigious of all publishers and not at all surprised that James T. Fields felt it unsuitable for his house; she had never thought it would be. Ticknor and Fields were so important that their imprint guaranteed the best.

Whittier then took the manuscript to John P. Jewett, who had published *Uncle Tom's Cabin* after its serialization in the *Era*, and Jewett agreed that the essays would make a pleasant small book for young people. Whittier called the essays prose poems. After one of their increasingly frequent afternoon drives, he wrote Larcom, "What signifies thy boast of riding with a poet? Didn't I ride with one too, and a Prose-poet in the bargain?"[16]

Jewett published the book in the fall of 1853 with the title *Similitudes, from the Ocean and Prairie*. Each of the "prose poems" begins by placing a child in a natural setting and then moves to a conclusion about morality or religion. Most of the similitudes celebrate the beauty and joy of God's creation, but the final statement is consistently that one must go beyond the physical world to the heavenly.

The book was well received. It sold for fifty cents (fifty-nine in gilt), and was advertised as an inspirational gift book. Larcom was pleased at its modest success and happy with the praise of family and friends. Her attitude was hardly professional: "Writing gets a poor remuneration in 'lucre' unless one can create a sensation by some sudden flash, which I, with my disposition to peace and quietness, shall never do," she wrote her friends. "Mr. Arthur [*Arthur's Home Magazine*] wishes to pay me for all I write for him; but he feels poor and I suppose has met with many reverses. He says he will send any books of his, at my order, or any number of the Gazette or Magazine subscriptions, I mean. Do you want any, or know of anyone who does?"[17]

She continued to write and found acceptances, if no money. The *National Era* published five of her poems in 1853 and the same number the next year. *Arthur's Home Magazine* was always receptive; in 1854 it printed three of her similitudes, four short essays, three poems by Herder, Richter, and Lessing translated "from the German," and three poems signed with the anagram Culma Croly. One of the poems, "Asa and Ira," is the story of two brothers, both of whose farms are afflicted with weeds, insects, and floods; Ira prays and moans and fails, but Asa prays and works and succeeds. "Life's a Railroad" laments the fact that people move so fast these days that they have no time to remember the important things. (This same year *Arthur's* was running Dickens's *Hard Times* as a serial.)

Various church and local papers liked her work. Larcom was never to make major claims—she always spoke of her poems as her verses, and even at the height of her fame questioned whether she should be called a poet—and she hesitated to approach the "big" papers or magazines. She did finally, on her mentor's urging, send two poems to the *New York Knickerbocker*, but was hardly surprised when she did not even receive an acknowledgment. She was beginning to request payment for her work, but not with much confidence that she would get it.

Failure to be paid could not stop her from writing. Rhyme and verse form came easily and provided a natural vehicle for the expression of moods, thoughts, feelings, and reactions to events in her immediate surroundings or the world. Her verses, as she freely admitted in later years, were primarily autobiographical, topical, and occasional. Many of the poems she wrote at this time reflected her experiences in the West; she also tried her hand at some based on features and legends of her own Essex County.

She saw a great deal of Whittier and his sister that summer, and in August joined them and other friends at the Free-Soil convention in Wolfeboro, New Hampshire. It was her first experience of the kind, and she listened approvingly to the speeches and attended the festive dinner.[18]

In an unexpected way the trip influenced her future. Years before, in Lowell, she had been fascinated by the New Hampshire farm girls, and had loved to listen to their tales and descriptions of the mountains, especially the mountains that held the headwaters of her beloved Merrimack River. The idea of mountains stirred her imagination, but she had never seen them. Rochester, where Emeline lived for a while, was in southern New Hampshire; the terrain was not very different from her familiar northern Essex or Middlesex counties, although from Rochester on very clear days she had seen the faint jagged line of summits on the distant horizon. At Wolfeboro she was much closer. The train trip to Alton Bay and the steamer up Lake Winnipesaukee to Wolfeboro carried her steadily nearer to the giants massed on the northern sky. After the conference the group went by steamer twenty miles up the lake to the quiet village of Centre Harbor and across to Squam Lake, almost at the feet of the majesty beyond. Even from a distance she felt joy at such beauty and a longing to know the mountains better.

Like all good people, Larcom was horrified at the Kansas-Nebraska Act as it was bitterly debated in Congress in the spring of 1854. The act would allow the two prospective states to choose whether they would enter the Union free or slave, and in effect repealed the Missouri Compromise. Whittier did everything in his power to defeat the bill, but it was passed late in May. Anger at southern dominance was increased when Anthony Burns, an escaped slave, was caught in Boston and, over a storm of protest and an attempted rescue that involved violence, was returned to the South. Even Emerson, who had stayed aloof, was finally enraged enough to enter the battle. Massachusetts abolitionists felt betrayed by their own people; their hatred of President Pierce, who seemed to have forgotten that he was a New Hampshireman, was matched by their contempt for the business interests that ignored principles for the profits on southern cotton.

The passage of the infamous act led directly to the formation of a new political party, called the Republican party, and to increased westward migration. If Kansas settlers were to choose whether they would be slave or free, then Kansas had better be settled by decent, God-fearing New Englanders who could not only make new homes, but establish a free state. Assistance societies sprang up, combining profit with principle in typical New England fashion; the societies lent money to the new settlers and collected a percentage of their earnings. Since the South had similar, though less organized, ideas about the settlement of Kansas, the result was violence and the eventual appearance of John Brown.

Much of Whittier's attention was devoted to the political situation, but he was not too busy to write Larcom, "Whenever I take up *Similitudes* or read a letter of thine I am impressed with the notion that thou shouldst write a story of sufficient length for a book by itself. It vexes me to see such a work as *The Lamplighter* [a best selling novel by Maria S. Cummins] having such a run, when you cannot remember a single sentence or idea in it after reading it. I am sure you could do better—give pleasure to thy old friends, and make a thousand new ones—and 'put money in thy purse' if I may be permitted to speak after the manner of a Yankee. Pray think of it—study thy plan well and go ahead."[19]

Obediently, she began to think about writing the story. It was to be set in the West, with characters based on her sisters but illustrating western attitudes and people.[20] Planning the book with Whittier and his sister was inspiring; she loved visiting, for she was fascinated by the quiet Quaker household and was finding in Elizabeth a friend as close as her beloved Ma and Becky.

Far less quiet but attractive in a different way were her friends the Robinsons. She enjoyed visiting them, too. They never had much money, but their marriage was a loving one and their family life affectionate. Both, in different ways, were clever, intelligent, and well-read. Larcom felt comfortable in their home and especially loved their children. The past she and Hattie had shared and escaped was a bond; their adult friendship began on easy terms and deepened as the years went on. William Robinson's wit and good humor covered an unswerving dedication to abolitionism that often caused him trouble. In 1854 he left the Lowell paper to become editor of the short-lived *Boston Commonwealth*, and the family moved to Concord. Robinson had grown up there, a schoolmate and close friend of the younger Thoreau boy and a regular at Mrs. Thoreau's melon parties. He was closely involved with the passionate abolitionist group that had its headquarters in Concord.

Like Whittier, Robinson encouraged and praised Larcom's work, but all the encouragement in the world from friends and proud family did not cancel out the fact that most editors still paid her in subscriptions and gratitude. What she needed was money in her pocket and direction in her life. During the late summer and early fall she continued to write her poems, to struggle with the long story that Whittier wanted, and to watch with interest and at times a desire to join in the campaigns that were pushing the settlement of Kansas. Her letters show increasing loneliness for her friends at Vine Lodge after Emeline went to Wisconsin, a growing emotional involvement with the political situation, and the assumption that she would eventually return to the West to live and work. Her distant sight of the mountains had made her determined to be among them, and in the spring of 1854 she taught classes in drawing and painting to earn money specifically for that purpose.

All her activity did not answer the question of what she was to do with her life. After the vigor of Lowell and the comparative openness and independence of the West, she found it difficult to fit herself into sedate and decorous Beverly. She knew she could stay there, living with Louisa or with Lydia and Isaac. Being aunt in residence, helping to run the house and rear the children, was a normal and respectable occupation for unmarried New England ladies. Making a home with Louisa, as they had once planned, would allow her time for writing, but the danger of becoming financially dependent on her family was intolerable. She had earned her own money for too long, and she knew that without her own means she would lose control over her life.

The family was ready with advice. They were proud of her, but it was, after all, rather odd for a woman to be so intelligent and so well educated, to insist on supporting herself and to be able to do so, to spend her time reading, writing, and painting when she should be thinking about getting married. They thought she was treating Frank badly and said so, even going so far as to accuse her of being a jilt.

She could not easily defend herself, for running away had not really solved the problem of Frank. The accounts of her relationship with him in her Vine Lodge letters from the spring of 1853 to the autumn of 1854 show a mind constantly vacillating. "He thinks some of coming out here next fall," she wrote, after explaining that she had not heard from him for a while, "and perhaps we will spend the winter, and return across the plains. . . . I am glad you can appreciate so well one who is dear to me (I can write to you so without the fear of being called sentimental). I become more and more convinced every day, that he has few equals in goodness, in upright manliness, and depth of feeling, whatever his faults may be."[21]

By September, however, she was deciding to "take a school," as she needed money and Frank wasn't coming until the spring; she felt she could bear a longer separation. "And on the whole I think I prefer a life of 'single blessedness' while there are good reasons why it should be so. This life is so much a little strip off the whole piece that I don't think it makes much difference about 'marrying and giving in marriage' unless one is sure that *the* one *is* the one, and no other. You know that I never arrived at that certainty; but have always loved Frank as a brother. . . . after what has passed I shall certainly go with him if he comes for me; only I care less about going the more I stay here, and get familiar with people and things again."[22]

Frank could make the decision; if he came for her, of course she would go. Two months later she wrote that they expected him around Christmas time, but she would not decide until she saw him "face to face. I am doubtful whether my going will be a good thing for *him,* and he may think so yet himself. . . . I am not so 'self-reliant and independent' that I can live and be happy without friends. But I think I could do very well without a *husband.*"[23]

She was honest about her doubts in her letters to Frank, but often that honesty sounds like a series of moves in some complicated game of approach and retreat. He planned to come east for Christmas; she wrote back that she had taken a school for the winter and therefore he decided not to come. She began learning new painting techniques and advanced studies of modern languages so that she could teach them: "You see I am making plans just as if there were no other prospect before me. Well, I don't know that there is; and if there should be, I should teach, rather than keep house. And I mean always, if I have health, to have resources of my own, to use as I please. You know I'm quite an old maid now—almost thirty—and not at all willing to resign my independence."[24]

By spring her mind and feelings had changed again.

I am glad you think so well of Frank; I love him warmly, but not passionately, as some do, or as *perhaps* I might love—I say this to you because you have known so much of my life, more of my inner life than my friends here do; I would not say it to them. . . . I'm sure I cannot tell why I have not gone to see him or he has not come to see me before now. I know that he has wished and tried to have me with him. . . . I *shall* refuse and defer no longer; I have not done it directly yet—I honor him, and believe that I could live happily with him, hoping for the better hereafter, when hearts shall be made plain. . . . but he, who has been so kind and noble to me, shall never know unhappiness through my coldness. I do not hear from him very often; perhaps I have told him too plainly how I feel.[25]

It was clear by the late summer that matters had reached an impasse; perhaps Larcom had indeed been too honest. Frank was not eager to make the long and dangerous journey east to discuss the possibility of marriage with a lady whose mind changed with every wind. He had settled happily into the life of Colusa, a small community on the Sacramento River with farms and small businesses to support the mining towns around it. At first he had tried to practice medicine, but discovered that there were already too many doctors.[26] Although several business ventures were not particularly successful, he had found the place where he belonged. If he traveled east it would be to bring his wife back to California, and the mixed signals he received hardly encouraged such an effort.

Larcom knew she was to blame, but when he did not come she felt rather insulted; her reaction mingled guilt, indignation, and relief to an uncomfortable degree. She was shown a letter Frank wrote to his mother, in which, she told Ma and Becky, "are some things you would not quite like, but I attribute them to one of his 'moods.' I do not think this long silence is proper treatment of me, even if I have given him cause, and I shall tell him so, if he gives me the opportunity—but I shall not write again unless he first writes me." Under the circumstances she was looking seriously for work. "Don't think I am in trouble. Not a bit! I'm determined that this world shan't trouble me, let it do its best, or worst! But I can't live without coppers in Yankee-land or anywhere; and then I, in common with everyone of my race, have work to do which I must be about."[27]

A position, as opposed to her temporary "schools," was not difficult to find. Eliza Holmes was leaving Wheaton Female Seminary because of her health and nominated Larcom as her successor. The school impressed her: it had dignity, prestige, high standards, and a strong religious orientation. The teachers seemed friendly and the girls were young ladies. The buildings were set in level countryside surrounded by woods; if the terrain was almost as flat as the prairie, that did not matter, for she was only committing herself for one term—two at the most. Feeling that she had solved her immediate problems, she began her teaching duties in December.

CHAPTER 6

Life at Wheaton

Wheaton, like Monticello, was a family-owned school of excellent reputation. The girls lived in private houses with a housekeeping couple and a faculty member in charge; thus Larcom found herself with ten girls in her care right from the beginning. The school year was divided into three terms. Originally she went for one term, possibly two, but she was to stay there officially for more than eight years, and afterward would return frequently as an honored visitor. In all that time she never grew to like teaching any better, yet most of her students remembered her with love and gratitude.[1]

Most teaching was drill from a text, but Larcom used Miss Fobes's method, presenting her material as a story lecture, encouraging girls to question and comment and to search on their own for further information. She wanted them to deal with ideas rather than facts, as she had learned to do at Monticello. One of her courses was botany and, instead of working in the classroom, she took her students out to the gardens and the woods where they could range about, hunting specimens. Then they gathered to compare, identify, and discuss what they had found. Occasionally she took a few older girls to Boston to look at beautiful houses, gardens, and vistas or to visit exhibitions of paintings.

On the negative side, she was incapable of discipline and reacted to bad behavior as to a personal insult. It was fairly easy for an unprepared student to trick her into a discussion that used up the

94

whole period. She was a much better teacher of bright students than of ordinary ones, but all the girls respected her genuineness, and for some she became a model and a lifelong friend. She founded a magazine, *The Rushlight*, and the Psyche Literary Society, both of which involved bright girls who enjoyed writing.

Each teacher had to take her turn at leading the morning prayers. The girls were very much impressed by Miss Larcom's sincerity, and did not guess how frightened she was at performing before a group. Only her strong sense of duty forced her to do it. She did like finding inspirational material and began to keep a scrapbook of her favorite passages.

She prepared her lectures and classes conscientiously, reading everything she could find that would enrich her subject. Part of her task was to help in the formation of character, and therefore she felt obligated to be available, especially to the girls in her house. Being always on hand cut into her time, but she could not resist any call for help or even companionship. Her room was bright and well furnished, with white curtains at the window and a carpet of her favorite green on the floor, but although she had a room of her own, she lacked the protective ruthlessness to keep the door closed. At first the duty was no hardship; she liked the well-bred young ladies and sympathized with their problems and aspirations.

When a group headed by Boston merchant Amos Lawrence established a contest for a song, words that fit some popular tune, to be sung at rallies and, presumably, by settlers heading to the West, Larcom sent some verses. Passage of the Kansas-Nebraska Act in 1854 had increased the steady emigration from Massachusetts to the West; by now going to Kansas was a crusade against the forces of evil, for enough right-thinking settlers would ensure that the territory entered the Union as a free state. To her amazement her "Call to Kansas" was the winner. The prize was fifty dollars, and her poem was printed in most newspapers. Delighted congratulations came from her family, from Whittier and Elizabeth, and from other friends. The Wheaton students, one of whom had heard the news through her father before it was officially announced, surprised her by singing the song in assembly one morning. Larcom, amazed, could only "start, lift both hands, and then, to hide her pretty blush and confusion, bury her face in them, while the girls clapped delightedly."[2]

The success of her prize song added to her small but growing literary reputation, although her payment was still subscriptions and letters of thanks. The habit of verse making was so ingrained by now that, even with her time not under her control, she wrote a great deal. A suggestion from Whittier had the force of a royal command, and she did try to work on that long story. She was far from happy, however, when he announced in the *Era* that Miss Larcom was preparing an "American story." The pressure upset her, although she replied to him calmly enough:

> I wonder if you can guess how frightened I was when I saw the announcement in the Era, that a book of mine would be published this season! I had begun to count it among the impossibilities, my time is so completely broken into little bits here. But when I saw that notice, I said "Now it *must* be done." Will it be a "breach of promise" if I shouldn't succeed in finishing it?
>
> I doubt my powers as a story-teller, more and more. Still, I am willing to try, and fail, if it must be so, for the sake of the experience. I can think of things enough to say, if they could only be made to hang together. And then, when I feel most like writing, a grave "must not!" rises before me, in the shape of a lesson in Moral Science, or a pile of compositions to be corrected, forty or fifty high. But the thing shall be accomplished, if it is among the possibles. I am somewhat in doubt about returning here another term, unless I can have more time allowed me. And yet I should hardly feel justified in leaving, it is so difficult to obtain a suitable teacher on short notice. The present term closes March 13th, and the next lasts from the first of April to July.[3]

With Hattie Robinson she was much more open. "How that book is ever going to get written I don't know. I could have cried, when I saw that Mr. Whittier had mentioned it, in the paper; for I had given it up in discouragement, myself. And then I didn't mean to have my name on it. Indeed, I should not have dreamed that I could write a long story, if Mr W had not told me I could, and advised me to try. Well, the notice has gone forth, and I am in honor bound to do something; but what will it be?"[4] On the same date she wrote to her Vine Lodge friends, "Only think—it is a year since I heard from F.—I wrote last, I'm sure I don't remember what." For friendship's sake she decided to write again, "but I don't want to be married to him, nor anybody else,—if I understand myself."[5]

Family concerns distracted her as well. Louisa Harrington's second son, Larcom, who had always wanted to follow his father's career, went on his first voyage, caught cholera in New Orleans and died there. Louisa was heartbroken, and normal grief was compounded by the fact that the young man was not a church member and therefore might be supposed to be eternally damned. His Aunt Lucy, who had cared for him during that year away from the Lowell mills, found her traditional religious beliefs challenged again. She wrote her Vine Lodge friends that she could not accept the idea even though she knew her thoughts were wicked by orthodox standards. Her emotional rejection of a mainstay of dogma added to the simmering ferment in her mind that she was not quite ready to voice at conservative Wheaton.

The same letter goes on to express her longing for some "good long talks with you" and proceeds to other important subjects. She had written to Frank, finally, "because I could not bear it without an explanation . . . I love him still, better than other men, but not as I could love, and he knows it." The letter goes on to comment on her recent reading and her ideas about her own writing:

No, Becky, I don't read much, except in "learned" books, for my scholars' sake. I have read *Ida May* and the *Lamplighter*, and think them good stories, but praised quite too much for their worth. *Ruth Hall* I hardly cared for to read, judging by the general flimsiness of Fanny Fern's writings, but if I have a chance, I shall. I want to read Miss Bremer's letters, and have the promise of them soon. After all, I don't feel as if any great American story has been written except *Uncle Tom*. I have Martha Russell's *Leaves From the Tree Igdrasyl*, which I think you would like, the first story, particularly. Mrs Stowe has just issued a new edition of the "Mayflower," which contains some capital things.

If I attempt to write a book, I should not dream of anything great; I should only attempt some sketches of American life, as I have seen it. If it were true to nature and life, and pleased my friends, I would not cry, if it did not have "a great run." Indeed I would not be the authoress of some books which have been popular, for anything. *Fashion and Famine*, for instance. Still I think the error was in the judgment of that writer, and not in her heart.[6]

Somehow all the activity at Wheaton made her aware of her own loneliness. For the first time in her life she was separated from Emeline, for George had exchanged the ministry for farming once again and moved to Lake St. Croix, Wisconsin, "with bears and wolves for neighbors."[7] The pattern of George's life was established: a series of acting pastorates, seldom more than a year at any one location. As he shuttled back and forth across the continent—New Hampshire, Wisconsin, Minnesota, California—Emeline and the surviving children dutifully followed.[8] Busy as she was, Larcom missed her sister. Certainly being out from under Emeline's maternal wing pushed her toward maturity, and certainly the sisters had disagreed about what Larcom's future should be, but they had been together or within visiting distance ever since she could remember. Nothing could quite fill the emptiness that Emeline's departure left. And although she did not want to marry Frank and live the kind of life he had chosen, letting go of him was hard. She did care for him; furthermore, there was a social value to being "engaged," and while marriage remained a possibility, however remote, it offered an alternative to a permanent commitment to teaching. She wrote to Hattie, "*You* can hardly know, loved and loving as you are, how lonely and cold the way seems to one who has no other heart close to hers, whose kindly throbbings lend strength in the hour of weakness.—I have felt it, but I do not now, because I believe there is such a thing as 'walking with God.' And if anything can brighten life, that will."[9]

When the term ended in mid-July she went home to Beverly, full of plans for the immediate future. Earlier she had written Whittier that she was getting nowhere with the story, but that she planned on writing it during the summer and giving the manuscript to Mr. Jewett, who was to publish it, in September. Within a few days, however, she was too ill to work or even travel. In fact, each year at Wheaton was to end with a period of illness or exhaustion—particularly when she had committed herself to something she did not really want to do.

As a child Larcom had had consistent good health, but ten years of confinement and the lint-filled air of the mills left her with problems both physical and psychological. As well as scrofula, she had a susceptibility to respiratory ailments. The prairie left her with malaria, which would recur later in her life. Another legacy of the mills was an almost pathological hatred of noise; the constant clattering of machinery had contributed to her near breakdown as a child. Certainly the Wheaton girls did not sound like the Lowell mills, but there were times when the shrill voices and constant chatter had a similar effect. Quiet was a necessity: "It could not be too quiet for me," she wrote Elizabeth Whittier. "At least, I never found a place that was."[10]

As well as physical ailments, there was the psychosomatic problem that she called "trouble with my head." It involved pain in her head and neck, dizziness, exhaustion, and at times an apathy so deep that she could hardly function. While there may have been a physical cause, these attacks, which began while she was at Wheaton, occurred whenever she was under pressure or faced with difficult decisions—in fact, when her life got out of control.

Her own sense of duty drove her to work very hard at her teaching, and her letters first hint and then state her wish to be free of it so she could do more writing. In a passage that occurs in a draft of *A New England Girlhood*, but was crossed out and not used in the book, she wrote, "I had some taste for pretty things,—(I like pictures). I had almost a covetous desire for books; not books indiscriminately, but the kinds I liked;—but what I did wish for more than anything else was freedom to do the things I liked to do. I was willing to sacrifice for that everything that girls generally find attractive."[11]

She was thirty when she went to Wheaton, a young and attractive woman with her pleasant face, rich, light brown hair, and smiling blue eyes. Her size added to her dignity, and, according to her students, she was graceful in movement and gracious and loving in manner. She dressed simply but well. Blessed with sisters who were extremely skilled at sewing, she wore well-cut and well-made dresses, preferring practical colors like dove gray and drab (a yellowish tan) that could be trimmed with bright ribbons and collars.

A photograph taken during these years shows her in what must have been a "best" dress. She is sitting, with one hand resting on a table near some books. Her hair, drawn away from her face into fullness at the back, shines in the light. Her tight bodice has white lace at its V-shaped neck, and the sleeves are very full at the shoulder, then tight on her arms. Her shawl has a deep ornamented border.

The huge skirt flows around her, and the whole dress has the rich gleam of heavy, dark satin.

One student remembered that "she always wore a band of velvet, cut short at the ends and pinned with a small pin, around her throat. This was becoming to her. One of her charms, after her sweet, strong face and kind eyes, was her voice, which had a low, rich quality of tone. Her laugh was delightfully hearty. She would laugh till she cried, and break out again as the ludicrous side of things struck her."[12]

The velvet band around her throat, which became a kind of trademark, hid the scars or sometimes the running sores of scrofula. The disease troubled her still, now psychologically as well as physically. She no longer thought of it as an affliction to be cured; it was beginning to seem disgusting and shameful, a secret that had to be guarded. Perhaps the contrast with the well-bred and carefully brought up students emphasized her ugly ailment, or perhaps the attacks became more frequent, but her self-contempt and loathing of her body grew as her discontent increased. Her letters show a range of moods that were probably connected with her health, either as cause or effect, although most of the time she retained her sense of humor; with gentle irony she wrote to Elizabeth Whittier, "In truth, I have not felt well since I came home, but there's no use in attempting to be 'delicate' when your looks contradict your words, I find."[13]

She was over her illness by August and set off on a series of visits, to Newburyport to stay with her sister Abby Haskell, to Amesbury to see the Whittiers, and then to Maine where John and Eliza Hanson now lived. As always, the presence of friends, freedom from restraint, and surroundings of natural beauty erased her tensions and allowed her naturally happy temperament full play.

Back at her duties, she began to keep a journal, although irregularly, for she liked best to write her thoughts in letters so that she could feel connected to her friends. Ma and Becky, Emeline, Elizabeth Whittier, Susan Hayes Ward (a former student), and Hattie Robinson were regular correspondents; she wrote a yearly letter to Philena Fobes, summing up all she had done and thought.

Her letters to Whittier have a composed air; they are almost essays on the beauty of nature and on her writing, and they are always cheerful. One she wrote at the beginning of the new year is typical of her side of their correspondence:

How have you been this magnificent winter? Frozen into the
Amesbury snow-banks? I am happy to see, by the *Era*, that your
ideas are not all in the icicle state. For myself, my thoughts
seem completely ice-bound. Look out for a terrible freshet by
and by!

But what a hearty, thorough going winter we have had of it!
First, the ice-storm made fairy-land or gnome-land of our woods.
The drooping birches, all in white, made arches all along the
footpaths, splendid glittering arches, beneath which none but
the *very lowly* might pass. The great pines could not stand the
shower of splendor that descended upon them; stout branches
fell with a crash, and lay across the road, overcome by the ex-
ceeding weight of glory.

Then the snow came, by wholesale; oh the grand great snow-
drifts that look as if they didn't mean to go away till next July,
how my eyes revel among their generous heaps! It is a pleasure
to see an abundance of anything that is neither ugly or wicked. I
don't know whether to include these very *free* and *freezing*
north-winds, under either of those categories or not. I conclude,
however that their *intentions* are benevolent, and that is the
main thing.

I have just been reading something of Chaucer, with a view to
that lecturing I told you of. What a reality there is in his May-
mornings! I can hardly believe my eyes, when I look up from my
book into the snow-drifts, my mind gets so full of sunshine,
daisies, and singing birds.

I want, very much, to *burn* that story, so far as I have written
it, and begin anew, in the spring. I have added but two or three
chapters since you saw it; and looking at it now that it has
grown cold, it seems to me miserably designed and put together.
I ought to have gained some ideas in the course of a year or
more; and I am unwilling to write a book that will not be worth
more than one reading,—if the power to do it is in me, and if it
is not, I would rather not write at all. There are too many *shams*
already. Will you advise me?[14]

One of her greatest pleasures was going to Boston, sometimes
with a few students and sometimes alone, perhaps meeting Hattie
Robinson or Beverly friends there. The Old Colony Railroad brought

her to the station at Kneeland Street, and the horsecars made getting about the city easy, although she usually liked to walk.

Boston in the middle 1850s was still a city of open spaces, elegant mansions, and wide, tree-lined streets.[15] The gold dome of Bullfinch's State House and the spire of Park Street Church floated over the Common. The well-to-do had deserted the old North End by now and their tall townhouses or large single homes were built on Beacon Street, Park Street, Pemberton Square, the lovely Colonnade Row on Tremont Street, Temple Place, or the airy gardens of Summer Street. The Common was an extended backyard, and it was delightful to watch the children playing games on the grass or sledding down the hill in winter, the girls sitting neatly on their sleds while the boys "belly-bumped" down the steep hill.

The paths through the Common made pleasant walks. One could look at the Old Elm, older than the city itself, or walk past the famous Tremont House, with its five granite pillars, or the brand-new Parker House, where important visitors to the city stayed. Larcom, with her seagoing heritage, loved the wharves where bowsprits of sailing ships seemed to hang across the streets. The port was busy, and in East Boston Donald McKay was building his fast and lovely clippers. On the smaller streets were the artisans' shops and bookstores in which to browse and perhaps make a modest purchase. Larcom quickly became familiar with these and with the galleries and exhibition halls in which paintings could be seen.

Bostonians had a fairly new place to stroll in the Public Gardens, with its conservatory and the curving paths among flower beds. The Gardens ended in a seawall on the west; it was picturesque in the extreme, but, unfortunately, the Gardens could be enjoyed only at certain times. The waters of Back Bay were fine at high tide or when the wind blew from the east, but the railroad lines that now cut across the bay prevented the free flow of tidewater through the Mill Dam. In fact, the stench of Back Bay at low tide was already a town scandal, and plans were in progress to fill in the mud flats.

Everyone knew that the city was changing. Population had grown so fast that space was desperately needed. Already the wharf areas of the small peninsula had been enlarged with land taken from the tops of the famous three mountains. Made land widened the neck that attached the city to the Roxbury countryside, and many people felt that this "new" South End would become the most fashionable place to live. Although a few built homes in the small filled area of Back Bay, individuals and developers were rushing to build up the South End, turning it into a place of "blocks" of tall, austere houses around grassy, flowering squares.

But there was more to the city than physical beauty or the variety of a seaport. It held within its extended territory the great minds of the time, the writers and thinkers whose work led and shaped the nation. The city took a quiet pride in itself that did not exclude those with the right qualifications: a midwesterner like William Dean Howells would naturally come to Boston if he wanted to be a writer, and a country boy from New Hampshire like James T. Fields could become the nation's most prestigious publisher. Boston knew itself to be the goal for intellect and talent; the probably apocryphal but undoubtedly apt story of the old Bostonian lady who asked, "Why should I travel? I'm already here," sums up the attitude of the old inhabitants.

For Larcom, a day in the city meant combining walks with perhaps a visit to an art exhibit at the Athenaeum, or attendance at an abolitionist meeting, or examination of the paintings at Williams and Everett's well-known gallery. There was also the chance of seeing on the streets or near the Old Corner Book Store some of the greatest minds of the age. Being in the city of Emerson, Longfellow, Holmes, Mrs. Stowe, her own friend Whittier, and others was exciting. She returned to Norton after such a day feeling as if she had indeed been on the edges of the great world.

She and most of her friends were intensely interested in politics. The new Republican party, formed in reaction to the Kansas-Nebraska Act and made up of Whigs, Democrats, and Free-Soilers who loathed slavery, had been further strengthened and unified by the arrest of fugitive slave Anthony Burns in Boston and the resulting violence, by the killing of settlers in Kansas by proslavery elements, and especially by the stupid, brutal, and nearly fatal attack on Charles Sumner by a southern congressman on the floor of the Senate. Whittier's letters and poems reflected his outrage, and he supported the Republican free-soil candidate, John C. Frémont, the romantic "Pathfinder" who had crossed the Rocky Mountains and claimed the lands along the Pacific for the United States. Larcom, like many abolitionists, saw him as the God-given leader of all right-thinking people.

Sometimes affairs in Kansas so troubled her that she toyed with the idea of going there herself, and she was fairly intolerant of those who did not share her views. She wrote Elizabeth: "What are we to do about Kansas? I verily feel as if I would fly out of myself with shame and indignation, sometimes. Alas! If I should even convert one after I get there, I think I could not stay away.

"And then the men are so vexing! I had a letter from a St. Louis friend of whom I thought better, all in the 'Peace! Peace!' style to slavery, although he says 'it is a curse,' blaming *Massachusetts* and the *radicals* for present troubles, but hoping Mr. Buchanan will prove a salve for them. Just think, three sheets full of that! I'd like to dip my pen in fire to answer him—or borrow J. G. W.'s."[16]

As political feelings intensified, Larcom found times when she could hardly keep quiet. She wished that the North could withdraw from the Union, as it was a disgrace to be connected with southern wickedness. She was not alone in her feelings; as she told Hattie with dry humor, "We are quite revolutionary here [at Wheaton]. Our young ladies held a meeting on the Fourth, and passed some stirring resolutions."[17] There was concern for their southern students, whose position among their sometimes overpatriotic classmates grew daily more difficult.

She spent several days of her spring vacation with the Whittiers. Back at Wheaton she wrote expressing her concern; Whittier was having a bad spell with his insomnia, and was very worried about the political situation. She added an invitation to come to Wheaton when he made a proposed visit to his cousins in Providence. Whittier replied that he did not call on her when he went to Providence because Norton was off the track, because a visit from a Quaker might damage her reputation, and because he did not go to Providence.[18] Larcom, clearly amused, answered, "I am entirely 'nonresistant' in matters pertaining to logic, and am but just lifting myself up from the overthrow of your weighty reasons for not coming to see me when you *didn't go to Providence.*"[19]

In a letter to Elizabeth, with a contrived humor that is not characteristic and betrays embarrassment, she asked what she should call Whittier when she mentioned him to his sister.[20] Apparently she was invited to use the family name, Greenleaf; she addressed several letters to him that way, before going back to the "My dear friend" that she used for those closest to her. In his case she was also making a kind of pun, and she frequently adopted Quaker plain speech in writing to him. He had called her Lucy almost from the beginning, but her respect for this older and famous man would not let her presume to break the formality of names without permission.

She saved money so that she could take the fall term off and began the summer rejoicing in the fact that there was no more school until December. She considered writing her "long story" in letters, and Whittier approved the idea. In August she stayed with the Robinsons; Hattie wrote in her journal, "Lucy Larcom came to spend a week with us. I like her very much. She has something to talk about, excepting gossip, help, and babies.—She has the table-tipping power, and Mary and she tried together, and got what pretended to be a communication from Elbridge."[21] Hattie, the skeptic, found the experience interesting. Larcom, although she never mentioned spiritualism except in the most abstract way, was apparently fascinated by its possibilities.

Her letter of thanks to Hattie warmly invited her to visit them in Beverly, where the family was awaiting the return of Isaac Baker from one of his voyages, commented on Kansas, the election and Frémont's defeat, remembered her summer visit with pleasure, and promised to come again. The next time she wanted to meet, or at least see, Thoreau. She had accepted Hattie's mockery of the eccentric writer, but now she had read *Walden* and could not think of its author as merely the butt of town jokes. *Walden* became a book she treasured and read over and over. She could still laugh at Hattie's comments on "Hennery," but her respect for him was immense. She may not have discussed the book with Whittier, who called it "capital reading but very wicked and heathenish."[22] For Larcom, both the magic of Thoreau's natural world and his message "simplify, simplify" were important.

During the summer she had more time to write, and she was trying to enlarge the market for her poems. Local papers, the *National Era*, and the *Boston Telegraph* were always pleased to take her work, but pay from them was poor. She no longer felt as much sympathy for Mr. Arthur of *Arthur's Home Magazine* when he was too poor to pay her, although she still sent him a fair amount of her work. Some of her similitudes appeared there, and a series called "Maiden Meditations," short essays that mused on familiar sayings. She wrote about shams and disguises, the "beautiful," getting acquainted, an allegory called "The Three Tapers," and a story that contrasts the flamboyant behavior of the night-blooming cereus with the quiet and unobtrusive beauty of the violet. Her prose works she signed with her name; for her verse she still used "Culma Croly." Her connection with *Arthur's* stopped completely, however, when its assistant editor, Virginia Townsend, whom she had known at Monticello, printed part of a personal letter without Larcom's permission.

She returned to Wheaton in December, feeling well after her long vacation, with a stock of poems she had written over the summer and fall. Her return was marked by a move to a new and much larger house, which she disliked for its largeness and because, she wrote, "I am disturbed by rooming within hearing of a *man's voice,*—almost as bad as the piano I had in the room next to me before. He is an inveterate talker, and confirms my belief that 'silence is golden.' "[23] In February Emeline wrote to say that one of her twins had died— the sixth child she had lost. Larcom read Mrs. Browning's *Aurora Leigh* and commented enthusiastically to Hattie, "A *grand* poem, isn't it? I think woman is *somebody* in these days, if all the talk and writing amount to anything. Miss Bremer's *Hertha* is in the same progressive strain; Aurora Leigh is a *grander* character altogether, I think, than Hertha."[24] She planned to join Hattie at an antislavery meeting in Concord and expressed approval of Emerson's strong abolitionist stand. She reread *Walden,* liking it even better the second time. There were moments of longing for Vine Lodge, which was becoming a symbol of happiness for her, and as usual she reported to her friends there, "I have not heard directly from Frank in more than two years. It does not look as though we should ever 'sit in your parlor chatting' again, does it? But I have not lost my *sisterly* interest in him; though I do not imagine there can be anything more between us."[25]

Another pleasant summer passed. Larcom wrote her poems and worked on a second little book, but it must have been clear to her and to Whittier that the "American story" would never be written. He still had ambitions for his protégée, however; once she had confided a dream of someday publishing a book of her poems, and now he began to insist that she try to do so. As always, but with some real doubts, she followed his suggestion and then reported what she had done, at the same time stating her theory of poetry:

Well, I called on Mr. Jewett, and asked him if he wanted to read some poetry. He replied that poetry was rather "out of his line," and suggested Ticknor and Fields. So last week I wrote to the latter gentlemen, and have just received a reply, which I enclose, with the inquiry whether your opinion agrees with theirs. If it does, I will put the Ms. to sleep for this winter, if not longer. There is no reason that I know of, why I should want them published *now;* and it may be much better to let them rest awhile. I said to myself, when looking over the pieces after I had arranged them to the best of my ability, "Rather slender, if you call this *poetry.*" And perhaps, if I wait, something will come to me which will put more stamina into the volume—if there ever is one. If I have begun to see my deficiencies, that ought to be one step forward. I have found great enjoyment in trying to speak out my thoughts this far, though "with stammering lips and insufficient sound," as Mr. Browning has it. I long and am ready to strive for nobler thoughts and more worthy utterances;—but the thought must come by inspiration,—and the utterance too, if genuine. After all, it is only to *live* the highest there is in one, and then speech, and all that is external will take its most beautiful form. I cannot conceive of a conceited poet—is there such a phenomenon. Or indeed I might ask, is there conceit in any true thing?

But I am wandering from the matter about which I began. I should prefer Ticknor to any other publishers, and regard his opinion on these matters highly. But he does not hint that he would *ever* be willing to examine my "specimens"; why he should say "good as they are," I don't understand, when he probably knows nothing about them.—But I used your name, as you gave me leave to do, and perhaps he thought that an equivalent for their merits.[26]

The literary world was delighted with the *Atlantic Monthly,* a new magazine founded by Francis H. Underwood, with a group of advisers that included Emerson, Lowell, Longfellow, and Holmes. Lowell served as the first editor (1857–61) and the others were major contributors along with Whittier, Thomas Wentworth Higginson, Edward Everett Hale, Harriet Beecher Stowe, and Harriet Prescott. From the beginning the *Atlantic* was a subject for discussion, and it soon drew attacks for its provincialism. It was thoroughly New England—in fact, Boston (and Cambridge)—in its tone and in its contributors, whose anonymity was not very carefully maintained. Probably this Brahmanism was not conscious policy; Boston was still the literary center of the United States, and neither Lowell nor James T. Fields, who succeeded him as editor in 1861, needed to go far to find what they wanted. Regardless of the attacks on its regionalism, no one ever disputed the quality of its contents or its high literary standards. To be published in the *Atlantic* was a great honor.

Whittier, of course, wrote for the *Atlantic*, and he decided that Larcom should, too. A response in one of her letters illustrates his mentoring style: "I received, a few days ago, the poem 'Across the River,' with a 'respectfully declined,' from the office of the new Maga. I was not at all surprised, only that I did not certainly know that you had sent it. With all deference to the judgment of the gentlemen editors, I think it is quite a decent little poem, with the changes you made; and it is a much greater pleasure to me, to know that you liked it, than it would have been to see it in print among acknowledged seers and songsters.—But I am sorry you had your trouble for nothing."27 Obviously he felt free to make changes and to submit the poem without consulting her, and she accepted his editing.

Whittier's interest in her and her work remained constant, and there were other positive elements in her life. She enjoyed being out-of-doors at Wheaton, she liked her students, and she had made several good friends among the faculty and in Norton. The sister-in-law of the town minister was a companion on walks in the woods, and later she enjoyed the company of Abijah M. Ide, editor of the Taunton paper, and a young man named Edwin Barrowes, brother of one of the Wheaton students. She had friends in nearby Providence, and there were always invitations to visit the homes of former students. She could get to Beverly fairly often, and her income allowed her the travel in the summer that almost made up for the enclosed life of Wheaton.

When the Robinsons left Concord and moved to Malden, she was sorry, for she had liked visiting the town and her vicarious connection with literary greatness. "I should think you must miss the Concord inspiration. It's just the pleasantest old New England town I ever was in. The air of it is different from the air of any other place. That peculiar stillness was delicious to me, for I hate a hubbub and stir, of all things. 'Give me peace and a dinner of herbs.' "[28] Harriet, who liked a fair amount of hubbub and stir and who had found Concord a little too conservative for her tastes, was glad to move. Malden, a town that a few years before had been another small country village, was now growing rapidly as transportation to Boston improved. Larcom came to feel very much at home in Harriet's well-run house with its profusion of plants indoors and lovely garden outdoors. The year before, William Robinson had begun writing his strong "Warrington" articles for the *Springfield Republican*, a paper secure enough not to have to worry about loss of circulation if the crusading writer offended readers.

In 1856 *The Congregationalist* reprinted her "Call to Kansas" and indicated that other poems would be welcomed. The paper was, as its name suggests, a religious one, the chief organ of the Congregational church in New England, although its circulation was not limited to the area; the Vine Lodge people, for example, were subscribers. It presented news of church matters primarily, and its editorials and features were moral and religious. It did not pay particularly well—a dollar or two for a poem—but it paid, and it was a respected paper. One of the real benefits it offered was the chance to review books, enabling Larcom to begin building a personal library. She wrote for *The Congregationalist* from 1856 to 1867. In 1857 she published nineteen poems, signed with either her initials or her full name, and the next year seventeen. After that the number gradually fell, and in 1866 and 1867 she had only one poem in the paper. Part of the reason was that as her popularity grew, better-paying markets became available. Furthermore, in 1857 the editor, C. A. Richardson, asked her if she would select the poetry for the paper for a small but regular salary.

In a letter to Hattie, Larcom punned that she wrote a weekly poem for the paper, "and it is weakly enough!"[29] Most of the poems are indeed weak; they are tritely religious and show none of the careful work that characterizes poems that were important to her. Even so, they were better than much of the verse that appeared there. As de facto editor, she continued the practice of having "selected" poems, which had been published in other places first, and original poems, labeled "For *The Congregationalist*." Of the approximately eighty poems she contributed to the paper, only twelve were good enough, in her opinion, to be reprinted in later collections of her work, and most of these were "selected" rather than "For *The Congregationalist.*"

Several are interesting for reasons other than poetic merit. "The Way of the North Star" (10 September 1858) is a dramatic dialogue between a husband and wife whose home is a way station on the underground railroad; "Sorrow on the Sea" (16 August 1859) says

> God's deep cannot quiet be
> 'Neath a slaver's boat.

A pleasant little poem called "Helen" begins,

> I knew a little blue-eyed lass
> Among the rills,
> When Autumn bleached the withered grass,
> And dried the hills.

The accompanying letter to C. A. Richardson says "The poem being personal, and not a very high order, in my estimation, I have preferred to use only my initials." It was written for a little girl (Helen Spaulding) who wanted something "on purpose for her" in *The Congregationalist.*[30]

If Larcom tended to dash off or dig up poems for the newspaper, quite the opposite was true of her contributions to the short-lived but prestigious magazine of the arts called *The Crayon.* The poems she submitted to it were for the most part more carefully done, and they represented her thinking as well as her craftsmanship. Of the twenty-five poems published in the magazine during its six-year existence, twelve appear in her collections.

The splendid insights that had come together with her reading of Emerson a few years earlier had, for the most part, remained unvoiced until now, and the background against which she finally spoke seems curious, for Wheaton was religiously oriented and completely orthodox. Whether the opposition stimulated her or she had just reached a point where she had to state her religious thinking, her beliefs make the subject of the most important poems that she wrote during this time.[31] "The Death of June" (*Crayon,* August 1855) is a long poem; after the introductory lines that proclaim the "death" of June and detail its beauty in a passage of the richly textured description of the natural world that she did so well, the different richness of July follows. All the description leads to her point:

The universe is one great, loving thought,
Written in hieroglyphs of bud and bloom.

Humanity is part of the thought, part of the loving God who is the thought. Only human sin prevents knowledge and happiness.

"Entangled" reflects her perception of the interconnectedness of all things and the joy that understanding brings:

Birds among the budding trees
Blossoms on the ringing ground:
Light from those? Or sound from these?
Can the tangle be unwound?

The tangle does not need to be unwound, for it is man's finite perception of God's work, and the perception itself, available to those who seek and are ready for the seeking, is beauty and joy.

Like William Cullen Bryant, one of her favorite poets as a child, Larcom accepted the invitation to come to Nature, but there she found not the majesty and universality of death but the being who guided the waterfowl to its home. In "A White Sunday" she described her own Sunday morning worship service under a blossoming apple tree while others were in church.

The world we live in wholly is redeemed;
Not man alone, but all that man holds dear.

Human beings are part of this wholeness; they are "human plants," but they have the ability to choose their way, and they may do themselves spiritual harm by concentrating on "their own impoverished lives" instead of God's world, thereby shutting off "light and growth." Some try to find answers in theology, but that can be "hard and lifeless." Even religion is too often a word for

transient fervor, or for duty cold,
Or vain, self-helpful works of charity.

Works mean nothing without the presence of God in one's life, and God can be found in Nature.

Emerson had been her catalyst, making her think and easing her fear of going beyond dogma. She added his ideas and some Boethian philosophy to her prairie vision and she accepted his universe—with modifications. Her "one great loving thought" was no impersonal oversoul, but the loving personal God of the New Testament. She had, in fact, reached a Christian transcendentalism that had little to do with the Calvinism of her childhood. Her beliefs made denominations seem trivial; the best people she knew were her Calvinist sister and the Quaker Whittier, poles apart but both good Christians. God was above dogma. Her own theology brought her moments of joy and comfort, but that strong childhood indoctrination gave her a vacillating hold on her beliefs; she was often attacked by doubt, guilt, and even fear at her own heterodoxy. She could not accept the old rigidity, with its built-in cruelties, but she was not quite secure enough to put it behind her. Religion was, after all, the most serious and important matter that a human being had to deal with. Larcom's religious quest, so important in her life, was never a search for belief, but rather for the expression of belief.[32]

The examination of nature leading to a statement about God and man is hardly original in American poetry. In fact, little of Larcom's work is original. Its attractiveness lies in her use of detail to create a sensuous description of the natural world she loved so well. The poems still communicate her appreciation of and joy in nature, and though to a modern reader the "message" may say little, it was belief that she shared with her audience.

These three poems and others written during the same period were a means of working out her own thoughts and a justification of her beliefs. At conservative Wheaton there were raised eyebrows and occasional sharp comments about Miss Larcom's refusal to attend church every Sunday; she was forced into defining herself against the prevailing belief. Staying away from church services that taught a doctrine she could no longer accept was not easy. She knew that some of her colleagues disapproved of her, and although disapproval was always hard for her to bear, she persisted with her usual quiet stubbornness.

By December 1857 Larcom had been at Wheaton for three years. Although she still thought of her position as temporary, she had settled into the routine of the school. Common sense (and her friends) told her how fortunate she was to have a good job in a fine school, a salary that was more than ample for a woman, a location close to the places that mattered to her, and good friends, admiration, and affection. Her future could move in this smooth, secure way as long as she chose.

Under the cheerful exterior that Emeline had taught her to present to the world, however, was a growing dissatisfaction and restlessness that she was ashamed to admit even to herself. She was just as irritated and bored with the mechanics of teaching as she had been in the district school and at Monticello. Lack of time to write distressed her; she hated having to contrive moments alone, and there were never enough of them. The long story she and Whittier had planned had dwindled into another version of *Similitudes* called *Lottie's Thought-Book*, a series of rather sententious letters written by a young girl to her mother—a long step from that representative American story. She wondered whether she could have carried out the original plan if she had more control over her life—if she could stand free, not hampered and bound by the expectations of society, able to develop and use her talents.

She repressed this kind of thinking and did not connect it with the increasing trouble with her head that plunged her into spells of mental paralysis. It was selfish and irresponsible to want a life with freedom to read, write, be outdoors, and talk with friends. If God had sent her to Wheaton and given her the responsibility of guiding young minds and characters, then it was her duty not just to do the work but to be satisfied and happy in it. If she was to stay—and what else was there to do?—she must accept her life and make the best of it.

CHAPTER 7

Esther and "Hannah"

Larcom's letters and journal over the next several years show a pattern of extremes and an increasingly divided self that moved her to question her own sanity as two important influences drove her in different directions.

On her spring vacation in 1856 she went to visit Eliza Holmes in Waterbury, Connecticut. Holmes had a cousin whom she described as "morbidly shrinking" because of a "little defect of the eyes."[1] Esther Humiston was probably tubercular, and she lived as a recluse, waiting to die and refusing to see anyone except her family and an assortment of ministers. Holmes rather ruthlessly engineered a meeting between the two women, sure that they would like each other.

Larcom was fascinated by what she and others saw as the saintly self-denial, rejection of the world, and resignation to God's will that Humiston seemed to epitomize. For some reason the image of beloved Esther in her chamber patiently waiting for God to call her to a better world caught Larcom's imagination. The two women met only once, but for the next four years they corresponded in a series of long, frequent, and loving letters.[2] Humiston became a confidante; more, she became an ideal.

From the beginning Larcom's letters were intimate. She told, for example, of dreaming of her father: "I thought he came to life, and oh what a void in my heart was filled when he spoke to me, but he said words that grieve me still, although I know it was a dream."[3] For the most part her letters were preoccupied—almost obsessed—with religious musings and her own failings. To a modern reader her concerns and intensity seem neurotic. In *A New England Girlhood* she described those bad years in Lowell as bringing out in her a morbid self-criticism; Esther Humiston had much the same effect. At times Larcom seemed to be exploiting her own misery; unhappiness was what Humiston wanted, so that she might counsel resignation, and unhappiness was what she got. Larcom's letters to her almost never presented the busy, productive side of her life.

Larcom shared the sentiments and sentimentalities of her age, but she could be sensible and practical as well. Those qualities deserted her, however, under Humiston's influence. Emeline had certainly counseled acceptance of God's will, but it was an active, not a passive, acceptance. One could affect life's quality by one's own attitude—it did not make one any warmer to complain about the cold. But Emeline was far away in Wisconsin, and Larcom missed her desperately.

Humiston's influence meant passive acceptance of life as it was. Therefore, as Larcom's discontent with boarding-school life grew, she interpreted her feelings as evil. As a good Christian in Humiston's terms, she had to love all people while withdrawing from them. She had to brood over her own sinfulness and question her activity. Doubt gnawed at her sense of self-worth: was the writing she loved so much worthwhile? Was the pride she felt in it sinful? Should she not give up all but her duties and try to become like Humiston?

With these conflicts in her mind, she was hardly prepared for nearly overnight fame. In the fall of 1857 the *Crayon* editors requested some poems. She had nothing new, so she dug out of her files some verses she had written years before and sent to the *Knickerbocker.* Since that magazine had not even bothered to answer, she had no hesitation now about sending the poem to *The Crayon.* It appeared in the December 1857 issue.

Once she had sent the poem, she forgot about it. Over Christmas vacation Lois Larcom was seriously ill with a "mortification" of the foot. Larcom shared nursing tasks with her sisters; when her mother was clearly recovering, she returned to Wheaton, tired and depressed, to find that she was charged with plagiarism. The *New York Knickerbocker* had published the poem without informing her and now claimed that she had stolen it.[4] Larcom was horrified. She was not very good at fighting for herself, but she could, she discovered, fight for her work and reputation. She wrote a politely sarcastic letter to the *New York Tribune* denying that she was a "literary thiefess" and giving details: that she had sent the poem but had not had even the courtesy of an answer. In fact, since the poem had been published without anyone telling or paying her, she would now reclaim her "stolen goods."[5]

The poem got a good response from the beginning, but the controversy had the effect of calling further attention to it. Everyone read it and liked it; in time it inspired several paintings and, twice set to music, became a frequently repeated concert song.

HANNAH BINDING SHOES

Poor Lone Hannah,
Sitting at the window, binding shoes:
Faded, wrinkled,
Sitting, stitching, in a mournful muse.
Bright-eyed beauty once was she,
When the bloom was on the tree:
Spring and winter,
Hannah's at the window, binding shoes.

Not a neighbor,
Passing nod or answer will refuse,
To her whisper,
"Is there from the fishers any news?"
Oh, her heart's adrift, with one
On an endless voyage gone!
Night and morning,
Hannah's at the window, binding shoes.

Fair young Hannah,
Ben, the sunburnt fisher, gayly woos:
Hale and clever,
For a willing heart and hand he sues:
May-day skies are all aglow,
And the waves are laughing so!
For her wedding
Hannah leaves her window and her shoes.

May is passing:
Mid the apple bough a pigeon coos.
Hannah shudders,
For the mild southwester mischief brews.
Round the rocks of Marblehead
Outward bound, a schooner sped:
Silent, lonesome,
Hannah's at the window, binding shoes.

'Tis November,
Now no tear her wasted cheek bedews.
From Newfoundland
Not a sail returning will she lose.
Whispering hoarsely, "Fishermen,
Have you, have you heard of Ben?"
Old with watching,
Hannah's at the window, binding shoes.

Twenty winters
Bleach and tear the ragged shore she views.
Twenty seasons;—
Never one has brought her any news.
Still her dim eyes silently
Chase the white sails o'er the sea:
Hopeless, faithful,
Hannah's at the window, binding shoes.

Regardless of its effect on a modern audience, the poem appealed to the same element in the popular taste of the day that loved story pictures. "Hannah" presented pathos and virtue. Her fidelity, her refusal to give up hope, her quiet industry, the pride that kept her from complaint and hid her broken heart: all these were qualities of a noble woman. The songlike stanzas made an attractive frame for these elevated thoughts. Art, after all, had to have a purpose, and that purpose had to be a good one. A poem should delight, of course, but even more it should make a moral statement or illustrate a virtue.

Years later, William Dean Howells, in *Literary Friends and Acquaintance*, wrote, in his usual patronizing manner, that "she was chiefly, and will be most lastingly, famed for the one poem, 'Hannah

Binding Shoes,' which years before my days in Boston had made her
so widely known. She never again struck so deep or so true a note,
but if one has lodged such a note in the ear of time, it is enough; and
if we are to speak of eternity, one might very well hold up one's head
in the fields of asphodel, if one could say to the great others there, 'I
wrote "Hannah Binding Shoes." ' "[6]

"Hannah" remained popular. It followed Larcom all her life, although she grew sick of it and at least once begged an editor not to
use it as an example of her work. For years she received letters asking who the original of "Hannah" was, and whether she had lived in
Beverly or Marblehead (both towns claimed her). Larcom patiently
answered that there was no original; the poem represented a situation all too common in coastal towns.[7] Eventually her answers became rather flippant. After her death, her obituary in the *Chicago
Journal* called the poem "an American classic, to be found in nearly
every American anthology."

Larcom was amazed by fame. The success of "Hannah" puzzled
her; it was so far from her best work. The letters of admiration and
gratitude from readers everywhere were hard to believe, and so were
the suddenly welcoming attitudes of unknown editors. Since the situation seemed unreal, Larcom took it calmly; her letter to Ma and
Becky described the controversy rather than the poem or the attention it was bringing her.

The success of "Hannah," with the resulting fame and admiration, solved no problems. Instead it further polarized her two conflicting aims: concentration on teaching and concentration on writing. At some point the idea of writing as a professional instead of an
amateur must have surfaced, for she told Ma and Becky, "I don't
want to have *that* [writing] my only means of getting a living, for the
hardest work of all must be to spin out one's brains."[8] Concentration
on writing tempted her if only she dared to take the risk, but financial security was a necessity; even her dear friend Greenleaf made
little money from his poems. And was it truly womanly to set
oneself up as a writer unless one was divinely driven, like Mrs.
Stowe?

More than the fear of trusting herself to her pen prevented her
from leaving Wheaton; there were difficulties because of her temperament. That very cheerful disposition that made her personally
popular was both a strength and a drawback. Philena Fobes, writing

after her former pupil's death, described her "large intellectual nature, poetic insight, moral and social qualities, and serene temperament," but went on to say that Larcom herself knew the "disadvantage of her happy, easy disposition, which, as she said, made it impossible to be anxious about her future. It combined with it a slight degree of mental inertia. . . . With one more drop of celestial ichor, or rather, one more spark of divine inspiration added to her rich gifts, what high creative genius she would have manifested, what impassioned strains she would have sung!"⁹

Sarah Jane Spalding, who later became her closest friend, diagnosed the problem a little differently: "You are a little too apt to consult the side interests of others in forming your plans, my dear Lucy, and amiable as this is, it sometimes defrauds you of your purposes, and entangles you in indecision. Isn't it so? If your spirit were not clear and even, holding its own poise in spite of circumstances, I fear you might suffer serious inconvenience from this very unselfishness of yours, this trying to think what A would like, and what B would like, and to walk along with all their wishes, when you had better stride on at your own pace, leaving them to catch up with you—the better for them if they do."¹⁰

Both of these comments are the counsels of affection; their point is borne out in other ways. Larcom's correspondence is dotted with letters, usually to close friends like the Robinsons, that literally dither: she will come on the twelve o'clock train, or perhaps the three o'clock if it looks like rain early, or perhaps, if the weather isn't good or the time convenient, she'd better come another time. There are enough of these letters to be significant; they suggest, on a small level, a real dislike of committing herself too definitely.

If small decisions were difficult and the opinion of others too important, big decisions, like leaving a comfortable and respectable teaching position, were clearly agonizing. Inertia (Larcom herself called it indolence), sensitivity to opinion, indecisiveness, and her fear of confrontation set up situations in which her only recourse was to drift, to let things happen to her. She had drifted away from unpleasant tasks in her childhood, as she had drifted away from the West and her commitment to Frank, and as she had drifted to Wheaton. She said later that Lowell had taught her self-discipline and the importance of work, but these qualities were superimposed on an easygoing personality that was not yet bold enough to take her life in her own hands. What both her friends missed was the fact that when she was in control, doing what she wanted to do, decisions were easy.

So she resisted the yearning to move—to go home, live with Louisa, and write—and stayed securely at Wheaton, enjoying her fame and trying to ignore any calls away from what still seemed to be her duty. But if common sense, practicality, a concept of service, and the example of Esther Humiston directed her life, the opposing voice was powerful. "I see nothing of thine lately," Whittier had written a year before. "I am sure thou must have found something to say in thine own clear simple and beautiful way during this long winter. Does not the voice say to thee as formerly to the Exile of Patmos, *Write!*"[11]

With Humiston counseling resignation, Whittier urging the value of her writing, and her own timidity opposing her desires, Larcom's mind was in chaos. The trouble with her head increased; sometimes she spent days shut away as much as possible, enduring pain and self-hatred. As her isolation and alienation grew, she turned more and more to Humiston, pouring out her unhappiness and turning herself inside out for the other woman's comments. The same topics occur over and over: religion, marriage, Frank, and scrofula. She described a "true marriage" as the "highest state of earthly happiness. The flowing of the deepest life of the soul into a kindred soul . . . two spirits made one to be a double light and blessing to other souls."[12] "There's ice in me, others tell me of it, and I feel it," she admitted, but felt only God could thaw the ice.[13]

In another letter she spoke of the "temptation" of marriage, suggesting that it might have been stronger for her if she were not so absorbed in study; "I thank God that He keeps me busy, and thus so I am relieved of the burden of myself." But Frank was not the right choice. "He is impulsive, passionate, and *seems* much younger than I. My feeling for him is the constant affection of a sister for a somewhat wayward brother, who is yet stronger in many aspects than herself. He has a high sense of honor, made up of the pride of a man, and the principles of a Christian. . . . We never did in *all* respects answer to each other, I doubt whether we ever should."[14]

Encouraged by Esther, she wrote to Frank, trying to save their friendship and perhaps ease her own sense of guilt. His answer dismayed her; he was willing to "give up all, will bury the dead past . . . to be friend, brother, anything I say. But with it he expresses such an utter loss of faith and hope, and seems so indifferent as to life and usefulness, that my heart sinks in me to think that I may have caused such a wreck." She begged Esther to tell her whether she should continue to write him: "I do not wish the remembrance of me to keep his thoughts from others; I want him to love and be loved, and not to live alone, like me. . . . And perhaps I can save him, for himself, for the world, and for God. He seems now in complete apathy; says he is too indolent to be very unhappy about it—and that is the worst feature about it, to me; for he is, or was, both ambitious and passionate."[15]

Her response to the renewed correspondence was divided. Distress at Frank's unhappiness was real, but underneath was the pleasant consciousness that she was still wanted. But she knew that she was not the same tall, attractive girl Frank had last seen in 1850, nor was he the romantic young man she remembered. Too much time had passed. Nevertheless, she thought of him lovingly, as she did of the youthful, adventurous dreams they had shared, and hearing directly from him again penetrated her loneliness and brought warmth. Years later, going through some old papers, she found Frank's letters and described them to a close friend, "some of them *love-letters* that I hated to burn, they read so true—and really made me wonder that I am not Mrs. Somebody—I don't know how I resisted when I was really so attached."[16]

Whatever discontent Frank's letters may have indicated, he had settled in at Colusa and was thoroughly at home there. He was elected county assessor in 1857 and was very much a citizen of his community.[17] The area around Colusa had been so heavily settled by southerners that it was called the South Carolina of California. All its elected officials were Democrats. In general, settlers in the West were little concerned with the issues that led to the Civil War, but Colusa was actively prosouthern. The political attitudes Frank displayed in his letters horrified Larcom, but she tried to ignore them and persisted with the correspondence, telling Esther each mood and sway of feeling. "I could almost believe I love him enough to go to him at once," she wrote, and then immediately backed down: "I am sure there are chambers in my heart that he could not unlock . . . I do feel that it is in me to love, humanly, as I have never yet loved him." This letter reveals the complexity of her problem and certainly suggests that part of her unwillingness to let go of Frank came from her own loneliness and sense of isolation: "I *long* for something to care for, something that needs me more than it needs anything else. Is it the mere womanly instinct? Surely, we were put on earth to be God's nurses, guardians, guides.—Esther, I think a mother must be the happiest being on earth. I can conceive of no greater loss to a woman than to live and die without children of her own. I have always had an intense craving of this kind; I want something that needs all my heart,—that belongs to me.—Sometimes I think this is more of the feeling that I have for Frank; it would be a sort of maternal feeling I should have for him, if I lived with him."[18]

The letters to Humiston are so consistently unhappy and brooding that it is almost shocking to turn from them to Larcom's letters to others and the activities and interests they record. At times it seems as if two different people were writing. Part of the difference may have been her writer's awareness of audience—that only Esther wanted to hear her unhappiness. Her letters to Ann Spaulding and to Elizabeth Whittier are certainly intimate and do reveal her conflicts, but only among other subjects, and their overall tone is positive. To Whittier she wrote, as always, either reports of her work or carefully composed essays about the natural world, intimate only in the sense that she knew he shared her delight. Her letters to Hattie Robinson were about her reading, her ideas, her family, her activities, and events in the political and literary worlds. She wrote of Isaac Baker's departure for Australia—"Lydia's Isaac and mine"—and how much he would be missed, or her amusement when Emerson's "Brahma" inspired a host of parodies, and Lucius Manlius Sargent's "Mr. Fum" insisted that no one had the slightest idea what the sage was talking about even though they all attended his lectures rather than be out of fashion.[19] She could smile at the criticism without changing her appreciation of the thought.

In the fall she wrote Hattie of her longing to be in the hills, and commented on the New York editor and dandy Nathaniel Parker Willis: "Willis, I perceive, gets very eloquent about the horse-show, in the *Home Journal*. I don't quite fancy his Willis-y way of talking about fine horses and fine women all in a bunch—but perhaps I don't appreciate horses." She added, briefly, "I am going [to Boston] partly to see the doctor—not that I am sick, but I found that I had somehow 'run down,' and I thought I would try to *run up* again."[20] During Christmas vacation she announced, "I had a meeting-house with a minister in it, among my gifts. I thought that was a *little* too much." Clearly this was family teasing and Hattie understood the reference, for it was not explained; she went on to talk about the books she received as gifts and her delight in reading Shakespeare and the history and literature of the Middle Ages. There was also an account of a visit to the Athenaeum and other galleries with the sculptor Margaret Foley, "who took me around to see artists and pictures; it was a feast to me. I saw the great painting of Florinda, great in size, I mean, for I don't suppose there is anything *great* in a group of women scantily clad, but it is a brilliant affair."[21]

Her renewed acquaintance with Margaret Foley, who had briefly been a mill girl, enhanced her interest in art galleries and exhibitions, although her hatred of crowds and noise still made her shun big social occasions. As she got to know more people in Boston her comfort there increased, and she was finding it very pleasant to be known and admired as the author of "Hannah Binding Shoes."

Even with brother Isaac away it was still delightful to visit her family in Beverly, and there were wonderful stays in Amesbury, where she sat and talked and dreamed before the fire with the poet and his sister, or walked with Greenleaf in the countryside. In Newburyport she had made a new acquaintance, another Spaulding— although she spelled it Spalding and there was only the most distant connection with the two sets of Spauldings Larcom already knew. Sarah Jane Spalding was the wife of the Reverend Samuel Jones Spalding, minister of the Whitfield Congregational Church.[22] She was about Larcom's age, and they shared many attitudes and beliefs. Both had Calvinist backgrounds, although Spalding had broken away much earlier. She had spent some time at Brook Farm and wrote occasionally for papers. Her religious belief was strong and secure, but there was nothing reclusive about it; she was well-read and intelligent, able to discuss issues and ideas as well as keep a sharp eye on events in her husband's parish. Larcom liked her at once, although she had no idea that she was beginning the most important friendship of her mature years.

Nor, though her letters to Humiston dwell on him and their past relationship, was Frank the only man she knew. Harriet Hanson Robinson said that "Lucy might have married, once when she was quite young, and again later; but for reasons of her own she declined,—reasons, the validity of which, in one instance at least, I did not see."[23] There are no real clues to the second suitor, but there are several possibilities. Among her papers at Wheaton is a sonnet (called that, but it does not use sonnet form; possibly it is a translation from French) by Alphonse Renaud, the French master, which hails her as a light bringer ("Lucy") and begs her to teach him her joy in life. There was the unidentified minister about whom her family teased her. Her letters to Edwin Barrowes indicate an easy friendship. He escorted her to social events in and around Wheaton; their small social group exchanged calls, went for long walks and sleigh rides, and attended lectures and concerts. When he went to New Orleans with the Massachusetts Fourth Regiment in 1862, he wrote her letters full of the details of army life. Abijah M. Ide, Jr., a journalist and part-time postmaster of Taunton, who published the local newspaper and liked Larcom's poems, was a frequent visitor to Wheaton and also part of the same social group. Then there were her letter friendships, particularly with the two editors of *The Crayon*, John Durand and William Stillman. In his biography, Stillman describes their first meeting: "Lucy Larcom, the truest poetess of that day in America who gave us more of her most charming poems. She was teacher in a girls school somewhere in Massachusetts, and I went to see her on one of my editorial trips. We went out for a walk in the fields, she and her class and myself, and they looked up to me as if I were Apollo and they the Muses; and we went afield in many things."[24]

There is no evidence that any of these men were more than friends, and there were other candidates for the role of second suitor. Larcom liked men and enjoyed having them as friends, and she had a genius for attracting people to her.

The cheerful, active woman who wrote inspiring poems, enjoyed walking in the woods, and loved good conversation with friends, and the pitiful creature who brooded over her sins to Esther Humiston were still the same woman; nowhere is the contrast so clear as in her letters and activities through 1859. This was, in a sense, a crisis year; she was thirty-five in March, halfway through her biblically allotted span of years. She wrote a private poem, designed for her friends, called "Thirty-Five," using the analogy of life as a hill, with the writer standing at its summit, looking back at what had been, and then preparing to descend the hill, confidant that what was to come would be better. The poem is very positive, and Larcom admitted that she did not often feel that way.

Earlier in the year she had written to Elizabeth Whittier, "I am living on here as usual, more weary of the monotony, perhaps, and yet more reconciled to it, and to my mortal lot generally. I believe it is all right, probably, yes, undoubtedly just the best place and the best work for me, though so different from the cloudy castles which I fear I shall never be vandal enough to destroy."[25] Resignation to her life brought a sense of its dullness. In a poem called "May Morning after a Storm" (*Congregationalist*, 27 May 1859) she described a tempest followed by a morning that is washed clean and beautiful:

> If thou art shaken with the winds of heaven,
> 'T will prove thou art alive.

She did not feel shaken by any storms at Wheaton.

Her letter to Vine Lodge a few days after her birthday was a loving and nostalgic recollection of days there, full of longing for the old confidences and friendship and, it now seemed, a time when she had been truly happy. On her spring vacation she visited Amesbury, where she and the poet climbed Whittier Hill to watch the sun set in the Merrimack Valley. She is the friend mentioned in his poem, "The Preacher," inspired by their walk. But by the end of the term she was in a "low, nervous, fussy state, quite beyond anything I ever before experienced," she told Hattie later.[26] In Beverly her spirits improved almost at once, perhaps because she had an exciting summer planned. She had been carefully saving money for a long and elaborate vacation.

Like Whittier's friendship, her visits to Boston, and her time outdoors, her summer vacations were a real source of strength. They restored her health and released her from the confinement of her teaching duties; they freed her from her tortured thinking as well. This year she began her travels in Rhode Island; from there she went to Newburyport, where she spent more time with her new friend Sarah Jane Spalding. She visited Mount Holyoke, considering the possibility of teaching there, but wrote Humiston, "I didn't like Mt. Holyoke school very well; it seemed too like a great machine that I didn't want to be ground in. I like it here as well as anywhere in a school, because there is more of nature allowed."[27]

And at last she did what she had wanted to do for so long: she toured the White Mountains. By this time the New Hampshire mountains had become a fashionable vacation spot with symbolic embellishments. Years earlier, Hawthorne's dark, romantic vision in a story like "The Great Carbuncle," for example, had presented the mountains as forbidding physical barriers and as forces working to destroy those whose quest for the shining stone was motivated by false desires. *Lucy Crawford's History of the White Mountains*, first published in 1846, gave firsthand accounts of disaster in the wilderness: lost climbers who died of exposure, or the landslide that buried members of the Willey family in Crawford Notch.[28] Tales of this kind became part of the folklore of the region.

Gradually the mountains became more accessible. Roads were built, and venturesome travelers discovered quaint valley villages or rented rooms in farmhouses; by the next summer they usually found that the farmer had extended his house and turned into a boardinghouse keeper. Towns located at road junctions or possessing a spectacular view became the sites of enormous hotels whose broad piazzas allowed visitors to stroll or sit in contemplation of the summits. "Doing the Notches" was the fashionable tour, and a whole social pattern developed around it.

What added to the attraction of the mountains was Thomas Starr King's *The White Hills; Their Legends, Landscape, and Poetry*, published in 1859.[29] Starr King, a famous preacher, not only gathered together legends and verse, he endowed the mountains themselves with religious and poetic symbolism, based on the simple physical reality that mountains pointed and led upward. They were, therefore, closer to God. The difficult climb to the summit paralleled the difficult climb through life, with its goal of reaching the highest point. The symbolism was clearly attractive; several years later Mrs. A. D. T. Whitney, launched on her career as a popular novelist, almost spelled it out in a novel. Her heroine, at a crucial moment of her life, travels to the mountains with a party of rather worldly relatives. One of Whitney's mentor characters, looking at the fashionables who give token glances at the splendid mountains on their way to dance, mutters, "It's no use for people to bring their bodies to the mountains, if they can't bring their souls in them!"[30]

In Lowell Larcom had admired the brisk country girls who seemed almost another kind of being because of their freshness and independence. Her curiosity about the mountains began then, and in the years that followed she had absorbed enough of the mountain mysticism, which fit so perfectly into her own religious thinking, that the journey became a pilgrimage. Nothing about it disappointed her.[31] The mountains proved to be everything she had expected. More than the fresh air, the trees and flowers that she loved, and the majestic beauty around her, she responded to the symbolism. One could climb and be closer to God. Her happiness spills out of an uncharacteristic letter to Humiston, "But isn't it delightful to give yourself up wholly to rest—to feel that you have nothing to do about living, only to receive whatever life has to give, and to give as you receive?—To move on naturally and without thought, like sunshine and cloud and breeze, or to be moved as the leaf is by the wind—to be shone on as the flower is by the sun—this is the life—one kind of life, and the Epicurean existence has its charms."[32]

Each year her return to Wheaton brought on a physical reaction; this year, perhaps because her vacation had been so glorious, the reaction was violent. All the things that troubled her, dismissed over the summer, were waiting when she resumed her teaching duties. To make it worse, she had a bad attack of scrofula, and its ugliness, contrasted with the clean, fresh beauty she had just enjoyed, was intolerable. If she remembered Emerson's statement that beauty is the mark God sets on virtue, it must have intensified her irrational feelings of guilt and disgust at her treacherous body.

The precariousness of her mental balance in the fall of 1859 showed especially in her attitude toward the disease. "I have to fight with myself to go anywhere and to see anybody—and *scrofula* is at the root of it," she wrote Humiston. "I feel it as a horrible curse, a *ban* almost—only that I know I ought not. I believe there is something in the nature of the disease that brings with it self-loathing and shame.—There is no one, not even my mother, who has any idea how I feel. In my heart I want either to get well or to die."[33]

And finally she confessed her greatest fear: that these uncontrollable changes of mood and the depression that she could not fight were signs of loss of sanity:

But I could not answer you, because I was passing through the shadow just then; feeling the weight of the curse,—for such is disease and mental depression—oh, these horrid scars that sin has left on body and soul! There is no other word for them. And to know and love the lovely and glorious, and yet feel all this in one's self—

The trouble in my head is somewhat abated. It appears and disappears so, I think the seat of it must be in the nerves. It is sometimes in my head and sometimes in my neck and back. I have thought it might be a spinal disease; and have sometimes been rendered so miserable by it,—though it is not really *pain*, —that I have considered seriously the possibilities of insanity. God preserve me from that! but I have often dreamed that I was so, within a year or two. I suppose that close and continued mental exertion is not good for me,—but it seems necessary;— and then too much physical exertion wearies me just as much. But I am so much stronger than I was before I went to the mountains, that I ought not to say a word. If I could afford to live as my constitution demands, perhaps I should be well. Only there would always be scrofula,—and how deep that goes, I do not know. Large and healthy-looking as I am,—I am ashamed to feel like a "whited sepulchre."[34]

Part of the horror of what she was going through stemmed from her isolation. In the really bad times she could not bear to have anyone near her; she closed herself off from friends and thereby intensified her own unhappiness. She knew her reserve was seen as rejection and coldness, but she was powerless. Even when Eliza Holmes came to Wheaton to teach for a short period, Larcom felt none of her former fondness for this friend, only an apathetic politeness that dismayed her. She seems to have reached a point where the opposing forces were equally balanced and she herself had no power over them. The result was not peaceful stasis but sterile, unproductive paralysis.

She gave up going to doctors, she told Humiston, feeling that "fresh air, good food, and proper exercise" were all that helped, although "they will not cure that taint that was born with me, and will only leave me at death, probably." And she went on, in that convoluted thinking that Humiston invoked, to question whether it was right to try to be healed, or even to pray for healing: "—and yet I should be afraid to ask to be healed here; I can see for myself some temptations that would immediately assail me if I knew myself sound in body, and what others He may know, I never can tell. It is my cross, I will bear it and *try* to rejoice in it."[35]

It is hard to interpret the "temptations" as other than sexual— wordly love that might interfere with love of God. Nor is it possible to tell from such fragmented information whether her self-disgust and loathing of her body really barred marriage, or whether her deep-seated rejection of marriage found in her physical condition a kind of cover. When she was well she enjoyed her strong, healthy body, but undoubtedly her repression of natural instincts contributed to her restlessness and nervous tension. She wanted children but feared she might transmit her ugly disease to them, and at thirty-five she must have been aware that her childbearing years were limited.

Larcom may have questioned the morality of trying to find a cure, but at some point in the winter she did go to a faith healer. And by late fall the extremes of her depression had eased; once again her journal recorded activity and thought as well as moments of despair.[36] She liked *The Afternoon of Unmarried Life*, finding it full of "common sense, healthy sentiment, and sincere piety."[37] Masson's *British Novelists* did not please her: "He makes a novel and a narrative poem about the same thing; but it strikes me that a novel is about as much like a *real* poem as a canal is like a river, wandering 'at its own sweet will,' or as a railroad is like a romantic by-path through the woods. In a true poem you go where the poetry carries you; in a novel you may carry poetry with you wherever you have to go."[38]

Application of contemporary standards of art raised a question: "I always find myself doubting whether Shakespeare was so very good a man. That he admired and could delineate all noble things is undoubted; but the low and ignoble are delineated often with equal apparent relish. Could one who was living his best do that?"[39] Her doubts about Shakespeare's personal morality were overshadowed by her love of his work. In fact, when a Wheaton student's voiced desire to hear and see a Shakespeare play in a theater caused a controversy over whether anyone who went to a theater could be a Christian, Larcom serenely ignored the arguments, the raised voices, and the tension and continued to teach Shakespeare in her literature classes.[40]

She had reservations about some of her contemporaries as well. The Oliver Wendell Holmes who wrote inspirational poems like

"The Chambered Nautilus" was someone she could admire, but her feelings about the creator of the Autocrat and the Professor were mixed. She read both series in the *Atlantic*, but when the Professor married the Schoolmistress, she was stirred to comment: "I like the *Atlantic* for its originality and variety, though I think that the religious newspapers have some reason for their occasional strictures. Holmes is always racy. —I don't feel quite as interested in the Professor as I did in the Autocrat, and I think that smart and cool way of cutting people to pieces does not indicate a wonderfully amiable disposition.—I wouldn't have been *that* Schoolmistress for a great deal."[41]

At Christmas Isaac Baker was home and leading the family festivities, including a performance at the town hall by an elocutionist who read from *The Rivals* and Shakespeare, but pleasure was overshadowed by political events: "John Brown to be hung tomorrow!" she wrote Hattie. "Do we live in Christendom? I think America needs missionaries from some more enlightened land."[42]

As usual, returning to Wheaton was hard, but this winter and spring she was outdoors as much as work and weather permitted. She increased her excursions to Boston, taking painting lessons each Saturday; she finally overcame her fears and accepted Margaret Foley's invitation to an artists' reception, where, to her surprise, she enjoyed herself. A session with the dentist relieved her of four teeth and "neuralgia," and she continued to select poetry for *The Congregationalist*, to write for *The Crayon* and the Taunton paper, to send out her poems, and to work on another group of similitudes and moral tales, to be called *Ships in the Mist*.

In January she heard that Hattie Robinson's son had died, and wrote a rather glib letter of condolence, including a passage that suggested that the child's death had been sent to test and strengthen the Robinsons' faith. Hattie had not developed a protective shell about dying children, and she was more agnostic than believer; in her pain she found the letter offensive and said so. Larcom's answer was much more sincere as she tried to spell out her own conviction of a loving and personal God. The near quarrel was averted, and by summer Larcom was making morning-glory drawings for Harriet for possible use on the child's memorial stone.

By 1860 Humiston's health was so poor that she could no longer read or write, and the correspondence ended. Larcom wrote instead to her young half brother, Franklin Carter, and planned to give her journal to Humiston when the latter was well enough to read it. The journal certainly records her depressed moods and her discontent, but it is neither so intimate nor so tortured as her letters to her friend.

About the same time she realized that she had not had an attack of scrofula since the very bad one in the early fall. More than a year earlier she had written to Humiston, "Is it certain the scrofulous tendencies are absolutely ineradicable? Some physicians tell me that it is not so, and of late I am beginning to believe that the right medicine and right living may effect a cure."[43] Her prescription for herself included good food, rest, exercise, and much time outdoors, and, although she could not know it then, the severe attack she had had in the autumn of 1859 was the end of the disease. The scars remained, and for the rest of her life she covered them with a neck-band or a high collar, but the pain and the running sores that had so sickened and shamed her never recurred. According to the account of a relative many years after her death, the "affection of the neck" was cured by the "lying [sic] on of hands."[44] With her attraction to spiritualism, it is not surprising that Larcom might credit a faith healer with her cure; it is much more likely, however, that her new regime healed this form of tuberculosis.

Being outside brought more than physical benefits or natural beauty, deep and real though that was to her. Her walks helped to satisfy her need for freedom, for in woods or fields she was rid of the walls that closed her in with the noise and clutter of human person-alities. Outside she could move as she pleased, to walk or pause or drift where and when she chose. For moments, at least, she con-trolled her life.

In the spring of 1860 she was in better health and working hard to accept Wheaton as the station in life to which it had pleased God to call her, or the place where she could do the most good, or even as a trial that she must endure to perfect her soul. She never hated Wheaton; she admired the school itself and had good friends there. What she did hate was the confinement of a boarding school with the accompanying rules, duties, and restrictions. In spite of her mo-ments of self-loathing, she never became a recluse. She continued to go to Boston to look at pictures and meet friends. She saw the young Prince of Wales on his American visit, she went to the opera with the Robinsons, and she was faithful in attending painting classes with a Miss Stetson in Studio Buildings. There were outings with her friends at Norton. She did not neglect her correspondence or her reading. She reviewed Owen Meredith's *Lucile* favorably and she was reading Swedenborg: ". . . wondrous wisdom and wondrous foolishness," she wrote in her journal. "It is hard to distinguish between what he knew and what he did not know, he is himself so certain that all he sees and relates is truth. His visions are often nothing more than analogies that anyone of perceptive intellect might take quickly, and why this seeing power should be claimed as peculiar to him and his followers, I do not understand."[45]

In April the announcement of Helen Spaulding's marriage reminded her of time passing, and again she wrote to her Vine Lodge friends with love and longing for the days when they had been together. She wrote of her loneliness, her guilt about Frank, her health ("My head is getting worn out, for one thing, and my nerves, too"), and wished for quiet. She thought about moving to Wisconsin, where Emeline lived, and longed for a home of her own.[46]

The end of the school year and her return to Beverly brought better health and spirits as usual. Isaac Baker had bought a small boat, called the *Beach-Bird*, and there were more family excursions, short boat rides or picnics by boat. Like all her family, Larcom loved being on the water, but it was Isaac who made the occasions possible and delightful. Her summer visiting again included the home of John and Eliza Hanson in Maine, and from there, full of the joy of the outdoors, she wrote Elizabeth Whittier, "I don't know that I shall be able to live in a house at all, by and by, it makes me feel so stifled,"[47] and later, "Goldenrod is *splendid*, nevertheless; but it belongs in a vase of the literary lady color, 'Deeply, darkly, beautifully blue.' "[48] Whittier's red-green color blindness made him love bright yellows, and Larcom had given him a dark blue vase to hold yellow flowers. She was in good spirits and looking to the future when she wrote him from Maine about her joyous outdoor vacation and a wish that she might someday publish a book of verse.

She had been writing fewer poems because she was working on the fourth and last of her little similitudes books, *Leila among the Mountains*, in which she tried to share with young people the beauty and moral strength mountains meant to her. But by this time she had published quite a large amount of verse, and Whittier, always zealous in behalf of his protégées, responded to her tentative hope by again insisting that she send a selection to Ticknor and Fields. He wrote to James T. Fields to urge their publication.[49] Larcom was reluctant, but unwilling to go against Whittier's commands; she was not at all surprised when Fields declined the suggestion. Much as she wanted a book of her poems, she did not think she was ready. A year earlier John P. Jewett had written to ask, "Have you a sufficient number of pieces of poetry of your composition to make a vol.? If so, would it not be wise to publish them?"[50] She had refused, possibly because she wanted the Ticknor and Fields imprint on her work. If her poems were good enough, eventually Fields would publish them. The refusal did not upset her. Emerson praised a poem of hers called "Elijah," and she had many admirers and a steady market for her work. Her journal entries, though they still showed changes of mood, were more consistently cheerful as they repeated her determination to accept her life: "I am out in the air every day, this cool, clear, autumnal air, that makes me forget certain haunting trials that seem like nightmares when I keep myself close. Mixing with nature so as to get saturated with it, in a sense.— one gains a blissful unconsciousness of self as a bearer of burdens; and life, both physical and interior, comes to be a pleasant thing.—I am not sure but the willingness to have more to do with those about me adds something to the general agreeableness. I don't like to be among so many, but I have determined to make the best of it, and the most of them, for their sake and my own."[51]

CHAPTER 8

War

Like everyone else in the autumn and winter of 1860–61, Larcom's attention focused more and more on political events. She and Whittier rejoiced over the election of a westerner named Abraham Lincoln to the presidency, although they would have preferred their hero, Frémont; they were horrified at the public burning of the *Springfield Republican* (in which William Robinson's "Warrington" articles appeared) in Virginia.

The Quaker Whittier, having worked so passionately in the abolitionist cause, was now dismayed at the imminence of the monster he had helped to create, and he backed away from war. Larcom saw it as a holy cause, and tried to explain her feelings to Elizabeth and Greenleaf:

How many times in these fearful days I have thought of you both, and wished I could speak to you! At such times as these, we want to look into the faces of our best friends, to assure ourselves that there is reality and stability in something. Not that I have any doubt that this struggle will yet have a glorious end,— but it is so strange to live in a revolution, and the thought of bloodshed is so dreadful!

Yet, although I cannot bring myself to think of the waste of noble and precious lives which must result from this conflict,— unless miracles are wrought for us;—although I cannot think of that without deepest sorrow, yet it seems as if my whole being had turned from peaceful to warlike. I wish I were a man, that I might offer my life for my country; I have urged my friends to go,—and I will work night and day, if it is needed, for the success of our cause,—for is it not freedom's, and truth's and God's? . . .

I know you do not believe in war: neither do I; it is barbarous, it is hateful; and yet, forced upon us as this is, there is an instinct of resistance to wrong within us all, the trumpet-call of Nature itself, that drowns at once all previous beliefs and theories. If ever there was a cause for fighting, there is now; and I am not sure but that a bloody struggle would be most humane, as it would be brief.

How dreadful to be speaking so, when the death of every soldier who falls represents mountains of heartbreak, rivers of desolation everywhere!

We have given up school for a day and a half, to make shirts for our soldiers. Mr. Wheaton furnishes the material, three hundred yards of flannel, which will be made up and ready for use tomorrow.

Our pupils from Georgia have left, intending to return to their friends, but I fear they cannot; they were very unhappy here, of course, and we could not ask them to stay.

I think that we are most in danger of forgetting our Highest Trust now that we can count upon troops and treasures without limit. We women will be greatly to blame if we believe that God would confuse the counsels of the rebels, and save us from war, even now. It isn't too much to ask of Him,—but I do not know what bitter lessons He sees we need. He is still the God of peace, and He "scatters those who delight in war."

How doubly beautiful the spring flowers seem in this mild season! Yesterday I went out and found violets in bloom. I gathered them with a kind of fear—they seemed so little at home with the thoughts that had possessed and shaken me so! There is a stern reproof in this awakening of Nature, in the calm beauty, born of love, that smiles at all things, warmer and brighter every day. But Nature did not attain her present place without terrible convulsions, without long conflicts of her yet unharmonized elements.

Perhaps I shall see you in May or June;—I may go to Newburyport for a day or two. I hope we shall have clearer skies before then.[1]

Lincoln's inauguration, Fort Sumter, and then the steady procession of southern states leaving the Union held everyone's attention; Virginia's betrayal was hardest to bear, as Whittier's "Massachusetts to Virginia," with its evocation of Revolutionary days, attested. On April fourteenth Governor Andrew called up the Massachusetts militia, and Boston became an army camp overnight. Troops drilled on the Common, flags flew everywhere, and the merchants decorated their shops with red, white, and blue banners. Looking back in later years, Larcom wrote, "I saw the first troops leave Boston for Baltimore and Washington, and was intensely roused. It was the only time in my life that I ever thought I would rather be a man than a woman, that I might go and fight and perhaps die for my country and freedom. I had to content myself with knitting blue army socks and writing verses."[2]

No one expected that it would take much time to put the southern rebels in their places, and the news of the attack by a Baltimore mob on the Massachusetts militia came as a shock. The attack occurred on the nineteenth of April, and Larcom, like all other patriots, at once saw the parallel. Eighty-six years before, on the same date, the "shot heard round the world" was fired, and the struggle that created the Union began. Her poem "The Nineteenth of April" contrasted the honor of one war with the dishonor of the other. The poem was printed in the *Transcript,* reprinted in *The Congregationalist,* and frequently anthologized in collections of war poetry and song.

Of course she kept on with her reading and comments in her journal:

People of sickly delicacy of taste say we must not (we women especially) gather such flowers [i.e., read medieval literature] and indeed it would be pleasanter if the bushes were not so muddy; but yet it is not so bad as if the blossoms were all canker-eaten at the heart, as in some modern gardens of literature. . . . I find Marsh's *History of the English Language* a well-written and well-studied book, and one from which I shall gain much aid in reading the old poets. I have become the possessor of Chaucer, and Prof. Childs' edition of the old Ballads, recently, and I feel rich.[3]

What does cause depression of spirits? Heavy hand and heavy heart, and no sufficient reason for either, that I know of. I am out of doors every day, and have nothing unusual to trouble me; yet every interval of thought is clouded, there is no rebound, no rejoicing as it is my nature to rejoice, and as all things teach me to do. . . . A new volume of poems by T. B. Aldrich just read, impresses me especially with its daintiness and studied beauty. There are true flashes of poetry, but most carefully trimmed and subdued, so as to shine artistically. I believe the best poetry of our times is growing too artistic; the study is too visible. If free- dom and naturalness are lost out of poetry, everything worth having is lost.[4]

On her birthday the girls filled her room with flowers, and she was grateful for the loving tribute. When she heard that Mrs. Stowe, whom she admired so much, had praised her work, she had to tell Hattie. "I was *really* pleased with the word of praise from Mrs. Stowe, because it is pleasant always to have the sympathy and ap- proval of one who is truly great, as I believe she is. Oh, if I could only have my time and liberty,—I know I could write much better than I ever have yet. But I won't be impatient, nor rebel against things as they are: for they must be for the best, in some way unknown to me."[5]

The war and all her activities so filled her mind that the news of Esther Humiston's death early in May was merely something to be accepted. Her journal entry paid tribute to her friend's beautiful life, but showed little personal grief or loss. The relationship had been such an odd one that it was easy for Larcom to elevate Humiston to the position of saint who had finally gone home.

Few of her war verses were later included in collections of her work. Like most patriotic poems, many are embarrassingly emo- tional. One, however, was different. Out of her mingled pain and exaltation at the war, the new scientific ideas beginning to circulate, and her deep religious faith came a very serious poem called "The Rose Enthroned." William Robinson, temporarily working at the *Atlantic*, read it and was so impressed that he showed it to James Russell Lowell, who was just finishing up his editorship of the maga- zine. Lowell accepted the poem, and it appeared in the June 1861 issue.

The poem begins with a description of the painful and violent creation of the world:

> It melts and seethes, the chaos that shall grow
> To adamant beneath the house of life;
> In hissing hatred atoms clash, and go
> To meet intenser strife.

After the chaos of the "warring elements" the world is populated by "slimy monsters with unhuman eyes" in generations that must die and be succeeded by others, for they cannot build a future.

> While mid the ruins of the work she planned,
> Sits Nature, blind and dumb.

> For whom or what she plans, she knows no more
> Than any mother of her unborn child:
> Yet beautiful forewarnings murmur o'er
> Her desolations wild.

Finally there is calm, and Beauty emerges on the new-formed earth:

> Within the depths of palpitating seas,
> A tender tint, anon a line of grace,
> Some lovely thought from its dull atom frees,
> The coming joy to trace:—

Six stanzas describe the coming of Beauty into the world and the hint of greater to come, until,

> In golden silence, breathless, all things stand;
> What answer waits this questioning repose?
> A sudden gush of light and odors bland,
> And, lo,—the Rose! the Rose!

> The birds break into canticles around;
> The winds lift Jubilate to the skies;
> For, twin-born with the rose on Eden-ground,
> Love blooms in human eyes.

Love enters the world (and clearly this is love and the rose with all symbolic interpretations) but only after long pain and violence as well as learning from "truth in errors past." Nor is the process finished:

And of some wonder-blossom yet we dream
Whereof the time that is enfolds the seed;
Some flower of light, to which the Rose shall seem
A fair and fragile weed.

For all her patriotic zeal and emotionalism, in her more thoughtful moments Larcom had to justify the struggle that turned a people against itself. War made sense only as a purification, a terrible but beautiful blood sacrifice that would finally expel evil. The world was still, under God's guidance, in the process of being made, and the upheaval in human life paralleled the geological growth of the planet.

The poem was another step in her career. Since the *Atlantic* published poems anonymously, guessing the authors provided a pleasant game for the literati until the yearly index came out. "The Rose" was briefly attributed to Lowell, but then opinion gave it to Emerson himself and it was read with appropriate seriousness. Larcom was amused and flattered. "Hannah" had brought her fame and the chance to make money; "The Rose" brought prestige. Young though it still was, the *Atlantic* was the literary summit of Boston, and Boston was the literary summit of the country. Publication there of a poem so serious and meaningful that Emerson seemed to be the logical author proclaimed her a true poet and a legitimate part of the literary world.

"The Rose" also brought her new friends. James T. Fields, who was to succeed Lowell as editor of the *Atlantic*, and his enchanting wife, Annie Adams Fields, sought out this new poet and attempted to draw her into their circle. Fields's role as a publisher was probably unique; he was not classed as a businessman, but as a man of letters, part of the literary group, and he and his wife made personal friends of the Ticknor and Fields authors. Larcom became a welcome guest at the famous Charles Street house, at least at smaller gatherings; it took time before Annie's gentle persuasion encouraged her to attend the larger parties. She did, however, begin to feel herself a part of the group of writers who frequented the Old Corner Book Store.

Nevertheless, the end of the school year found her very tired and longing for the rest that would come, "up among the mountains with friends who love noise and confusion as little as I do, I shall be at peace. A blessing will come to us, among the hills."[6] Unfortunately, for once the summer failed to offer its usual healing magic.

The Battle of Bull Run in July made appallingly clear the fact that the troops seen off with such pride and high spirits in the spring would not be coming home in a triumph a few months later; far too many would not come home at all. Larcom's enthusiasm weakened under such a blow. Then she and the Whittiers had planned to spend a few weeks together in her beloved mountains, but Elizabeth's doctor recommended the sea instead, and their plans had to be canceled. Aside from a week in New Hampshire with James and Annie Fields and a short visit to Newburyport and Amesbury in August, Larcom stayed in Beverly most of the summer. Lacking the usual rejuvenation, she had to leave Wheaton early in the fall to go home and rest.

Her malaise disappeared with the onset of cold weather, and her journal entries were more cheerful by late October. Every Saturday she went to Boston for lessons in painting flowers and leaves, resulting in studies done in rich, bold colors firmly enclosed within thin, dark outlines, just as the rich talents inside her were bound by the thin, dark lines of womanly propriety. Though she sometimes questioned the expense, she found that the act of painting, with its necessary concentration, relaxed and calmed her mind, letting her escape temporarily from both personal and national worries.

There was much to escape. At the end of October the engagement at Ball's Bluff proved that nobility of purpose alone could not win battles; the military fiasco involved three Massachusetts regiments, whose tallies of dead, wounded, and above all, prisoners, echoed all over the state. Antietam reinforced the message. There was general dismay in literary Boston after that battle at the news that Dr. Holmes's son, young Wendell, had been seriously wounded. There was another kind of dismay for some when his father, after searching the battlefields for his wounded and missing son, wrote up the whole experience for an *Atlantic* article.[7]

At Wheaton the students and teachers knitted, as women did all over New England. Neither her knitting nor her verses were enough for Larcom; she began to think about other ways of helping, like going south to teach escaped slaves. She talked about moving to New York, too, but only in a vague kind of way.

The longing for freedom and more control over her own life never eased: "How I should like to live a free life with nature one year through!" she wrote in her journal. "Out in the bracing winds, the keen frosty air, and over the crackling snowcrust, *wherever I would;*

and then in summer, seek the mountains or the sea, *as I chose;* no study, no thoughts, but what came as a thing of course; no system, but nature's wild ways, which have always their own harmony, evident enough when one enters into them, though understood by no mere observer."[8]

She needed something to help her face her problem, and she was to have it. Early in January 1862 Rebecca Danforth, making a long visit to her eastern relatives, came to Wheaton for a few days. For Larcom it was a catharsis to talk to this old friend who knew her so well that little had to be explained. Her journal entry describing Becky's visit questioned for the first time her devotion to her teaching duties at the expense of her own talent, adding that she was hardly paid enough to make the sacrifice worthwhile.[9] If God had given her the talent for writing verses from which readers found comfort and inspiration, perhaps that was her life's purpose rather than teaching. Perhaps she was wrong to resign herself to a kind of life that limited her so. After the visit her journal shows an important change: she no longer questioned whether she should leave Wheaton, but wondered how she could manage if she did. Of course she did nothing immediately, but tentative planning occupied her spare hours.

Shortly after Becky's visit, Larcom left to spend a few days at home before Isaac Baker's departure for Sumatra. She always hated to see him go, but this time she felt sadder than usual, perhaps at the thought of the summer without land and water excursions and the company of this genial brother who was so much the center of the family. The same long journal entry that mourns his departure records a week of visiting, including a short stay in Amesbury, and finishes with her account of a day in Boston visiting galleries:

A picture first: Church's "Icebergs," a most wonderful portrayal, too. It is ice glorified with polar sunshine. It leaves me with memory of something as beautiful and transparent in color as one might imagine a spirit's robes to be; indeed, I could scarcely think of the ice mountains moving away, as I looked at them, into a gathering haze of soft sky-tints that seemed less impalpable than their own hues, as otherwise than living conscious realities. The nearer masses were cloven as if by the sun's rays, so bright, so clearly cut were the crystal seams that opened down into pure apple-green waters, pouring here and there through some fantastic arch or grotto which the ice had shaped for itself in breaking.[10]

From Boston she went to Waterbury, Connecticut. She had corresponded with Esther Humiston's half brother, Franklin Carter, and was impressed by his "fresh, young, generous heart."[11] He and his mother urged her to come to the house where Esther's room was kept as a shrine and where the atmosphere was so quiet and peaceful that Larcom felt herself on holy ground. By mid-June she had decided to take a long leave from Wheaton, to have a good vacation during the summer and fall, and then to go back to Waterbury for an indefinite stay during the winter. She was sure she could work well in that quiet home, and perhaps there she could make up her mind about her future.

In the end the decision about her future happened rather than was consciously made, and it was impelled by family concerns, what she later called "a harvest-time for Death."[12] Her nephew, Charles Harrington, a student at Brown where his "dissolute" behavior was distressing his mother and aunt, was suddenly converted. He joined the church and then the army. He was in one battle, wrote home of his dislike of the strange steaminess and the vast straggling forests of the South, came down with a fever, and died. Larcom wrote a touching entry in her journal about the nobility of his sacrifice and the joy of his conversion, but she, like the rest of the family, was terrified at what his death did to Louisa. The last of the sons she had borne to young Captain Harrington was gone; there seemed nothing much to live for. Charlie's death was followed almost immediately by that of sister Adeline's husband.[13]

The loss of Charlie made young Franklin Carter even more dear; during her visit to Waterbury Larcom had written in her journal, "I thank thee in my childless and homeless state, for this adopted and inherited one, at once brother, son, and friend."[14] He, Eliza Holmes, and Esther Humiston's mother were urging her to come to Waterbury and, indeed, to make her home there. She could have Esther's room, and in that sanctuary she could find all the peace and stillness she needed. Carter's admiration pleased her, and sometimes his intelligence and enthusiasm reminded her of another Frank, although this young man had a much clearer sense of an orderly future. Perhaps in her more sentimental moments she saw him as the son that she and Frank Spaulding might have had. She reacted to news of his engagement with the "half-jealous feelings of a mother," as she confided to her journal, but was soon able to share his joy.[15] Carter and his wife remained her friends for life.

She stayed with Louisa most of the summer; not until late August did she feel free to travel, beginning in Newburyport to visit her sister Abby Haskell and then her friend Sarah Jane Spalding. With the latter she attended services at Andover Theological Seminary and went to lunch at Harriet Beecher Stowe's home. She knew how highly Mrs. Stowe regarded her work, that, indeed, Stowe considered her an American Mrs. Browning, but even that praise and her status as a recognized poet could not quite erase her shyness in the presence of someone she admired to the point of reverence.[16]

Her visit to Amesbury was a little disappointing; there were other guests, and she did not like sharing Elizabeth and Greenleaf. She could not escape the war: at Haverhill John Hanson was getting ready to leave as chaplain to the Massachusetts Fourth Regiment. In a letter to Whittier she compared the autumn beauty of nature to the darkness of the war news, "like a green island in a sea of blood." The letter ends, "It is almost as beautiful as it can be, everywhere I go. Perhaps the dark contrast of all other thoughts makes it seem so; and yet it may not be that, altogether: I have had level Septembers for so many years, that the beginning of Autumn in a hilly country is almost like a new creation to me."[17]

Like so many patriots, she was suffering growing disillusion and disgust at the realization that the sacred cause was not so sacred to everyone. When the war began, Lowell lawyer Benjamin Butler, who had been a Democrat, supporting the Fugitive Slave Law and Jefferson Davis for president, suddenly turned his coat and, through political influence, became a Union general. Rumor held that he was using his position to add to his and his brother's fortunes. He ignored the instructions of Governor Andrew, and later, as the occupying general in New Orleans, won for himself the title of "Beast" Butler; in fact, his behavior was so bad that he was a factor in swaying English public opinion toward the South. Lincoln removed him from that post, but already Butler, a shrewd politician to whom many people owed favors, was too powerful to be pushed aside. His behavior sickened and shamed loyal citizens, many of whom never forgot it.[18]

Among the mountains Larcom could ignore Butler and others like him, and her own problems as well. In November she returned to Beverly briefly, then went to begin her winter's visit to Waterbury, that haven of peace where she could be in touch with Esther's spirit and have all the quiet she needed.

One of the things that Larcom still had to learn about herself was that she never wanted quite as much quiet as she thought she did. Years before, when her illness in the mills sent her back home to Beverly for rest, she had finally chosen to return to Lowell. She wanted both quiet and activity—stillness and stir—but, more important, she wanted control of both. Either one, forced upon her, became intolerable. In November, shortly after her arrival in Waterbury, she wrote to Elizabeth Whittier that she thought herself on "sacred ground . . . to come so close to the mortal life of one whom I knew only as a spirit, sleeping in her bed, sitting in her little, low-windowed room."[19] Ten days later, however, she was writing to the Robinsons, asking them to send the Boston papers. "I feel myself at a woeful distance from the 'hub of the universe'; losing Boston I seem to have lost the center of gravity, and jollity too. They all *think New York* here," she wrote, and put a three-month limit on her supposedly indefinite stay.[20] As for complete quiet and writing, she was reading German with a friend and directing a reading group of local ladies. She and William Robinson exchanged literary gossip: "The book-world did not blossom very freely at the holidays, it seems. I hear that Hawthorne considers Gail Hamilton's book *the* best of the season; Longfellow also admires it. She certainly is a very eloquent scold; it seems to me that her originality consists in taking the contrarious side, in everything."[21]

Being away from Wheaton gave her enough distance to see her life more clearly. She admitted to Annie Fields that she was "most childishly homesick," and went on to say that as far as writing was concerned, she would be more productive if she were a washerwoman, for at Wheaton she wrote from "irrepressible desire, which yet conscience insisted must be repressed" if she were to be faithful to her duties.[22] Actually, as she eventually learned, she might need quiet for the act of writing, but she needed the stimulus of people and events to generate the ideas that made her poems. Much of her best work was done against what she saw as barriers to her writing, and her themes grew from her observation of the world around her. Frustrations came when she was trapped in either the world of activity or the world of silence.

Her visit ended abruptly in February when a returning ship brought news that Isaac Baker had died of fever in Sumatra five months earlier. Larcom rushed home to be with Lydia. "You will imagine my sister's loss—may guess at her sorrow as I cannot," she wrote Hattie, "though I see how it has taken away the very foundation-stone of her happiness for this world."[23] But this time her grief was as much for herself as for her sister. It was years before she could deal with Baker's death and the emptiness his loss made in her world. Lydia was heartbroken but, true to her tradition, controlled; there was both comfort and sadness in her new baby, who would never see his father. All the family mourned, and Louisa, still grieving for her son, felt the blow in a special way. Isaac had helped her with legal and financial matters all through her widowhood and had been a surrogate father for her sons as well as the center of the Larcom family. In fact, Louisa's fragile health declined so sharply that, fearing consumption, the family sent her off to Emeline in April, hoping the change of scene, the fresh Wisconsin air, and Emeline's presence would help her regain her strength.

Larcom forced herself back to Wheaton for the spring term, but her grief was constant and almost at once the trouble with her head began. She could hardly wait for summer and the mountains. She made an attempt to go south to teach the freedmen, despite the disapproval of her family and friends, but her application was turned down. She kept busy, going to Boston nearly every weekend, visiting galleries, calling on her ever-growing number of friends, and enjoying the novelty of her own celebrity as Miss Larcom, the poet whose lovely verses inspired others to seek the best in life. She saw much of Annie Fields, whose kindness and charm had helped her overcome some of her diffidence and fear of crowds by drawing her into smaller entertainments at the Charles Street house; now she was a source of comfort and encouragement. Larcom's memorial for Isaac Baker, published in the August 1863 *Atlantic*, was a sad little poem called "Hilary," far from her best work.

At the end of the spring term she left Wheaton quietly; it is not clear how definite she was about returning there. Lydia needed her, and she does not seem to have made any decisions beyond that point. Isaac Baker's little boat lay unused; the family avoided the kinds of expeditions and amusements that he had made so delightful. Larcom spent time in Campton with James and Annie Fields again, then joined Elizabeth and Greenleaf on the Isles of Shoals. They stayed at the Laighton's Appledore House, enjoying its hundred-foot-long drawing room with black walnut walls and large windows that overlooked the sea.[24] Other acquaintances joined them, for it was a popular resort and Whittier always encouraged his close friends to vacation when and where he did.

There were several happy days before the urgent message came: Louisa was gravely ill in Wisconsin. She longed for Beverly and her family, but was not well enough to travel alone. Larcom left for the West at once, but she was too late. Louisa died before she could get there, and, ironically, the train carrying her body home passed her sister's westbound train on the way.

Larcom poured out her sorrow in a letter to Annie Fields:

> This cup of grief has been very bitter to me;—as bitter as it could be made, it has seemed to me. I had not the comfort of gratifying her last wishes in any one thing. I expected she would be well enough to accompany me home; her great longing was, to see Beverly once more, and to see me. But I could not even look upon her face in death, or see her form committed to the earth.
>
> —And with her, my pleasant dream of home dissolves—it was she who said she would make a home for me wherever I would choose. It is lonelier than ever—the earthly outlook, but I must not yield to selfish regrets. She has gone home, in a sense more real than we often say it of the dead. Her whole family had gone before her,—husband and four children had left her one after another. Her heart seemed broken when her youngest son died in the army, last year; she never recovered her strength after that blow. I cannot mourn, when I think of that glad reunion of a household in heaven but I cannot help the great blank that her death and my brother's have made in my life. I miss them both so much! These family ties I find grow stronger as I grow older; to lose anyone to whom we belong, and who belongs to us, in any sense, makes earth so different a place.
>
> Will you care to look at the enclosed, as you have glanced at other verses of mine? They can be returned to Beverly if not the thing for the Maga.—I wrote from a sudden feeling of how I wished some women would feel.[25]

Larcom's stay with Emeline was bittersweet. Louisa's death, like Isaac's, was a personal loss that not all her firm belief that she would see them both again could ease. She had not even been able to say

goodbye to these two people she loved so dearly. And being with
Emeline awakened so many memories. The romance of beautiful
Louisa and her ambitious sea captain had brightened Larcom's childhood; now they were gone. Gone as well were her own young and
hopeful days when the future seemed to stretch out forever, offering
so much—and so different a dream. Seventeen years before, the little
band had left Massachusetts to conquer the West, and a young and
eager Lucy Larcom had been in love with a dream and a man. The
correspondence revived in 1859 had not lasted; politics, not personal
feelings, ended it. Frank's prosouthern sympathies filled her with
contempt. Too many of the men she knew were fighting for the
cause, enduring the horrors of war, pain, and death, while Frank sat
safe and uninvolved in California.

As always, her emotion was expressed in verse. Out of memories,
pain, loss, and dedication came a kind of statement—the poem she
sent in her letter to Annie Fields, "A Loyal Woman's No." It is in the
form of a refusal to marry:

> No! is my answer from this cold, bleak ridge,
>   Down to your valley: you may rest you there.
> The gulf is wide, and none can build a bridge
>   That your gross weight would safely hither bear.

Assuming that all human beings must grow, and using the ascent of
a mountain as the symbol for that growth, she looked at the common belief that in marriage the stronger and better-educated man
should lead the woman, and found that her suitor was unable to
climb. Because she was "weak, as others are."

> I might,—I will not hide it,—once I might
>   Have lost, in the warm whirlpools of your voice,
> The sense of Evil, the stern cry of Right;
>   But truth has steered me free, and I rejoice.

But her suitor saw only her "flowery levels," not the "heaven-smit
summits"; he was "not man enough / To grasp [his] country's measure of a man." She accused,

> You lure me to the valley: men should call
>   Up to the mountains, where the air is clear.
> Win me and help me climbing, if at all!
>   Beyond these peaks great harmonies I hear:—

The harmonies came from heroes, male and female, who climbed the mountains, no matter how much effort, pain, or sacrifice the climb cost them. Therefore,

It charms me not, your call to rest below.
I press their hands, my lips pronounce their vows:
Take my life's silence for your answer: No!

The poem appeared in the December 1863 *Atlantic* and was immediately appreciated for its strong statement of true womanly nobility and patriotic feeling. Women had the task of upholding standards, and this bold refusal to be degraded by marriage was a fine sentiment.

Larcom claimed that the poem was not autobiographical, but no one close to her believed it. Of course it was a shaping of her own experience rather than a record; it certainly owes something to Whittier's "The Yankee Girl," which the mill girls had liked so much. It is, in a sense, a ruthless poem; one can only wonder if the *Atlantic* found its way to Colusa and what Frank thought if he read it. Clearly those who were "not man enough" included those who ignored the cataclysmic struggle going on, those who, for example, sat safe and uninvolved in California. The language is sharp and scornful: "gross weight," "grovelled," "fettered and forsworn," "weak," "falters . . . creeps," "ignoble souls" are all terms directed at the cowardly and complacent suitor. Given Larcom's feelings about mountains as symbols of the way to God, the mountain-valley imagery is even more savage. There is energy and anger in this poem seldom found in her more contemplative work.

There would be no more guilt or remorse about Frank; she had been right to refuse him. She would never forget the young dream they shared and all that it meant to both of them, and she was grateful that she had had the experience, but all possibility of marriage with him ended for reasons that were perfectly justifiable. Instead of a possible husband, he was transmuted into part of a romantic and sustaining image: two people, divided by distance, time, and belief, yet remaining true to each other and their youthful love. But she wrote the real man out of her future.

The last year had been shattering, and Larcom came out of it changed. She was thirty-nine. In spite of early physical maturity, in many ways she had remained young, with a heart full of hopes and despairs and doubts and plans, and with the confidence of youth that something nice would happen soon. She had come perilously close to a nervous breakdown, and she had learned a great deal about herself: particularly that her success as a teacher brought her no happiness at all, while her writing did. She had hung on at Wheaton for too long, just as she had, for different reasons, hung on to Frank too long. Security was not worth the price she had paid for it. Furthermore, if her belief in a loving, personal God who cared about even the fall of a sparrow was as strong as it should be, then her fears were unnecessary, even sinful. In that sense separating herself from Wheaton became an act of faith; if she was following God's will, opportunities for living usefully would come.

Immediate, of course, was the fact that she was needed in Beverly. Lydia's sweetness of character had not been embittered or diminished by her loss, but she was very lonely. She showed her happiness at having her sister with her by choosing plants from her own lovely garden to make Lucy's room a green bower. Larcom found that her own grief was easier to bear when she shared it with her family. Practically, too, the bustle of moving her belongings, especially the large number of books she had accumulated, and the furnishing of a bedroom and sitting room for her in Lydia's big house were distractions good for everyone.

Although part of her plan was to give herself more time to write, Larcom at once arranged to earn some money by part-time teaching at Ipswich Academy and private classes in literature, botany, and painting. Except for her own self-respect and independence, there was no great need for her to work, for the whole family was prosperous. Isaac Baker's estate—consisting of the house, several parcels of land, and a sizable investment in bank stocks—would keep Lydia and the children in comfort. Louisa's inheritance from her husband had been carefully invested (at the advice of Isaac and brother Benjamin); she left over eight thousand dollars to be divided among her surviving relatives. Adeline, the wealthiest of all the sisters, sold the new house on Thorndike Street and moved into another one she owned, closer to Lydia and to Dane Street Church. Benjamin was just over the hill on Essex Street, where he ran a prosperous florist business.

Larcom took advantage of her unusual leisure. She read everything she could find, and for a while was artist rather than author. She was especially fond of painting the small, inconspicuous plants that grew close to the ground; her studies of flowers, lichens, and mosses were often Christmas and birthday gifts to close friends. She did not forget the war or her personal grief, but she kept busy. During the winter she was a visiting teacher of composition at Wheaton; she went there every two weeks to read and discuss the students' essays. Her visits were social events as well as work, and her friends there were delighted to entertain her. Edwin Barrowes remained her correspondent and her escort at Norton. She continued to meet Hattie both in Boston and in Malden. Once she started teaching in Ipswich, it was an easy matter to go by train from there to Newburyport, sometimes to see Abigail, but more often to spend time with Sarah Jane Spalding. Mr. Spalding, like so many New England ministers, had spent his year as chaplain of a Massachusetts regiment, but he was home now, and the family was once again established in the comfortable parsonage on Green Street.

Mrs. Spalding was exactly the kind of friend that Lucy needed. She was deeply religious, but in a sensible, non-neurotic way; she would never take to her bed and wait to die. She and Larcom discussed books, issues, ideas, and occasionally people comfortably together. They had friends in common, notably Whittier, and Mrs. Spalding knew the Stowes and the irrepressible Gail Hamilton well. She admired and encouraged Lucy's verse writing, and insisted on its importance as the expression of a God-given talent. The most significant friendship of Larcom's maturity grew steadily.

Probably sometime in 1863 she had taken a bold step in the direction of a career by sending some of her work to the *Independent.* Although this New York weekly was nominally a religious paper, it was widely read for its news and features; at times it was far more political than religious.[26] It took a stand against slavery and the Fugitive Slave Laws and attacked the morality of religious leaders who did not support abolition. Its circulation went from ten thousand in 1852 to thirty-five thousand in 1860, then at least doubled by 1870. It published Stowe's *Pearl of Orr's Island* as a serial in 1861–62. Henry Ward Beecher wrote for it regularly, and for a while was its editor, working with and then being succeeded by Theodore Tilton; the Beecher-Tilton scandal in the 1870s nearly destroyed the paper, but it survived until 1928.[27]

For a while it was literally a big paper, using nine-column blanket sheets: "These big sheets were furnished uncut, and many readers who thought them too sacred to mutilate found . . . it was necessary to lay the sheet down in the middle of a good-sized room to fold the pages back. Subscribers complained that Congregationalists were becoming differentiated from people of other faiths by their long arms."[28] Regardless of its politics or religion, the *Independent* was a widely read paper with a reputation for the high quality of the literary work it published. Because of its standards and the fact that it paid well, its contributors were the most popular and important writers of the day.

Curiously, for her first attempts Larcom reverted to anonymity; two early works that internal evidence indicates are hers were unsigned. One was a story about Margaret, a sculptor, who learned her art through love; an editorial note said the paper hoped for more work from this "new pen" (25 June 1863). "Songs for Our Baby" (14 January 1864) is hers, and "The Weeping Prophet" (23 November 1864), a poem inspired by a bas-relief done by Margaret Foley, was signed "L. L."; later she claimed it. From then on, she used her full name.

She was forty years old in March of 1864. Ann Danforth Spaulding came east to visit her family, and although the old Vine Lodge intimacy could not quite be recaptured, Larcom was happy in her friend's company. The *Atlantic* published another of her patriotic poems, "Re-Enlisted" (May 1864), which was described (correctly) by one critic as "maudlin."[29] Again she tried to go south to teach in the schools for freedmen; she had an interview, but her application was refused. Whether she really wanted to go south or whether the possibility was simply an attempt to escape and be useful is not clear.[30]

During this time she visited the Whittiers as often as possible. In the summer of 1864 Elizabeth had a bad fall while staying at the Isles of Shoals and died in September. Her death was another great personal loss. In a little over two years Larcom had lost so many who were dear to her; she wrote Susan Hayes Ward, "I don't wear pink bows and drab dresses any more. . . . black is the hue that I have adopted . . . I have not been permitted to lay it aside for two years or more; it has been a harvest-time for Death in our own family these seasons. And my innermost friends have also gone home, one after another, until I do feel sadly alone."[31]

Elizabeth's death changed the mentorial relationship between

Whittier and Larcom to a friendship of near equals. The two women had been such close friends that the poet felt Larcom shared his grief more than anyone else could. Through the autumn they read Tennyson's "In Memoriam" together before the fire as the long evenings closed in, and Larcom commissioned a friend to do a portrait of Elizabeth from photographs.[32] It cost more than she could sensibly afford to spend, but the comfort it brought Whittier justified the sacrifice.

Living on a day-to-day basis, Larcom seems to have made no long-range plans. Shortly after she had gone to Wheaton, she wrote Miss Fobes a comparison of her life to "epochs, similar to geological ages," when changes moved her to "a new life in a new world."[33] Lowell, the West, and Wheaton had been worlds that she had grown into and beyond; then, like Holmes's chambered nautilus, she had gone on to something else. Now she once again waited for the next opportunity.

CHAPTER 9

Our Young Folks

The sudden death of William Ticknor in the spring of 1864 ended the illustrious partnership of Ticknor and Fields and gave Fields control of the firm. To some extent Ticknor had been the conservative businessman and Fields the literary adventurer who established strong personal relationships with his authors.[1] Fields's attitude was paternal; the venerable Brahmins felt that he was taking care of them and trusted his devotion to their interests. The entertainments at his home—Annie's salons and the famous breakfasts—were essentially an adjunct of the business; indeed, the firm had paid for the Charles Street house and it, like the Old Corner Book Store, was what a later age would call superb public relations. Visitors to the Old Corner never forgot the comfortable atmosphere or the hearty sound of Fields's laughter coming from behind the green curtain that separated his office from the rest of the store.

With Fields as the senior partner and young Howard M. Ticknor and the pleasant chief clerk, James R. Osgood, as junior partners, the reorganized firm was called Fields, Osgood. Fields sold the shop on Washington Street; it was long outgrown and he had wanted to make a change for quite a while, but Ticknor had not agreed. The new firm moved into a remodeled building at 125 Tremont Street, where the ground floor became showroom and offices, with Fields's own office and an "authors' room" on the second floor. There were other ways to expand: he bought the *North American Review*, started a new magazine called *Saturday Evening*, with Thomas Bailey Aldrich as editor, and, since he was very busy, soon hired a promising young westerner, William Dean Howells, to be assistant editor of the *Atlantic*. Seeing a market that was not being properly exploited, he decided to start a magazine for children.

Fields had no doubt about the success of any of his projects, and certainly not of *Our Young Folks*. He could call on all the best-known writers in the country as contributors; their names were bound to attract readers. Although the magazine was for children, he knew that it would be read by adults as well, as indeed it was. For his editorial staff he created an organization that would work as long as he controlled it. Howard Ticknor was the office manager; the three editors were Gail Hamilton, Lucy Larcom, and John T. Trowbridge. Their duties were not very clearly defined. Each was to contribute to the magazine, to be in charge of some department (Larcom had the puzzle pages), to give advice, and to read and recommend manuscripts, although only Fields had the authority to accept them. Larcom was involved in the planning, and during the autumn she and Annie spent time and thought on a name for what they called the "Little *Atlantic*."[2]

Whatever Fields's reason for choosing the three editors, it was certainly not based on their friendship or their ability to work together. Larcom wrote Hattie, "Do you suppose Gail and I shall become acquainted? I have not met her yet since the once at Newburyport some years ago. I have no anxiety to be entered upon her list of friends—shouldn't like to have a 'complaint' made of me in public. But I think her *New Atmosphere* is a good sort of book,—it's to the point, surely; and it will do for us maiden sisters to be pitying the married women, and trying to oil their rusty hackles, especially as we have never felt them grinding."[3] A year and a half later she answered a request for the autographs of all three editors: "I have never met with Mr. Trowbridge, and do not see Gail Hamilton except accidentally, once or twice a year."[4]

Mary Abigail Dodge was a talented young woman whose articles under the name Gail Hamilton appeared in various papers. She was a friend of Whittier and of Mrs. Spalding; Larcom had met her through the latter and had given up trying to like her almost at once. It is easy to see why: Hamilton's self-confidence, her insistence on the center of the stage, and, above all, the breezy, affectionate irreverence of her manner toward Whittier prevented any kind of closeness between the two women.

Hamilton took the last part of her pen name from the town of her birth, Hamilton, Massachusetts. She came from a prosperous family and had been very well educated. She taught English in a high school in Hartford before going to Washington, where, on the recommendation of Sara Lippincott (author and editor Grace Greenwood), she spent two years as governess to the children of Gamaliel Baily, publisher of the *National Era*. In 1860 she came back to Hamilton to care for her ailing mother and began to write for various papers. Fields published her *Country Living and Country Thinking* in 1862; *A New Atmosphere* (1864) was an analysis of the social values that, in her eyes, made married women little better than slaves. Fields, who liked her—most men did—described her as "eccentric, a queer bird with plenty of cleverness in her beak and wings," and a later critic called her "a sort of Margaret Fuller watered down, and also peppered up."[5]

Her attitude toward her new position showed in a letter she wrote to a friend: "My connection with the 'New Magazine' will be as close as I choose to make it. I shall have none of the labor to do, the scissorings, selecting, etc. I should never undertake anything of that sort, it would be very irksome to me, but advice, you know, and opinion, I am always ready to give without much urging."[6]

The third editor, John Townsend Trowbridge, was a New Yorker who had moved to New England and had already made a name for himself as a writer of adventure stories for boys; in his lifetime he wrote about forty books. Although he was named editor, almost at once he left on a tour of southern battlefields to write articles and eventually a book about the war.

Our Young Folks was advertised in the autumn; its first issue appeared in Janaury 1865 and was as successful as its publisher had known it would be. Contributors for the first year, besides the three editors, included Harriet Beecher Stowe, who wrote essays about family pets and the importance of treating animals well, Thomas Bailey Aldrich, Thomas Wentworth Higginson, Whittier, Lydia Maria Child, Louisa May Alcott, Rose Terry, Elizabeth Stuart Phelps, Oliver Optic, and Mayne Reid. The well-known physical culture expert Dio Lewis wrote about the need for outdoor exercise for all children, even girls; Longfellow's "Christmas Bells" appeared, along with four of Larcom's poems. Each issue contained several pages of riddles, puzzles, and games, many of them contributed by the Robinson family.

As Fields had anticipated, the readership of the magazine included adults as well as children, and his authors were happy to write for it. Everyone knew how important it was to train the young mind, so a contribution was a piece of work that benefited society as a whole. Besides, Fields paid well. In many cases he offered a bonus or an extra-generous payment to a writer who would agree to publish only with him, hardly a difficult decision since he controlled so many prestigious publications. He was able to attract both new and established writers that way.

For Lucy Larcom the new position was a step that carried her fully into the literary world, giving her a definite and recognized place, a modest but secure niche in the world of letters. The job brought another kind of security as well. Her regular salary of fifty dollars a month was enough to live on; extras, like books and travel, were easily earned from her poems or an occasional private class in literature. With financial security came freedom of movement, for her duties were flexible enough to allow her to control her activities. She could read manuscripts as easily on the beaches of Beverly or in the mountains of New Hampshire as in the Boston office of Fields, Osgood, but when she went to the city she had a place there. It did not take long to establish the balance of stillness and stir that she had always wanted.

The indications that the war was coming to an end added to her pleasure. She wrote her Vine Lodge friends,

> We have been shaken, literally, all this noontime by guns from the fort at Salem, in honor of the Richmond victories. Cannot we hold up our heads now? O, I am glad to be a *free* American. I wish you were here to go with me to the May meetings again, in Boston. You may have heard that Garrison intends discontinuing the Liberator, as it is no longer needed, and that he counsels the breaking-up of the Anti-Slavery Society for the same reason. The "reformers" are having a grand quarrel over it, already.
>
> I hope I shall get out to see you before many years. I don't know how far this editorial work will confine me at home. But "Ticknor and Fields" are a gracious firm, and they will make things as pleasant for me as possible. It is a privilege to work for large-hearted people.[7]

Every week or two she spent several days in Boston, combining all the things she enjoyed doing with time at the office, picking up and returning manuscripts and books for review, and visiting her widening circle of acquaintances.

Although she would have liked to put "Hannah Binding Shoes" behind her forever, she was flattered when she was asked to write a companion poem for the *Atlantic*. She dutifully produced one called "Skipper Ben," a sentimental and overstrained description of Hannah's husband's feelings as he is about to be shipwrecked (July 1865). Again the response was favorable; in her mail came a letter from that influential arbiter of taste and literature, Thomas Wentworth Higginson:

> I want to thank you for your poem of "Skipper Ben" which touched me very much, and adds to our store of pure New England poetry. Whittier never wrote anything truer to the soil, and you have access (as shown in this poem and in "Hilary") to certain fine musical modulations which lie beyond him. This poem may not take root so absolutely in the popular heart as did "Hannah," but it cannot fall much short of that, I should think; while it reaches a higher domain of art.
>
> Rivers of tears might be shed over either, and that suggests, after all the only remaining criticism;—whether the most distressing tragedy is not always, spiritually speaking, a mistake, and whether to have let in a smile of higher peace upon the surviving life would not have been nobler, after all. This touches high questions of art and faith, and is perhaps going farther than I have a right.[8]

Whittier's opinion of the poem was equally favorable; after reading it in company with James and Annie Fields, he wrote, "It is the best poem that has been printed there [the *Atlantic*] for the last two years. It is all right—without a flaw."[9]

The war, which still inspired Larcom and other poets to write fairly bad verse, came to an official end with Lee's surrender in April, but celebrations were cut short by the terrible news of Lincoln's assassination. Larcom could not bear the thought of the crowds at the memorial service in Boston; she heard all about it and about Garrison's eulogy from the Robinsons.

The summer brought a long visit from Emeline and her children, but Larcom kept busily at her work. Many of her poems now were for or about children, written for her own magazine, and she was thinking about a new kind of effort, a collection of excerpts from various sources designed to help the reader with his or her spiritual growth. There were other such books, usually put together by ministers, but in general she disliked them. She chose writings that had helped her, so the collection would be a very personal statement. In fact, the basis of the collection was the scrapbook she had made at Wheaton for morning prayers. She discussed the idea with Fields, who was interested in the book.

In the fall she visited New York for the first time, staying with Wheaton connections, then returned home to resume her usual pattern. After one of her visits to Malden, Hattie wrote in her journal, "She is splendid, so modest and humble and good, pious without bigotry, good without pretense.—She ought to have made some good man happy long ago."[10]

Harriet's point of view was that of an extremely happy wife; her love for her husband and his for her, their shared concern for their home and children, shine through her journal. William Robinson clearly respected his wife's intelligence and identity and made her a part of his outside life. Out of her own happiness she wanted others to be happy, and especially this old friend whom she so admired. The issue of marriage became a source of friendly argument (perhaps at times not so friendly) between them during the next few years.

The winter was a very busy one for Larcom, complicated by the fact that she was severely troubled by rheumatism, so that she decided to spend no more winters within reach of the Beverly east winds. Her rheumatism may have provided a tactful excuse, since the difference between the east wind in Boston and in Beverly was minimal; she was more and more attracted to the city, but after all the arrangements that had been made in Lydia's house, was reluctant to admit that she preferred to be in Boston for the busy winter season. In February she succumbed to the lure of fashion, bought a pair of the new heeled shoes, and was temporarily unable to walk as a result.[11] She rejected an offer to start a school of her own in the rapidly growing upper Mississippi River area. She did some teaching of composition and painting, but most of her effort and energy was divided between the work of the magazine and the preparation of her little devotional book. Summer, as usual, meant the mountains; carrying her work with her, Larcom visited the Fieldses' home in Campton, New Hampshire, and then made a tour of other mountain resorts.

In Beverly the beautiful September weather once again called for family expeditions. She wrote Whittier about one of them, a drive through Gloucester, Pigeon Cove, and Annisquam, adding, "Some day early next week we are going again in a boat, out among the islands in our harbor. I dread it a little, for I have not sailed in *our* waters since 'Hilary' went away. But I have been laying ghosts all summer, and I find that in doing so, they change to angel-presences."[12]

Doing the kinds of things they had done with Isaac and Louisa was hard, but finally rewarding, and out of it, as always, came a poem (a much better one than the mournful "Hilary") that illustrates her ability to create a picture as well as, finally, to place the two deaths in perspective. Its combination of natural beauty, personal feeling, and public statement is typical of the work of her mature years:

BITTERSWEET SHADOWS

Off we drifted, yesterday,
Till the sea-foam dashed the spray
  Of the woodland bittersweet,
Leaning from a sunlit cove
Where amid salt winds it throve,
  Swaying to the tide's low beat.

Oh, the afternoon was fair!
Murmurous echoes swept the air,—
  Sighs of pines and dip of oar:
Every breeze that passed us, went
Laden with some rare wood-scent,
  Loitering down the dreamy shore.

And we lingered, loitering too,
Where the heavy cedars threw
  Shadows on the water's gold;
Till again in glee afloat,
Like a bird our idle boat
  Skimmed the wavelets manifold.

Then, the crystal channel won,
In its deep the shallop shone,
  Sails of silver, prow of pearl:
Hidden ledges brake that dream,
Sucking down the flash and gleam
  Underneath their high-tide swirl.

Free again, broad sunshine found,
Slid the boat on, greenly wound
  With its veil of bittersweet,
Tangling round the sunk rock's edge,
Catching streamers of sea-sedge
  From the sheen beneath our feet.

Anchored in the dusk, a spell
From the folds of twilight fell
  On the bay's black, star-strewn floor:
Awe with that weird glitter crept
Shuddering through our thoughts; we stept
  Gladly on firm land once more,

Trailing home the bittersweet:
Such dim ending was but meet
  For an afternoon so rare.
Was the date of yesterday?
Years since then have slipt away;
  Few such memories they bear.

No todays like that remain:
Joy is flavored now with pain;
  For the best of all our crew,—
Helmsman, gentlest passenger,—
Lie so still they will not stir,
  Though the sea should drench them through.

So our shallop floats no more
Where the low, vine-tangled shore
  Dips its orange-golden fruit
To the splashing of the wave:
Only white flowers for a grave,
  Now our serious hands will suit.

Still the sun shines, and we drift
Homeward on the current swift,
  Those who went before to meet.
All things beautiful grow sad:
Yet even grief is sometimes glad;—
  Shade us, Life, with bittersweet!

(*Poems*, 1868)

Time and Emeline's bracing companionship helped her. She would always miss Isaac, Louisa, and Elizabeth, but the naturally cheerful side of her nature was again dominant. Her letters for this period are full of news, literary gossip, comments on national affairs, and humorous accounts of her own not very expert attempts at housekeeping.

The literary event of the winter was Whittier's *Snow-Bound*. His sister's death had set him thinking and remembering, and the result was his evocation of the New England past that he shared with so many of his readers, no matter where they lived. Its success, both critical and financial, was enormous, and it erased forever the abolitionist label that often frightened away editors and readers. Larcom's *Breathings of a Better Life* came out in the fall, in time to have excellent Christmas sales; in fact, it was reissued many times over the years.[13]

For the winter, following her plan, Larcom moved to Boston, "boarding herself" at Mrs. Burnham's house on Pine Street. Her friends, distrusting her domestic competence, called frequently, bringing gifts of food. "And the cakes came like a Godsend," she wrote Hattie, "for I was intending to go out in the morning and buy something for breakfast. But I waked late, and my fire was dead gone out, and I was halt with the rheumatism, so that I was very thankful to eat your mother's 'bullets' washed down with chocolate. . . . I enjoy 'roosting' up here very much. It is really pleasant, because I have the sunshine."[14]

In spite of the painful bouts of rheumatism that persisted well into the spring, Larcom enjoyed the winter in Boston. Being there meant that she could take even more advantage of all the city had to offer, and she particularly liked such things as buying mayflowers for sale on the street as the last of a major snowstorm melted away. Probably through the influence of Annie Fields she worked with the North End Mission, a nondenominational group that tried to make life easier for the rapidly growing mass of foreigners in that part of the city.[15] She became interested in clubs for working girls and gave as much time as she could spare to those two charities.

She had not heard directly from Frank Spaulding for years, although news of him came from Emeline. He had made himself completely a part of his California life and had been elected tax assessor and then recorder for Colusa County. The end of the Civil War only strengthened the strong pro-South sympathies of the area; it became a refuge for southerners who could no longer tolerate conditions in their old homes. A local history records, "On election day [1864] an incident occurred which showed the intensity of the conflict. Dr. Spaulding, who had not been out of bed for two weeks, caused himself to be hauled to the polls, and when he reached there a hundred or more of his fellow Democrats gave him an ovation in cheering him till the court-house rang with their applause."[16] The end of the war and the news of Lincoln's death caused riots. When troops came to keep order and arrested the ringleaders, the soldiers were later charged with kidnapping. Frank Spaulding was elected county judge in 1867 and held the position until ill health forced him to resign.

Sometime in 1867 he wrote directly to Larcom. According to her account to Harriet Robinson two years after the fact, he told her that he still loved her and tried once again to persuade her to marry him.[17] If she did not, he was going to marry someone else. At the time Larcom wrote to Ma and Becky,

> I have come to be the busiest old maid you ever knew. It is something to have all your romantic dreams turned out of the house, and the door barred against them. One takes a grim comfort in making up one's mind to a sheltered loneliness for life. I am thinking of going to housekeeping soon—a sort of summer house in Beverly, with a niece for "maid of all work." It is better than being in Boston always.
>
> And our "Dr. Frank" is really married! His wife is a niece of an ex-governor of South Carolina, I hear. I am sorry he has a kindred spirit in his Southern proclivities, but I hope he will be happy.
>
> He sent me a "farewell," and I received it, with sorrow that he will not let me be a friend,—but without any regret. We should never have thought of each other as anything *but* friends; then he might have kept so. On my part, it was all an illusion.[18]

Since she had long ago put aside any possibility of marrying Frank, her reaction to "having all your romantic dreams turned out of the house" seems curious. After seventeen years Frank was more dream than reality, so much time had passed since the days when she had thought seriously of marrying him. But she had nurtured another kind of dream: youthful romance raised to idyllic friendship that stretched across time and distance. It was a sustaining dream that could be taken out of memory and used when needed, and it had become part of her image of herself. If she could think of Frank as still "first" in her affections, someone always part of her life, she assumed that he would think of her the same way. One of her poems, "A Whisper of Memory," clearly written to Frank, voiced her desire to remain a constant presence in his life, a beautiful memory, like "the fresh dawn," "a streamlet," "the Indian summer's laden air. . . . A breeze-like sweetness of remembered hours!" The memory of their love, somehow more beautiful because never fulfilled, was a source of comfort and strength to her, and she wanted it to work the same way for Frank. The announcement of his marriage changed the image and hurt her pride.

Frank's marriage and her friendly arguments with Hattie Robinson led to some thinking and writing about women and marriage, but at the time she wrote her Vine Lodge friends she was enjoying herself too much to be very troubled. It had been a custom for Whittier's circle of friends to meet somewhere, usually at the Isles of Shoals, for a few days each summer. This year, however, as a result of Larcom's discovery, a group of them went to Bearcamp River House in West Ossipee, New Hampshire, for several weeks, almost taking over the small hotel. It was an old stage tavern by the river on the road between Lake Winnipesaukee and the mountains; it sat on a dirt road near the railroad station, and to the north and west were glorious views of the Ossipee and Sandwich ranges. There was a superb view of Mt. Chocorua, which both Larcom and Whittier (and millions of tourists since) considered the most beautiful of all the New Hampshire mountains.

During the day the guests wandered off on their own or made expeditions to various points of interest. Whittier never went far from the hotel, but liked to stand and gaze at the river or at a stately tree. He had a favorite elm to sit under, and his friends knew enough not to join him there unless invited. In the evenings they gathered by the fire—Whittier was the fire builder, and again, no one dared usurp his prerogative—recounting the day's adventures or telling legends and stories of the region. Whittier was the dominant figure; Larcom was the one "whose presence brought sunshine into the grayest day."[19]

Since his sister's death in 1864 Whittier had had several relatives staying with him, and eventually his niece, another Elizabeth Whittier, became a permanent resident of the house in Amesbury. She was in her early twenties when she came to Bearcamp, bringing several of her young friends, and their presence made the vacation even more delightful for the elders. In fact, it was so happy an experience that it became an annual event; people came and went, but usually the group included Larcom (sometimes with Lydia Baker and her children), Lizzie and her friends, Whittier's Cartland cousins and his friends the Pitmans, Mrs. Spalding, and others. Both Whittier and Larcom wrote "mountain" poems as a result of these visits.

After returning in the fall from her travels, Larcom again established herself in Lydia's house in Beverly and found rooms in Boston. There were a great many visits to Malden, usually for dinner and overnight, and now she often went to the Robinson parties. Her usual partner was a minister, Gilbert Haven, who later became a Methodist bishop; one of Harriet's journal entries is typical. "Last eve Lucy came out, and we sent for G. Haven and we had a great 'crack' till half past eleven ended by an argument on 'religion' or what is called that."[20] Hattie was annoyed when the report of an evening of charades with Lucy Larcom, "the distinguished editress," appeared in the local paper.[21] One evening they spent the time discussing the experience of the Lowell years. Conditions at the mills had changed so much that the famous "mill girls" were now almost forgotten history. Haven suggested that either of the two women should write about the time, and although they did nothing about it then, the idea stayed in both their minds.

The June 1867 issue of the *Atlantic* had another of her poems, "The Red Schoolhouse." She was finding a great deal of pleasure in writing for children. Many of her verses reflected her own happy childhood or the growth and activity of her beloved nephew Harry Baker, who figured as "Hal" or "Prince Hal." She had three poems in the *Independent* in 1867 and six the following year. "Swinging on a Birch Tree" (10 October 1867), originally in her own magazine, brought a delighted response from Whittier: "How came thee to know about 'Swinging in [sic] a Birch Tree'? Thy verses took me back to old Haverhill and boyhood."[22]

In March Lois Barrett Larcom died. There had been little intimacy with her busy mother when Larcom was a child, but in her adult years they grew close. She felt the loss, although the grief that Lois Larcom's daughters felt was relieved by their thankfulness that her suffering was ended.

Her mother's illness had kept her away from Boston. On her return she was surprised and horrified to discover an unpleasant situation developing at the publishing house. Late in the autumn Gail Hamilton, reading an *Independent* article about authors and royalties, decided that Fields was cheating her. Never one to submit or even proceed quietly, she immediately confronted her publisher. Fields, whose attention that winter was completely given to the visiting Charles Dickens, tried charm and conciliation, thinking that she would forget the whole thing (including her demand for back royalties); when his tactics did not immediately succeed, Osgood tried but was so hostile that he made matters worse. Hamilton left *Our Young Folks*, but not the controversy; she wrote an account of her claim to all Fields's authors. The most significant response came from Sophia Hawthorne, who, discovering that her royalties were less than they had been for her husband's books, decided she too was being cheated and summoned her formidable sister, Elizabeth Peabody, into battle. As a result, a tribunal of leading citizens "heard" Hamilton's case and decided that, although there was no deliberate wrong, Hamilton had been treated unfairly. They ordered Fields to pay a portion of the amount she had asked.[23]

Fields and Annie, although stung by Hamilton's disloyalty, were ready to forgive, but Hamilton was not. Instead she wrote up the whole situation in *The Battle of the Books*.[24] Its long, tongue-in-cheek subtitle was typical: "Recorded by an Unknown Writer, for the Use of Authors and Publishers: To the First for Doctrine, to the Second for Reproof, to Both for Correction and for Instruction in Righteousness." There were ramifications; Fields was embarrassed, of course, and many writers wanted explanations of their arrangements with him. Fields had always done business in a paternalistic way, "taking care" of his authors and, of course, his firm. Now he began to feel that the world was going in the wrong direction. It pained him deeply to be mistrusted. That he deliberately cheated anyone seems unlikely; it is much more probable that without Ticknor he was careless in handling and keeping accounts and records, and often his decisions about favored status were made subjectively. Until Hamilton's challenge brought the situation to light, no one thought much about it.

Throughout the scandal Whittier and Larcom stayed loyal to Fields. Whittier was fond of both antagonists. He apparently tried to persuade Hamilton not to publish her book, but when he failed he stayed neutral. Fields was his old friend and, like so many people, he could not bear to hurt Annie. But he liked Gail Hamilton, enjoying her wit and her affectionate irreverence; who but Gail Hamilton would write a letter to the venerable institution that Whittier had become beginning "Dear Sheik"? His letter to Fields was brief and wrong. "I can't help thinking you might have managed her more shrewdly. . . . It won't amount to much anyway, and will cost more than it will come to the writer, I am sorry all round."[25]

Larcom's feelings were not so divided; Hamilton had never been one of her favorite people. She was, however, in a position to understand the situation, since, as she confided to Harriet Robinson (who in turn confided it to her journal), she herself had never received a penny for her steadily selling *Breathings of a Better Life*, which was going into extra editions.[26] She could understand Hamilton's demands, but was appalled at the way she chose to deal with them. Even though Larcom herself had been a victim of Fields's informal bookkeeping, there was no temptation to break away from his kingdom. By the autumn of 1868, with Hamilton gone and Trowbridge away, Larcom became sole editor of *Our Young Folks*. "She is to have full charge of the 'Young Folks,' " Hattie recorded, "and is troubled over it—as its affairs are in a mussed condition."[27]

Furthermore, one of her long-held dreams was about to come true: Fields planned to publish a collection of her poems, and she was busy getting them ready. Undoubtedly appreciation of her loyalty had something to do with Fields's decision, but by this time she was popular enough that such a book was sure to sell. She was to have ten cents a copy for each volume after the first five hundred, and, as the sole editor of the magazine, she would receive a salary of one hundred dollars a month.[28]

In her letters from this time there is no evidence of a divided self. Her religious questions seemed to be resolved; perhaps leaving the orthodoxy of Wheaton helped, or the sensible influence of Sarah Jane Spalding, or the trauma of the deaths of Louisa Harrington, Isaac Baker, and Elizabeth Whittier. Even more likely, the satisfactions and successes of her life proved her faith: the opportunities were sent and she took them. As editor of a children's magazine she could do as much for young people as she had done while teaching, and therefore she was making her contribution to the world.

Her own references to her health were different, too. There were occasional complaints about being too busy, especially during the time she was sole editor of the magazine, but not many. Once in a while she mentioned her head, but her tone was brisk; for example, a note to Mrs. Spalding asked, "What if I take a bundle of papers and come down to N. for a day or two this coming week? . . . I am *obliged* to stop and rest for some days—My head will not stand the strain any longer."[29] When she did mention an illness, it was specific, like her rheumatism, or the "neuralgia" that was cured by a visit to the dentist, or one of the colds to which she was susceptible.

In fact, during these years she worked out a way of life that exactly suited her. Freed from concern about money, she lived modestly but according to her own pleasure, with one foot in Boston and the other in Beverly. Her past timidity about the Old Corner crowd had vanished, and under Annie Fields's gentle but firm guidance Larcom attended more and more of her dear friend's salons, receptions, and breakfasts. She did not get over her hatred of crowds and noise, but she learned to control it. The people she met liked her work; they also liked her company. Howells remembered that "she was above everything cheerful, and she had a laugh of mellow richness which willingly made itself heard."[30]

Even her ever-lengthening vacations in the mountains carried out the balance of stillness and stir that was so important to her. She spent part of her time with the Whittier group or with her sisters and other friends at major resorts like Bethlehem, where each afternoon guests sat on the wide hotel verandas or promenaded the length of the great boardwalk. She "did the Notches," the fashionable tour around the White Mountains that was a prescribed part of New Hampshire travel. She loved the drama of the Notches. Crawford's stark rock faces held the grim memory of death by avalanche; at Franconia the great walls of rock barred the way, then seemed to move aside at the traveler's approach to display the smiling valley beyond. But she also liked to spend time alone, renting a room in a farmhouse where she could be quiet, look at the mountains, and write. Mail from Fields, Osgood followed her, and she dutifully kept them informed of her whereabouts.

Poems came out late in 1868, just in time for the Christmas sales. It was dedicated to Elizabeth Whittier, "by one who owes its best suggestions to the inspiration of her friendship," but the introductory poem suggests that Larcom was quietly dedicating it to all her beloved dead. She went back through her printed works and chose the ones she liked best; Fields and Whittier, who were advising her, both insisted that she use "Hannah Binding Shoes," although she herself was tired of it. A few unpublished poems were included. The sixty pieces were arranged thematically under the headings "Hillside and Seaside," "Child and Woman," "From Without" (nature poems), "War Memories," "Miscellaneous" (generally poems she liked), "Devotional," and "The Coming Life."

Reviews of the book were favorable. "They [the poems] contain many beautiful thoughts, delicate fancies, and descriptions of nature. Nor do they lack the all-harmonizing and enriching undertones of sadness, the maturer strength which only life-experience can give to the poet's song. It is not too much to say that the book will be recognized and welcomed as a real addition to the poetic literature of the day," wrote the *Atlantic Advertiser and Miscellany* (February 1869). The *Atlantic Monthly* review was less gushing but approving; its writer, probably Howells, still thought she had never done anything as good as "Hannah." Larcom must have smiled to herself when he characterized "Prudence" as "charmingly easy and life-like; the touches are very light, but each tells . . ." (January 1869).

Predictably, the one hostile response came from New York. The *Round Table* (8 May 1869) headed its review "Is Lucy Larcom a Poet?" and answered itself with a resounding negative. It attacked her content, verse forms, and grammar, and ended with a charge of plagiarism, this time directed toward "The Rose Enthroned."

Except for the last part, Larcom read the review with amusement. She wrote William Robinson asking him to deal with the plagiarism charge in one of his newspaper articles, giving him the necessary information. "I never saw the 'Birth of the Lily' in the *Continental*, —but I think its author saw 'The Rose Enthroned.' This latter was written in 1860, and published in June, 1861,—through *your* mediation, you know. The *Continental* was not started until 1862." She recalled the fuss over "Hannah," and ended cheerfully, "This 'Round Table' man evidently has New England on the stomach, sadly disagreeing with him. He evidently thinks the singing of bob o' links a dangerous heresy. I rather think they will keep on singing and that the nightingales will have no objection, whatever the bats may have to say about it."[31]

The poems are both public and private; they move from a personal thought or experience to a generalized message for the world, which may or may not be directly stated. The famous "Hannah," for example, starts from fact, the commonplace fact of coastal towns that men were lost at sea and women mourned them, and moves to a glorification of the feminine virtue, fidelity. "Three Old Saws," which begins,

> If the world seems cold to you,
> Kindle fires to warm it,

is Emeline's philosophy of life. The poems "From Without" are reflections of her struggle to define her own religious beliefs. There are verses based on local legend or famous people, and several that came from her reading of Germanic epic.

For the most part her readers saw visual detail, generalization, and didacticism, all of which they liked, and did not realize how very personal her poems were. Under the public disguise, her openness, her ability to write out her innermost thoughts and conflicts with increasing freedom, gave her a release that was usually denied to women. The issue of privacy, of what to tell, was one that had worried her; a few years earlier she wrote in her journal, "I have questioned whether it was womanly and right to give the deepest natural gushings of one's heart to the common circulation of printed type. And yet what is genuine, natural, of the inmost life, is all that ever reaches other hearts to do them good, and perhaps it would be selfishness to withhold. I would rather seem weak and foolish than insincere."[32]

If her poems were limited by her own sense of what poetry is and does, she was effective for her audience, which shared her standards of literature and the arts. Like Whittier and the other patriarchs, she used poetry to convey a message, although she and they would have contended that the message itself was the poem. At some point in the world of nature, described in her richly textured style, she found a clue to insight about life or the human being's place in God's world. As someone who had been given the ability to see and to tell what she saw, she had an obligation to share what she knew with others. The publication of *Poems* was a triumph and a justification. It permitted Larcom to think of herself as a poet—not, of course, a Whittier or a Longfellow, but still, in a modest way, a poet. She had, it seemed, at last found the world in which she belonged.

Letters of appreciation continued to arrive. Harriet Prescott Spofford wrote a glowing review for *Galaxy Magazine* (February 1869) that brought Larcom much satisfaction. She sent a copy of the book with a modest letter to Thomas Wentworth Higginson, that influential critic and writer whose importance then is so hard to understand today.[33] She saw no harm in maintaining a good relationship with a reviewer who already admired her work.

Although being sole editor of *Our Young Folks* did not chain her to a desk, Larcom did make changes in the way she organized her life. Now she needed to spend even more time in the city and she had less time to do her own writing. The latter fact, which would have been a source of worry at one time, appeared only occasionally as a mild complaint in her letters. One hundred dollars a month was a good salary, and if she needed more, she had only to write a poem.

Much of her thinking and writing in 1867 and 1868 had to do with marriage and with her own position. Undoubtedly the news of Frank's marriage was a major cause, but so were the discussions she had with Harriet Robinson. Harriet's journal records one of their encounters; she was visiting relatives in Salem and went to Beverly to call. "Lucy was at home and we sat in the arbor and talked woman, marriage and other subjects. Lucy thought that no married woman of her acquaintance was as well off as she, and she envied none of them. I told her that she was as yet an undeveloped person, on account of her single state—if any of her married friends do envy her condition they have learned wisdom enough not to own it. I suppose she is her own mistress and can think her own thoughts, and if she *can* do anything there is nothing to hinder."[34]

Harriet would in the future become an active feminist; her journal indicates that, while she herself was very happy, she was aware that the duties of marriage caused waste of talent. Of the brilliant Harriot Curtis, once coeditor of the *Lowell Offering*, whose career as a writer had been lost when she married, Hattie wrote that she was "desperately unhappy" and had "buried her talents in a napkin."[35] Hattie was rational enough to see both sides and eventually wrote that, while Lucy would have made a wonderful wife, she would have been "lost to the world—if she had done her duty at home."[36]

Larcom's arguments may have been as much to convince herself as her friend or the world, but there is no sign of regret. She did seem to feel a need to explain herself, to insist that she was doing what

God wanted her to do with her life, and above all that her choice was a wise one for her. One of the poems she wrote about this time is a kind of credo. Called "Unwedded," it describes a woman who never married, yet has a happy and satisfying life:

> For out of her life goes a breath of bliss,
>   And a sunlike charm from her cheerful eye,
> That the cloud and the loitering breeze would miss;
>   A balm that refreshes the passer-by.

She knows that "many a mother, and many a wife, / Draws a lot more lonely." Once she had the kind of "romantic dream"

> That keeps the world rosy with mists of youth,
>   And holds her in loyalty close and warm,
>   To her fine ideal of manly truth.

Aiming for happiness will not bring it; service and work and love will,

> For the heart of woman is large as man's;
>   God gave her his orphaned world to hold,
> And whispered through her His deeper plans
>   To save it alive from the outer cold.

> And here is a woman who understood
>   Herself, her work, and God's will with her,
> To gather and scatter His sheaves of good,
>   And was meekly thankful, though men demur.

> Would she have walked more nobly, think,
>   With a man beside her to point the way,
> Hand joining hand in the marriage link?
>   Possibly, Yes; it is likelier, Nay.

She has the love and respect of friends who are "good women and faithful men," and her influence is strong and good. As her life goes on,

> Transfigured under the sunset trees,
>   That wreathe her with shadowy gold and red,
> She looks away to the purple seas,
>   Whereon her shallop will soon be sped.

She reads the hereafter by the here:
A beautiful Now, and a better To Be:
In life is all sweetness, in death no fear.—
You waste your pity on such as she.

There is an interesting footnote to the poem. After it was published in *Poems*, she wrote Harriet Beecher Stowe: "I hope you have by this time received a little volume of my verses. *Poems* it seems presumptuous to call them, but I did so, as that was, on the whole, the most convenient name to use. . . . And I wanted to tell you that one of them, 'Unwedded,' was the result of a certain conversation we had at Mrs. Fields' some time since. I think the last line is almost a literal repetition of a remark you then made. It lingered in my mind, and finally came out to 'point a moral' in the way you see."[37]

Given the circumstances of Stowe's life—her financial responsibility for her entire family and Calvin Stowe's constant sexual demands—it is hardly surprising that she would feel that a single woman who was useful and productive was in no need of pity.[38]

The whole poem shows security resting on accomplishment. Part of Larcom's slow growth of confidence came from letters by readers of *Poems* and *Breathings of a Better Life* thanking her for the moral beauty and spiritual guidance the books offered. She was very proud of *Breathings*, considering it the best thing she had ever done and a real contribution. Then, too, the publication of her book of poems gave her assurance, for she had complete faith in Fields's literary judgment. Recognition, approval, belonging, and gratification all combined to give her a stronger sense of self-worth than she had ever had, and to confirm that she had "understood / Herself, her work, and God's will with her" and had made the right decisions.

She made no great claims for herself or *Poems*, but she was proud of it, and so were her friends. Mrs. Spalding wrote gleefully that it was already sold out in Newburyport and Boston bookstores and people were asking that it be ordered. Whittier was loud in its praise, and seemed to feel, with reason, that he had had a great deal to do with its existence. He certainly had given a great deal of advice and he continued to do so, unaware that his advice was not as welcome as it once had been.

Many of Whittier's letters to Larcom and others show his editing methods. He changed words, lines, and passages, often for valid reasons, but just as often to suit his own taste; he liked "tinkering" with poems. In helping Larcom to select the material for *Poems*, he worked in the same way; one of his letters praised the poem "On the Beach" and then practically rewrote it.[39]

As a novice Larcom had been grateful for this kind of help, but now she was a well-known poet and an editor who made judgments about other people's work. Her gratitude to and affection for Whittier were unchanged, but her poems were her own. Of course she said nothing to this valued friend; she simply stopped sending her work to him. When he finally asked why, she had an affectionate and tactful answer ready: "But you have taught me all that I ought to ask: why should I remain a burden on you? Why should I always write with you holding my hand? My conscience and my pride rebel. I will be myself, faults and all."[40]

It was not simply her own success that gave Larcom more confidence in herself and her work; she was finding a new kind of reinforcement. Until her connection with the magazine, her only model as a writer was, of course, Whittier. She had met and was on friendly terms with others, especially the Old Corner Book Store regulars, but these friendships were not close. With Whittier the relationship had always been primarily that of master and novice, although on Elizabeth's death it approached more closely a friendship of equals. What Whittier did for her, particularly in the dark times at Wheaton, cannot be minimized: his steady insistence that she was a poet and should keep on writing shaped her life. Rewriting her work, however, was another matter, although for a long time neither of them questioned the infallibility of his judgments.

Larcom had met other women writers, of course, but on a social level; she had not felt that she was one of them. She reacted to Stowe, for example, with almost paralyzing reverence. But in the offices of *Our Young Folks* she met and worked with many more women who wrote.

Larcom's life had not really fitted her for the average woman's role, even though she usually tried to assume a version of it. In Lowell she had lived among young women who prided themselves on their abilities to earn their own livings and to learn. She had had a certain measure of independence in the West, and at the same time she had seen marriage reduce women to drudges. She had also known Philena Fobes, who occupied her executive position without apologies for usurping a man's place. The women writers that Larcom now met were ladies, in every sense of the word, but they were writers as well. The younger ones felt no need to apologize or to hide behind a pen name. Most of her new friends were not active feminists, although some did become so, but all of them had one foot outside woman's sphere, and were, in a sense that they themselves might not have seen or admitted, professionals. Yet they remained womanly.

When Larcom began work at Our Young Folks, she took her duties seriously enough to write to two editors, the venerable Lydia Maria Child and the active "Grace Greenwood," for advice. A former student remembered the sense of awe she felt as she watched Larcom and Greenwood walking down Tremont Street together.[41] Greenwood (Sara Jane Clarke Lippincott) was an important source of practical suggestions. She was about Larcom's age, but had begun her professional career much earlier and was a well-established writer by 1854 when she began editing The Little Pilgrim, a magazine for children.

Child was in her sixties by the time Larcom and she became acquainted, with a distinguished career behind her. She had virtually invented children's magazines and had been considered among the most important women writers in the country until her outspoken and too early Appeal in Behalf of that Class of Americans Called Africans (1833) caused her to be temporarily ostracized and denounced. She and her husband left New York and moved to Wayland, Massachusetts, in the 1850s; here she wrote The Progress of Religious Ideas, a tolerant examination of religious beliefs that amazed Theodore Parker because it was written by a woman. Larcom wrote her for advice about running the magazine and a pleasant correspondence developed; both women agreed that a children's magazine needed a "mother" in charge.

Besides these two editorial colleagues, Larcom met the women who contributed to the magazine. The youthful Elizabeth Stuart Phelps already had stories published in Harper's and the Atlantic, and was working on a book to be called The Gates Ajar. Abby Morton Diaz, a former Brook Farmer who grew up in a family of antislavery activists, was another beginning writer of stories and articles; she would contribute the popular "William Henry Letters" to Our Young Folks before they were published in book form. Harriet Prescott (Spofford) was a long-established writer; she and Harriet Beecher Stowe, in fact, were the only women invited to the famous *Atlantic* dinners before the festivities became (for a while) exclusively male. Rose Terry (Cooke), poet and short-story writer, also contributed to *Our Young Folks*, as did Harriet Winslow Sewall, well known as a poet. Diaz and Sewall became Larcom's personal friends.

The most important of these writing women to Larcom was Adeline Dutton Train Whitney. The daughter of a wealthy Boston shipowner, she was married and the mother of several children; from her town house in Boston, her comfortable home in Milton, and her summer place in New Hampshire she had written a pleasant little book called *The Boys from Chequasset* to amuse her children. She followed that with *Faith Gartney's Girlhood*, which, in modern terms, made the best-seller lists.[42] *A Summer in Leslie Goldthwaite's Life* was serialized in *Our Young Folks* in 1868 and then published by Fields, Osgood.

It is easy to see what Whitney and Larcom had in common. *A Summer in Leslie Goldthwaite's Life* is about young girls—except for the first one, all her books are about young girls—and the inspirational effect of mountains (specifically, the White Mountains), which led her heroines to a better understanding of themselves and of God. Whitney dedicated the book to "the memory of my dear friend Maria S. Cummins [author of *The Lamplighter*] and of days among the mountains made beautiful by her companionship," but in a later edition (1893) she added a tribute to Lucy Larcom. Another book, *We Girls*, was serialized in the magazine before its publication; these and two more made up a popular series called "Real Folks." Whitney's religion was mystical rather than pious, and she knew how to tell an interesting story; her girls are believable and well-drawn characters. The books are feminine novels of initiation, in a sense, for the young girls grow up to find identities and religious belief in the world. Other books examined domestic problems and the lives of city working girls, always concerned with the necessity for women to build useful, fulfilled, satisfying lives and their importance and power as controllers of the home. All these themes were ideas that Larcom shared.

Larcom met other women besides writers. Mary Bucklin Davenport Claflin, whose husband was lieutenant governor and then governor of Massachusetts, became a friend. Mrs. Claflin was an important social figure and a prominent hostess, but she was also active in various causes, particularly the establishment of women's degrees and the well-being of women students at Boston University. Alice Freeman (Palmer), the first woman president of Wellesley, was another new acquaintance.

These women widened Larcom's vision. They did their work openly, without any need for apology or explanation, yet without being "unwomanly." If they wrote, they did so under their own names. For the first time Larcom found peers. As her world opened out, she stopped questioning her past behavior and decisions and felt that she had indeed found what God wanted her to do with her life.

CHAPTER 10

In and Out of the City

Ulysses S. Grant was elected president in 1868. He remained a hero, although it was unfortunate that he owed so many favors to Ben Butler, who continued to make himself a scandalous force in Massachusetts politics. Miss Alcott wrote a charming book called *Little Women*, and everyone went to look at Hiram Powers's statue, "Clytie." In May of 1869 the celebrations for the linking of the transcontinental railroad brought the West suddenly closer; in October New England trembled with earthquake shocks. In spite of Whittier's attempts to suppress it, Gail Hamilton's *Battle of the Books* was published, causing another kind of shock.

Larcom found everything that went on interesting. Her social world expanded; she went frequently with Abby Morton Diaz to events at the Saturday Club, usually meeting the Robinsons and other friends there. She was still shy with strangers, but she was finding that her world held fewer strangers than before. Instead there were acquaintances who admired her work and enjoyed her company.

She sold her first poem to *Scribner's Magazine* for twenty-five dollars, and her "Mountain Sonnets" appeared in the July 1870 *Atlantic*, but the most important event was the realization of another dream: early in 1870 she moved into a home of her own. She rented sunny, spacious "rooms" in Beverly Farms. Although all the Larcom family farms had by this time been sold to incoming summer people, there was still a great network of relatives in the area.

But she had chosen the location for its attractiveness and also for a very practical reason: Lydia's house in Beverly was a long walk from the train station there, while the apartment in the Farms was only two houses away from the depot.

She hired a woman to do the heavy work and, since she did not want to be alone and was completely bored by domestic duties that might interfere with her writing, usually had one of her nieces or young cousins staying with her to act as housekeeper and companion. One relative remembered the period clearly, describing Larcom in her forties as a "beautiful, gracious figure with flowing, abundant brown hair and a most benignant face."[1] Lydia's daughter Lizzie Baker lived with her most of the time; they were much alike and created a pleasant atmosphere so that friends and relatives loved to visit. Her neighbor Captain Josiah Obear frequently lent his horse and carriage for drives about the country; another neighbor, Oliver Wendell Holmes, chatted when they met in the village.

She loved having her own place—having, for the first time, so much control over her surroundings. Her letters were full of invitations to call; she even learned to cook several company meals so that she could invite friends to a dinner she made herself. James and Annie Fields, who had bought a house in Manchester, frequently drove along the shore road and stopped in for conversation or a cup of tea. She entertained Celia Thaxter and Mary Livermore as well as her usual friends, and Whittier came occasionally. His niece Lizzie was a frequent overnight visitor, usually bringing one of her friends, as was a cousin's daughter, Mary Larcom Ober.

There were woods and fields nearby, and Larcom was able to indulge her love of the outdoors, but what satisfied her most was her view of the sea. It was a narrow view, restricted by trees and houses, but even its limitation could inspire. "A Strip of Blue" (Atlantic, December 1870) was a poem that she herself liked; she often asked that it be chosen as representative of her work rather than the ubiquitous "Hannah." It is a long poem, beginning,

> I do not own an inch of land,
>   But all I see is mine;
> The orchards and the mowing fields,
>   The lawns and gardens fine.
> The winds my tax-collectors are,
>   They bring me tithes divine,

Wild scents and subtle essences,
    A tribute rare and free;
And, more magnificent than all,
    My window keeps for me
A glimpse of blue immensity,
    A little strip of sea.

Ships sailed across the strip of blue, arousing the imagination and seeming at times like souls with "familiar names." Although mountains were more important to her now than the sea, Larcom never forgot the impression of its majesty that came from her childhood; the sea was another representation of God's power and beauty. Her brief view held its own kind of advantage, for,

A part is greater than the whole;
    By hints are mysteries told.
The fringes of eternity,
    God's sweeping garment-fold,
In that bright shred of glimmering sea,
    I reach out for, and hold.

Such beauty is both earthly and divine, encouraging the mind to drift and yet anchoring it in substance.

Here sit I, as a little child:
    The threshold of God's door
Is that clear band of chrysoprase;
    Now the vast temple floor,
The blinding glory of the dome
    I bow my head before.
The universe, O God, is home,
    In height or depth, to me;
Yet here upon thy footstool green
    Content am I to be,
Glad when is opened unto my need
    Some sea-like glimpse of Thee.

Perhaps the poem remained a favorite with her because it was written out of real happiness and contentment, for at this point Larcom had what she truly wanted from life.

One friend who did not visit her in Beverly Farms was Harriet Robinson, whose feelings for Larcom were at the moment a little strained. Both of the Robinsons supported women's rights, and as her children grew and she had more time, Harriet was becoming involved in the movement, just as William supported it with his pen. She was an active planner of the Women's Suffrage Fair held in Boston in 1871; when she asked for a poem for its paper, Larcom wrote back that she was too busy, adding, "You know I'm way behind the times—I am not even a 'Suffrage Woman' yet, though I haven't the least objection to the rest of the women's having it. But you see I'm constitutionally 'on the fence' and never could see yet whether it was worth while to crow for either side or not." She went on to wish the "enthusiastic believers" success, adding that "if the suffrage carries, as it will, I hope it will be a blessing to everybody. All the people I know and respect seem to be in the movement, and still I 'don't see it.' "[2]

The offended Hattie decided that Larcom did not want her name connected with the suffrage cause. In truth, whatever Larcom felt about the movement, she was not ashamed but afraid to have her name associated with it. For one thing, it was confrontational; more important, however, was the fact that her newfound security did not stretch that far. Dependent as she was on the public, she literally could not afford a label that might alienate some readers and editors. She remembered that Whittier's audience had been limited while he was using his poems for the abolitionist cause. She could not take the chance, and she steered carefully through the middle. Nothing in her letters shows whether or not she saw that her own life provided the freedom and autonomy that most women lacked.

Her writing was never allowed to venture outside the patriarchal definitions of poetry. Even her poems about women did not attack the status quo; they attempted to point out gently some of the things that were wrong. Her "Sylvia" (*Atlantic*, December 1872) was a "woman's poem" that went back to something she had written years ago on the prairie. Sylvia was about to be married, and "No voice had made her name so sweet" as her lover's. But after marriage the years went on with their constant work and exhaustion, and

> He called her "wife" in accents gruff.
> Why should she for her girl-name yearn?
> Was she not his? Enough.

But she did yearn for it, for "dreary weeks and years" although

Life was not sad enough for tears;
Her heart more slowly broke.

Gradually, in spite of her husband's pride in her ability to work, she died; and in her last moments, as he recognized his loss, he also realized what he had done to her. Finally,

The warm-breathed, fresh magnolia-bloom
   In hands that never stirred
He laid, with one beseeching word,—
"Sylvia!"—that pierced death's gathering gloom.
   Her soul smiled back: she heard!

Under the sentimentality of the poem, which was, apparently, what most readers perceived, lies an attack on male attitudes, but it is certainly a gentle one. It is, in fact, an explanation, respectfully submitted, to the patriarchy. How consciously she wrote is impossible to know; it was a sentimental age and she was part of it, yet it is very hard to believe that Sylvia's hearing her name as she died made up for years without identity. "I am glad you like 'Sylvia,'" she wrote Annie Fields. "I'm afraid it is only too true and common a picture."[3]

She certainly had strong feelings of solidarity with other women, and she was indeed aware of their problems, but she simply could not throw herself into a battle of any kind. She could, however, write poems about women; it was her way of understanding and helping, although not a way that the fiery Hattie Robinson could appreciate. An earlier poem, "Weaving," had emphasized the connection between black women who grew cotton and white women who wove it into cloth. Including "Sylvia," the five poems she wrote for the *Atlantic* between 1871 and 1874 are about women. "Mehetabel" (June 1871) dreams a dream that her mother scorns and her lover cannot be part of, but the dream never comes to pass and her life is wasted. "Phebe" (October 1872) joyously finds her lover. "Sylvia," of course, marries, loses her identity, and dies. The heroine of "A Gambrel Roof" (February 1874), a local legend, is a clever wife of Revolutionary days who outwits her husband's decree that no tea shall be served in his house by entertaining her friends on the wide roof. The very different "Goody Grunsell's House" (September 1874) describes an ugly, dismal house haunted by the ghost of a failed marriage, for "spectre and fiend will roam / Through the heart that is not love's home."

Her "Loyal Woman" is more than a patriotic poem; it is really about a woman's integrity and what marriage can do to it. Prudence, the "Little Old Girl" who first appeared in *Our Young Folks*, has been trained to be a good wife by having all beauty, joy, and freedom cut out of her life. "Getting Along," written ten years earlier for *The Crayon* (July 1861) gives the thoughts of a woman in a loveless marriage who knows that her husband married her for her money. "Hepzibah" (*Independent*, 22 January 1874) again concerns names, but in an ideal way; Hepzibah's name is given (and consecrated) as she is christened, used to the bride at the altar and by her loving household, and finally at her death "the old-fashioned name / Woven into her life" has gathered "a meaning some new world is waiting to claim." "Old Madeline" (*Independent*, 6 July 1871) is another Hannah, remaining faithful to a dead love; the woman in "Her Choice" (*Independent*, April 1874) married a farmer instead of the fashionable gentleman she might have chosen, and years later could say that though "Woman's lot at best is hard," marriage to a man with ideals and integrity redeemed hardship.

In general these poems are explorations of women's lives; they lead to no thesis, except, perhaps, that human beings need to be honest, that they need to find the best way to live their individual lives, and that marriage must be a true union of souls as well as bodies if it is to have any reality or worth. If Larcom's "Unwedded" is quietly triumphant, it is not smug; she never saw her way as the only right way, one that all other women should follow. It was indeed right for her, but she never claimed she had found perfection. She always, for example, gently regretted not having children of her own. But she had nieces and nephews, work she loved, a measure of fame, a sense of usefulness, security in her religious thinking, friends, and a home, and she was very happy.

Trowbridge returned to *Our Young Folks* in the spring of 1870, and Larcom gave up her position as editor-in-chief with mixed feelings. As editor she had made no major changes; the magazine continued to offer a balance of stories and poems aimed at entertaining children while it instructed them in morals and manners. Larcom enjoyed and was good at selecting manuscripts, planning attractive pages, talking to writers, and encouraging their work. Unfortunately, she hated to reject anything; she wrote time-consuming letters offering suggestions for changes or naming other magazines that might accept

Lucy Larcom.
Courtesy of the Essex Institute, Salem, Mass.

Emeline Larcom.
By permission of the Marion B. Gebbie Archives and Special
Collections, Wheaton College, Norton, Mass.

Captain Benjamin Larcom.
Courtesy of the Beverly Historical Society, Beverly, Mass.

Lucy Larcom.
This may have been one of the publicity pictures available to fans
who wrote asking for an autographed picture. On some copies,
"Brown's Famous Pictures No. 23" is printed under the photograph,
with her dates incorrectly given as 1826–1894. Courtesy of the
Essex Institute, Salem, Mass.

Monticello Seminary, Godfrey, Ill., ca. 1870
By permission of the Marion B. Gebbie Archives and Special
Collections, Wheaton College, Norton, Mass.

Wheaton Seminary, 1849–1879.
By permission of the Marion B. Gebbie Archives and Special
Collections, Wheaton College, Norton, Mass.

Advertisement for *Our Young Folks.*
Atlantic Monthly, January 1865.

MR. WHITTIER will contribute a prose article for the second number; and he, as well as other leading writers, will frequently furnish appropriate poems and prose articles.

In addition to the writers named above, regular contributions will be furnished by

RICHARD H. STODDARD, author of "Adventures in Fairy Land."
COL. THOMAS W. HIGGINSON.
GRACE GREENWOOD, editor of "The Little Pilgrim."
THE AUTHOR OF "The Little Susy" Books.
THE AUTHOR OF "Dream Children."
MRS. A. D. T. WHITNEY, author of "Faith Gartney."
MISS MARIA S. CUMMINS, author of "The Lamplighter."
MISS LOUISA M. ALCOTT, and others.

Engagements are also in progress with several other writers of celebrity, whose names will be duly announced. Many of the most prominent contributors to the ATLANTIC MONTHLY will lend their aid in making the magazine acceptable to the young people.

ILLUSTRATIONS.

Every number of OUR YOUNG FOLKS will contain capital pictures, drawn and engraved by our best artists. The valuable aid of Mr. DARLEY has been secured, and the first number will be enriched by designs from his pencil. This number will also contain drawings by Mr. VEDDER and Mr. CHAMPNEY. A finely engraved steel portrait of some popular author will be given in the first number of each volume. The portrait in the opening number will be that of THOMAS HUGHES, author of "Tom Brown's School Days at Rugby."

The Publishers of OUR YOUNG FOLKS will endeavor to furnish to their young readers a magazine whose monthly visits shall be always welcome, and shall be expected with pleasure. They will coöperate with the Editors in procuring for OUR YOUNG FOLKS whatever is excellent and original in

STORIES AND SKETCHES,
  BIOGRAPHY, HISTORY, AND POETRY,
    TRAVEL AND ADVENTURE,
      OUT-DOOR AND IN-DOOR SPORTS,
        GAMES AND PUZZLES,

and every variety of miscellany, entertaining and instructive, serious and comic. They are confident that a magazine conducted on the plan which they propose, will supply a want long felt in the households of our land.

SIZE AND STYLE.

The size of OUR YOUNG FOLKS will be that of the CORNHILL MAGAZINE, or somewhat more than two-thirds the size of the ATLANTIC MONTHLY. Each number will contain not less than sixty-four pages. The magazine will be electrotyped from new and beautiful type, and handsomely printed at the University Press, Cambridge.

TERMS.

SINGLE SUBSCRIPTIONS, Two Dollars a year. Single Numbers, Twenty Cents.

CLUBS. Three Copies for Five Dollars; Five Copies for Eight Dollars; Ten Copies for Fifteen Dollars; Twenty Copies for Thirty Dollars: and an extra copy *gratis* to the person forming the Club of Twenty.

POSTAGE. The postage must be paid by the person subscribing.

CLUBBING WITH THE ATLANTIC MONTHLY. The *Atlantic*, ($4.00 a year,) and *Our Young Folks*, $2.00 a year,) will be sent together to one address for Five Dollars.

☞ *All subscriptions are payable in advance.*

SPECIMEN COPIES of the First number will be sent to any address, as soon as published, for Ten Cents each.

All letters respecting the magazine should be addressed to the Publishers,

TICKNOR & FIELDS,

135 WASHINGTON STREET, BOSTON, MASS.

Lucy Larcom.
Drawing used as the frontispiece in *Lucy Larcom's Poems* (1884).
Courtesy of the Beverly Historical Society, Beverly, Mass.

the piece. And, given the fact that she thought about money as little as possible, she was nearly hopeless at handling a budget and equally bad at meeting deadlines. She found business and detail tiresome, especially when they interrupted her own writing or prevented her from going to the mountains.

As usual, her friends were more upset than she was. Mrs. Spalding had written of the improvement in the magazine. "'The Editor's Talk,' which used to be a series of pop guns disgustingly trying to hit somebody all the time, has become thoughtful, tender, and winning, showing that neither wisdom nor wit is synonymous with snubbing."[4] Now she protested: "I can not feel reconciled that you should rise from your editorial chair, for you fill it, my dear Lucy, gracefully and usefully. I have hoped that when once used to the business details, you might find leisure and freedom in it. I think your judgment is admirable, in its mixture of courage and gentleness, and whatever you think best, is doubtless so—but I am sorry."[5]

The Spalding home in Newburyport was by this time a real refuge and delight to Larcom. Mrs. Spalding was what Ma and Becky had once been: trusted and completely compatible. Bright, well-read, aware, and deeply religious, she provided exactly the support Larcom needed, even to tactful criticism when it seemed necessary. It is clear from her letters that she valued Larcom as both friend and poet. Larcom sent her as a gift a copy of *The Friendships of Women*, a book that glorifies friendship between women as a fine example of the Platonic ideal of love.[6] The three Spalding children—Mary (fourteen), Annie (ten), and Edmund (five)—all adored Aunt Lucy; the girls dressed up and pretended to be Miss Larcom, and Edmund planned to marry her when he grew up. One quiet guest room over the ell was named her room. It particularly pleased her that she could offer some assistance to the Reverend Samuel Jones Spalding, who had tackled the enormous task of putting together the Spalding/Spaulding genealogy; Larcom was able to give him details about the Lowell branch of that huge family.

If she was unhappy at giving up her editorial authority, it did not trouble her for long. She needed time for more than her own work. Fields, Osgood had asked Whittier to do an anthology of poems for children, and he agreed, provided that Larcom would help him. Even had she wanted to refuse she could hardly have done so, for she owed both Whittier and Fields too much. *Child-Life* (1871) was the first of three anthologies that she and Whittier worked on together.

At first the collaboration was sheer pleasure. They met in Amesbury or Beverly Farms or among the mountains to discuss their choices, and as often as not the work time turned into the philosophical and religious discussions they both so enjoyed. But the division of work was an unequal one: she collected the poems and was responsible for having them copied out, then had to prepare them for publication and read proof. For this she received a flat sum, either three or five hundred dollars. Whittier read the poems, made the final choices, and received the royalties. His name went on the volume, and he acknowledged her assistance in the preface. She did not really mind and agreed to work on a second volume. Whittier's company was pleasant, and she liked to feel that she was helping him. The tiresome part of the work could be done at the office, where she still had a desk and clerks to help.

James T. Fields was making plans to retire. The chief reason that he gave was his desire to devote his time to writing and lecturing, but undoubtedly the trouble with Gail Hamilton and Sophia Hawthorne, with the resulting loss of prestige that undermined the Fields image, had influenced his decision.[7] When on 2 January 1871 the firm became James R. Osgood and Company, there was no immediate change. Fields and Annie remained the center of social life for literary Boston, and everyone flocked to his lectures. For the authors, too, life seemed to go on in the same way. Osgood had his own kind of charm, and of course they had known him since his junior clerk days.[8] He never married and, although he had a long friendship with journalist Kate Field, he seemed to seek and enjoy primarily male companionship. Osgood's autumn lists for 1871 and 1872 were brilliant, but fairly early in his ownership there were signs of trouble. When he expanded *Every Saturday*, it failed. *Our Young Folks*, possibly because Osgood could not do the same kind of inspired juggling act that Fields did so well and therefore could not control his editors, became a problem that he solved by selling the magazine to Scribner's. Before that he sold *Every Saturday* and even the *Atlantic Monthly*, the brightest star in his sky, to Hurd and Houghton.

Freed from her duties as chief editor, Larcom wrote and visited more. She even had a brief fling at political activism when a group of citizens protested the closing of a home for disabled soldiers in Roxbury. She took part in the lobbying, but the crowds and noise upset her so much that she literally had to run from the room. In addition, the surgeon-general's smooth manner offended her. So, to a lesser degree, did William Robinson, who supported the official position. "Well, I'll say no more about it," she wrote him, "only that it looks a little strange, when ten thousand has been appropriated by the State, and an official receives eight thousand for distributing it, he should grumble at the most natural applicants—the disabled soldiers just turned out of their Home at Roxbury." She went on to make another point; Robinson had apparently criticized the North End Mission. "I wish you had asked *me* about the North End Mission before para-graphing it. . . . The work is *really* done by women of all sects,—I would say 'ladies' if the word were any better—Unitarians and even *Radicals* among them. And within two or three weeks of my leaving Boston, I saw and talked with three or four fallen women who were trying to reform, under the influence of the Mission. Two of them are in the Home in Rutland Street to remain until they find places to work.—Now, my dear friend, it is painful enough to go down into the mire after these people,—but to have one's efforts gently sneered at by a friend is more painful still."[9] Neither reproof harmed their friendship.

She had a busy summer with Emeline and some of her children staying with her. She kept a quiet corner in which to write, but more people than ever called at her pleasant rooms, especially the young women friends of her niece. Lizzie Whittier was a frequent visitor. Some of the poet's admirers did not approve of her, feeling that she was not taking proper care of her uncle, who, in his mid-sixties, was very frail and subject to severe colds. Lizzie, with her friends, her interest in causes, and the three years she went south to teach freed-men, did not seem to realize the full sacredness of her charge. Mrs. Spalding, fussing over the situation, lamented that "Mrs. Grundy" prevented dear Lucy from moving into the Amesbury house so that the poet would get the care he deserved.[10] There is no reply to this letter, nor is there evidence that Larcom had any desire to give up her freedom and become an unpaid housekeeper, even for her old friend. She liked Lizzie and, with her sympathy for young girls and the memory of her own lost girlhood, admired but did not encourage the young sacrificing themselves for their elders. She knew, too, that Whittier himself was not among the complainers and was, indeed, very proud of his niece and happy to see her young companions. Lizzie came often to Larcom's Beverly Farms home and usually brought friends. One of them, Maria Dowdell, who later became a doctor, wrote a letter full of pleasant gossip to her admired Miss Larcom:

> Have seen the wonderful Mrs. [Celia] Thaxter and was not favorably impressed by her. She has a very silly laugh, for one thing. Suppose someone has told her that she has a sweet musical laugh and so she displays it on an average every two minutes whether there is anything to laugh at or not. I told Mr. Whittier I did not like her, should never think of her as a friend and compared her just a little with you yourself, when he paid you a beautiful and deserving compliment, "O, it is rare to find anywhere one so true and natural as Lucy."
>
> Yesterday Lizzie's Portland friend came and stayed till this morning. I was there to tea, and liked him very much. I do hope something will come of it. L. and I were going to Boston this morning had it not stormed. Hope to be able to go tomorrow. He will be there so I don't expect to see much of L. Poor me without a beau will have to entertain myself as best I can alone, but I expect we shall have a pleasant time [and] not return before Saturday, perhaps.[11]

Lizzie's "Portland friend" was Samuel T. Pickard, a newspaperman and editor of the *Portland Transcript*. He became a Bearcamp vacationer and, after he and Lizzie married, was very close to Whittier and a good friend to Larcom.

The second Peace Jubilee, which was held in Boston, brought visitors from everywhere. One hundred thousand people, according to the *Independent* (17 June 1872), came to the Coliseum to hear a chorus of twenty thousand voices sing patriotic songs. A huge organ had been built for the occasion, and, besides musical groups from various countries, the feature was Johann Strauss and his Vienna Orchestra. (To escape the horror before he was forced to comment on it, Boston's famous music critic John Sullivan Dwight left town.) Tactfully, the festivities were held from 17 June to 4 July (Bunker Hill Day to Independence Day); deeply moving to many was the presence of southern regiments at the celebration.

The rest of the summer was intensely and abnormally hot, and Larcom spent most of it in New Hampshire. As usual, she took work with her. The idea of owning, not renting, a home of her own persisted; as soon as she returned, she began special savings to buy a farm in New Hampshire, either in Tamworth or West Ossipee.

Visits to Adeline Whitney in Milton and Mary Claflin in Newtonville, where she met the admired English author George MacDonald, occupied her in the autumn, but these visits and other travel in the city were made difficult by a strange disease that attacked horses all through the East. Boston became suddenly unfamiliar: "There were no cars, no teams; the queer sight was presented in a great city, of the driveways as clear as the sidewalks; of nobody needed to guard the crossings or unsnarl the 'blocks'; of stillness like Sunday, day after day; of men harnessed into wagons,— eight human beings drawing, slowly and heavily, what any poor old prickle-ribs of a horse, that had life left in him at all, would have trotted cheerfully off with. A lady's trunk was a cartload; and a lady's trunk passing through the streets was a curiosity; you could scarcely get one carried for love or money."[12]

The lack of horse power left the city vulnerable, and the fire of November 1872, which started in the North End, swept into the center of Boston and burned for three days. There were strong winds to drive it and no horses to bring fire-fighting equipment. About one-third of the city was destroyed: lives, homes, and businesses were lost. One of Osgood's warehouses went, and old Trinity Church, which had just welcomed its new rector, Phillips Brooks, burned to the ground.

Larcom was staying in Somerville, a rural suburb of Cambridge, with Harriet Minot Pitman, a childhood friend of Whittier's and one of the Bearcamp vacationers. The Pitman home was another place she liked to visit, often with Harriet Winslow Sewall, another poet, who was a friend of both women. The three were frequent traveling companions, for they shared a love of mountains.

On the night of November ninth they saw a glow in the sky over Boston "like a great volcano in the east."[13] They waited through anxious days when it seemed that the whole city would burn; as soon as the fire was controlled, groups and individuals rushed to help. Larcom and her friends worked in the North End, among the poor but respectable Portuguese families who had lost everything.

She was chiefly concerned with young women from the sewing sweatshops connected with various stores; their places of employment no longer existed and they were desperate. The work went on well into December, and Larcom, like other women, put aside her personal concerns for the time.

She went back to Beverly for Christmas and was kept there by a series of snowstorms well into the new year. From Beverly Farms she wrote Whittier one of the long verse letters they both enjoyed, explaining why she would not be able to make a promised visit to Amesbury and going on to describe the beauty of the winter world around her and at the same time her restlessness away from the stimulation of the city. Even when the weather cleared her return was delayed, however, because a smallpox epidemic followed the fire. It was March before she resumed her busy city life; she and Whittier were guests for a week at the Claflin home on Mt. Vernon Street. Their hostess gave several parties that brought together the literary, political, and social lights of the city, and held a quiet celebration of Larcom's forty-ninth birthday.

Although she had known that Osgood was planning to sell *Our Young Folks* (its last issue was to be October 1873), Larcom had been too busy to worry about her future. The collaborations with Whittier would bring predictable sums, the *Independent* and other papers and magazines took her poems, she could always do part-time teaching, and she and Osgood had plans for future writing. Mary Mapes Dodge, who was to edit *St. Nicholas*, wrote warmly, asking her advice and begging her to write regularly for the new magazine.

Even had the magazine stayed in Osgood's hands, it is questionable how long Larcom would have remained with it. Her correspondence and the comments of contemporaries show that she made and retained friends easily, yet she had a major clash with John Townsend Trowbridge, her associate editor. At the time she began work on the magazine she did not know him, but several undated letters show that they became friendly; one contained a warm invitation to visit his family in Arlington: "Come on the 12 o'clock train and spend the night. I little thought it would be so long before you would visit us." He went on to say that they would get together and plan the November issue as soon as she decided what was to go in it.[14]

The trouble developed after Trowbridge became chief editor. Details are obscure, since the two pertinent letters in the company's letter book were written on onionskin paper in purple ink that has faded to illegibility in places.[15] One account says that Larcom, "angered at her demotion, took offense that she was not consulted in matters of acceptance, illustrations and layout. Trowbridge . . . found Miss Larcom's work less than competent."[16] Trowbridge's letters support that view; however, Larcom was not angered at her "demotion." It took place in spring 1870; a year later she wrote a friend, "My life in the office of *Our Young Folks* was one crowded with work to distraction. I was rejoiced when Mr. Trowbridge took my place, and left me at liberty to live here in peace. Even the reading of mss. is not very perplexing here,—and they follow me still."[17] One reason for accepting Larcom's words is that the arrangements were handled by Fields; given his and Annie's fondness for Larcom and his tact, it is unlikely that he would have allowed her to be hurt or angry. There is, in fact, an opposite possibility: she and Fields might have agreed that a position demanding so much detail and business sense was not something she could do well or happily.

Trowbridge's first letter in the book said, "I am so astonished at the tone of your letter, that I am constrained to request that you will return mine that I may see what I wrote in my haste that so offended you." A week later he wrote, "At length, after two years and a half, . . . I did (very hesitantly, I assure you) venture to ask you—at the beginning of a new year—to be a little more explicit in your descriptions of the mss. you returned to me."[18] The copy of this letter is twelve pages long; in it he denied that he had been "ungentlemanly," tried to explain why he hadn't consulted her much, and said that he did not think of himself as her superior. The postscript, however, threatened: "On rereading your letter and seeing how positively you assert that your work with the magazine is not designed to save me labor and that you do not intend to make any change in your manner of doing it to oblige me, I consider it will be as well for me not to send you any more mss. It will give me but little more trouble to assume the entire reading of these myself." Perhaps the fact that Trowbridge, "in spite of the firm's pleas for economy, . . . felt himself forced to hire a third person (his wife) at an annual $1000" had something to do with the situation.[19] Larcom continued to read submissions and kept her feelings about Trowbridge to herself. She remained on polite terms with Osgood, and the situation does not seem to have troubled her very much.

She was more concerned over the misfortunes of her friend William Robinson, who had been ousted from his job as clerk of the legislature. Robinson had enjoyed his closeness to working politics, his membership in the powerful Bird Club, and his status as a well-known political writer. In all these positions he had fought the good fight against the forces of evil, Democrats, and especially Ben "Beast" Butler. Solid Boston Brahminism loathed the sound of Butler's name as much as his politics, and Robinson scorched him in the papers.

But political forces and alignments were changing. Charles Sumner, once a hero, was looked on with disfavor for criticizing Ulysses S. Grant. When Sumner introduced a bill proposing that the names of Civil War battles be taken off regimental flags to ease bitterness, the Massachusetts legislature responded by censuring him—an act that brought Whittier back into politics, where he led the fight to remove the censure from his friend. His efforts were finally successful; in the next legislature the censure was rescinded, and Whittier went home to Amesbury. But no one could help when Ben Butler staged a coup to get Robinson out of his clerkship; in fact, the move was supported by some of Robinson's old political allies, acting in the name of expediency.

Loss of the clerkship was a blow to his party, but it was personally devastating to Robinson; in fact, it was a loss from which he could not recover. He never minded a good fight, but the fact that the coup had been aided by trusted friends was hard to accept. Hattie was terribly worried about her husband. He still had his audience, of course, through his Warrington articles, but the center seemed to have gone out of his life. Even the huge party to celebrate the Robinsons' twenty-fifth wedding anniversary in the fall and the magnificent gift of forty-five hundred dollars collected from his friends did not revive his spirits.

Aside from concern about this old friend and indignation at what had happened to him, Larcom was satisfied with her world. In a letter thanking Annie Fields for her birthday gift, she wrote, "it won't do for me to have many more birthdays, unless I choose to give it up that I am lost in the abyss of old womanhood, and I feel rather too frisky for that, as yet."[20] Over the years she had gradually gained weight, and she was by this time rather an imposing figure. Whittier, in a letter to Harriet Minot Pitman that he knew Larcom would see, wrote teasingly, "As to anybody's intrinsic *goodness*, the less said the better. Take Lucy Larcom for example. If she is any better than one of the wicked it is because she is more providentially made than her lean and scraggy sisters with nerves naked to the east wind. Don't give her a bit of credit for it. I don't."[21] She was still attractive enough that she could be teased about men. The year before there had been a young Mr. Williamson, and she wrote Lizzie Whittier, "I am used to being called *a jilt*, though not among the young folks. A woman of my years and size would cause a tremendous crack in breaking any boy's heart, I guess!"[22]

Elizabeth Stuart Phelps told an anecdote about Larcom and Whittier and Larcom's "dreaminess, or absence of practical attention, of which her friends were lovingly and laughingly aware."[23] The two had gone for a ride and were driving up a steep hill.

The load—on the lady's side—was not light. Lucy Larcom was talking, and she talked on. I think the subject was the life to come. At all events, it was some abstract theme, grave and high.

The horse grew unruly. The buggy lurched and rolled. Whittier grasped the reigns valiantly, anticipating a possible accident, and centering his being on the emergency. But Lucy talked on serenely.

The horse threatened to break. The danger redoubled. The buggy sagged heavily, on Lucy's side. Still, peacefully she murmured on.

"Lucy!" exploded the poet, at last. "Lucy! If thee does not stop talking till I get this horse in hand, thee will be in heaven before thee wants to!"

Whether created by "providential" flesh, by temperament, or by Emeline's precepts and her own self-discipline, Larcom's cheerful, warm serenity, her ready laughter, and her care for others had certainly made her a woman whose company was prized and whose friendship was cherished. She herself was aware of the other side of the coin, however; people who do not betray their feelings are often thought not to have any. One of her most serious poems, written two years earlier, reveals a vulnerability that perhaps only her very closest friends understood:

THEY SAID

They said of her, "She never can have felt
    The sorrows that our deeper natures feel":
They said, "Her placid lips have never spelt
    Hard lessons taught by Pain; her eyes reveal
    No passionate yearning, no perplexed appeal
To other eyes. Life and her heart have dealt
With her but lightly."—When the Pilgrims dwelt
    First on these shores, lest savage bands should steal
To precious graves with desecrating tread,
    The burial field was with the ploughshare crossed,
    And there the maize her silken tresses tossed.
With thanks those Pilgrims ate their bitter bread,
    While peaceful harvests hid what they had lost.
    —What if her smiles concealed from you her dead?[24]

Sometimes presenting a cheerful face to the world was wearying;
this poem reads almost like a cry for understanding. She had certainly been trained, in the proper behavioral code for New England
ladies and gentlemen, not to burden the world with her troubles and
emotions, but sometimes she longed for others to see beneath the
serene surface to the vulnerable human being who lived there—in
herself and in other women reared in the same Puritan code. She was
not unhappy, but she had borne her share of grief and pain and
learned how to live with them.

Her serenity was to be tested. By April she was back in Beverly
Farms with plenty of work to do, looking ahead to a long visit by
Emeline and some of her children. Her chief work for the summer
was reading proof for *Child-Life in Prose;* her own collection of children's poems as well as the Lowell story that was teasing her mind
had to take second place. She planned short visits to Annie Fields at
Manchester and Sarah Jane Spalding at Newburyport, and in late
summer would join Whittier and other friends in her beloved New
Hampshire.

As spring passed, however, she began to worry about her future.
She was not afraid of being without money, for by this time she
knew her poems and other kinds of writing would sell, but she still
felt that depending solely on her writing was too precarious. She

wanted a regular income, for in seven years she had established a life that was perfect for her. Now her home, her travel, her place in Boston, and above all her freedom of movement were threatened. An alternative, living with Lydia in Beverly, was always available, but it was not what Larcom wanted. The offer of a teaching position at Bradford Academy, a girls' school northwest of Boston, brought on a kind of crisis; there was always a chance that this was a sign of vocation and, more practically, it paid an excellent salary.

Teaching in a boarding school was not attractive, but it had to be considered even as she sought a way to keep the life she prized. In late June or early July she had a meeting with Osgood to discuss future work; she took advantage of the occasion to ask for some kind of steady connection with the company, using the editorial skills she had learned in the last seven years. It was hard for her to ask, but she stressed the difficulty of writing while teaching, as well as her potential usefulness to the firm.

Osgood's answer shows a complete lack of understanding or concern under its bland surface:

After thinking over the whole matter very carefully I do not like to advise you on literary or commercial grounds to decline the school proposition, if it is a favorable one. Literary matters are, as you know very well, rather precarious, and altho' the two or three plans which we have talked over are decidedly promising and *must* be carried out, yet I hardly feel as if there could be enough such in the future as to justify the payment of a regular salary. Besides, it seems to me that you might do both—i.e. teach and do such literary work as might be needed from year to year as well. Of course I have very little idea what the labor of teaching is, but it scarcely seems incompatible with a certain amount of literary and editorial labor.

We want the little children's poems for next year's publication; I would rather not do it this year, because we must give the two Child-Lifes (poetry and prose) a chance to run together this season. Did we agree upon any price for this? You might go on and finish it and put it in our hands to keep over. We would pay you for it as you wanted it.

Then we want the mountain book from Mr. Whittier, and any other *specialty* in that direction (or any other direction) which

he is willing to edit and give his name to. I suppose he would
not work with any one except yourself; at all events you can do
more towards inducing him to do such books than any one else.

The *Idyl of Work*, I judge from your letter, will be ready for
Spring publication. Let us have it by the 1st of January, please.

"Woman-Life" and the Juvenile Books are back of all these
things and ought to be considered in making up a verdict.

If you can combine teaching and literature you can make
more money and make everybody happy. What say you?[25]

She could see nothing to do but accept the position at Bradford and
make what she could of it. For someone who wanted to teach, the
opportunity was excellent; it paid well and the academy had a good
reputation. Even though she had written Lizzie, "If I could only earn
money enough at home to keep things going comfortably, nobody
would catch me in a school,"[26] Whittier's comment to Mrs. Pitman
was enthusiastic: "She is at Bradford in elegant rooms and is paid
$800 per year over and above board and expenses for lecturing to a
class on English literature etc.—3 hours 4 days in the week. It is
much better than living alone in Beverly."[27]

Neither Osgood nor Whittier understood what taking the teaching
job meant to Larcom; it was not better than living alone in Beverly.
It was, in fact, a disaster. Part of the arrangement was that she should
have half of each day for her own work, but the problems and responsibilities of teaching spilled over into her personal time. She no
longer had the patience or the commitment that had enabled her to
teach well at Wheaton no matter how she felt. One or two girls were
helped by her; most found her preoccupied, distant, and unap-
proachable.[28] Her habit of having her own worship service on Sundays, preferably out-of-doors, generated sharp criticism; ironically,
this deeply religious woman was accused of atheism.

By late fall she began to experience nearly forgotten symptoms:
nervousness, apathy, and trouble with her head. Once again she felt
confined; she desperately missed the life she loved and the place she
had made for herself, and she had lost control of her life. Her long
weekends at home hardly gave her time to see her friends and relax
in her own surroundings, and she was seldom able to get to the city.
All her activities there had to be given up, and she longed for the
company and stimulation as well as the sense of being part of a busy

world. By spring she was so unwell that she was hardly able to go anywhere and could barely force herself to write.

Child-Life in Prose came out in the late autumn. Larcom had been paid for her editorial (and secretarial) work on the book, while once again Whittier received the royalties. He mentioned in the preface that he had had advice from the lady who assisted him with *Child-Life*, but this time he did not mention the lady's name. Earlier he had written, "I've got the sheets of our *Child-Life*, and like it hugely. But I think now I shall take the credit all to myself. If it had not looked nice and good, I should have shirked it, and left it all on thy shoulders."[29] The letter sounds like a joke, except that he did indeed take all the credit.

Larcom had undoubtedly said that she did not need to be mentioned, but it is unlikely that she expected to be taken at her word. She had learned by now the importance of keeping her name before the public. The omission hurt; what had been a labor of love for an old and dear friend was tarnished by the slight. Whittier's later comment sounds somewhat shamefaced: "The *Hearth and Home's* notice of 'C. L. in Prose' gives me all the credit for this last volume. I deferred to what I thought was thy wish in not directly using thy name in the Preface, but I ought in justice to both of us have given it."[30] It is hard to understand Whittier's behavior; certainly he felt honest affection for this friend whose career he had helped to shape. His action was clearly the result of insensitivity rather than any deliberate malice; he seems to have accepted her surfaces very quickly.

The return to anonymity and the year at Bradford seemed like regression to the days at Wheaton, but much worse. She was back in a school, confined by rules and schedules and commitments, and again unknown. At Wheaton she had been much younger; now she seemed to have lost all that she had gained. The achievements of the past ten years were swept away, and in her darkest moments it seemed that she had not the strength to begin again. Her fiftieth birthday in March was hardly joyous, nor did she feel "frisky" as she had just a year before. Although there is no evidence, the tensions and discomforts of menopause may have added to the very real unhappiness of her life.[31]

If the year at Bradford was a dark night of the soul that left her shaken and unwell, she came out of it with a cold determination never to allow herself to be so trapped again. She made a conscious decision that she would never change: nothing would get her back in a school again. No matter how she had to live, there were to be no more panics that drove her to seek financial security at the cost of everything that mattered. In fact, during the last months at Bradford she planned a way to manage her life. While she never liked to think about money, she could be a hardheaded Yankee when driven to it.

Accepting the fact that she would probably never find another editorial job, she counted her assets. There was money in the bank and she could count on payment for the next collaboration with Whittier. She had promised Osgood a collection of her own poems for children as well as a story about Lowell days, and had worked on those two assignments during the year whenever she felt well enough. A poem now brought her between twenty-five and forty dollars. She could teach private classes or an occasional course at her friend Miss Johnson's school. She could accept the commissions to write on specific subjects that she had been too busy for in the past. Fields suggested that she prepare lectures for schools and women's groups; she kept that idea as a possibility, though public lecturing did not appeal to her. The important thing was to overcome the fear that lack of money would make her a pensioner, however welcome, on her family. She wanted to keep what she had: her home in Beverly Farms, her winters in Boston, her travel in the mountains. She would have to give up the dream of a farmhouse in New Hampshire, but she could hold on to the rest.[32]

Her plan, finally, was to line up enough work so that she could always see a year ahead and, with that period secure, stop worrying and enjoy her life. Again she fell back on faith; if what she was doing was right, God would send the opportunities. There were to be no more panics like the one that sent her to Bradford; that was a mistake she would not repeat. In June, weary and ill, she put the lost year at Bradford firmly behind her.

CHAPTER II

Finding the Way

Although she needed rest, Larcom made a few visits and a short trip to the mountains before she began her new way of life. Sooner than her family liked, she arranged to teach two adult classes in literature. These classes, organized by friends (Mrs. Pitman in Somerville and Miss Anne Page in Danvers), were given to audiences who were proud to be instructed by a famous poet and willing to pay for the privilege.

When Boston came to life again in the autumn, Larcom felt as if she were returning after years in exile. There were changes in the city; the downtown section, devastated by the fire, was being rebuilt, mainly with business blocks, stores, and warehouses. More land had been claimed from Back Bay, and a grand boulevard, called Commonwealth Avenue, was to run westward from the Public Gardens. Most of Larcom's favorite haunts were untouched, however, and she could visit them at her leisure to see what was new. Mr. Prang's art store, for example, introduced a European custom that seemed delightful: special cards to be sent to friends at Christmas. Best of all, of course, was dropping in to the Authors' Room at her publishers and again being part of the literary world.[1]

For the winter she found lodgings in the South End—that part of the city that had been designed for gracious living but abandoned for the made land where the bay was filled in. Now the tall blocks of houses were for the most part respectable and attractive boardinghouses. Larcom's was on the edge of Back Bay, and she frequently went to hear Phillips Brooks, the rector of burnt Trinity Church, who held services all over the city until the new building in Copley Square was finished. The "high" Episcopal service seemed a little ridiculous to a stiff-kneed Congregationalist, but she would have put up with worse to hear Brooks preach.

Her fears that she had lost her place in the literary world proved groundless, and her fame was confirmed by a curious request from the editors of the *Daily Graphic* and *Hearth and Home*, the latter a frequent buyer of her poems. They were asking the one hundred "best known men and women in America" to investigate spiritualism for the paper. She apparently did not accept the offer, but it was good for her self-confidence to be named in that way.[2]

She was only amused when the aging Emerson's poetry anthology, *Parnassus*, came out and she found "A Loyal Woman's No" credited to Anonymous, but her friends were angry. She wrote soothingly to Hattie, "But isn't it much more an honor to be there impersonally—the best way to enter a philosopher's Paradise—so that I can know that neither personal prejudice or preference had anything to do with that Loyal Woman of my brain?—But then, as you say, and as I hear from other sources, there are a great many things in the volume poor enough for me to have written under my own name."[3]

Childhood Songs came out early in the spring of 1875 and was very well reviewed. Her poems "for and about children," as she put it, are light, pleasant, and for the most part appealing. One of them, however, illustrates the occasional lapses that occurred in her work, as if she had stopped listening to what she was saying. "What the Train Ran Over" is a memory of the children from the lane who once played in fields now cut by railroad tracks; unfortunately, it is not until the end that the reader discovers that the children the train is running over are not real.[4] Her contemporaries, however, were not disturbed by the grisly image; reviews and comments in letters were full of praise.

In May she delivered the manuscript of her Lowell story, *An Idyl of Work*, to Osgood. She was very tired and still very nervous, and the winter and spring had been a mixture of good and bad. Earlier she explained her failure to write or visit Hattie, "I ought not to read or write or stay indoors much—so my tired brain and the doctors say; and I am going to try electricity for my jaded faculties. I *have* dissipated a good deal, within a month, but must cut these things short, I find."[5] The electricity treatments helped her, and her "dissipation" made life more interesting; unfortunately, it cut into her writing time and added to the pressure that she could hardly bear. When she handed over her finished *Idyl* and left the city for Beverly, she planned to work on the third anthology, then join Whittier and their friends at Bearcamp. She was counting the days until the long vacation in the mountains that would restore her health.

An Idyl of Work was the most serious and sustained piece of writing she had ever attempted, and she put a great deal of herself into it, recalling the days when she was a young woman full of dreams and ideals. She tried to illustrate the brief flowering of the Lowell experiment and the lives and qualities of the girls who were part of it. While she was still at Bradford she had learned that Frank Spaulding was seriously ill; news of his death in December 1874 came while she was working on the story and deepened her nostalgic remembrance of things past. Although the book is about girls, its most important male character is a young doctor, noble and manly in his dreams and aspirations.[6]

Much to her sorrow, the book was not successful. Some critics liked it, but only friends and former mill girls bought it; financially it was a complete failure, and the reasons are fairly clear. The opening scenes in Lowell, when the flooding of the river gives the girls an unexpected holiday and they gather for a long walk in the country, are attractive. There is a reality about them that gives them life. The plot, however, is weak and contrived, full of coincidence and dependent on characters who seem to have no other necessity in the tale. There is no suspense, even in a near seduction; the reader knows good will triumph. In fact, her plot is no stronger here than in the atmospheric but shapeless stories she wrote for the *Offering*, and the *Idyl* makes it clear that she could never have written the "long American story" that Whittier had urged: fiction was not her strength. Her factual approach to the lives of the mill girls for the *Atlantic* six years later, however, was beautifully handled.[7] As an evocation of time and place, *An Idyl of Work* is pleasant, but as a story it falls apart. Her use of blank verse instead of prose probably did not help sales either.

Two of her characters do stand out. Although she insisted that she was creating composites, not using real people, her Esther is clearly Emeline, "tall and strong, with gold-brown hair" from whose "large,

fair, well-ordered" mind "sunny light / Seemed ever to flow outward." She is guide and comforter to the other mill girls. Though
dedicated to a life of single usefulness, at the end she marries the
young doctor and they go west to help develop a new world.

Another girl, Minta, represents the breezy mountain girls who
had so fascinated Larcom as a child. Minta has a local suitor, a "first-
love fallacy," who, since she came to Lowell, offends her with his
"accustomed mastery of will" and his "scoffing at her taste for
books, / Which spoilt her for a housewife." Minta decides he
"would be the one most uninteresting book / To take for life-long
conning." In the end she chooses to ignore marriage for a while and
teach girls in a statement that certainly expressed Larcom's belief:

Human beings
God made us, then he added womanhood.

Larcom put a great deal of her experience, feelings, and thought
into the *Idyl*, and its failure was a deep disappointment; perhaps the
measure of her hurt, as well as the nervousness from which she still
suffered, showed in her reaction to the *Independent*'s review. While
he praised the story, characters, and incidental poems, the reviewer
disliked and mildly ridiculed her blank verse. Normally Larcom's
response to bad reviews was temperate, but this one offended her.
She stopped sending her poems there, and later explained to Hattie,
"I have not sent them anything since they let one of their whip-
persnappers write an impertinent notice of the *Idyl* as an editorial. It
was too rude a thing for any well-bred paper to do, so I thought I
would not count myself as one of their staff [her name had been
consistently listed on the masthead as a contributor to the paper]—
at least until reparation was made."[8] It was unlike her to cut herself
off from a prestigious and profitable market.

By the end of her first year of supporting herself by her writing,
Larcom could say at least that she had not failed. She had made a
good start, but she was too intense and forced herself to do more
than her fragile health would sensibly permit. Eventually she would
learn to pace herself, to keep better control and balance of time and
work, but now she was trying to do everything at once. She was
completely exhausted; her head pained her and she had to struggle
against the old apathy to get her work done. As a result, her tense-

ness and nervousness increased. Underneath was always fear of a real illness that would prevent work.

Only the thought of the mountains sustained her; she was sure that the long vacation she had planned and saved for would bring the mental and physical health that she needed. After she handed in the manuscript for the *Idyl* she turned immediately to the last piece of work before she could be free, the third collaboration with Whittier. *Songs of Three Centuries* was an ambitious collection of poems that Osgood had scheduled for the Christmas sales. She began the work reluctantly; she longed for leisure and the mountains, and she had never wanted to do the book. Three hundred years of English and American poetry made too large a pot from which to select. And, much as she wished to, she could not quite forget the circumstances of the last book she and Whittier had worked on together.

By August, still tied to the city and work, she was barely suppressing her anger and resentment. She wrote to Mrs. Claflin, newly returned from Europe, thanking her for her descriptive letters and then explaining her present situation,

I have scarcely walked to the beach this summer,—for why?—I have been so busy about a book, Mr. Whittier's book—a compilation of English poetry which Osgood wished him to make and which he agreed to do, with my help. It is to be published this fall, and there is the hurry and fatigue of it; my head has been nearly used up, through the warm weather. If I had supposed it would be one third as hard, I would have refused to do it, without a year's time.

This seems like complaining, but there is nobody to blame about it. I only know that I have lost the beauty of the summer, poring over books.

Mr. Whittier has made a flying call here, once or twice and now he has gone to West Ossipee, N.H. where I am to join him and try to finish the book. He has taken several of his young-lady friends with him, as is his wont, so that I feel no fear about his having company and a good time, while I am delayed, as I must be, by a sudden cold, which keeps me housed. I shall go in a day or two, if I feel better.

Mr. Whittier has seemed very well whenever I have seen him,

and I have heard of him as being in unusually good spirits among his friends.[9]

Larcom worked on long past the time that she usually left on her travels, always with the knowledge that her collaborator was enjoying himself at Bearcamp. She felt trapped. Cutting out, copying, and readying material for the printer were demeaning tasks that seemed to negate all that she had achieved, but hardest to bear was the thought of her friends in the mountains. It seemed unforgivable and was probably the precipitating factor in the clash that occurred when, complete with papers, books, and bad feelings, she was finally able to join the others at Bearcamp. Given her avoidance of confrontation, it is unlikely that there was a real quarrel, but she let her hurt and anger show, and she resented any attempts to hurry her with the details of the book.

Her stay in the mountains was brief. Later Whittier wrote her with suggestions for more poems to be included and an apology: "I am *very* sorry that thy feelings were so hurt by our dispute at Ossipee. I think I explained the circumstances of peculiar anxiety and worry. Rather than feel that such a life long friend was estranged I would prefer to have the unfortunate book in the Red Sea deeper than Pharaoh's chariot wheels. But two sleepless nights and utter nervous discouragement account for, if they do not excuse, the matter. Heaven knows how hard I have all my life striven to control this nervous excitability. But let it pass. Thee *know* that I am the last person living to harm the feelings of any one, much less a dear friend, if I can help it."

That Larcom was not ready to let it pass is suggested by a second letter from Whittier, undated but probably later:

Thee are quite right in thinking that I did not know much about what was said on the evening thee refer to. I only know that I was sleeplessly worried about my brother's affairs, and the hurry of getting out the book. I was sick, and feared that thee had made thyself more sick by riding so far and late in the sharp wind, and, if I remember right, thee was unreasonably persistent in denying that there was any need of returning proofs promptly. When one is unreasonable himself he is in no mood for tolerating the same thing in others. I dare say that I was a fool, but that's no reason thee should make thyself one, by dwelling on it. Lay it all to dyspepsia, Ben Butler, or anything else than intentional wrong on the part of thy old friend. We have known each other too long, and done each other too many kind offices, to let it disturb us.[10]

Through the fall she was still tied to the book, which did not, after all, come out in time for Christmas sales. Whittier had learned a lesson; her name was mentioned, her work was credited, and he arranged to share the royalties with her. Even that act, however, was qualified: the royalty checks came to him and he gave her her portion. *Songs of Three Centuries* was an immediate success. It was enlarged the next year and was reissued six times within the collaborators' lifetimes. Suitable recognition and payment for her work certainly made Larcom feel better about the book, but the pressure of putting it together had done serious damage to her health and to the friendship. On the surface the breach was healed, but the relationship was never to be quite the same.

In December she went with the Pitmans to Professor Thayer's house in Cambridge to hear Emerson read his "Immortality." The best part of the occasion was the chance for a long talk with Longfellow, who was so kind and showed such interest in her poems. There were few such outings, however; she was very busy and never quite well during the winter and spring that followed. Because she felt unwell, her writing proceeded more slowly than she wished, and that intensified her nervousness.

William Robinson, whose health had continued to fail, died in March. Larcom felt personal grief for this old friend who had helped her so often, and even more grief for Hattie. She wrote a brief but loving letter and was not surprised that Hattie's reaction was to throw herself into work. She spent the next year collecting her husband's articles, writing a long introduction, then publishing the book as *Warrington's Pen-Portraits* and literally going on the road to sell it. She was paying tribute to the husband she had so deeply loved and admired.[11]

Larcom was not able to attend either Robinson's funeral or Lizzie Whittier's wedding to Samuel T. Pickard in April, although she was very happy about the latter.[12] She decided against going to Philadelphia for the Centennial celebrations even though most of her friends went and she had wanted to see the work of her sculptor friend, Margaret Foley, a marble fountain shipped from Rome for the celebrations. The thought of the crowds discouraged her and she really could not spare the time.

One of the things she had learned was that anthologies paid well; now she proceeded with two of her own, *Roadside Poems for Summer Travellers* (1876) and *Hillside and Seaside in Poetry* (1877). Both were small volumes that could fit into a pocket or handbag so that the traveler could, while gazing at some lovely scene, enhance his perceptions with suitable verse. She was also working on a series of four articles for *St. Nicholas*, for each of which she received sixty dollars. Part of the impetus toward hard, steady work came from her determination that this year nothing should prevent a real vacation, and in particular a long stay in the mountains to revive her soul and refresh her tired head. Of course she would take work with her, and of course she would join the Whittier party at Bearcamp.

After a round of visits to friends, she set off for the mountains. The hotel was overflowing with friends, all ready to enjoy themselves. A second edition of *Songs* was coming out, but the changes were slight and could be done at a leisurely pace, so there was no pressure attached. The vacation was dominated by bears and bear stories and bear steaks for dinner; several groups climbed Mt. Chocorua (Larcom, her nephew, and Samuel Pickard were in one) and camped there, so that their campfire could be seen at night by their friends below. From one group of campers came stories of hearing bears growl all night long. Whittier, enthralled by the bear stories, wrote verses called "How They Climbed Chocorua," about the climbers and their prudent retreat from the bears; he had Larcom read it aloud as if it were by an unknown author:

The next day . . . Lucy Larcom and some others of the party prepared a burlesque literary exercise for the evening at the inn. She wrote a frolicsome poem, and the others devised telegrams, etc, all of which were to surprise Whittier, who was to know nothing of the affair until it came off. When the evening came, the venerable poet took his usual place next the tongs, and the rest of the party formed a semicircle around the great fireplace. . . . By and by telegrams began to be brought in by the landlord from ridiculous people in ridiculous situations. Some purported to be from an old poet who had the misfortune to be caught by his coat-tails in one of the Knox bear-traps on Chocorua. It was suggested that he might be the author of the poem read at the husking. Lucy Larcom, who, by the way, was another of the writers popularly supposed to be very serious minded, but who really was known among her friends as full of fun, read a poem addressed to the man in the beartrap.[13]

Larcom's poem attributed the growls and howls not to bears, but to the poet's process of composition. She ended "To the Unknown and Absent Author of 'How They Climbed Chocorua' " with the following stanzas:

> By its tones of dismay, melancholy and loss,
>   O'er his coat-tails' sad ruin;
> There's a moan in the pine, and a howl o'er the moss—
> But it's he—'t isn't Bruin!

> And the fire you see on the cliff in the air
>   Is his eyeballs a-glarin'!
> And the form that you call old Chocorua there
>   Is the poet up-rarin'!

> And whenever the trees on the mountain-tops thrill
>   And the fierce winds they blow'em,
> In most awful pause every bear shall stand still—
>   He's writing a poem!

Her verses led Whittier to suggest that the poet caught in the bear trap had better make his will, and, with suggestions and laughter from the group, he did so, remembering everyone present:

> Here I am at last a goner,
> Held in hungry jaws like Jonah;
>   What the trap has left of me
>   Eaten by the bears will be.

> So I make, on duty bent,
> My last will and testament,
>   Giving to my Bearcamp friends
>   All my traps and odds and ends.

The bequests are various.

To Lizzie Pickard, from my hat
A ribbon for her yellow cat,

and to Larcom, suffering from her annual hay fever,

If a tear for me is shed,
And Miss Larcom's eyes are red—
Give her for her prompt relief
My last pocket-handkerchief!

Except for her hay fever, which descended upon her each August twentieth and this year had followed her to the mountains, Larcom had a cheering and delightful stay at Bearcamp. She went on from there to other familiar spots, settling finally for a long and solitary stay in a quiet farmhouse near Jefferson where she could read, rest, walk, and work at her own will while she enjoyed a view of the majestic Presidential range. She went for the first time to the top of Mount Washington, a long and fearful journey by wagon, and fell in love with the stark, dramatic beauty of what seemed to be the top of the world. She stayed three days at Summit House, liking the place and the Dodge family who owned it. The experience was important to her spiritual life and became a regular part of her annual mountain pilgrimages. So high above the world, closer to God, it was impossible to think of pressures, illnesses, personalities, and irritations; they had no meaning. The strong winds that blew steadily across the summit seemed to cleanse her of petty troubles and to free her mind to think about the things that really mattered.

Her vacation improved her health, although she was still not well when she returned to work and city life. One of her chief pleasures, her visits to Whittier and the Amesbury house, with all its happy memories, was no longer available, for Lizzie Pickard's marriage had caused a major change in her uncle's life. Approaching his seventieth birthday and never in good health, he disliked the prospect of living alone, dependent on a paid housekeeper. He made arrangements to live with his cousins, the Misses Johnson and Mrs. Woodman, who had recently bought a big house in Danvers, although he kept the Amesbury house as his legal address.

There are conflicting accounts of Oak Knoll and Whittier's residence there. It is sometimes described as a beautiful old mansion and the Johnson ladies as lovely women who cared for their famous cousin; other accounts suggest a kind of Gothic pile in which Whittier was almost a captive. British critic Edmund Gosse described his visit to Oak Knoll with William Dean Howells in anything but attractive terms:

> Doubtless in the leafy season Oak Knoll may have its charms, but it was distinctly sinister that December morning. We rang, and after a long pause the front door opened slightly, and a very unprepossessing dog emerged, and shut the door (if I may say so) behind him. We were face to face with this animal, which presented none of the features identified in one's mind with the idea of Mr. Whittier. It sniffed unpleasantly, but we spoke to it most blandly and it became assured that we were not tramps. The dog sat down, and looked at us; we had nowhere to sit down, but we looked at the dog. Then, after many blandishments, but feeling very uncomfortable, I ventured to hold the dog in conversation while I rang again. After another pause the door was slightly opened, and a voice of no agreeable timbre asked what we wanted. We explained, across the dog, that we had come by appointment to see Mr. Whittier. The door was closed a second time, and if our carriage had still been waiting, we should certainly had driven back to Danvers. But at length a hard-featured woman grudgingly admitted us, and showed us, growling as she did it, into a parlor.[14]

Overseas visitors and Pilgrims (Whittier's name for the hoards of unknown admirers who liked his poems and therefore felt free to invite themselves unannounced and unwelcome to his home) were not the only ones dismayed by the dogs; Gail Hamilton, making a surprise call, was attacked by them and had to run from the grounds.[15]

With her memories of Amesbury and with the shadow of their near quarrel in her mind, Larcom was not comfortable at Oak Knoll. She wrote Horace Currier, a Newburyport friend who shared Bearcamp vacations, "Celeste and I had a pleasant call on Mr. W. at Danvers. He is as delightfully situated as any man could ask to be, and his friends ought all to be glad for him,—even though he does not need them so much as formerly."[16] But to Lizzie Pickard she was more open:

I have seen him once this winter at Mrs. Claflin's, and that is all. Sometimes I wish the old times could come back as when I used to be so at home with you all at Amesbury, and saw him so often,—for you know how I value his friendship. But he almost never calls upon me now, and I never was one who could run after even my best friends, when they seemed to be having a better time without me.—And then it is foolish to expect to *keep* anything, in this changeable life. I suppose it is something better, even for ourselves, to lose what *we* think is best for us. The spirit of anything good can never be lost, so I shall always be grateful for that pleasant share of mine in the Amesbury life, in your Aunt Lizzie's time, and after. Perhaps in the better life coming, we shall renew the old friendship in a better way for all of us.[17]

Probably a change in their relationship would have occurred anyway with the breaking up of the Amesbury household, but Larcom could have accepted it more easily without the memories of her own resentment and her sense of exploitation and betrayal. She never tried to minimize all that she owed the poet, and she could accept the fact that life changed and so did people; nevertheless, what looked at that point like the loss of the old special friendship hurt her badly.

During the winter of 1876–77 Larcom alternated between bouts of illness or extreme tiredness and days when she felt well and could be out and about the city. She still pushed herself to work, both at her writing and the occasional class she taught. When she was unable to finish her course at Miss Johnson's school in Boston, James T. Fields stepped in to help. "The trouble in my head grew worse with constant work," she wrote Hattie, again explaining her failure to write or visit, "and I have given it up—the work I mean, and the head almost went too. Mr. Fields offered to read three of his lectures in place of my lessons, or else I should be plodding on still."[18]

She was beginning to find a compensation for the loss of Whittier as a constant in her life, the strong man to whom she could turn as a source of wisdom and approval. Even after she had broken away from his mentoring they still sent each other copies of their work and spent time together discussing the beliefs they shared. With the old relationship changed, however, she was ready for someone to fill the emptiness. She had gone to Trinity Church frequently during the winter, drawn, as were so many, by the personality and preaching of its rector, Phillips Brooks. When she met him, the famous preacher and the famous poet found that they shared a great many beliefs and attitudes.

Brooks came to Trinity Parish in 1869, having already made a great reputation as a preacher and minister in Philadelphia (and as the author of the carol "O Little Town of Bethlehem").[19] He came to a church in trouble, for Trinity's congregation was steadily moving from the older section of the city to the new Back Bay. The thirty-four-year-old rector had the task of presiding over the buying of land in what is now Copley Square and planning for a new church at the same time that his magnificent sermons were rebuilding church attendance. The fire of 1872 destroyed old Trinity; for four years Brooks conducted the services of the church in borrowed buildings and meeting rooms all over the city, until the new church, built in Romanesque style by architect Henry Hobson Richardson, was consecrated in February 1877.

Regardless of denomination, people flocked to his sermons—three on Sunday and one on Wednesday evening. Brooks had a splendid presence (he was six feet four and weighed about three hundred pounds) and great oratorical skills, and his message led away from the harshness of Calvinist Congregationalism to a God of love. It is easy to see why Larcom was drawn to him; according to one account, Brooks saw "God, man, and nature, inextricably interwoven, spiritual and material, a living organism, working out God's purpose." And bound up in the first, the "unity of man, divine and human, spiritual and physical, the indissolubility of his personality."[20] Since his belief matched those to which Larcom had independently fought her way, it was an enormous satisfaction to hear it from so impressive and legitimate a source. She became a fairly regular attendant at services (although she still did not much like the ritual), and as her friendship with Brooks grew, there were frequent talks in the minister's large, fire-warmed, comfortable study in the rectory. Even before she knew him his sermons helped her, and to find that he shared her beliefs and respected her work and her spiritual gifts strengthened her self-confidence and her courage to continue the sometimes frighteningly insecure life to which she was now committed. He reinforced her belief that if she was doing God's work, the opportunities would continue.

Whittier had emphasized her poetry, but Brooks stressed her religious thought, a difference that was to be significant. Whittier, and to a lesser degree William Robinson, had been approving fathers, but the much younger Brooks became a friend, and their growing compatibility lessened the need for the poet's support. As her reliance on Whittier ended, her hurt feelings eased and finally disappeared altogether. If they met less often now, they met as old and dear friends.

By spring, thanks to a real rest, visits to friends, her usual pleasant routine of galleries, concerts, and bookstores, and the avoidance of "literary work," she felt very well, ready to deal with the unexpected loss of her rooms in Beverly Farms to her landlord's newly married son. Her sister's house welcomed her, as usual, but while there would always be a bed for Aunt Lucy, the busy household could not offer her the privacy and space she needed. She could, however, store the accumulation of seven years there, and it was not very long before she found compensation in a new sense of freedom. Perhaps she had grown past the need for a home, and by this time saving the rent money was important. "I am going to wander about this summer, I do not yet know where,—nor where I shall turn up when winter comes," she wrote cheerfully to Mrs. Claflin, and went on to misquote *Paradise Lost*, "'the world is all before me, where to choose' . . . I am deeply grateful for the improved health I enjoy. I now have a head which I dare to use—with moderate care. For three years, previous to this winter, my brain has seemed like a weight of lead which it was very hard to carry about, and which might at any moment crush me. I have learned a lesson about over-work, which I mean to profit by,—though not in a pecuniary sense. Don't be surprised if you hear me as retired to some 'Home' for indolent and indigent old ladies."[21]

Once the business of moving was finished, Larcom began a round of visits. She went with Mrs. Spalding to Vassar, where Annie Spalding was a senior; the highlight was a long conversation with astronomer Maria Mitchell. She attended the Wheaton Anniversary celebration, enjoying the renewed contact in spite of extreme heat and crowds, and went from there to New Haven where her friend Franklin Carter was a professor at Yale. By the end of July, after enduring a heat wave followed by violent thunderstorms, she was more than ready for the mountains. She traveled by steamboat to Portland, where she stayed for a few days with the Pickards, then went by rail to Bethel, Maine, a small town near the New Hampshire line. She wanted to try the Maine side of the mountains, and Samuel Pickard had recommended the area. Larcom brought more trunks with her than usual, for she planned a long stay and needed her books, pens, paper, lap desk, and portfolio to keep on with her work. This year it was a series of commissioned articles for the *Art Journal* about the relationship between landscape and poetry.

Her friendship with both Pickards had become closer. In fact, just as Brooks replaced Whittier, so Pickard took the place once occupied by William Robinson; both were personal friends, but they were also connected with papers and interested in her as a writer. Pickard was certainly eager to publish her work in the *Portland Transcript.* She reviewed books for him, including Harriet Robinson's memorial to her husband, and they decided that she should write a newsletter about Boston activities, or any other subject she found interesting, and send one whenever she chose. (She did a similar kind of thing for the *Boston Advertiser.*) Her newsletters were a pleasure to write, for the essay was the form with which she was most comfortable; its shortness allowed her to "craft" her prose as she liked to do.

Bethel proved to be the perfect place for her. "I do not think my friends could understand the great effort it has been for me to rouse myself to any exertion," she wrote Annie Fields, "even when the object to be attained was a very delightful one. Near the mountains I am a different person; and I feel here, as if I were regaining my former vigor. Certainly my head is getting rested,—and that seemed to be the source of all my fatigues." She went on to describe the place, ". . . about a mile from the village, with the river winding through the wide meadows before me, and the White Mountains cut sharply on the sky in the distance. . . . The sunsets are something beyond my dreams, almost, at times. The mountains lie mainly west from here, and such illuminations as they receive from the late light and the afterglow!"[22]

Whittier and his friends were at Bearcamp, but Larcom stayed contentedly in Bethel; for one thing, she suffered no hay fever attacks there. A local history mentions proudly that Miss Larcom spent much time at Bethel, describes the wide view from Sunset Rock, and quotes her poem, "On the Ledge," written there.[23] On very clear days she could see the buildings on the summit of Mount Washington, thirty miles away.

Altogether it was a happy and much healthier woman who returned in the fall, briefly to Beverly and then for a longer visit to Newburyport and Mrs. Spalding. Her stay on the top of Mount Washington waiting for the clouds to move away had inspired a poem, as the mountains so easily did. "In a Cloud Rift" appeared in *Harper's* (August 1878). She had a significant experience when she either slept out or fell asleep on the mountain, and from that came "Asleep on the Summit," a poem of childlike simplicity, ending,

> Cradled and rocked by wind and cloud,
> Safe pillowed on the summit proud,
> Steadied by that encircling arm
> Which holds the universe from harm,
> I know the Lord my soul would keep,
> Among the mountain-tops asleep.[24]

Her visit on the mountaintop led to another new experience. The Dodge family, who owned Summit House, also owned the Hamilton Hotel in Bermuda, and they invited her to be their guest there for as much of the winter as she could spare. Larcom was delighted, both with the idea of a new and exotic place and the sea voyage it entailed.

There were, of course, things to do in Boston first. In December Whittier was seventy; his publishers and admirers decided that he should be honored. *Literary World* solicited poems in his praise from everyone who had ever set pen to paper; one of the *Atlantic* dinners was arranged for him. The influx of Pilgrims to Oak Knoll increased, although the dogs were still on duty.

Larcom called on him a few days before his birthday. "Miss Page and I went to see Mr. Whittier,—and had the entertainment of entertaining *him* with the reading aloud of some of those seventieth birthday poems which are to fill the next *Literary World.* They came to him while we were there. I don't think he *quite* relished the idea of being so toasted, and it seems to me not quite the way, to send around and ask everybody who has ever printed verses to write some on the occasion. Spontaneity is the charm of all these things. Of course he will feel bound to some sort of gratitude, and of course very nice things are said of and to him."[25]

The *Atlantic* dinner featured Whittier, Emerson, Holmes, and Longfellow on the platform, seven courses, and innumerable speeches, including the one in which Mark Twain compared the three venerables to three western bad men, causing shock in his audience and enraged reactions in Boston newspapers.[26] Ladies were not invited; the doors opened at half past ten to allow them to enter, having, presumably, dined elsewhere. Larcom did not attend, but she did see Whittier often during his fairly long stay in the city, usually at the homes of friends like the Claflins, and they enjoyed each other's company as if there had never been a breach in their friendship.

Shortly after the New Year she left for Bermuda, where she stayed until March, extending her visit by two weeks. She liked the sunshine, the roses that bloomed in midwinter, the perpetually spring-like weather, the lovely and different hues of the sea, the excursions in little boats over the crystal-clear waters, the unfamiliar constellations, the tales of shipwrecks and pirates, and the pleasant company at the hotel—all of which she duly chronicled in a newsletter for the *Transcript* (20 March 1878) and a poem called "Bermoothes" (*Harper's*, November 1878). The vacation was exactly what she needed; she returned in good health with her cheerfulness restored. Distance and change of scene always helped her put her life in perspective. Although there would still be times when she pushed herself too hard, generally she was learning to control and balance work, rest, and pleasure.

For the next two years her life was busy but stable. There were some bouts of illness, but for the most part she felt well and energetic. Her reputation as a poet was secure, and she had no difficulty finding outlets for her verses. There were more *Atlantic* poems, a few in *Harper's*, many in *St. Nicholas*, and she had a long list of popular if not so prestigious magazines that happily accepted her work. Several newspapers, as well, considered her a regular contributor; her newsletters for the *Portland Transcript* and the *Boston Advertiser* were well received and were reliable sources of income.

The article she had done for the *Art Journal* was expanded into a book, *Landscape in American Poetry*, for which she wrote the entire text; it is a handsome book with illustrations by Boston artist John

Appleton Brown.[27] To avoid any teaching she followed the suggestion Fields had given her and worked up some lectures. They had
titles like "Girlhood and Womanhood in Poetry," "Women Poets,"
"Woman as a Lyric Poet," "The Authuriad," and "The Holy Grail."
One of them, "Women Poets," shows how this woman poet saw her
own treatment:

> The writings of women, whether in prose or verse, have not al-
> ways been judged with absolute candor by man.
>
> Sometimes overpraised, sometimes passed by with a super-
> cilious smile, as quite beneath criticism, and sometimes looked
> upon patronizingly, as the best that could be expected of her, it
> has not been easy for woman to find the true measure of her
> own powers, or the just value of her own productions. She has
> sometimes seemed ashamed of her own literary work, simply
> because it was done by a woman. And so she has frequently kept
> her claim to the authorship of beautiful poems carefully con-
> cealed though the air around her was ringing with their melody,
> and everyone was asking for the singer who sang so sweetly.
>
> These remarks, of course, do not apply to the present. We live
> in an age which is more just to woman than any preceding; an
> age in which flattery has given place to fairness, and indif-
> ference to sympathy; an age in which woman may cultivate her
> natural talents, and be honored in whatever honorable work she
> does, by men and by women alike.[28]

Although speaking in public made her nervous, her lectures were
popular and provided another predictable source of income. Her audiences were women's groups, church groups, schools, and lyceums.
She received twenty-five dollars for each, and lecturing demanded far
less time and was not a sustained commitment. She liked writing
the lectures for the same reasons she enjoyed the newsletters; the
short, concentrated form gave her the chance to work unhurried
over the careful prose she enjoyed most.

Early in 1879 she wrote Lizzie Pickard that she was busy, feeling
better, and working hard. Although her bank account was getting
low, she would not teach. She commented on another writer's
efforts: "Mrs. Thaxter was at Mrs. F[ields]'s painting China plates by
the dozen; she seems to have exchanged poetry for pottery. I doubt

not she finds it more profitable business; she must make plenty of money."[29]

The *Atlantic* birthday dinner for Oliver Wendell Holmes was turned into a "breakfast," so ladies could attend. The earliest *Atlantic* dinners had included two women, Harriet Beecher Stowe and Harriet Prescott (Spofford), but Stowe's insistence that no wine be served in her presence inhibited the gentlemen and the dinners quickly became exclusively male,[30]—until, much later, protests from feminine writers like Gail Hamilton inspired the "breakfasts," usually beginning at two in the afternoon, to which all authors might be invited. The seventieth birthday celebration for the Autocrat was held in the Brunswick Hotel, and literary "stars" gathered to dine, talk, and listen to speeches.

Larcom's partner for the breakfast was William Winter, the New York drama critic and poet; at their table was Thomas Wentworth Higginson. Winter described the occasion in his reminiscences:

> The privilege fell to me of escorting to the table that accomplished gentlewoman Lucy Larcom . . . I sat at her right, and on her left sat Thomas Wentworth Higginson,—stalwart among progressive thinkers, intrepid iconoclast of intrenched abuses, who, in the serenity of a lovely and honored age . . . represents all that is highest and therefore best in American literature. Our talk, I remember, ranged gayly over many themes, lingering for a moment on wine. The current potation chanced to be claret, and Miss Larcom, who did not taste it, was insistent (in a low tone) that I should ask Mr. Higginson to take a glass of wine with me—as, immediately, I did. His response, most courteously made, was to raise to his lips a glass of water. "But," I said, "you do not honor the toast—which is the health of our fair companion": whereupon he swallowed a teaspoonful, perhaps, of claret, with obvious impatience. I was afterward informed that he was a rigid, inveterate, iron-bound apostle of total abstinence! If his eyes should ever rest on these words he will be amused to learn that Lucy Larcom, notwithstanding all her demure gravity, was not averse to a joke, and that she was then trying her hand at a little playful mischief, of which both he and I were to be the victims.[31]

Her winter and spring were organized around two important writing tasks. *Breathings of a Better Life,* the little devotional book she had published in 1866, had sold steadily although she had never received any money from it. But her publishing house was going through major changes, and now there was to be a new enlarged edition for which she would receive royalties, so that at last she could profit from this best selling of all her books. She enjoyed the revision, and when it was finished she turned to another pleasant occupation: a long blank-verse poem that was to open her next collection of poetry.

Wild Roses of Cape Ann and Other Poems came out in November 1880. It is, as its title suggests, a book with a strong regional flavor, Larcom's chief contribution to local-color writing. It opens with a blank-verse poem (she had worked hard on improving her skill at the form) interspersed with lyrics describing Essex County's rocky coast, its history, its people, and its natural beauty. There are poems based on local legends and a great many that center on the outdoor world, including her mountain poems. There are tributes to the great minds: "R. W. E.," "J. G. W.," and "O. W. H.," each written to imitate its subject's style. There are poems from the West as well. "A Prairie Nest" and "Through Minnehaha's Veil" recall her youth; "A Whisper of Memory" and "In Vision" are memorials to Frank Spaulding. A group of religious poems at the end attempts to communicate the lessons life had taught her and the joy and security she had found in her faith. One thing the book does not include is "Hannah Binding Shoes," although letters in praise of that work still arrived.

Of all her collections, this one is the most personal, for it captures and brings together so much of her life. The sonnet to Emerson, for example, is a very public tribute, but in light of her own experience it is a very private statement. "Doors thou hast opened to us, thinker, seer," she began, and went on to say that his voice, "From great expanses beyond time and space" stirs "the sluggish soul new paths to trace," so that finally

> The mention of thy name, like Nature's, brings
> A sense of widening worlds and ampler air.

The tribute is general and public, but it also describes the personal and specific effect Emerson's thinking had on Larcom's life.

Poems like "They Said" or "In Vision" are intensely personal, re-flecting feelings that she seldom talked about, but she had always been able to cloak her autobiographical subjects in a generalized public statement of experience that she shared with her contempo-raries. Those who knew her well had the clues to the private reality.

Both Longfellow and Holmes wrote warm letters of congratula-tion, which she prized. The book was well reviewed; a delighted Whittier wrote to Holmes, "Has thee seen Miss Larcom's 'Cape Ann'? I like it, and in reading it I thought thee would also. Get it and see if she has not a right to stand with the rest of us."[32]

Wild Roses received so much praise that she expected it to sell well, but she was disappointed to note that the second and third editions meant only between two and three hundred copies. "One certainly cannot live by 'poetry,'" she wrote Whittier ruefully.[33] Nevertheless, she was content with her life. She had proved she could earn enough money to live as she wished; while she would never be rich, she felt successful in the things that really mattered.

CHAPTER 12

Working Close to
the Margin

Larcom would later reject the word "career" when applied to her life.[1] It was too harsh and masculine a concept to suit the acceptable image of a woman poet singing her songs. Nevertheless, by 1880 she was certainly established as a working writer with increasingly professional attitudes, and her letters began to show a stronger interest in advertising, in reviews, in the appearance of her books, and in business matters generally. There were two reasons for her changed attitudes. She was no longer an amateur; writing had become the business of her life. Furthermore, she was dealing with a new publisher, whose methods forced her to act and think like a professional. When she returned from Bermuda in the spring of 1879, a major change had taken place: James R. Osgood and Company had become Houghton, Osgood and Company.

When Fields took over in 1864, his immediate moves were toward expansion—new authors, new editions, new magazines. The firm was secure enough to handle anything, and until his financial policies and ethics were challenged and his self-image damaged, he seems to have had no problems. Osgood had seemed a suitable successor to Fields, since he was charming and congenial, loved books, and enjoyed the company of authors, but while his style was similar, his capabilities were not. He tried to follow the same pattern, but what Fields could often do through sheer force of personality was beyond

Osgood. Almost at once there was trouble, and he divested himself of magazines instead of working to build up circulation. He seems to have been a very poor businessman; his focus on immediate cash rather than long-range planning led to shortsighted deals at the annual trade fairs.[2]

William Ticknor had liked doing business with a reliable printing company called Hurd and Houghton; when Fields took over, the business relationship ended: "Between Henry Oscar Houghton and James T. Fields there could be little sympathy. Fields, the senior by six years, of heavy build but a dandy in dress, genial, generous, relaxed; Houghton, taut, unpressed, guarded, imperious, forthright and implacable. Charm was one of Fields's stocks in trade; integrity was Houghton's. James T. had a short memory; Henry Oscar a long one."[3] The firm of Hurd and Houghton grew, created the Riverside Press, with its reputation for fine printing, and ventured into publishing. They published Gail Hamilton's *Battle of the Books* in 1869 and bought the *Atlantic Monthly* in 1873.

It is hard to imagine two more different and incompatible partners than Osgood the charming man about town and Houghton with his rock-ribbed Vermont integrity, his precision, his awareness that publishing was a business, all allied to his love for the appearance of a book as well as its content. Houghton was not often loved, but he was respected and trusted. He also had a talent for finding good men. The group that came into the new partnership with him included his future partner, George Mifflin; his literary adviser and editor, Horace Scudder; and his chief assistant, Francis Garrison, who had learned publishing by helping his famous father with the *Liberator*.

As anyone might have predicted, the partnership between Osgood and Houghton was fairly soon stretched to its limit and the firm was dissolved. Part of the separation agreement, in very simple terms, was that Osgood kept the books and Houghton kept the authors, assuming that they were willing.

From the first Larcom liked Henry Oscar Houghton, finding him on the whole easier to deal with than Osgood. He might be—and was—a hard businessman, but he was scrupulously honest and she understood his integrity and appreciated his forthright approach. She, unlike some of the authors, had no trouble deciding between J. R. Osgood and the new Houghton Mifflin company. Neither, for all his personal fondness for Osgood, did Whittier; both went with the new firm. William Dean Howells, on the other hand, stayed with Osgood; he resigned as editor of the *Atlantic Monthly* and was replaced by Thomas Bailey Aldrich.

One of Henry Houghton's first decisions was to move the company offices to Park Street. A newspaper account many years later described the "large and brilliant reception, with Thomas Hughes, author of *Tom Brown at Rugby* as the guest of honor. And among the other guests were included such great names as Longfellow, Holmes, Aldrich, James T. Fields, Horace E. Scudder, Washington Gladden, Charles Francis Adams, Judge Hoar and Senator Hoar, Elizabeth Stuart Phelps, Lucy Larcom, Mrs. A. D. T. Whitney, Sarah Orne Jewett, and Rose Terry Cooke."[4]

Larcom's account of the same event to Lizzie Pickard is more personal:

> I took a Pullman Car [from Portland],—only one person was in it besides myself,—and did not get very tired. But—the train did not arrive until half past one, and when I got up to 4 Park Street, having stopped on the way to leave my packages and buy a pair of gloves, it was perhaps quarter past two and Mr. Hughes had just left, so I did not see him. However, I had a very pleasant time, and attended to some little business-matters which needed seeing to, and met many very nice people. The greatest lions, however, had come and gone—Bjornsen, Holmes, Longfellow, and others. Your uncle was not there.

> The rooms were very pleasant, carpeted throughout with something that looked almost exactly like your parlor-carpet; the desks were all taken out, and there were only bookcases and refreshment-tables, the last very elegant. My bonnet looked as well as anybody's I saw, and my old gloves would have done well enough. But as I stayed and had a sort of private lunch with the publishers and Mr. Fields, perhaps the additional "style" was just as well. (Perhaps they invited me on account of my bonnet! Who knows?)[5]

It had taken a long time to develop the kind of professional self-confidence that would let her be comfortable in such a gathering. She had developed another kind of professionalism, too, the ability to ask for what her work was worth even if she had to clothe her requests, especially to friends, in layers of tact. When Samuel Pickard asked for a poem and offered five dollars for it, she wrote back that she would accept that sum, but, "If you were not editor of the *Transcript*, I should of course have no interest in sending anything there, as I receive usually from twenty-five to forty dollars for a magazine poem."[6] Since she continued to send poems, she must have received her price.

Besides reflecting her growing professionalism, Larcom's letters from this period showed her living the busy and varied life she wanted. She kept a fairly firm schedule, using the mornings to work on her writing, but her afternoons and evenings were full of activities. Occasionally she mentioned getting away from the city to rest her head, but her retreats were brief.

When she had gone to Bradford in 1873, time and distance forced her to give up her charity work with the North End Mission and the working girls' clubs. On her return to Boston she was prevented by time and lack of money from participating, although she did keep in touch with the girls' clubs. Occasionally she arranged that payment for a poem should go directly to a charity, but she could not often afford that loss of income. She was distressed at not making some contribution, and she and Brooks worked out a kind of individualized charity. Among his parishioners was an invalid girl named Elsie Ada Locke. Larcom interested herself in the child, visiting when she could, but more often writing long, friendly letters that tried to build up the girl's confidence and also to be as informative as possible. They are full of news, descriptions, and personalities, and range over many topics, from her belief that Wordsworth was the poet who "most deeply and truly understood woman at her best,—as God meant her to be," to a description of her first Watch Night service at Trinity Church (1880), to her pleasure at swimming in the waves at York Beach when she joined the Spaldings there, to an analysis of her niece Lucy, a Greek and Latin scholar whose life "has been one of sacrifice and hard work for her family's sake." The letters presented a kaleidoscopic view of her life, but they were lively and interesting, designed to make the invalid feel part of a wider world.[7]

Larcom's summer was the usual mixture of pleasure with friends, then privacy and solitude among the mountains; she joined the group at Bearcamp for as long as her hay fever permitted. Whittier was there, of course, with the Pickards, the Cartlands, and other friends. It was a very happy time—the last summer there, in fact, for only a few days after their departure at the end of September, Bear-camp Hotel burned to the ground and was never rebuilt.

The unusually icy winter of 1880–81 kept Larcom housebound for longer than she liked, but she had plenty of work to do. The *Atlantic* commissioned her to write an article about the Lowell mills, and for it she had to sort through both papers and memories. She was moved when a letter from a school in Kansas arrived that described the celebration of the state's twentieth anniversary, with her Kansas prize song as a feature; many of the students at the school were the children of former slaves. A legacy of two hundred dollars from a former student ensured her summer travel, and Whittier sent her a copy of his latest work, *The King's Missive*, which arrived just in time for her birthday.

Even though James T. Fields had not been well, his death in the spring came as a terrible shock to all his friends. Whittier, whose friendship with his publisher went back forty years, was shattered. His consciousness of mortality, his own years, and his fragile health pervade the letters he wrote at this time; they are full of his belief that he would not last much longer. Larcom reacted predictably, mingling her own sense of loss for this good friend with deep sympathy for Annie. She spent the month of June at Thunderbolt Hill: "Mrs. Fields is very brave and cheerful: she spends much of her time out among her flowers, and in looking over her husband's correspondence when she is in the house; and I write and read, and look out at the sea, which is all around us. Sometimes we walk or ride together."[8] In their conversations Larcom attempted to return some of the comfort Annie had given her when Isaac and Louisa died.

Before that visit she had stayed with Emeline (again living in New Hampshire) to plan her *Atlantic* article with her sister's memory to supplement her own. She had started the work with William Dean Howells, but while she was writing he left the editorship of the *Atlantic* and was replaced by Thomas Bailey Aldrich, whose ideas were, apparently, a little different. He wanted a more personal approach and made suggestions for changes in what she considered the final version. Eventually she wrote him flatly that she was not going to make any more changes, since she was tired of the whole thing.[9]

As much as she cared for the drama of the mountains, she could find beauty and significance in the quiet meadows of the Spaulding farm. She had always liked painting the unobtrusive small plants that grew close to the ground, and she found a moral lesson in these and the wildflowers of the apparently unproductive land. One of her poems about these barely noticed living things, "Fallow," appeared in the October 1881 *Atlantic:*

> I like these plants that you call weeds,—
> Sedge, hardhack, mullein, yarrow,—
> That knit their roots and sift their seeds
> Where any grassy wheel-track leads
> Through country by-ways narrow.

Man may tear down—"plough the arbutus from her hills, / Hew down her mountain laurel"—but nature responds by filling the seemingly worthless land with her own small beauties that, unnoticed and unwanted, are still God's creation and in the end will inherit the earth.

> Her wildwood soil you may subdue
> Tortured by hoe and harrow;
> But leave her for a year or two,
> And see: she stands and laughs at you
> With hardhack, mullein, yarrow:

> Dear Earth, the world is hard to please:
> Yet heaven's breath gently passes
> Into the lives of flowers like these;
> And I lay down at blessed ease
> Among thy weeds and grasses.

Nothing, in spite of finite human perceptions, is useless or unvalued in God's sight, no matter how small and humble.[10]

"Among Lowell Mill Girls" appeared in the November 1881 *Atlantic.* It was a nineteen-page article, a well-written and informative account of a time and place and her role in it. She stressed the good things and, predictably, the sanctity of work, not as doctrine but simply as a prevailing attitude. The article brought a number of letters from women who had themselves been in the mills and appreciated what she had written. She was pleased that

Hattie Robinson approved, and more than a little surprised to find her article taken seriously by groups interested in labor, social conditions, and women workers.

There were still, to her annoyance, letters about "Hannah Binding Shoes," generally asking for "facts"—who was Hannah and where did she live. Larcom's answers often held a note of flippancy, or perhaps boredom, as she not so patiently explained that there was no "original" for the poem, that Hannah could have lived anywhere along the coast, and that her story was a common one. Samuel Pickard told the story of an uninvited visitor to Amesbury (one of the Pilgrims) who rushed at Whittier, babbling his happiness at meeting the author of that great poem, "Hannah Binding Shoes." Whittier, hiding his amusement under his Yankee poker face, allowed the visitor to gush on, then simply said, "Then let me present Miss Lucy Larcom."[11] If the story in one of its many versions is true, then, judging from the fan mail, the visitor must have been in the minority.

Neither did Larcom enjoy the increasing number of requests for personal information, usually from editors of anthologies or biographical encyclopedias. Her work, not her life, was what mattered. Either she refused or she replied with a kind of set paragraph giving almost no details beyond places and work. It was a consistent attitude that she eventually explained to her publisher:

If you please, I don't want to be biographied and put into the "Thirty Portraits." . . . I do object to giving dates for several reasons, one of which is that I do not desire annual letters of congratulation or condolence, or birthday celebrations, which would only remind me of the neglects and failures of my life. Those anniversaries I prefer to keep in the silence of my own memory and conscience; they are far from being joyful occasions to me, and I do not know that I need give the public permission to force such reminders on me. . . . I do not in the least object to having it understood that I have entered upon what Victor Hugo called "the youth of old age," and am cheerfully looking westward towards a new sunrise. But I prefer to see it all through that *slight veil of mist which makes life, as well as nature, so much more picturesque.* I should not enjoy the mountains upon which I am looking today half as well, if I could see the milestones and the telegraph-poles and the rail-way-stations which I suppose cover their slopes. So please let the dear public have its illusions about me, until I am dead,—or leave it for me to write my own autobiography—when I am too tired and too old to do anything else![12]

She did admit, in response to another query, the personal nature of her verses. "I can read my own autobiography in them very well, and so can some of my friends who know me best. My impulse in writing them has been to set my life to music as best I could;—a life that has always had to be occupied with many things besides. In verse I have found the most natural and free expression of myself. I do not claim to have written much poetry; perhaps only some true rhymes."[13]

Whittier spent a great deal of time during the following winter in the city, and the two friends met frequently, usually at Mrs. Claflin's welcoming home on Mt. Vernon Street. No trace of the old mentorial attitudes remained. They were simply two friends who had known each other nearly forty years and had important memories in common.

"I have been busy, but in very discursive ways," she wrote Sarah Jane Spalding, who complained at not having seen or heard from her since Christmas. "Several opportunities came, to write to order for magazines or papers, and the earning of my daily bread is still the first necessity for me . . . I always feel compelled to respond to a proposition which says, 'We will give you so much, if you will do so much,' and I put letter writing and everything else aside, for business." The letter goes on to tell of going to Wellesley College with Mrs. Claflin and Mrs. Hemenway to hear Shakespeare readings, to the Chauncey Hall School reunion, and to see "the Greek Play—but I did not go to see Oscar Wilde. I thought he was not worth the effort."[14] There were, in fact, times when friends were almost too kind with their invitations to make long visits or, harder to refuse, to go to concerts, lectures, exhibits, and other social and cultural events. Larcom enjoyed all of them, sometimes to the point of neglecting her work when the wolf was not actually knocking on the door.

Spring brought two sad events, the deaths of Longfellow in March and Emerson in April. Loss of these giants seemed to change the face of the world. For their poetic colleagues at all levels there were

verses to be written. Larcom regretted that she had not known Longfellow better; he had often invited her to call on him at home, but
her diffidence about intruding on the great prevented her from taking the invitations seriously. At the time of his death she was com-
pleting a piece for *St. Nicholas* called "Longfellow and the Children," and she was able to incorporate a memorial into the ending.

Two of the "greats" had gone, but others remained; in June Harriet
Beecher Stowe celebrated her seventieth birthday. Instead of an
Atlantic dinner, the celebration was a lawn party at "The Elms," the
Claflin estate in Newtonville, where two hundred guests, including
the whole literary establishment, gathered to hear tributes read and
recited to the great lady. Larcom was present, of course, although she
found the crowds oppressive and spent as much time as she decently
could in the cool house, talking quietly with friends.[15] Whittier had
written a poem for the occasion, but as usual he got someone else to
read it.

After the reception Larcom went home to Beverly and prepared for
her summer travel, which ended in September at Saratoga, New
York, where she and Hattie Robinson presented papers on the mills
and the mill girls at the yearly meeting of the Social Science Association. Larcom enjoyed seeing the resort town and meeting the
members of the Association, including Thomas Wentworth Higginson, F. B. Sanborn, Clara Barton, and Maria Mitchell, and her presentation went well.[16]

When she returned home in October she found waiting for her a
copy of Elizabeth Stuart Phelps's new novel, *Dr. Zay*, sent by the
author. She read it at once, then wrote her appreciation, "But *Dr. Zay*
—I thank you very much for her. The book is one of your strongest. I
did wish she would not marry—just as everybody else does,—but my
theories of love lean over toward friendship so far, that if I wrote
novels, I suppose very few of my heroines would marry. I should have
too high ideals for them; and then I suppose they would all have
something of a 'divine chill' about them, as far as the earthly passion
goes. But 'Dr. Zay' knew herself, or *you* knew just how she would
feel."[17] Her comment reflects her concern over some of her nieces
who were in no haste to marry; she feared that they were following
her example, which might not be best for them. A woman with something to contribute to the world, like Dr. Zay (or Lucy Larcom) might
reject marriage, but most women would serve better by creating a
home and bringing up children.

Very often now she was asked to write poems for special occasions, and many of these requests were for hymns. Writing hymns brought little or no money, but they were easy enough to do, since her childhood memorization of so many had built the pattern into her mind, and hearing her words sung as part of a worship service was a great satisfaction.

There were several long-range projects ahead of her. It was time for another edition of that excellent seller, *Songs of Three Centuries*, for which she would do most of the work. The New York publisher Worthington was planning a book celebrating the thirty most famous women in America; Larcom was asked to write one section and to be the subject of another. Reluctant as she was to be "biographied," she agreed. She was assigned the life of Clara Barton, and her own story would be told by her friend Adeline Whitney. The title page announced the book to be an "authorized record of the lives and deeds of distinguished American women of our times," and the dedication honored women and the men who could appreciate the work of all people, regardless of gender.[18]

Larcom handled her assignment with care. After many letters, she had two meetings with Clara Barton, who had recently been appointed (by Governor Ben Butler) to head the women's reformatory at Sherbourne, Massachusetts. Her chapter is workmanlike, clear, and informative. The same cannot be said for the chapter about her, for Mrs. Whitney chose to emphasize her friend's "motherliness"—perhaps to get around those precise details that Larcom was so unwilling to give—and the result is overly sentimental.

While she worked on the Clara Barton chapter, she was looking over her poems again; her publishers had decided that it was time for a collected edition of her work. The new enlarged version of *Songs* took some of her time, but the steady income the book brought made work on it worthwhile.

Spring brought a round of visits to her friends while she worked on the Barton article and some poems. August found her in Maine, visiting the Pickards in their cottage on Peake's Island in Casco Bay before she went to the mountains. Whittier's group found a new gathering place after Bearcamp burned, a farm in Centre Harbor owned by the Sturtevant family. It was a quiet place between Lake Winnipesaukee and Squam Lake, with a view over the smaller lake to the mountains—near the spot where Larcom had her first sight of the distant White Mountains years before. The house was big, the cooking was good, and there were pleasant walks nearby; a huge pine inspired Whittier's poem "The Wood Giant." Larcom stayed there briefly, then went on to Mount Washington. From Summit House she sent a glowing report to Whittier. "The sky-scenery, especially, has been beyond anything I have hitherto seen. I came up in a sunset of bewildering splendor, and we had sunrises, Northern lights, the full moon, lunar rainbows, and yesterday the storm cleared off with a double rainbow that formed itself into a circle, almost, instead of an arch, in the center of which we saw the shadow of this summit reflected against the clouds, from the setting sun behind." She urged him to try to see the summit, explaining that the road up "is really no harder and no more frightful than coming up through the Notch, and the house is perfectly comfortable."[19] Whittier preferred staying south of the Notches, but he always liked Larcom's descriptions of the places she visited, just as she always liked writing or telling him about them.

The mountains usually gave Larcom health and energy, but in late September of 1883 she fell seriously ill. She was in Bethel, and either she got as far as the Pickard home before collapsing or they managed to get her from Bethel to Beverly. What the illness was is not clear; later she mentioned dysentery, fever, and spinal weakness in connection with it, and two years later said that she had had malarial troubles the last two years. Whatever the precise nature of her ailment, she was very ill indeed. As she began her slow recovery, the friends who feared for her life now began to worry about her future, since she would not be able to work for a while.

Whittier, always at his best when real trouble came to someone he cared about, set about soliciting contributions for her from their friends. One of them, Harriet Minot Pitman, responded willingly, but saw a problem: "I am very sorry about Lucy's illness, and am glad that you have taken the case in hand. I am happy to enclose a check for a hundred dollars. It seems to me very desirable that she should be taken care of now, and not to have to work or worry until she is fully able. I know that you will do what is wisest. How will you reconcile her to accept a gift.—She is very independent, and very proud."[20]

Whittier apparently made her accept the money by convincing her that it came from an anonymous benefactor.[21] "If I were not too weak to resist anything just now, or if I knew who it was whose kindness wakes my thanks and my rebellious pride, at the same moment, I might rebel," she wrote him. "I have never allowed myself to have any anxiety about money-matters, and indeed, have been able to work close enough to see the year's income before me, with a margin, and to keep out of debt, and have felt myself better off than most folks. . . . But words are of no use. I thank the givers for their overflow of friendly thought toward me, a thousand times more than for the money itself." With a touch of her old humor she went on, "To put me down, properly, Worthington's book has arrived, in which I am caricatured in a wood-engraving. I might have known it would turn out so."[22]

Whittier followed up the anonymous gift with a larger-than-usual royalty check, and Larcom, feeling stronger, replied, "I think your 'annuity' is more valuable to me than any other I am likely to receive, for it stands to me for the continued generosity and friendship of years. But I hope you have not given me more than what you judge a fair share of the spoils. I am glad the books sell so well—and for the check I thank you sincerely." The letter goes on to say that Maria Dowdell, now a doctor, had been to see her, and that writing still taxed her strength; it ends, however, with a burst of energy. "But what matters for personal ailment when the demagogue [Ben Butler] that disgraced the State for a year is made to go back to his own kind. I respect the manhood of Massachusetts as I feared it would not be possible to do again. It is my misfortune that my brother and nephew—in the house—are Butler men,—I am so ashamed that they are, I do not think it wise to agitate the subject at all."[23]

Even from her sickbed Larcom watched Ben Butler's latest activities. In the years after the Civil War Butler's flamboyant career flourished. As a one-term senator from Massachusetts he had pushed to impeach Andrew Johnson and served on the Reconstruction Committee that supervised the plundering of the defeated South. He tried seven times to be nominated or elected governor, and succeeded only when he turned his coat again and ran as a Democrat. Along the way he had added to his wealth and power; scandal clung to him, but nothing was proved. As governor he should have received an honorary degree from Harvard. The Trustees, however, refused to give it, partly because of their dislike for him and his ways, and partly because he had accused the Harvard Medical School of body snatching, a charge that dwindled away without proof but was not forgotten.[24] In November 1883 he was defeated in his try for a second term as governor.

Once Larcom was well enough to hate Ben Butler again, her improvement continued. The only work she attempted was a newsletter, called, appropriately, "Convalescence and Reading," in which she told of her pleasure in rereading Emerson.[25] She returned to Boston in December, aged by her illness; the rich brown hair was streaked with gray and there were deeper lines in her face.

Houghton Mifflin planned an illustrated catalogue of their authors; Larcom would have preferred to be left out, and she was insistent that if a picture was to be used, it should be only with her approval. The woodcut in *Our Famous Women* she considered a "frightful caricature" and felt that having another one "before the public" was "almost a matter of self-defense."[26] There were plans for a collection of her poems, which at first she envisioned as *Poems* and *Wild Roses* put together; she wanted to leave out *Childhood Songs* but to include the incidental poems from the *Idyl*. She also agreed, for fifty dollars, to do the Whittier Calendar for 1885, a small date book with suitable quotations from the poet for each day.

Larcom celebrated her sixtieth birthday with Lydia but was immediately back in the city, working busily though not happily on the calendar. Since there had been other Whittier calendars, she had to check to make sure she was not repeating quotes, and that took too much time. "I enjoy doing it," she wrote Frank Garrison, "but I think I should have declined had I foreseen how much time it would take. . . . The lady with whom I live has made two calendars (George Eliot) and she says she could not do one for less than a hundred dollars . . . I do not intend to retreat from a bargain made in my ignorance, however,—though I am not sure I can do the work in the time specified."[27]

Harriet Robinson sent a verse play to her friend with a request for honest criticism. Since her husband's death, Robinson had become active with suffrage and women's clubs and was writing for several papers. Larcom praised the play's "originality of the plot and of the idea," the "power of representing situations," and the "poetic force of much of the language." Over the verse she became businesslike: "What I should most criticize—just as I should if it were my own—is the rhythm; and on that account, I should not offer it for publication without careful revision. There are certain rules for blank verse which are even more strict than the rules for rhyme, though indeed, they are the same, as to intention. . . . letting it go as it is might kill it as a poem. I think good blank verse very hard to write, and my own frequent failures have made me study it the more carefully."[28] She had not forgotten the review of the *Idyl* or the failure of that book.

There were a few mild "malarial" attacks in the spring, and her latest living arrangement, a room in her brother Benjamin's house, was not working out well; her room and the house were "not at all comfortable, the noisiest possible, I think. It is a relief to go to the city and *rest*. Who would believe it?" she wrote Annie Fields.[29] Whether the problem at Benjamin's house was noise or Ben Butler, Larcom spent most of the spring in the city, finishing both the Whittier Calendar and the selection of poems for her book. She took treatments with "wet sheet packs to get the malaria out of me," and particularly enjoyed meeting friends and sitting or strolling in the Public Gardens, which seemed lovelier each spring.[30] Once her work was done, she and Abby Johnson left for a tour of Nova Scotia. They sailed from Boston to Halifax, then traveled by train across the province, lingering in the Evangeline country and sailing on Minas Basin. They came home from Digby, stopping over at Bar Harbor; at Portland Miss Johnson went on to Boston while Larcom headed for Bethel and work.

She stayed in the mountains through October, returning in time for the appearance of *Larcom's Poetical Works* early in November. The book was far more ambitious than her original concept; it contained nearly three hundred of her poems, grouped as "Earlier Poems," "War Memories," "Verses for Occasions," "Childhood Songs," "Wild Roses of Cape Ann," and "Later Poems." There was a portrait with an autograph and illustrations; the cover had a laurel wreath and the lettering was in gold and black.

It was a handsome book and Larcom should have been proud of it, but when it arrived she sat down to write her indignation. "The outside startled me somewhat," she told Garrison. "I have never seen my name without a handle before, and I do not like the looks of it. . . . *Must* the whole edition go so? I should be content with either the 'Miss' or the 'Lucy' as you chose; but as it is it has a mannish sound very unnatural to me. You know women never call each other by their surnames alone—except in some rudely playful way, in imitation of their brethren. . . . I feel very much as if I were not wholly clad, without my prefix."[31] To Henry Houghton she wrote that the last name alone was "bad taste. It seems to class me among 'them literary fellows' but I do not want to be a 'fellow' at all."[32] Her protest was effective; later volumes were titled *Lucy Larcom's Poems.* Once the change was made, she could enjoy the first collected edition of her poetry and the good response from the public and reviewers that followed.

After another busy winter, she spent the summer with an artist friend in a cottage at Bethlehem, New Hampshire. Ellen M. Carpenter was an established painter who had studied in Worcester and Boston, then Paris and Berlin, and by this time was noted for her scenes of the American West and her portraits.[33] She was equally well known as a teacher, and it was her custom to take small groups of painting students abroad or to various locations at home. Larcom enjoyed being with such a group, and when she was not doing her own work, painted with them or visited with other vacationers. The cottage faced the mountains, and the studio and living conditions were attractive. She called on and walked with William Dean Howells and his wife, who were in the next cottage. She thought Bethlehem a very "public place," with a "good deal of calling and visiting going on."[34] From there she went to spend a week at her beloved Ossipee Park, then to Centre Harbor. She did not return to Beverly until mid-October.

In the spring she took a room in Miss Carpenter's apartment and studio in the Hotel Byron, a residential hotel on Berkeley Street. She was adding several artists to her list of friends, satisfying her lifelong love of painting and opening up still another world. Carpenter rented a room to two Boston University students, and Larcom enjoyed hearing about their studies and the difficulties of coeducation. Several of her former students who had married and settled in Boston sought her company and included her in more invitations than she could possibly accept.

Her room was within walking distance of Trinity; predictably, she began to study the history and doctrine of the Episcopal church. "A friend who has undertaken to Episcopize me," she wrote Mrs. Spalding, "has sent me a pamphlet . . . which strikes me as quite as good an argument for the Romish Church as for the one intended." No matter how her Congregationalist attitudes were offended by high-church lavishness, she was still drawn to Trinity, both by Brooks's sermons and her "increasing home-feeling in the worship at Trinity Church."[35] Her letter to Mrs. Spalding goes on to describe some talks on Buddhist theosophy she was attending, as well as the usual concerts, lectures, and visits.

When her publishers asked her to make an index of first lines for the new edition of her poems, she was able to reply rather crisply that she simply had no time, and if they wanted one, they had better get someone else to do it.[36] She could not take the time for something that would not bring any money, but she was now able to refuse without feeling that she was shirking her duty.

Her little devotional book of 1866 was still in print and continuing to sell, and Houghton Mifflin felt that another would be a good idea. Called *Beckonings for Every Day*, it was to be a calendar with a daily inspirational or thought-provoking message. The idea suited her; the work would not tax her health and the result would satisfy both her financial needs and her feeling of purpose and usefulness. Most of the summer was given to the book; a series of letters to Frank Garrison, her editor, show clearly that she had a precise picture in her mind of its appearance as well as its content.[37] She courteously but very firmly argued points like the title, the spacing and arrangement of material on the pages, the use of blank pages between months, and the undesirability of carrying a quotation over to a new page. Larcom, concerned with looks, and Garrison, concerned with costs, had some trouble agreeing. At one point Larcom brought in what she clearly considered to be a weighty argument: "That method of arrangement was the idea of Mr. Fields. . . . He thought it better taste to begin the page with a new paragraph when possible. I don't think it would have occurred to me, but I used to find that his ideas about such things were generally correct."[38]

The polite argument continued from Centre Harbor, where she stayed for a month, from Ossipee Park, from Bethlehem, and from various other stops in her three months in the mountains. By September she had read proof and sent it back with her corrections, only to be dismayed at the results, for the printers had not followed instructions: "For myself, I would rather not have my verses reprinted at all, than not have them as I arranged them. . . . I care *so* much, indeed, that, little as I can afford it, and little as I am to blame for the matter, I would rather incur the expense myself, than not have the verses changed back, at least in some important cases."[39]

Assertiveness won, and her letter thanking Garrison for making the corrections went on to another concern, ". . . the color of the bindings. I should much prefer some delicate tints—pearl grey, pale olive green, and very light brown or fawn color. . . . Nothing has been said about the price of the book. I hoped it would not be more than one dollar; still, we all want it to be brought out in neat and attractive style."[40]

This preoccupation with the appearance of her books was to continue for the rest of her life. Ironically, the sophistication in publishing matters and the necessity for taking control (even if through a kind of emotional blackmail such as her offer to pay for the changes herself—at a sacrifice) that Larcom showed must have been generated by Houghton; Fields the paternal would never have allowed his authors to worry about such things. If Houghton's authors had to be much more businesslike, however, they did know that he was scrupulous in his financial dealings. Too, Larcom's arguments for an attractive appearance were shrewd, for both Houghton and his partner, George Mifflin, loved a handsome book.

On the whole Larcom's efforts were successful, as was *Beckonings for Every Day*. Her friends liked it, it sold well, and buyers wrote her their appreciation and gratitude. The woods and mountains inspired poems, one of which, "The Wood Thrush," was accepted by the *Atlantic* (November 1886). Her success and her long stay in the mountains had their usual effect: she returned to Beverly in the autumn of 1886 in good health and high spirits.

CHAPTER 13

"A Delight to Live in this World"

A decade later, Larcom looked back on the period of her life beginning in the early 1880s and wrote, "I cannot tell you what a different world I have been living in for the last ten years. . . . Life grows larger and brighter every day."[1] Her success in managing her life and her improved health had much to do with her happiness; equally important was the support and encouragement of Phillips Brooks, whose high opinion of her work and contributions resolved any lingering doubts about religious belief or about the choices she had made. Yet her letters, especially toward the end of this period, reflect two attitudes: personal happiness and sadness at changes in her world.

One event in particular forced awareness of change. When she returned to Beverly in the fall of 1886 she found a town boiling with a small-scale civil war. In Larcom's childhood Beverly Farms had been an area of sturdy, hardworking fishermen-farmers; her own family came of such stock. A few wealthy Bostonians had bought land and built summer houses there before the Civil War, but their numbers increased afterward, and by 1880 some seventy "outsiders" had built summer residences.

Apparently the trouble began the year before with a proposal in Town Meeting to extend streetcars to Beverly Farms. A spokesman

from the Farms stated the Boston millionaires' ground for opposition: he feared "'Beverly citizens would avail themselves of a fine
ride and visit the beaches and drives' during the summer."[2] Beverly
citizens, needless to state, reacted with rage to the implication that
they might contaminate their own beaches.

From a public meeting came the suggestion that Beverly Farms
should incorporate as a separate town. Its supporters claimed that
the Farms was a rural area, while Beverly was becoming a busy shoe-
manufacturing center; that the Farms "natives" (most of whom by
now worked for the summer people) were so isolated that they could
hardly attend town meetings; that if Beverly became a city the
neighborhood would be ruined; that with separation the "native"
would have a lighter tax burden. Town spokesmen answered that the
distance was all of four miles, that a village of under two hundred
registered voters was claiming more than three quarters of the
town's seacoast, and that the separation would increase Beverly's
taxes astronomically. Their most effective weapon was the charge of
"tax dodging"—Bostonians paying taxes not in Boston, but in a place
where they controlled the assessment. It was a touchy issue all over
the state at the moment; Nahant, Milton, and others were held up as
horrible examples of towns lost to incomers. The legislature voted
down the bill for incorporation in March 1886.

The millionaires did not give up; instead, they began a campaign
to raise money and to make sure the next legislature would be in
favor of their bill. Newly elected members were invited for expense-
paid visits to the Farms; lobbyists were hired all over the state to
persuade legislators. Once again the bill came before the legislature,
and this time it had a great deal of support.

The Beverly group was taken by surprise when defeat of the first
bill did not stop the movement, nor had they anything like the financial resources of their opponents. As it turned out, they did not
need to do much, for the attempts at influence were so flagrant that
by spring of 1887 the bill was temporarily laid aside in favor of bribery and corruption charges.

Larcom had never liked what had happened to the Farms—familiar
land and the gorgeous seacoast shut away behind the walls of large
estates, and the roads clogged with summer people—but she had
friends among the summer colony, just as she had friends and relatives among the "natives." A John Larcom testified at one hearing; he

was supposed to show the rural nature of the area but was forced to admit that the only real "farm" left was a small part of one of the estates. Beverly people, if not as wealthy as their opponents, were certainly as well born, and they were disgusted at the snobbery and servility, as well as the ignoble methods, of the whole controversy.

Moving to Boston in December did not remove Larcom from the controversy, for what had been a local problem was now a statewide scandal. But she was glad to get back to the city; she felt well and her room at the Hotel Byron was bright with sunshine. It seemed that all of her friends were in town, and there were the usual activities that she always enjoyed. She was able to give time to the working girls' associations again, and every morning she attended the half-hour service at Trinity Church. At Easter she went so far as to take communion there for the first time. Whittier had not forgotten his efforts to ensure her at least minimal financial security. Drawing on his Quaker connections, he arranged with Philadelphia philanthropist George W. Childs to set up a pension of one hundred dollars a year for her.[3] With reluctant gratitude she accepted the money, which enabled her to stay in Boston longer than she had originally planned.

The report from the committee investigating bribery and corruption charges came back to the legislature early in May. While it did not charge bribery, it strongly condemned the methods used to influence legislators; nevertheless, the bill was passed and sent to the governor. Larcom could not stay detached. Her participation included attending some small meetings and the legislative hearings, but she was much wiser now than she had been twenty years earlier when she tried to lobby for Civil War veterans and instead ran in panic from the crowded State House. She contributed not active protest but the use of her name, influence, and pen. She wrote letters and articles for Beverly and Boston papers, helped draft petitions, and wrote to or called on friends who could help through their connections with newspapers and magazines. Samuel Pickard's *Portland Transcript* was widely read outside of its own territory; she felt that if he would "say a word in the *Transcript* to show what right public sentiment on such matters is, it will be valuable, as coming from an unprejudiced source."[4]

On 17 May Governor Oliver Ames vetoed the bill and condemned the means used; a week later the House sustained the veto. "I am so glad about the veto, I must say so to somebody. I feel more thankful than anything else, for I did not want any part of our dear old town to disgrace itself by the doings of its inhabitants," she wrote cheerfully to one of the leaders of the Beverly group.[5] Feeling well and triumphant, she began a summer of travel to some new places, including an exciting trip down the Saint Lawrence River to Quebec and Montreal, before she joined friends at Centre Harbor. Her last visit was to the home of Franklin Carter, now president of Williams College.

For all her triumph when the Beverly battle was won, in a longer view she saw what happened there as part of a larger movement that distressed her. The sordid behavior went beyond the town's still-intact borders; it was hard to maintain pride in the integrity of Massachusetts lawmakers after the influence of money was made so blatant. Ben Butler was not, after all, unique, only more clever than others equally willing to sell their honor. For one who could look back on the idealism of abolitionist and pre–Civil War days, one who remembered childhood stories of Revolutionary heroes like her own privateer grandfather and who had been held on her father's shoulders to see Lafayette, the fall was tragic.

She was aware of scandals in Washington, of the pervasive business morality with its greed and vulgarity. Brought up to believe in the sanctity of work, she was shocked by reports of labor unrest and events like the Haymarket riots. She knew that all these things went on elsewhere in the country, but, with her intense love for her own place, she did not want them to contaminate Massachusetts.

There were changes in Boston, too. Larcom had an adventurous soul and she was never opposed to or afraid of change in itself, but she saw both sides of progress. It was convenient for a tall, heavy woman to be mechanically lifted to upper floors in high buildings, but it was another thing to visit Elizabeth Whittier Pickard in the hospital where she was recovering from injuries suffered in an elevator accident. The new electric streetlights were brighter, but it was sad to lose the almost ceremonial lighting of the gas lamps at twilight. Less than ten years had passed since the members of the Arts and Science Society sat in the Athenaeum and heard music from Boston University (then just down the street at 18 Beacon) coming through Mr. Bell's new invention, but already one could talk from Boston to New York; soon people would have these instruments in their homes. Somehow the handwritten note seemed a more gracious way of communicating with friends. Emerson had been right: things were indeed in the saddle, riding mankind.

The physical changes in the city distressed her less than the intangibles, for she sensed with a bewilderment shared with others that Boston was no longer the moral, cultural, and intellectual center of the country, just as it was losing its role as the literary center.[6] If Boston was no longer exceptional because it had brought the world up to its standards, that was fine, but the unfortunate truth seemed to be that the city, and New England as a whole, was changing for the worse.

Even closer were changes in the literary world. Fields, Longfellow, and Emerson were dead, and the survivors—Holmes, Lowell, and Whittier—were old and fragile. The new realism of Howells and Twain, while she found it attractive in some ways, did not satisfy her standards of literary value: there was no moral message, no guide to what life should be. As early as the 1860s she had recorded in her journal her objection to poets like Thomas Bailey Aldrich, whose poems were beautifully crafted but lacked honesty and spontaneity and had no message that could inspire, and she repeated the thought years later. "But poetic feeling . . . seems to me at a low ebb," she wrote Harriet Robinson; "everything takes a materialistic turn."[7] Even the local colorists, like Sarah Orne Jewett and, particularly, Mary N. Murfree (who wrote as Charles Egbert Craddock), both of whose work Larcom admired, did not seem to her to carry their ideas far enough.

As for Walt Whitman, by Larcom's definition he did not write poetry at all. She saw *Leaves of Grass* in 1860 or 1861 and made one comment about it; when she and Harriet Robinson were discussing the design for a memorial for the latter's dead son, Larcom wrote, "I liked that hand and butterfly better than anything I have seen; my only objection to it would be the association with Walt Whitman's book. But very few would think of that."[8] At roughly the same time she made the journal entry that compared the occasional muddy bushes of medieval literature with blossoms that "were all canker-eaten at the heart, as in some modern gardens of literature."[9] While she does not name the canker-eaten gardens, the probability that she meant Whitman is strong; her reasons for finding his work unattractive are easy to discern and go beyond his open celebration of sex.

His glorification of the body, the self, and the physical world omitted the spirit and the way to God; there was too much earth and not enough heaven. His presentation of women, however strong and healthy, as existing to satisfy male needs and to bear children was the opposite pole from the view Larcom had expressed in the *Idyl of Work:*

> Human beings
> God made us, then he added womanhood.

Whitman's message was not poetic, and what Larcom, who enjoyed the tension between strict verse form and lively thought, would consider the formless and straggling mass of his work hardly deserved attention.

It was difficult to like what was being written and published, the poem that was beautiful in form but offered no inspiration, or the novel that presented realistic accounts of life but failed to lift and teach the reader. Sometimes even attractive work was hard to fit into her definition of literature. "I have seen Emily Dickinson's poems, and enjoy their queer gleamings and shadowy incoherences. It does not seem as if her mind could have been fairly balanced. But her love of nature redeems many faults," she wrote a friend.[10] Her comment is logical in the context of her society and her own work. Neither she nor her contemporaries were quite ready for Dickinson. Thomas Wentworth Higginson had praised Larcom's "Hilary" and "Skipper Ben," two poems in which sentimentality dominates, and it is difficult to imagine anyone who thought these were fine poems responding as we do today to Dickinson's work. (Perhaps we should give Higginson more credit than we do for seeing anything there at all.)

Larcom's comment was not unfavorable so much as bewildered, suggesting that she was attracted to Dickinson's poems but that the attraction was overwhelmed by what she called the "shadowy incoherences." Larcom's own contemplative poems lead the reader gently and smoothly to a conclusion and make use of a variety of strict verse forms; she, like even the most sensitive of her contemporaries, was unable to appreciate the demands that Dickinson made. What Larcom called "her love of nature" identifies what the two women poets had in common: a starting point in small, everyday, natural things. But while the ideas were often similar, the packaging was shockingly different.

As a professional writer who wanted her work published and paid for, Larcom stayed aware of the changing literary world. Sometimes she seemed to be caught between two elements that had once been fused and were now drifting apart: literature and religion. Her own kind of writing was slowly becoming old-fashioned, although her audience was still wide and faithful. She may have drifted into the position she finally took, but two letters suggest conscious choice. "I love to write and I suppose I shall go on trying to express myself in this way, always. The material fact that I have never earned more than enough with my pen than to meet, with difficulty, the necessary expenses of living does not in the least discourage me, or make me willing to write the trash that 'pays.' That is where I am now, on the literary question, and that is where I am content to remain,"[11] she wrote to Hattie, and in one of the yearly letters she still sent to Philena Fobes, "I have not suffered as many have—I have only had ordinary trials and losses and matter of fact struggles with circumstances, but I have often been in danger of succumbing to lower standards than I believed in. But it has been the one effort of my life to keep in sight the highest and best, and to be satisfied with nothing less."[12] Her decision was clear: she would continue to write as she believed, and, if she was ever forced to choose between literature and religion, she would choose religion.

Whittier was not changing, and although she had not been his protégée for many years, she certainly considered him the head of the literary group in which she belonged. She never objected to being classed with him, as she usually was, one near-contemporary critic claiming that she was the feminine of American literature as Whittier was the masculine, an evaluation that was essentially meaningless since neither term was defined.[13] Her work was like Whittier's, not because she echoed him deliberately but because they wrote out of the same tradition, values, and background. The village life she would describe in *A New England Girlhood* differed very little in its essential values from the farm life he described in *Snow-Bound*. If Larcom was becoming old-fashioned, she was doing so in the best of company.

Whether Whittier was aware of change is questionable; he was far more isolated than she, and by this time was so wrapped in venerability that only a fool or a brash westerner would dare negative comment. Several letters indicate that he saw himself, along with

Holmes, Lowell, and Longfellow, as forever set on the highest literary peak. "I have often," he had once written Holmes, "since I met thee in Boston, thought of thy remark that we four singers seem to stand isolated—set apart as it were in lonely companionship."[14] Although the letter goes on to say that fame is not as important as love, it reveals his sense of the poet's status and importance. His rather endearing arrogance certainly never conceived of time passing him by, and in one sense he was right, for during his lifetime neither his popular nor his critical rating changed, regardless of new literary trends.[15]

Although she still followed Whittier, it was with Phillips Brooks that Larcom discussed her problems and found reinforcement for her feelings. She continued to write hymns, and gradually her verses became more purely religious in their content. She found so much happiness in her own spiritual adventures that she wanted to communicate her joy to others. The change in her direction was slow and did not affect her finances as much as it might have. The magazines and newspapers to which she regularly submitted her work did use occasional religious material, though not as much as the purely religious papers; the latter paid far less, however, than the *Atlantic*, *Harpers*, *St. Nicholas*, or the *Independent*, and eventually her small income would have dwindled, but there were still commissions for work that she wanted to do.

Larcom's awareness of changes that she could not like did not send her into a state of melancholy or make her withdraw; she may have been unhappy over what was happening, but her personal life had never been richer. "I am not writing—or rather am not printing—as much as I did a few years ago," she wrote Susan Hayes Ward. "Somehow *living* itself gets so interesting I cannot stop to set it down in black and white. But that keeps finances low. . . . My health is better than for years, and I feel as if I were only beginning life, having found a glimpse into some of its secrets. Indeed it is a delight to live in this world and in these years of our Lord."[16] The experiment begun when she left Bradford had worked; her faith that God would provide her with opportunities proved to be true. Once she stopped worrying, her naturally cheerful temperament was again dominant. So, although she looked at the world and sighed, she remained happy; her personal joy and her sorrow at changes fused into a gentle nostalgia that was not a rejection of the present but a respect and regret for old values that were being lost.

As if to strengthen Larcom's feelings for the past, Mrs. Wheaton had asked her to accept a commission to write a history of Wheaton Seminary as part of its fiftieth birthday celebration. Since the *Our Young Folks* days when her life became so full, Larcom had made only brief visits to the seminary. It was delightful to go now and find that she was revered for her work, loved for herself, and that her connection with the seminary was a source of pride. Both the Psyche Literary Society and *The Rushlight* flourished.

While she was working on the sketch, she went often to Wheaton, planning her travel so that she passed through Boston on a weekend and could hear Phillips Brooks preach at Trinity Church. Unfortunately, the period was punctuated with bouts of the same "malarial" illness she had had in 1883, although never as severe. She grimly went to bed, then as soon as she could, got back to work again, trying to finish the *Semi-Centennial Sketch of Wheaton Seminary* in time for the Anniversary celebration on July first. The end of the task did not, however, mean an end to her visits to Wheaton.

The girls who greeted her with such love and respect were not, of course, her own students; they were a generation who had grown up reading Miss Larcom's poems. Her visits, very frequent after this, were great moments for the students, who combed the woods for wildflowers or autumn leaves to decorate the guest room for her arrival.[17] She gave lectures, but the girls remembered best that she joined them on their nature walks, calling attention to birds, flowers, and trees, and enjoying it all as much as they did. She sometimes conducted the morning devotional exercises, using New Testament texts, and there were talks with small groups of girls who never forgot her sincerity and her radiant face as she described her spiritual journey and her secure belief in a loving, personal God. The warmth and the joy she felt on these visits finally removed any darkness from memories of the years she had spent there. Once more Wheaton became part of her life, and it was an added delight when many of the "old girls" who had been her students arranged visits so they could meet her there.

The Wheaton Sketch had kept her busy for a year and paid well; she was working on a new edition of *Beckonings*. There were newsletters, lectures, and magazine poems for immediate needs, and friendly responses to her work. She was told that the critic Fitz-Greene Halleck preferred her "The Brook that Runs into the Sea" to Tennyson's "The Brook."[18] With a fair understanding of her own verse, Larcom thought the comparison flattering but silly. She found much more satisfying Adeline Whitney's use of "The Rose Enthroned" to make a major point in her latest novel, which concerned, among other things, the reconciliation of Darwinism and Christianity.[19]

New York editor and critic E. C. Stedman had written a book on American poetry in which he mentioned the "orchard notes" of Miss Larcom.[20] Her friends were indignant at the brevity of the label, but Larcom was not; she answered his request to use some of her poems in his forthcoming *Library of American Poetry* affirmatively, but added, "I would rather *not* have 'Hannah Binding Shoes' used as a specimen poem, unless the editorial heart is set upon it. I have so often wished I could get her away from her window!"[21] She thought either "A Strip of Blue" or "Climbing to Rest" (*Cottage Hearth*, February 1884) more characteristic of her work. She wrote a temperance pamphlet, called "The Cross and the Grail" (1887), at the direct request of Frances A. Willard.[22] *The Crystal Hills* (1889), a book of sketches of the White Mountains by F. Schuyler Mathews, contained three of Larcom's mountain poems and one of Whittier's. It was published by Louis Prang as an attractive gift booklet. Her Christmas poems for several Boston papers had become traditional. Letters praising her work arrived daily, and there were frequent requests for permission to use her poems in various collections as well as occasional proposals to set some of them to music. "Hannah" still brought appreciative responses and queries.

In the midst of all this activity she again turned her attention to the problem of a home. She had been living in a scattered way since she left Beverly Farms, with different boardinghouses in the city, long visits to friends, and rooms in family homes in Beverly. She had, in fact, almost lost track of several trunks and boxes of books and papers that awaited her in various attics. It was time to find a reasonably permanent center.

Both Whittier and Mrs. Spalding urged her to settle in Newburyport, where she had so many friends. Whittier was spending much of his time now in Amesbury or with his Cartland cousins, who had bought one of the big captain's houses on Newburyport's High Street. Mrs. Spalding wanted her closest friend nearby. Larcom briefly considered the possibility, but the distance from Boston was too great. She ruled out that city, too, telling Elsie Locke that there "I know too many people, and am too fond of seeing them, so that work gets neglected."[23]

In the end, to no one's surprise, she settled on Beverly. It had always been her legal residence, and it remained her home, even though it, too, was changing. Its cottage industry, shoemaking, had grown and generated factories; the population had increased, new homes were built, and there was talk about becoming a city. Nevertheless, Larcom's roots were there, and the town occupied a pivotal place in her divided existence, conveniently placed between Boston and the New Hampshire mountains. And, no matter how busy she was, she needed her family, both for security and for the nieces and nephews, and now their children, who took the place of the children she had never had.

Once before she had tried rooming in her brother's house, but the arrangement had not worked well. Benjamin's daughter Mary Abigail was a particular favorite, so Larcom again moved into the house, this time with more space and privacy, for she spoke of her "rooms" in the house where she had once had "a corner." She was busy for a while supervising painting, papering, and moving, calling in her scattered belongings, and finding "pictures, books and old tokens that have been packed away for years. It is both pleasant and painful to have one's life come back in this way."[24] In all her activity she was not too busy to remind Houghton Mifflin to advertise the new edition of *Beckonings* for the Christmas sales.

Her rooms became her legal home for the rest of her life, but she admitted to Sarah Jane Spalding that "I feel quite rich when I think I shall have a shelter of my own, though I may not use it much."[25] Boston still lured her; by the end of December she found that the house was too cold (she hated having to get up in the morning and make her own fire) and decided she really could not get things in order until spring. She needed to be in the city and announced her intention of shutting herself away from everyone to do some work. A confidential parenthesis in a letter to Mrs. Wheaton gives another reason: "Between ourselves, I will tell you that I have an imperative need of dentistry that will probably deprive me of my teeth, and make a hermit of me perforce for a few weeks. I begin to wish I had lost them *all*, years ago, since they would not last me as long as I needed them—."[26]

It was easier to find a place to live in the city. Miss Carpenter had moved to the Hoffman House, a residential hotel at 214 Columbus Avenue, and while she was in Paris, Larcom occupied her room. The choice was a happy one; the hotel became her winter home for the rest of her life. It was comfortable and convenient, and from its sunny bay windows she could look down the wide street to Trinity and the spires of the other Back Bay churches.[27]

The Wheaton Alumnae of New York planned a breakfast to honor Miss Larcom, and Susan Hayes Ward invited her to be a guest at the Ward home in New Jersey. She had been asked as well to be part of the celebration of Monticello's fiftieth anniversary; money to travel west was a problem, but the opportunity to do something for the school that had done so much for her and to see old friends at the same time was too appealing to refuse. She assumed that Monticello wanted a sketch similar to the one she had done for Wheaton.

Still more interesting was a suggestion that had come from her publishers. They were planning a new series of books called *The Riverside Library for Young People*, small, inexpensive books, but "exceptionally high order of literature, good English, interesting matter, by trained authors." Some of the books were to be "personal reminiscences, where the subjects treated are likely to be interesting to fresh young minds." They wanted Larcom to begin this part of the series, using her time in Lowell and "those other experiences which belonged to a New England country girl's home and surroundings. . . . you need not, of course make the book specifically autobiographic. The personal element would be valuable, but it need not be made unduly conspicuous."[28]

The request demanded a certain amount of consideration. It was sustained work and it was prose, which always called for more concentration and craftsmanship than did a poem, and she also had to ponder the problem of autobiography. How open should she be? There were no terrible secrets in her life, but she still found it unladylike to reveal too much personal information to the world. On the other hand, it would be interesting to write about her childhood, and her experiences might help young readers.

The visit to New York turned out to be far better than her expectations; the breakfast, with the chance to see so many of her former students and the sincere and loving tributes paid to her, made her both humble and happy. Staying with the Wards was another delight; although she had known Susie Ward since her first term at Wheaton, and though they had kept in touch in a friendly if irregular way, she had met the family only briefly before. Of course, she knew a great deal about William Hayes Ward, a Renaissance man who was an ordained minister, a teacher of science and Latin, superintending editor of the *Independent*, and a writer of poems, articles, and literary criticism. He was also a student of Assyriology, and a few years earlier had headed the first American expedition to Babylonia and Baghdad, sponsored by the University of Pennsylvania. He and Larcom were immediately compatible; in fact he was able to persuade her to write for the *Independent* again. She enjoyed talking with Ward's son, Herbert, and with a visitor, a young Middle Eastern student who, after he returned home, sent her the leaves of a willow tree from the banks of the rivers of Babylon.[29] The only unfortunate aspect of the visit was that she felt compelled to shut herself away for part of each day to work on her Monticello sketch.

At the end of April she left for the West. It was more than annoying to discover that Monticello wanted not an elaborate historical sketch but merely a poem.[30] The school had changed considerably since her time; it seemed to have lost its intellectual standards and to be little more than a popular finishing school. If she was disappointed in Monticello, however, the rest of the trip brought compensations. She saw her old friends Miss Fobes and Miss Eaton, both long retired, and, after so many years, Ann Spaulding and her family. From there, of course, she went on to Emeline's home in Minnesota, enjoying the "grand scenery of the upper Mississippi" again, and she rested "in what seems like an immense cloverfield. The air is sweet, and the horizon wide, and I enjoy the freshness and breadth of it all."[31] Best of all was being with her sister and seeing the children, now adults, once again. She and Emeline discussed the possible book and remembered childhood experiences and friends together; there was sadness, too, for Emeline and George were preparing to move to California to join Charles Spaulding, and Larcom doubted that she would ever see her sister again.

The poem she had written for the *Independent* was called "The Beckoning West"; the newsletter she sent back to the *Portland Transcript*, however, makes it clear that for Larcom the West had long since ceased to beckon. In fact, even with the joy of being with Emeline, she could hardly wait to get back home. It was nearly time for the mountains and she had decided to write the book that Houghton Mifflin wanted. With no pressure she could take her time and work at a slow, careful pace. She packed plenty of paper to take with her on her travels.

Again she discovered a new place to stay, and as usual had to tell Whittier about it. From Tip-Top House on Mount Moosilauke she wrote a long letter of description:

> In a howling storm which has encased the house with icicles and frost-fringes, and broken the telephone-wire so that we have no communication with the world below, I write down to you, because I want to tell somebody what a good time I am having, and how grand it all is.
>
> I have been up here one week today. I had a little suspicion of hay-fever hanging about me at the "Moosilauke" below,—but nothing of it dared follow me here. There has been every variety of weather, mostly warm and pleasant,—some days so still and sunshiny that it was delightful to sit or lie down on the brow of the mountain, and look away to the great northern and eastern ranges. We see them all, and I have learned to fix the places of the peaks, and call them by name. I do not believe there is another summit which is so good a point of view for the rest. The Franconia range is nearest and grandest, in the northeast, and the White Mountains, Mount Washington usually in a cloud, rise immediately behind. Ossipee Mountain and Lake Winipesaukee are prominent features in the southeastern view. We see them from the dining-room windows. Then in the west the lovely Connecticut valley stretches away to Camel's Hump in the Adirondacks.
>
> The clouds make wild work in the great ravines on every side of the mountain. I never saw so much wonderful cloud-scenery in my life before. I have stood right in the middle of a red sunset-

cloud and looked through it at the purple and crimson sunset lingering over Lake Champlain. It seemed so strange to be up in the sky, looking out at sky-scenery.

I could not begin to describe the beauty and the glory I have lived in this week; but I feel as if it had "struck in."[32]

The dark side of her love of openness and freedom is reflected in an earlier confidence to Elsie Locke: "I do not like lonely dreams, but I have a good many of them,—that is, I am alone in some great space, on some mountainside, or on the brink of a boundless sea."[33] This inversion of the things she loved is reminiscent of her comment years before that Emerson could lead one into lonely spaces with no resting place; it suggests that, for all her contentment, there were still moments of fright in her life and she still felt the need for balance and control.

Moosilauke was so beautiful that she stayed longer than she had intended, and after meeting friends at Centre Harbor she returned home to begin a very busy autumn and winter. With no deadline she frequently put planning and making notes for the autobiography aside for more interesting and immediate work (and income) and other activities. There were still hearings on the Beverly–Beverly Farms division and she, like others, wrote to friends and relatives all over the state asking their support and influence with their legislators. There were frequent meetings with Phillips Brooks. *Songs of Three Centuries* was to have a new edition, and she planned another devotional book. She wrote a favorable review of Harriet Hanson Robinson's suffrage drama, *Captain Mary Miller.*

Not until February did Larcom begin the first draft of her autobiography; Houghton Mifflin wanted it for the Christmas sales, and she was well aware of the advantage of that date. By August she was writing Horace Scudder "I am glad to have a little latitude with the book, for I find that my head will *have* to rest awhile. . . . I *am* interested in doing it, and I find that it will be somewhat locally historical. I begin to think that everybody's private history takes in the whole world." The rough draft, she went on, was "crudely completed, as far as I intended to go with it, but the final rewriting needs to be done with especial care, and not in haste."[34]

Once started, she worked lovingly and carefully on her rewriting; in November she was still reading proof, regretting that the proof-

readers "will have some trouble with some of the pages I have returned, I had to make so much correction of my own errors."[35] The
book was available for the Christmas sales, but barely.

A New England Girlhood, Outlined from Memory was and still is
an enchanting book.[36] In telling the story of her childhood, Larcom
could use her talent for creating pictures with words; her presentation of life in the second quarter of the nineteenth century is rich in
details that create a strong sense of time and place. On a personal
level, however, the detail is carefully controlled, so that the picture
is impressionistic rather than photographic. Earlier she had written
Henry Houghton that she preferred to see her life through the
"slight veil of mist" that showed the mountains but hid the telephone poles.[37] That feeling and the belief she shared with her contemporaries that biography, like any other kind of writing, was valuable only as it provided guidelines for others, certainly shaped her
own work. Comparison of the rough draft with the printed page
shows her concern to avoid revealing too much.[38] She cut the perceptive self-analysis bound up in her phrase "stillness and stir," an
essential clue for understanding her life, and she considerably soft-
ened her admission that what she really wanted most was freedom
to do the things she liked. She did not mention her long relationship
with Frank Spaulding at all.

Yet the veil fell selectively, modifying only what was too personal,
and much of what she re-created is vivid: the family life, the economy of a household, the character and life of the Lowell days all
seem very real. Most alive is the picture of a happy childhood, with
rules, constraints, and tasks balanced by love, security, and a
glorious kind of freedom.

> The cars rush into the station now, right over our riverside play-
> ground. I can often hear the mirthful shout of boys and girls
> under the shriek of the steam whistle. No dream of a railroad
> had then come to the quiet old town, but it was a wild train of
> children that ran homeward in the twilight up the narrow lane,
> with wind-shod feet, and hair flying like the manes of young
> colts, and light hearts bounding to their own footsteps. How
> good and dear our plain, two-story dwelling-house looked to us
> as we came in sight of it, and what sweet odors stole out to meet

us from the white-fenced inclosure of our small garden,—from peach-trees and lilac-bushes in bloom, from bergamot and balm and beds of camomile![39]

The same memory that generated the tasteless poem, "What the Train Ran Over," was much more lively and attractive in prose, just as the Lowell section was far better than the blank verse *Idyl of Work*.

Six chapters dealt with her Beverly childhood, five with Lowell, and one with the West. There was some attempt at disguise (Emeline became Emilie; Lydia, Lida; Louisa, Louise) and, most apparent when the book is compared with other sources of information, there was a definite glossing over of real pain—the death of her father and the terrible time in Lowell when she was so ill and unhappy. The whole Lowell section was affirmatively written, for her purpose was to show the importance of work, not just as a duty but as a builder of character and confidence in the young women who shared the experience. She talked very little about the West, but did include a description of Monticello and Philena Fobes.

Her publisher's suggestion had, in fact, come at the right time; part of the attractiveness of the book comes from that nostalgia that underlay her thinking, her own happiness combined with her sense of time gone by that could never be recovered. The result was a controlled nostalgia—not a simplistic urging to return to the past, but a looking back with love on parallel childhoods, her own and that of the country. Her earlier comment to Scudder that "everybody's private history takes in the whole world" certainly applies, for it was as much a time and a way of life that she chronicled as it was an individual experience. She tried to capture and frame a simpler world, and the result has the retrospective glamour of lost qualities: order, decency, and a balance of duty, work, and pleasure. Modern readers find the religious messages and the advice to girls difficult to digest, but the book is worth reading both for itself and for the social history it offers.

The book turned out to be longer than expected, and it was dedicated "To my girl-friends in general; and in particular to my namesake-niece, Lucy Larcom Spaulding." All the reviews were favorable, even the ones from New York, and it was sold out by the end of

December. Although it may have been written for young girls, it was read by both sexes and all ages; many of the letters she received came from older people who remembered similar childhoods.

The *Atlantic* praised the book both as social history and as literature, commenting favorably on her "honesty as well as her writing" and predicting "it will not be the young who will draw the greatest pleasure from the performance" (March 1890).[40] The reviewer for *The Nation* began with the statement, "It is difficult to convey by brief notice the charm of this simple autobiography of early years in New England," and then went on to summarize the content, deciding finally that the book was "healthy food" for the young (9 January 1890). *The Dial*'s reviewer clearly disliked what he called the ascetic, Puritan life that the author described, "But whatever may be the limitations of Miss Larcom's subject, her treatment of it is admirable. Nothing better of its kind has come under our notice than *A New England Girlhood*" (March 1890).

The book was a critical and popular success, but at first it brought little money, as Larcom ruefully told Harriet Robinson. "My letters are all full of compliments of *A New England Girlhood*, which has as yet brought me only about two hundred dollars. How can writers live by writing?"[41] But she was truly pleased with the response she had received, and the book continued to sell.

CHAPTER 14

Last Years

Although Larcom had originally questioned the idea of an auto-biography, she enjoyed the writing and was pleased with the result. She wanted to follow it with a sequel, a book about the prairie that would tell Emeline's story, but her publishers suggested that she wait. Her disappointment was eased by an attractive alternative. There were devotional books that she felt impelled to write, to share with others what life had taught her: that God is a loving presence and a friend, and that death is only the passage to a larger, freer, and more beautiful world.

Writing these three books dominated her life from 1890 to 1892, and they mattered immensely to her. She explained to Mrs. Spalding, "This and last year's little book seemed to insist on being written, and they seemed to put everything else out of my head. I have hardly remembered that there was such a thing to do as write verses. More and more I feel that I must follow such impulses, and not choose what to do myself, although other things might bring me more money. I want to give others the best that has come into my life—to make the entire result of living *count.*"[1]

Each of the three books that meant so much to her was dedicated to someone who had shaped and influenced her life. *As It Is in Heaven* (1891), her thoughts about life after death, was for "P. F. [Philena Fobes] the inspiring teacher and friend of my early womanhood . . . by her grateful pupil." The widening of her life, the sense of connection, her perception of all created things as one, the beliefs on which she constructed her life, all began at Monticello and had grown through the fearful, tentative hesitation of the Wheaton days to absolute security and joy.

The Unseen Friend (1892) was for Whittier; it was, she wrote him, "what the idea of Christ is and has been growing to be with me, as blended with the idea of the life unseen."[2] Later she added, "Through thee, my friend, I have come to see this [God as friend] very clearly. I have always thought of thee as a spiritual teacher. And then of late years to have had in addition the teachings and true friendship of Phillips Brooks has been a great and true help. I thank God that you two men live, and will always live—as he says to you—and that I have known you both."[3] Her dedication calls him the "Most beloved and most spiritual of American poets whose friendship has been to me almost a life-long blessing."

Everything about these books mattered to her, and once again there were many letters to her Houghton Mifflin editors about covers, styles of printing, cost, and advertising. One, to Frank Garrison, is typical:

I was in at Estes and Lauriat's after seeing you yesterday, and Mr. Sanford said he would take a dozen or fifteen copies of As It Is in Heaven, bound in morocco, for holiday sale. He thought the price rather high, however.

I made the discovery while there, that nearly all of Roberts Bros. little books, about the size of mine, are for sale in Morocco, this season, in style almost exactly like those I have had done "in brown"—limp covers, rounded corners, and title placed on the cover just as I have had As It Is &c. It almost looks as if they had copied that. The only difference I saw was that some had padded covers. The price was $2. or $2.50, and the shade of brown was exactly what I wanted for mine, but could not make the binders understand. Any of your people can see what they are, as 'E. and L.' had quite a display of these little books and DeWolfe and Fiske had some also.

Now if they have stolen my patent, which 'H, M' did not care to use, I think that at least my little books, Breathings, Beckonings, &c, should be obtainable in the same style. People want a handsomely bound book for a holiday-gift, and my friends have always said they wished mine were to be had in nicer binding. If it is too late to put them upon the market now, might there not be some ready for Easter and another Christmas?

As to my sense of color—isn't it just possible that, instead of its being an overplus in me, there is a lack of it in somebody or other connected with the binding-work? I am sure I do not wish to have less. Perhaps I should be a profitable person to employ as cover-critic. But I am afraid I should sweep away all those high-art designs that seem to me so weak and unmeaning, and should come down to the simple basis of plain lettering.

This is for yourself only: not a *firm* document.[4]

Her sense of need still drove her beyond her strength. During the fall of 1891 and the following winter and spring she had several bad bouts of the "grippe," which forced her to bed. As usual, when she began to feel better she rushed back to her work sooner than she should have.

Worship at Trinity Church was a vital part of her life, and Brooks remained a steady source of strength. She had first taken communion there in 1887, impressed by the minister's invitation to all people, whether members or not, to participate. Now she considered a major commitment, joining the church. The act could never be for her, as it was for some, a semisocial event; she had not been an active church member since she belonged to the little brick church on the prairie, and her hesitation was an indication of just how seriously she took church membership. Brooks respected her feelings even as he discussed the subject with her and argued the importance of being part of a church.

She joined Trinity Church on 19 March 1890. Her journal entry describes the event as quiet and undramatic, leaving her with a mixture of the "home feeling" she so often mentioned and a realization that nothing had really changed.[5] Her sense of beginning life again she credited to Brooks; when he became Bishop of Massachusetts in May 1891, she was glad for the honor and for his chance to spread his message over a wider field, but she was sorry he would no longer be her pastor. She predicted, correctly, that there would be fewer meetings with him, but she was happy when he called on Whittier and her two beloved friends met, and when he joined her on a visit to Wheaton and she could share him with the young girls there.

Busy as her life was, she managed to continue to see Hattie Robinson, Annie Fields, Mary Claflin, Adeline Whitney, and her artist friends, to get to know new people like Sarah Orne Jewett, whose work she admired, and to make frequent visits to Sarah Jane Spalding. She was actively involved again with working girls' clubs in Boston, her lectures, and the usual cultural round. Since the battle of Beverly she had stayed active in the town's Improvement Society, although she usually had to decline invitations to purely social events. The exclusively male Beverly Historical Society made her an honorary member, and she wrote poems for and attended outings sponsored by the Essex Institute. She earned just enough money to keep a comfortable balance in the bank and to follow the pattern she loved so well for her life: winter in Boston, late spring and early summer (wild rose time) in Beverly, and August through October in the mountains.

Although she concentrated on the devotional books, she accepted commissions when she needed money and the project was attractive, like her "In the Ossipee Glens" for *New England Magazine* (October 1892) or "Looking Back on Girlhood" for *Youth's Companion* (21 January 1892). *Songs of Three Centuries*, still a major source of income, went through an important revision; she and Whittier met several times during the winter, enjoying the work and companionship, with past troubles long buried.

She kept up with her reading and letter writing, although the latter was now restricted to dear friends and inescapable business matters. Many of her letters are retrospective, as if she was assessing her life and work; there is no suggestion in them that she regretted any of her choices. Some forms of looking back, however, annoyed her almost as much as the "Hannah" letters that still arrived. "And don't you think it is getting a little tiresome—this posing as factory girls of the olden time?" she wrote Hattie Robinson. "It is very much like politicians boasting of carrying their dinner in a tin-pail in their youth. What if they did? I declined having anything to do with Factory-Girls' Day at the Mechanics' Fair—because I do not believe in looking at them as a separate *class*. It is undemocratic. I am proud to be a working-woman, as I always have been,—but that special occupation was temporary, and not the business of our lives, we all knew, girls as we were. Classify people, and there is always a self-constituted higher class looking down upon them: there is the work-problem we are to meet—and the only meeting ground is a common human nature."[6] She may have meant her comments as a tactful warning, since Harriet was beginning to work on her book about Lowell, *Loom and Spindle*.

Even had Larcom been able to start the book she longed to write about the prairie, Emeline would not have seen it. She died very quietly one Sunday morning in July 1892. "It seems to me that her loss is greater than any I can possibly have," Larcom wrote to Harriet Robinson. "We were often writing to each other, and there never was any break in our affection, since my childhood. I think she was almost a perfect woman."[7] Still, the loss was easier to bear than many earlier ones had been; Larcom was sixty-eight and she did not expect to wait long to see her sister again. Her last book, *At the Beautiful Gate* (1892), contains about eighty-five poems, some collected earlier and some written since the collection of 1884. The dedication reads, "To my dearest sister Emeline, who taught my childhood to see that poetry and religion are one, I dedicate this collection of my songs and hymns, which has just missed her earthly approval."

By August Larcom had finished selecting poems for the book and was enjoying the breezes on the top of Mount Moosilauke. First newspapers, then letters from Gertrude Cartland and Lizzie Pickard brought news of the eighty-six-year-old Whittier's serious illness, followed by his death. She hurried home and stayed at Mrs. Spalding's for the funeral, a simple service in the Amesbury garden he had loved. There were four honorary pallbearers: Larcom, Mary Claflin, Alice Freeman Palmer, and Elizabeth Stuart Phelps.[8] A few days later there was a memorial service at his old home in Haverhill. The arrangements seemed perfect, just what he would have wanted. Larcom's faith made her loss temporary and bearable: "Now that he is released into immortal freedom, he comes closer to us all. I feel as if I knew him better, and he me, than we ever did. He makes the larger, better life of heaven more real to me," she wrote to Lizzie Pickard.[9]

With true New England caution, Whittier had never let his financial circumstances be known, and the size of his estate was a surprise; according to some accounts, it was more than one hundred thirty thousand dollars. He left Larcom five hundred dollars and the copyrights to their three books for her lifetime; the main part of his estate went to Lizzie. Larcom was grateful that she had been remembered, and wrote in a reminiscent mood,

I found it very pleasant to be at the old Haverhill homestead; it seemed as social and home-like as if *he* were there, too. He once took me there in a chaise from Haverhill, many years ago.—I have dreamed of him lately, sitting by the fireside chatting in the old way, as when I used to visit him and Aunt Lizzie. She was more to me than almost any friend,—more even than he. I always thought of them as one—and now they are together again. They cannot be far away. I want to keep near them in spirit, so as to find them at once by and by.—I am glad I did not even know that he was rich. He used to want to pay my bills when we were at West Ossipee, etc., but I declined, for I supposed he was almost as poor as myself—though I know that of late years his books have paid well. I am very glad he left me the copyrights of the books I compiled with him and indeed, it was only right, as I worked hard on them. The *Songs of Three Centuries* nearly cost me my health, the publishers rushed it so. I was good for nothing for three or four years after, as far as writing went. But he never knew the cause,—He was one of the exceptional cases among writers, of making money by his books. I gave up the attempt long ago, and made up my mind to write what would help others in some way, without much pecuniary reward. And I have been happy in doing so, for I have had large returns in gratitude and love.[10]

Samuel Pickard was Whittier's literary executor, charged with the responsibility of arranging for an authorized biography. He seems to have asked Larcom to write it, but she refused, partly because of her health and partly because, as she explained, "Mr. Whittier many times said to me apparently in earnest and jest both—'Don't *thee* ever go to writing about me!' It used to hurt me a little, as if I would parade his friendship in any way! I could not do after he died what I would not when he was alive—unless I knew he was willing—and he never hinted any wish of the kind, certainly. I have already been asked to furnish 'Recollections' for two periodicals, and have declined."[11]

She thought Pickard should write the biography himself and offered her help and advice. "I think Mr. Whittier had a wish that just a straight-forward story would be written about him, the plain facts of his life, and put the material into your hands as the person he could be surest of, just to tell the truth. He may have feared that his women-friends idealized him too much,—and some of his men-friends, too. At any rate, he did want you to write his life, and he knew you so well that he knew just what to expect of you. I think he was wise in his choice, and the book will be better for being entirely yours."[12]

She lent Pickard the letters she had at hand and promised him others, but requested that anything of hers be returned to her. She was especially concerned about the verse letters she and Whittier used to amuse each other with, and repeated an earlier caution: "He called forth such warmth of feeling from us who knew him well, the expression of our feelings might not always be understood by strangers. I think I could never have copied from his letters to me in the way Mrs. E. S. Ward [Elizabeth Stuart Phelps] has done in the *Century*. . . . But it makes an interesting paper—and scores of women could doubtless furnish one equally interesting if they had her gift, for we all know how enthusiastic he was in his attachments to his women-friends—and also how impartial." She added, apparently in answer to a question, "It is strange about those mistakes as to dates. I fancy he was not very accurate in such matters. It seems to me that the dates given to some of his poems by himself must be wrong—as I recall them."[13]

Although Larcom was pleased to think she could be of some use, there was little chance of her active help with the Whittier biography. Through the spring of 1892 she had been very tired. She felt no specific illness, simply a lack of energy. On her long visit to Wheaton in June the girls and some former students who joined her there noticed that while her interest and affection were as strong as ever, she needed more rest than usual. In the mountains she felt nearly well, but in October her tiredness intensified and she was very ill. "You know how hard I found it to walk up your hill," she wrote to Harriet Robinson. "The trouble has been increasing all summer—a severe cough was added, only now relieved, and for a month I have been shut into the house, doing nothing hard, and not allowed to go up and down stairs. The difficulty seems to be with the heart, and I am under medical treatment—improving, but shall always have to be careful about over-exertion of any kind. I am told to stop letter-writing, even. It seems strange to be so cramped, but I realize that though I look well, I have very little strength. Hard! when there is so much I want to do!"[14]

By the end of November she was able to go out but had been warned to restrict herself to moderate activity. She took time to sort through papers and letters, for so serious an illness made her think of what she wanted to leave behind, and she burned many of her personal papers. A few weeks later she moved to her comfortable room at the Hoffman House, where once again she was able to attend services at Trinity Church and see Brooks and other friends. There was business to take care of as well; she was trying, with Houghton Mifflin's help, to get some idea of the income from Whittier's bequest and her own work. The devotional books were the most profitable things she had ever done, and her *Breathings* and *Beckonings* were still in print and still selling well. It was important now to know what income she could count on, since she would not be able to work as intensely as before.

By the middle of January, however, she was again in bed; she wrote explaining her condition to Harriet. ". . . there is organic trouble of the heart, with both valves. The lungs and bronchial tubes are in wrong condition; I sometimes raise blood, and I have profuse local perspiration about the chest at night. In fact, I suppose I have been steadily 'running down' the last year or so, but have gone on just as if I were well. Now I am brought to a stop, and am told that I must never do any more *hard* work." She commented that the suddenness of General Butler's death was startling, but did not say that he would be a loss, and then went on, "Somehow I feel nearer Emeline and Mr. Whittier—as if we knew each other better now than before they went away. I should like to leave my life and work here, just where I can go on with what is waiting for me elsewhere, but there is a Master of Life who takes care of all that."[15]

When her serious illness was reported in the papers there was instant response. Letters and gifts poured in. Her family spent as much time with her as possible; they hired a nurse for her, and Emeline's daughter Lucy came to take care of her aunt. Mrs. Spalding wanted her in Newburyport and the family wanted her in Beverly, but she was too ill to be moved. Wheaton girls past and present were in constant attendance; if Larcom had needed proof that she was loved and that she had served others, it certainly came during her illness. They came to take care of her, to visit and talk, and to do anything they could for their beloved Miss Larcom, including taking over financial arrangements.

There was an epidemic in the city; Phillips Brooks, keeping his busy schedule, came down with what his doctors first thought was a cold, but which turned out to be diptheria. On 23 January, after an illness of only a few days, he died. Larcom was not unprepared for his death. A few days before he became ill she had had a "dream or vision" in which she was sitting with Brooks and other friends in a firelit room, when an unseen door opened. Brooks's face "lighted up as if in response to a greeting" and he got up and seemed to follow someone out of the room. "It was Whittier whom he saw," Larcom told her niece. "We didn't see him, but we knew it was he."16

After his death, Larcom seemed to loosen her hold on life. Her condition gradually worsened and she had bouts of considerable pain. There were days when she seemed to recover; on the eleventh of April Lucy Spaulding wrote a friend that she planned to take her aunt home to Beverly soon.17 The two women talked about the past when Emeline and Lucy were girls in Beverly and Lowell, or life on the prairie, for with Emeline's daughter Larcom could let her mind wander freely in the past. When she was strong enough, she went through old letters and journals, destroying everything left in her possession that seemed too private. Among the things burned were the journals from the 1860s and 1870s, with their references to Frank Spaulding and other too-personal matters. All her letters from Emeline went, and the younger Lucy promised to burn her aunt's letters to her mother.

Other times Larcom was nearly unconscious and seemed to be existing in a mystical world very near her beloved dead. Each period of recovery was followed by a worsening of her condition, with much pain at night, until it was clear that she was dying. She was not frightened. Whatever religious doubts had troubled her during her life were formal; she never for a moment questioned the reality of God or that she would see again all those who, according to her belief, had merely gone on before. Phillips Brooks, Elizabeth and Greenleaf Whittier, Emeline, Louisa, Isaac, and so many others— death simply meant that she would be with them all again.

Any regrets for the work she still wanted to do were canceled by her belief that God would call her where He needed her. She had been able to use her mind and her creative power in work that mattered because it brought comfort and inspiration to others. And she had experienced what few women of her generation knew: the chance to explore different worlds until she found the one in which she belonged. She could look back on a life that had been lived with intensity; if she had made some mistakes and missed some experiences, she had had so much that others were denied: recognition, dear friends, respect, and love.

Her last poem, "Dreaming and Waking," appeared in the *Independent* (13 April 1893); it affirms that one dreams "in vain / Of heaven" unless by "soothing human grief and pain" one has learned "That earth itself is holy ground."

From the fifteenth on, she was frequently unconscious. She had been reading a book by Phillips Brooks called *Perfect Freedom*, and in her semiconsciousness she murmured the word "freedom" over and over.[18] She died early in the morning of 17 April.

The death of Lucy Larcom rated headlines in Boston papers and notices in literary magazines and newspapers throughout the country. The *Boston Globe* called her "the best of our minor poets." After a simple but well-attended memorial service at Trinity Church, there was a quiet funeral at Saint Peter's, Beverly, for family and friends. She was buried near her sister Louisa in the Harrington family plot, not far from the spot where once a child went early one morning with a beloved older sister and saw the ocean as an immense blue wall. Her headstone is shaped like a writing desk, with a quill pen and her name and dates carved on its slanting surface.

Larcom left an estate estimated at five thousand dollars. Lucy Larcom Spaulding (Clark) and Harry Baker were her executors. The copyrights Whittier left her reverted to Elizabeth Whittier Pickard; Larcom's own copyrights went to Lucy Spaulding and her brother Theodore. She left three hundred dollars apiece to Lydia and to Benjamin's daughter, Mary Abigail; Octavia, Abigail, and Adeline were each left a hundred dollars.

Lydia survived her sister by three years; Sarah Jane Spalding, Harriet Hanson Robinson, and Adeline Whitney lived on into the early years of the twentieth century. Robinson's book about Lowell, *Loom and Spindle* (1896), has an affectionate tribute to her almost lifelong friend. Former and present students at Wheaton put together a memorial volume of *The Rushlight*, edited by Susan Hayes Ward, full of their loving memories and including information from Philena Fobes and Eliza Holmes. Mrs. Whitney published a small volume called *White Memories*, three poems as tributes to the three greatest human beings of her time: Larcom, Whittier, and Brooks. Beverly's Episcopal minister, Daniel Dulany Addison, rushed into print with a biography the following year. Her work continued to be read, reprinted, and anthologized. Undoubtedly the recognition she would have appreciated most came from the Appalachian Mountain Club, which recommended that a mountain in her beloved Ossipee range be named for her. Predictably, the mountain is close to Mount Whittier, but not nearly so tall.[19]

Her life can be summed up in two tributes, one private and one public. From Sarah Jane Spalding to Daniel Dulany Addison:

She was so loyal in her friendship, when once her affection was given neither silence nor absence weakened the tie, and the chances and changes of common society had no power over it. Immortality was real to her, and friends who had passed away she still held in the vividness and warmth of her interest. In this respect she was remarkable. Life to her was one—whether in the seen or unseen existence. It was life from God and with God. The kingdom of heaven was within her in a peculiar sense. This faith gave her the atmosphere of serenity which was so evident in her face, and felt in her whole presence. . . . Everything in literature which was good, and true, and beautiful she enjoyed, everything in nature, and socially she met and accepted persons at their best; petty and discordant subjects retired as something foreign and out of place where she was.[20]

From Justin Henry Shaw, in an article called "The Centenary of a New England Poet" in the *Boston Evening Transcript*:

This week came the one hundredth anniversary of one of the most beloved, and to me one of the best of our New England poets. Lucy Larcom of Massachusetts developed from humble origins to be in many ways a wonderful woman. She was first of all a young Lowell mill hand, then a bookkeeper in that mill, and for a while a pioneer teacher in the wild West, returning to be an important teacher in Massachusetts, and later an editor, writer, lecturer and religionist; and finally became one of a distinguished circle of a generation just gone.

Miss Larcom has been dead more than thirty years, and one imagines that her poems and some of her minor works must have been obscured by the present great output of so many publishers, and by the more limited interest in such books as she gave to the world, yet her work on the whole, and especially her poems, appears today, upon comparison, to have greater worth than heretofore, and to appeal more and more to those she probably intended to reach.[21]

Lucy Larcom's own assessment of her life and achievements would undoubtedly stress her religious contribution: her struggle toward a secure faith and her ability to use her writing to share that faith and to comfort and inspire others.

Distance changes the perspective. It is her courage and her life, with all its strengths, inconsistencies, compromises, and strategies, that seem admirable. She certainly had the career she denied, just as she achieved the autonomy and control that her standards, and perhaps her fears, never allowed her to admit she wanted. She was restricted by health, money, and conditioning; the two former were limitations both men and women might know, but the latter is specific, for she both upheld and evaded woman's role in order to go her own way.

She would certainly have denied her driving ambition and her quiet determination to be something out of the ordinary, to use her talent and her mind, and to live life more or less on her own terms. In her own way she expressed that Emersonian individualism that dominated her times, with boundaries and compromises determined by necessity and gender. She was neither an intellectual giant misplaced in time like Margaret Fuller nor a genius like Emily Dickinson, and she should not be judged against them. She was a talented and highly intelligent woman and writer who spoke for her time and who made the contributions she herself approved to the world she chose to live in.

NOTES

Libraries Whose Holdings Are Frequently Cited

BHS   Beverly Historical Society, Beverly, Mass.

BL   Beverly Public Library, Beverly, Mass.

BPL   By courtesy of the Trustees of the Boston Public Library, Boston, Mass.

EI   Lucy Larcom Papers, Essex Institute, Salem, Mass.

HL   By permission of the Houghton Library, Harvard University, Cambridge, Mass.

HN   By permission of The Huntington Library, San Marino, Calif.

MHS   By permission of the Massachusetts Historical Society, Boston, Mass.

RBH   Quoted by permission of the Rutherford B. Hayes Presidential Center Library, Fremont, Ohio.

SL   Harriet Hanson Robinson Papers, Schlesinger Library, Radcliffe College, Cambridge, Mass.

UV   Lucy Larcom Collection (7005-b), the Clifton Waller Barrett Library, University of Virginia, Charlottesville, Va.

WL   Marion B. Gebbie Archives and Special Collections, Wheaton College, Norton, Mass.

Introduction

1. Nina Baym, "Melodramas of Beset Manhood: How Theories of American Fiction Exclude Women Authors," *American Quarterly* 33 (1981): 123–39.

2. In *Whittier's Complete Poetical Works* (Boston: Houghton Mifflin, 1894) the poem is called "Eva." I saw the sheet music as part of a Victorian

display in the Essex Institute; the song is dedicated to Harriet Beecher Stowe and the music is by Manuel Emilio. Whittier rhymes Eva with "give her," "receive her," "never," "believer," and "river." He also rhymes "poor" and "shore."

3. Elaine Showalter, *A Literature of Their Own* (Princeton: Princeton University Press, 1977), 24.

4. Robert Penn Warren, *John Greenleaf Whittier's Poetry* (Minneapolis: University of Minnesota Press, 1971), 44.

5. Daniel Dulany Addison, *Lucy Larcom: Life, Letters, and Diary* (Boston: Houghton Mifflin, 1894), v.

6. Ann Douglas, *The Feminization of American Culture* (New York: Knopf, 1977), 230.

7. Addison, *Life*, 18.

8. WL, undated fragment.

9. Barbara Berg, *The Remembered Gate: Origins of American Feminism* (New York: Oxford University Press, 1978), 5.

Chapter One. Free as a Child

1. Lucy Larcom, *A New England Girlhood, Outlined from Memory* (Boston: Houghton Mifflin, 1889), 260 (hereinafter *NEG*). This autobiography is the major source of information for this section. It covers her childhood in Beverly and Lowell and gives some information about the West. "Recollections of L. L.," written for the *Lowell Offering* (1845, 211–16, 220–23) when she was twenty-one, treats some of the same material, but in a different manner; it has a youthful flippancy. I have modified some of her statements as a result of comments in letters written years later and directed to close friends rather than the public. Her notes and rough drafts of her autobiography, which are in the Beverly Historical Society and the Massachusetts Historical Society, have provided other information.

2. Information about the Larcom family comes from several sources: William F. Abbot, "The Genealogy of the Larcom Family," *Essex Institute Historical Collections* 58 (1922): 41–48, 129–50; Beverly Vital Records; Census figures for 1840–90; letters by and about Benjamin Larcom in the Beverly Historical Society and the Beverly Public Library; wills and deeds in the Essex County Courthouse, Salem; and books such as Edwin M. Stone, *History of Beverly, Civil and Ecclesiastical* (Boston: Munroe, 1843; reprint, Salem, Mass.: Deschamps, for the Friends of the Beverly Public Library, 1975); D. Hamilton Hurd, *History of Essex County*, 2 vols. (Philadelphia: Lewis, 1882); and Mary Larcom Dow, *Old Days at Beverly Farms* (Beverly, Mass.: North Shore, 1921).

3. Katherine Loring, *The Earliest Summer Residents of the North Shore and Their Houses* (Salem, Mass.: Essex Institute, 1932), 6. Reprinted from *Essex Institute Historical Collections* 68 (1932): 193–208.

4. For further information, see J. D. Forbes, *Israel Thorndike, Federalist Financier* (New York: Exposition Press, 1953, for the Beverly Historical Society).

5. Robert Rantoul's *Autobiography* is the handwritten story of his life (1778–1858). It has been bound by the Beverly Historical Society, which owns it, and is full of information, anecdotes, and the opinions of this leading citizen. He talks at length about Thomas Barrett (268–70), whom he admired. Larcom describes her grandfather, too; she dwells on his French charm, but she does not mention his four wives.

6. Barbara Welter, "The Cult of True Womanhood, 1820–1860," *American Quarterly* 18 (1966): 151–74. The description of women's voices (and lives) as "muted" comes from Edwin Ardener, "Belief and the Problem of Women," in *Perceiving Women*, ed. Shirley Ardener (New York: Halstead Press, 1978); see also Elaine Showalter, "Feminist Criticism in the Wilderness," *Critical Inquiry* 8 (Winter 1981), 179–205.

7. Larcom, *NEG*, 30.

8. Larcom, *NEG*, 117. The house on the lane, now Wallis Street, was replaced by a movie theater in 1934; after a varied history it is again called the Larcom Theatre. The section of town in which it stands is now heavily built up and bears no relation to the open fields that Larcom knew.

9. The miniature of Charlotte Ives Larcom Welch is in the Essex Institute, Salem, Mass.

10. Larcom, *NEG*, 125.

11. Larcom, *NEG*, 85–86.

12. Larcom, *NEG*, 42.

13. *Boston Transcript*, 27 July 1889.

14. Larcom, *NEG*, 106.

15. Larcom, "Recollections," 211.

16. This incident, like several others, is told in both *NEG* and "Recollections," 214. The youthful account has more detail and more humor.

17. Larcom, *NEG*, 48.

18. Larcom, "Recollections," 212.

19. Larcom, *NEG*, 128. According to the account of an anonymous Beverly citizen, when the house on the lane was torn down "hundreds" of her poems were found under the attic floor. Since she was probably eight years old when she left there, the number is unlikely.

20. The second house Larcom lived in is difficult to locate. It was probably the home of her grandfather Barrett, which was on Essex Street and had a

garden that bordered Central Cemetary. At the time Barrett was married to his fourth wife, who was not Lois Larcom's mother.

21. Larcom, *NEG*, 142–45. See also Edward Battis, "The Brig *Mexican* of Salem, Captured by Pirates, and Her Escape," *Essex Institute Historical Collections* 34 (1898): 41–63.

Chapter Two. The World of Work

1. A great deal of excellent research has been done on the Lowell mills and the mill girls. See Hannah Josephson, *The Golden Threads* (New York: Duell, Sloan and Pearce, 1949); Thomas Dublin, *Women at Work: The Transformation of Work and Community in Lowell, Massachusetts, 1826–1860* (New York: Columbia University Press, 1979); Philip Foner, *The Factory Girls* (Chicago: University of Illinois Press, 1977). Most useful to me was Benita Eisler, *The Lowell Offering* (New York: Lippincott, 1977). Contemporary accounts include Larcom's autobiography; her article "Among Lowell Mill-Girls," *Atlantic Monthly* 48 (1881): 593–612; and Harriet Hanson Robinson, *Loom and Spindle* (New York: Crowell, 1896; reprint, Hawaii: Press Pacifica, 1976). Robinson was a lifelong friend of Larcom.

I have given this section of Larcom's life no special emphasis; she herself got very tired of being labeled a "former mill girl," as if that were the only thing she had ever done.

2. Eisler, *Offering*, 15–16.

3. Eisler, *Offering*, 19–22.

4. Robinson, *Loom*, 58, 38. Robinson includes brief biographies of the young women she knew best, and her chapters 4 and 5, on the mill girls, are lively and informative.

5. Larcom, *NEG*, 117.

6. The section of Lowell in which the mills were located is now a national park; visitors can tour the mills and the area. Lucy Larcom Park is a small green oasis along a canal in the middle of the city.

7. Larcom, "Recollections," 213.

8. Harriet Hanson remembered him, too; always more outspoken, she named him in her book. See Claudia Bushman, *A Good Poor Man's Wife* (Hanover, N.H.: University Press of New England, 1981). This book has been very helpful, especially with information about William S. Robinson, although I do not agree with all of Bushman's interpretations.

9. Larcom, *NEG*, 154.

10. Emit Duncan Grizzell, *Origin and Development of the High School in New England Before 1865* (New York: Macmillan, 1932), 76–82.

11. Larcom, *NEG*, 166.

12. Robinson, *Loom*, 97–98.

13. Larcom, *NEG*, 182. The machinery, or its noise, is the only consistent complaint throughout her account of the mills; it is also the closest parallel to Melville's picture of factory girls. For the rest of her life Larcom hated noise, even locking herself away from the sound of Fourth of July firecrackers.

14. The logbook of Edward Harrington (1812–1844) is in the Essex Institute. He describes details of the voyage of 1840 in the brig *Oregon*, but much of the text reveals the young captain's longing for his wife and children and his ideals and plans for the future. After his text (and after his death) there are poems in a different hand, presumably Louisa's, and the first stanza of the hymn, "Come, Ye Disconsolate." The Essex Institute also owns Louisa Larcom Harrington's autograph album, dating from before her marriage and containing entries from family and friends. See also the article by George E. Brooks, Jr., "A Salem Merchant at Cape Palmas, Liberia, in 1840," *Essex Institute Historical Collections* 98 (1962): 168–74. The land Harrington bought, in back of the Beverly City Hall, is still residential, with several large houses on it. Thorndike's house, considerably modified, is now the city hall.

15. Larcom, *NEG*, 190.

16. Notes to *NEG*, BHS. The phrase seems vital to me in understanding her life and its contradictions, and I find it interesting that she chose not to use it in the final version.

17. Sarah Bagley and the very different mill experience she represents is briefly discussed by Eisler, *Offering*, 38–40; see also Josephson, *Golden Threads*, 199–203, 247–66; Foner, *Factory Girls* 53–73, 101–17, 165–68, 174–76; Dublin, *Women*, 114–25. Bagley edited a magazine called *The Voice of Industry* and was active in the Ten-Hour Movement; she was also the first licensed woman telegrapher.

18. Eisler, *Offering*, 36.

19. Robinson, *Loom*, 69–70.

20. Thomas Bender, *Toward an Urban Vision* (Lexington: University Press of Kentucky, 1975), chaps. 4 and 5.

21. Larcom, *NEG*, 226.

22. WL, 18 August 1841, and 11 February 1842.

23. It is difficult to tell exactly which children went to Lowell and which ones stayed in Beverly. The older ones certainly did not go, although Emeline joined the family later. Lydia and Jonathan seem to have been in Lowell but returned to live in Beverly. From available information, Lucy and Emeline were alone in Lowell for at least two years before Emeline's marriage.

24. Larcom, *NEG*, 240.

25. Philip James Bailey, *Festus: A Poem* (London: Pickering, 1839; reprint,

Boston: Mussey, 1845). I found *Festus* truly unreadable, but I am grateful to
it for generating a delightful piece of criticism. Robert Birley, *Sunk without
Trace: Some Forgotten Masterpieces Reconsidered* (London: Hart-Davis,
1962), sums up its wordy absurdity: when Festus marries, "Their brief hon-
eymoon of 2241 lines of discussion is interrupted by the end of the world"
(201). Passages quoted in the text are on pp. 178 and 206.

26. Robinson, *Loom*, 114–18, reproduces Clementine Averill's letter.

27. Several stanzas give the flavor of the poem:

> Oh, could ye have seen her—that pride of our girls—
> Arise and cast back the dark wealth of her curls,
> With a scorn in her eye which the gazer could feel,
> And a glance like the sunshine that flashes on steel!
>
> Go back, haughty Southron! thy treasures of gold
> Are dim with the blood of the hearts thou hast sold;
> Thy home may be lovely, but round it I hear
> The crack of the whip and the footsteps of fear!
>
> . . . .
>
> Full low at thy bidding thy negroes may kneel,
> With the iron of bondage on spirit and heel;
> Yet know that the Yankee girl sooner would be
> In fetters with them than in freedom with thee!

28. Quoted in Samuel T. Pickard, *Life and Letters of John Greenleaf Whittier*, 2 vols. (Boston: Houghton Mifflin, 1895), 291.

29. John Greenleaf Whittier, *A Stranger in Lowell* (Boston: Waite, Peirce,
1845).

30. Robinson, *Loom*, 109.

31. Foner, *Factory Girls*, xxii.

32. Caroline Kirkland, *A New Home: Who'll Follow?* (New York: Francis,
1839). Kirkland used the pseudonym "Mrs. Mary Clavers" originally. Eliza
Farnham, *Life in Prairie Land* (New York: Harpers, 1846).

Chapter Three. Living the Dream

1. The chief sources of information in this section are *NEG*, Larcom's
letters, and the poems and essays she sent to the *Lowell Offering* and various
newspapers. Her travel diary is in the Massachusetts Historical Society. The
issue of *The Rushlight* (the literary magazine she founded at Wheaton) done
as a memorial after her death contains reminiscences by friends from her
days on the prairie (*The Rushlight: Special Number in Memory of Lucy*

Larcom, ed. Susan Hayes Ward. Boston: Ellis, 1894. Trustees of Wheaton Seminary). Stephany Roller's "Lucy Larcom. A Portrait of Nineteenth-Century America" (Senior thesis, Wheaton College, 1962), has details of her life on the prairie and some pictures of the area.

2. Larcom, *NEG*, 263. Apparently George had bought the land before going west.

3. Wayne E. Fuller, *The Old Country School: The Story of Rural Education in the Middle West* (Chicago: University of Chicago Press, 1982), 40. See also Polly Welts Kaufman, *Women Teachers on the Frontier* (New Haven: Yale University Press, 1984). Some of the "shared experience" of Kaufman's first chapter is like Larcom's, but she did not go west sponsored by any group. She did share the "strong sense of mission and . . . romantic view" that Kaufman names as motivating forces (6).

4. Quoted in Addison, *Life*, 32–36. The letter is dated 9 June 1846.

5. *The Spaulding Memorial*, 2 vols., ed. Samuel Jones Spalding (Boston: Mudge, 1872) gives dates and facts about D. A. Spaulding and his family as well as about George and Frank Spaulding. All the relationships were very distant. S. J. Spalding's wife later became Larcom's closest friend.

6. Roller, "A Portrait," gives many of these details.

7. This story is told in an undated fragment in the Essex Institute. The fragment, part of a letter, was probably written about 1882 for Mrs. A. D. T. Whitney, who was writing a sketch of Larcom's life at the time. A poem, "The Negro Boy and His Spelling Book" (*National Era*, August 1849) was based on this incident.

8. Philena Fobes, *Rushlight*, 38.

9. Fobes, *Rushlight*, 36.

10. BHS, notes to *NEG*.

11. BL, 2 January 1849.

12. Correspondence after Larcom's death between her niece, Lucy Larcom Spaulding Clark, and her biographer, Daniel Dulany Addison, indicates that Addison made changes in his manuscript when George Spaulding objected to the way he was portrayed. He felt that Larcom's description of his "call" to the ministry sounded as if he was not sincere. Letters are in the Massachusetts Historical Society.

13. Larcom, *NEG*, 266–69.

14. Fobes, *Rushlight*, 43.

15. Eliza Holmes, *Rushlight*, 19.

16. Octavius Thorndike Howe, *Argonauts of '49. History and Adventures of the Emigrant Companies from Massachusetts, 1849–1850* (Cambridge: Harvard University Press, 1923), reproduces much of Isaac Baker's journal and gives information about this venture. The logbook of the voyage, kept by Joseph Carrico, is in the Beverly Historical Society. See also "California

Letters of William Goodridge of Beverly," *Essex Institute Historical Collections* 78 (1942): 376–86.

17. Howe, *Argonauts*, 97.

18. Howe, *Argonauts*, 130.

Chapter Four. A Separate Path

1. Information in this chapter and several following chapters comes primarily from Larcom's correspondence with Ann Danforth Spaulding and her sister, Rebecca Danforth. There are many of these long, detailed, and affectionate letters and I regret not being able to quote them more fully.

2. Larcom's letters to and from Henry Spaulding are in the Illinois Historical Society.

3. UV, 10 March 1851.

4. This advertisement ran in *The Congregationalist* throughout 1859. Similar ones appeared in other papers. Medical texts, such as Rene Dubos and Jean Dubos, *The White Plague: Tuberculosis, Man and Society* (Boston: Little, Brown, 1952), explain the disease and show the prevalence of forms of tuberculosis, but the advertisement gives the contemporary perceptions of scrofula. The folk remedy for the "king's evil" had been the touch of the ruler's hands.

5. UV, 5 April [1851].

6. BL, 11 June 1851.

7. BL, 26 September 1851.

8. Holmes, *Rushlight*, 18.

9. UV, 30 October 1851.

10. UV, 5 December 1851.

11. UV, Seminary, no date.

12. UV, 17 January 1852.

13. UV, 3 April 1852.

14. Nina Baym, "Portrayal of Women in American Literature, 1790–1870," in *What Manner of Woman*, ed. Marlene Springer (New York: New York University Press, 1977), 213.

15. UV, 5 April [1851].

16. I was not able to locate the original publication of this poem. It is in Larcom's third collection, *Wild Roses of Cape Ann* (1880). My guess is that it was written between 1870 and 1875, when she was writing about women, marriage, and herself. Several of the poems from this period appeared first in this collection.

17. To Mary Hall, MHS, 28 February 1890.

18. HL, 12 April 1852; UV, 3 April 1852; BL, 24 April 1852.

Chapter Five. Marking Time

1. EI, 10 January 1853.

2. John B. Pickard, ed., *The Letters of John Greenleaf Whittier*, 3 vols. (Cambridge: Harvard University Press, Belknap Press, 1975), 10 May 1849, 2:138–39. Unless otherwise stated, all Whittier letters quoted are from this text.

3. J. B. Pickard, *Letters*, 2:207.

4. It has not seemed worthwhile to argue points or make an issue of errors made by some of Whittier's biographers; many of these are tacitly corrected by my text. Generally, biographers have concentrated on their subject and made assumptions about other figures in his life, and errors are thus perpetuated. For example, most biographers give Whittier credit for arranging publication of Larcom's first book of poems. In fact, he arranged publication of the small book of moral essays, *Similitudes*, in 1853; her first book of poems was published fifteen years later when she was an established poet and a magazine editor working for James T. Fields. For the most part, biographers have assumed that only one kind of male-female relationship is possible: Whittier's protégées must have been in love with him. Few attempts have been made to examine the other side, the evidence from the women themselves. It has been easier to lump them together as would-be wives.

Even the biographers who write responsibly slight the personal identities of the women writers Whittier helped; Larcom, for example, seems to exist as the recipient of letters. John A. Pollard, *John Greenleaf Whittier, Friend of Man* (Boston: Houghton Mifflin, 1949), and Edward Wagenknect, *John Greenleaf Whittier: A Portrait in Paradox* (New York: Oxford University Press, 1967), are both creditable biographies. Albert Mordell, *Quaker Militant: John Greenleaf Whittier* (Boston: Houghton Mifflin, 1933), is so thesis-ridden that, in his efforts to prove Whittier a neurotic male coquet who teased and manipulated the women in his life, he ignores obvious facts. Larcom fares badly at his hands; Gail Hamilton is treated even worse, with less justification. For a useful survey of Whittier biographers and their approaches as well as an analysis of changing critical attitudes to his work, see Jayne K. Kribbs, "Introduction," in *Critical Essays on John Greenleaf Whittier* (Boston: Hall, 1980).

I have relied on two authorities: John B. Pickard's splendid three-volume edition of Whittier's letters with factual, temperate introductions to each section, and Samuel T. Pickard, *Life and Letters of John Greenleaf Whittier*, 2 vols. (Boston: Houghton Mifflin, 1895), and *Whittier-Land* (Boston: Houghton Mifflin, 1904). The latter's firsthand accounts are affectionate and undoubtedly subjective, but they are full of detail and anecdotes. John B.

Pickard's notes have saved me hours of time that would otherwise have been spent identifying Larcom's friends; I am very grateful.

5. To Esther Humiston, MHS, 1 May 1859.

6. UV, 23 September 1853, 12 January 1854, 15 May 1854.

7. EI, 10 January 1853.

8. UV, 14 December 1852.

9. The anonymity or pseudonymity of women writers has been discussed by several scholars; for an excellent account, see Mary Kelley, *Private Woman, Public Stage* (New York: Oxford University Press, 1983).

10. SL, 13 January 1853.

11. To Susan Hayes Ward, 25 August 1855, quoted in *Rushlight* (63); to the Robinsons, SL, 24 July 1857, 18 December 1857, 2 April 1858.

12. To Philena Fobes, EI, 8 May 1858.

13. Larcom, *NEG*, 65.

14. One woman at least did not feel that Emerson's thinking was only for men. In *Rose in Bloom* (Boston: Roberts Bros., 1876. Reprint. New York: Grosset and Dunlap, 1918) Louisa May Alcott has Mac present Rose with a copy of Emerson's *Essays*, 279–80. Alcott, of course, had grown up with these ideas.

15. J. B. Pickard, *Letters*, 8 July 1853, to James T. Fields, 2:221; and 3 September 1853, to Lucy Larcom, 2:233.

16. J. B. Pickard, *Letters*, 28 July 1853, 2:222–23.

17. UV, 15 May 1854.

18. Whittier wrote his account of the convention as a newsletter for the *National Era*, 15 September 1853; J. B. Pickard, *Letters*, 2:227–32. Larcom does not say whether she traveled with the Whittiers, but she probably did; Whittier liked to organize groups of congenial friends to vacation and travel together.

19. J. B. Pickard, *Letters*, 14 May 1854, 2:256–57.

20. I draw this conclusion from pages of manuscript in the Massachusetts Historical Society that are clearly the beginning of a story set in the West. It is undated and not identified in any way, but there is nothing in any other collection that seems remotely like the beginning of a novel.

21. UV, 18 April 1853.

22. UV, 23 September 1853.

23. UV, 17 November 1853.

24. UV, 12 January 1854.

25. UV, 15 May 1854.

26. Apparently doctors swarmed to the goldfields. According to Joseph Jackson, *Anybody's Gold* (San Francisco: Chronicle Books, 1970), 71, in 1851 the tiny mining town of Rich Bar had twenty-nine doctors.

27. UV, 16 September 1854.

Chapter Six. Life at Wheaton

1. *Rushlight*, 98–106. These accounts of her teaching are by former students; I have not given individual attributions, but have tried to summarize the memories and give a general picture.

2. Susan Hayes Ward, *Rushlight*, 85. The song was five stanzas long, written to be sung to the tune of "Nellie Bly." The first stanza starts off with patriotic fervor:

> Yeomen strong, hither throng!
> Nature's honest men;
> We will make the wilderness
> Bud and bloom again.
> Bring the sickle, speed the plow,
> Turn the ready soil.
> Freedom is the noblest pay
> For the true man's toil.
> Ho! brothers! come, brothers!
> Hasten all with me,
> We'll sing upon the Kansas plains
> A song of Liberty.

3. WL, 22 February 1855.

4. SL, 16 February 1855.

5. UV, 16 February 1855.

6. UV, 11 May 1855.

7. UV, 8 October 1856.

8. *The Congregational Year-Book* (Boston: Congregational Sunday School and Publishing Society, 1897) gives a record of George Spaulding's wanderings. He was in Genesee, Wisconsin, from 1854 to 1856; Hammond, Wisconsin, 1859–62; Marine, Minnesota, 1863–64; Eau Claire, Wisconsin, 1865–69; Depere, Wisconsin, 1869–70; Littleton, Massachusetts, 1870–71; Alstead, New Hampshire, 1871–72; Marshall, Minnesota, 1873–75. After that date he had no church but lived in Northfield and St. Paul, Minnesota, until in 1887 he and Emeline moved to California. He bought land in Beverly in 1859, and Louisa Harrington's will suggests that he had borrowed money from her. It is worth noting that for all his problems with his health he outlived both his wife and his sister-in-law.

9. SL, 14 June or July 1855. "July" is written with "June" above it.

10. *Rushlight*, 63; the letter is dated 25 August 1855. Several letters are quoted in the volume that do not appear in any of the collections.

11. BHS, manuscript.

12. Caroline Stickney Creevy, *Rushlight,* 91. The photograph is in the Essex Institute.

13. HL, 27 July 1855.

14. HL, 7 February 1856.

15. To reconstruct the Boston of Larcom's time I have leaned heavily on Walter Muir Whitehill, *Boston: A Topographical History* (Cambridge: Harvard University Press, 1959, 1968, 1979); and *King's Handbook of Boston* (Cambridge: King, 1885). I would like to thank J. H., whose love for and local knowledge of the best of cities added to my pleasure in finding Larcom's haunts.

16. HL, 16 June 1856.

17. SL, 9 July 1856.

18. J. B. Pickard, *Letters,* May 1856, 2:295.

19. WL, 2 June 1856.

20. HL, 16 June 1856.

21. 20 August 1856. Harriet Hanson Robinson's journal is in the Schlesinger Library, Radcliffe College, and was made available to me on microfilm. It is a delight to read for its author's vigorous personality, her love for her husband and family, and her comments on people and politics. The dates are probably approximate rather than exact, for she let her entries run on as long as they needed to, without regard for dated pages; often she wrote up a week or so at once.

22. There are several references to Thoreau in Larcom's letters to Harriet Robinson, who clearly looked on him as a restless and irresponsible wanderer, even though he was a boyhood friend of her husband. Larcom shared the joke until she read *Walden;* after that, although she admits that he is a "curiosity" (SL, 21 November 1856), her remarks show her interest and admiration. Apparently she never did meet him. Whittier's comments are in a letter to James T. Fields, J. B. Pickard, *Letters,* 14 August [1854], 2:267.

23. To Elizabeth Whittier, WL, 16 December 1856.

24. SL, 3 February 1857.

25. UV, 17 April 1857.

26. WL, 22 September 1857.

27. WL, 30 October 1857.

28. SL, 18 December 1857.

29. SL, 24 July 1857.

30. To C. A. Richardson, BPL, 21 April 1858.

31. Two of the poems discussed here, "White Sunday" and "Entangled," were not published in the *Crayon.* Written in her early years at Wheaton, often these poems were ways of thinking out her beliefs. Some, including "Entangled," were first published in the *Taunton Courier,* but she thought

enough of them to use them in her *Poems* (1868), where they were grouped under "Early Poems."

32. Larcom was always an omnivorous reader who turned to books for ways to think about problems. At this point most of her reading was theological; she found especially helpful the published sermons of F. W. Robertson, an English clergyman; another Englishman, F. D. Maurice, fascinated her. He was a controversial figure whose peculiar theology lost him his Cambridge professorship. His mystical vision of the church (all churches) as one divine family and of all things as signs and parts of God was branded heretical, but it either matched or clarified Larcom's views.

Chapter Seven. Esther and "Hannah"

1. Holmes, *Rushlight*, 23.

2. Larcom's letters to Esther Humiston are unlike anything else she wrote, even more internal than her letters to Ma and Becky. Chiefly they are about religion, both her exploration of her developing beliefs and her study of ministers, sermons, and theological works; they occasionally reveal her personal feelings about love, marriage in general, and marriage to Frank Spaulding in particular. Important as these letters are in revealing her conflict, they make very dull reading. She sometimes uses the kind of affectionate, even passionate, language that Carroll Smith-Rosenberg has pointed out as characteristic of some women's friendships, suggesting that women's lives were so circumscribed that their strong attachments were often to other women ("The Female World of Love and Ritual: Relations between Women in Nineteenth-Century America," *Signs* 1 (1975): 1–29). The two women met only once, but from that meeting to Humiston's death, her influence on Larcom was strong, if hard to understand.

3. MHS, 15 September 1856.

4. The poem was attributed to "Mercy More," a name given by the magazine.

5. MHS, 12 February 1858; also quoted in Addison's biography.

6. William Dean Howells, *Literary Friends and Acquaintance* (New York: Harper and Brothers, 1900), 123. The continuing popularity of the poem became a real source of annoyance. Thirty years later literary critic Edwin Percy Whipple wrote, "Again, some of the most popular and most quoted poems in our literature are purely accidental hits, and their authors are rather nettled than pleased that their other productions should be neglected while such prominence is given to one. . . . Miss Lucy Larcom, when she pictured 'Hannah Binding Shoes,' did not dream that Hannah was to draw

away attention from her other heroines, and concentrate it on herself."
Whipple, *American Literature and Other Papers* (Boston: Ticknor, 1887),
128.

7. The Beverly Historical Society owns the journal of Sarah Trask (1828–
92) whose story is similar to Hannah's. Larcom may or may not have known
about Trask; the situation was almost a sad commonplace. See also Mary H.
Blewett, "'I am Doom to Disappointment': The Diaries of a Beverly, Massachusetts, Shoebinder, Sarah E. Trask, 1849–51," *Essex Institute Historical
Collections* 117 (1981): 192–212.

8. UV, 10 May 1858.

9. Fobes, *Rushlight*, 44–45.

10. EI, 25 August [no year].

11. J. B. Pickard, *Letters*, 20 February 1857, 2:323.

12. MHS, 1 June 1858.

13. MHS, 2 August 1858.

14. MHS, 2 December 1858.

15. MHS, 28 February 1859.

16. To Sarah Jane Spalding, BL, 14 November 1892.

17. Justus H. Rogers, *Colusa County. Its History and Resources* (Orland,
Calif., 1891). The book is a record of the early history of the town and
county. References to Frank Spaulding and his brother Charles are scattered
throughout.

18. MHS, no date (Dear Esther, it is Sabbath afternoon again). Internal
evidence indicates that it follows a letter dated 28 February 1859. Many of
Larcom's letters after her return home sound as if she is almost ready to
rush to California. That impulse must have been checked by other factors
besides her own indecision; letters to Ma and Becky over this period tell the
ongoing story of "our relative, Mrs. Wilson" who had been west, came back
with great difficulty, then started west again. Her party suddenly disappeared, captured by the Indians, and, when Mrs. Wilson could not keep up,
she was killed (UV, 17 April 1857).

19. SL, 2 April 1858. Sargent's piece appeared in the *Congregationalist*, 23
April 1858.

20. SL, 4 October 1858.

21. SL, 15 January 1859.

22. Sarah Jane Parker Toppan Spalding (1822–1904) became the closest
friend of Larcom's mature years. She came from a well-to-do Portsmouth,
New Hampshire, family and was Samuel Jones Spalding's second wife. They
had three children, of whom Larcom was very fond. Spalding's letters show
her to be educated, well-read, and intelligent; she shared Larcom's religious
concerns and was a constant source of support. Both J. B. Pickard's notes
(2:335) and her obituary in the *Newburyport Herald* call her a writer, and

Pickard says she was a "former Brook Farmer." I suspect that she wrote for children and/or in religious papers, and her letters indicate that she reviewed books, but I have not been able to find definite information about her writing.

23. Robinson, *Loom*, 106.

24. William J. Stillman, *The Autobiography of a Journalist* (Boston: Houghton Mifflin, 1901), 228–29.

25. HL, 21 January 1859.

26. SL, 7 November 1859.

27. MHS, 18 September 1859.

28. Lucy Crawford, *Lucy Crawford's History of the White Mountains*, ed. Stearns Morse (1845, 1860; reprint, Dartmouth College edition, 1966; Boston: Appalachian Mountain Club, 1978).

29. Thomas Starr King, *The White Hills; Their Legends, Landscape, and Poetry* (Boston: Crosby and Ainsworth, 1868). Since this book came out the same year that Larcom made her first journey to the mountains, she may have had it as her guidebook. Certainly the ideas she held of the mountains parallel those presented in the book.

30. A. D. T. Whitney, *A Summer in Leslie Goldthwaite's Life* (Boston: Fields, Osgood, 1868), 63. Larcom met Whitney when this story was serialized in *Our Young Folks* while she was editor.

31. Larcom kept a careful accounting of expenses; in a small leatherbound book containing shopping lists and memoranda, she listed the train and stage fares and the hotels at which she stayed. Present-day travelers to the White Mountains will be interested to learn that it cost her, for example, fifty cents to stay overnight at the Flume House; the price apparently included meals. A journey of two weeks seems to have cost about twenty-three dollars. Her itinerary was the traditional White Mountain "loop," and she chose the best-known and most available places for her first trip. Later she sought out less fashionable places. The notebook is in the Wheaton College Library.

32. MHS, 11 August 1859.

33. MHS, 2 October 1859.

34. MHS, Sat. eve, October 1859.

35. MHS, 18 December 1859.

36. The journals from which I quote are at Wheaton; later ones are in the Massachusetts Historical Society. The volume dated 1861–62 has many pages torn out; volumes covering the later 1860s and 1870s were destroyed by Larcom or her niece because they were too personal.

37. Larcom, Journal, 21 November 1859. Anne Judith Penny (Brown), *The Afternoon of Unmarried Life* (New York: Rudd and Carleton, 1859). It is not at first easy to see why Larcom felt this book to be applicable to her own

situation. The English writer is talking primarily about the plight of a woman after her father dies and her brother inherits the estate. Its message, however, is that a single woman has a place in God's world and can find happiness doing her duty to others.

38. Larcom, Journal, 7 December 1859.

39. Larcom, Journal, 18 January 1860.

40. *Rushlight*, 104.

41. To Susan Hayes Ward, EI, 21 February 1859.

42. SL, 1 December 1859.

43. MHS, 25 September 1858.

44. From a talk given by Mary Larcom (Ober) Dow, the daughter of one of Larcom's Beverly Farms cousins, probably presented in 1934. Copies of the talk are in the Beverly Historical Society and the Beverly Public Library. This talk is the only place in which she or anyone else mentions Larcom's scrofula or its healing. Since Dow gives almost no details beyond saying that the healing occurred in Larcom's thirty-sixth year, I have tried to work out a kind of scenario based on what her letters show of her state of mind during that year. These indicate a severe attack of the disease shortly after her return in the fall, and that sometime during the late fall or early winter she probably went to the faith healer. She would not, of course, know that she had had her last attack, but beginning in 1860 her letters and journal entries, while they still show extremes, are not so tortured and neurotic. (She still had trouble with her head under stress.) I am convinced as well that the end of her correspondence with Humiston improved her mental health.

45. Larcom, Journal, 28 April 1860. Some of Swedenborg's ideas crept into the eclectic religion she was constructing for herself.

46. UV, 11 April 1860.

47. HL, 22 June 1860.

48. HL, 25 August [1860].

49. J. B. Pickard, *Letters*, 8 October 1860, 2:473.

50. MHS, 7 November 1859.

51. Larcom, Journal, 18 September 1860. Hints in her letters and journal suggest that among the "trials" was the necessity for close contact with someone who disliked and criticized her, probably because of her unconventional religious attitudes.

Chapter Eight. War

1. To Elizabeth Whittier, EI, 23 April 1861.

2. EI, undated fragment, probably for Adeline Whitney about 1882 when she was writing a biographical sketch of Larcom.

3. Larcom, Journal, 20 January 1861.

4. Larcom, Journal, 2 March 1861.

5. SL, 8 March 1861.

6. Larcom, Journal, 2 June 1861.

7. Catherine Drinker Bowen, *Yankee from Olympus* (Boston: Little, Brown, 1959), 164–74.

8. Larcom, Journal, 28 December 1861; emphasis mine.

9. Larcom, Journal, 11 January 1862.

10. Larcom, Journal, 5 April 1862. "Icebergs," by Frederick E. Church, attracted great praise in its day, then disappeared from sight. It was rediscovered in 1979 after hanging unnoticed for many years on an English wall and sold at Sotheby's for $2.5 million, at that time the highest price ever given for an American painting. See "A $2.5 Million Find," *Newsweek*, 5 November 1979, 115–16.

11. Larcom, Journal, 25 December 1861. Franklin Carter was roughly the same age as Larcom's nephew, Charles Harrington, whose "dissolute" behavior at the moment was causing his family much pain. Larcom even asked Whittier to advise her whether Harvard or Brown would better save a young man with wild ways. Her concern over Charlie's behavior and its effect on his mother is a running theme in her journal for several years, but no matter how worried she was, her ruling passion functioned. Her poem "Monica and Augustine" (*Congregationalist,* 4 February 1859) was an attempt to draw a parallel and comfort her sister by pointing out another wayward son whose mother's prayers were answered.

12. EI, 28 November 1864.

13. Larcom's journal suggests that there may have been a death in her sister Abigail's family as well.

14. Larcom, Journal, 4 May 1862.

15. Larcom, Journal, 4 August 1862. Carter had a distinguished academic career. He taught at Yale and became president of Williams College.

16. Larcom heard of the comparison thirdhand. According to Calvin Stowe, his wife said, "I am rejoiced that we too have a Mrs. Browning this side the water." Calvin Stowe told Sarah Jane Spalding, who promptly relayed the news, regretting that her duties as hostess at a dinner party for a group of ministers prevented her from further questioning (EI, 31 December 1861).

17. Clarke Historical Library, Central Michigan University, 5 September 1862.

18. Butler's mother had been a mill boardinghouse keeper in Lowell, but there is no indication that either Larcom or Hattie knew him then. William Robinson probably did. Information about Butler comes from Robert S. Holzman, *Stormy Ben Butler* (New York: Macmillan, 1954); Howard P.

Nash, Jr., *Stormy Petrel: The Life and Times of General Benjamin F. Butler* (Rutherford, N.J.: Fairleigh Dickinson University Press, 1969); and Margaret Thompson, "Ben Butler versus the Brahmins: Patronage and Politics in Early Gilded Age Massachusetts," *New England Quarterly* 55 (1982):163–86. His name recurs through Larcom's and Whittier's letters; for both he was a symbol of wrong and corruption.

19. HL, 24 November 1862.

20. SL, 4 December 1862.

21. SL, 28 January 1863.

22. MHS, 18 December 1862.

23. SL, 18 February 1863.

24. Oscar Laighton, *Ninety Years at the Isles of Shoals* (Boston: Beacon Press, 1930), 101.

25. MHS, 11 September 1863.

26. Frank Luther Mott, *History of American Magazines*, 4 vols. (Cambridge: Harvard University Press, 1957), 2:367–79.

27. Theodore Tilton accused Beecher of adultery with Mrs. Tilton. Beecher's church elders eventually acquitted him of the charge. For a full account, see Milton Rugoff, *The Beechers* (New York: Harper and Row, 1981).

28. Mott, *Magazines*, 2:146.

29. James C. Austin, *Fields of the Atlantic Monthly* (San Marino, Calif.: Huntington Library Press, 1953), 177.

30. Attempts to help and educate former or escaped slaves had begun before the war and continued as more northern-held territory allowed workers to go south. The program was supervised by the American Missionary Association; in Boston the Boston Educational Commission organized and recruited teachers and other volunteers. After the Emancipation Proclamation, efforts increased, and the project was institutionalized with the Freedmen's Act of 1865. See Joe M. Richardson, *Christian Reconstruction. The American Missionary Association and Southern Blacks, 1861–1890* (Athens: University of Georgia Press, 1986), and Jacqueline Jones, *Soldiers of Light and Love. Northern Teachers and Georgia Blacks, 1865–1873* (Chapel Hill: University of North Carolina Press, 1980).

Annie Fields's journal entry (27 December 1863) mentions Larcom's interview with a Miss Hannah Stevenson and says that Larcom thought going south might help her poems; Fields adds, "[she] possesses valuable ability and energy both of which will make her restless if not employed." The journal is in the Massachusetts Historical Society. Why Larcom was turned down remains conjectural. It seems unlikely that she really wanted to go; she may have seen the useful commitment as a way of improving her poems, but her subconscious reasons may have been based on a need to get

away from the sadness of the past year and the trap that teaching had become. Perhaps her ambivalence showed at the interview; it is also possible
that she gave Whittier's name as a reference and that he, knowing her state
of mind and her family's disapproval, did not recommend her.

31. EI, 28 November 1864.

32. The portrait of Elizabeth Whittier was done by an artist named Helen
Reed. After Whittier's death, Larcom did her best to make sure the portrait
went to Lizzie Whittier Pickard so that it would return to the Whittier
home in Amesbury, where it now hangs.

33. To Philena Fobes, WL, 10 January 1855.

Chapter Nine. Our Young Folks

1. I have used a variety of sources for information about James T. Fields
and the publishing house. See Austin, *Fields*; Ellen B. Ballou, *The Building
of the House: Houghton Mifflin's Formative Years* (Boston: Houghton
Mifflin, 1970); Warren S. Tryon, *Parnassus Corner. A Life of James T. Fields*
(Boston: Houghton Mifflin, 1963); Carl Weber, *The Rise and Fall of James
Ripley Osgood*, Colby College Monograph no. 22 (Waterville, Maine: Colby
College Press, 1959), and many articles about the Old Corner Book Store.
Each of these works presents a different point of view. I have tried to use the
information but to keep Larcom's perceptions of people and events when-
ever possible.

I strongly disagree with Tryon on two points. He says, "The running of the
magazine Fields left largely to its editors" (290). Larcom's letters do not support that statement, and Fields, I think, was too experienced to leave so
much responsibility in the hands of three amateurs. My own feeling, although there is no direct evidence, is that Fields kept control and that the
guiding spirit of the magazine was Annie Fields; her influence on that magazine and the *Atlantic* was strong. For examination of her influence, see Rita
Gollin, "Subordinated Power: Mrs. and Mr. James T. Fields," in *Patrons and
Protégées: Gender, Friendship and Writing in Nineteenth-Century America*, ed. Shirley Marchalonis (New Brunswick, N.J.: Rutgers University
Press, 1988), 141–60.

The interpretation of Whittier's letter that mentions the "lack of domestic peace" at the Fields home (7 February 1866) as "treachery that would
really have destroyed the Fieldses' happiness" (343) is clearly wrong. J. B.
Pickard proves Wagenknecht's contention that the letter was a private joke
(3:119, n. 3) by quoting a passage from Gail Hamilton; I would add that the
letter is precisely the kind of shared humor that Larcom and Whittier frequently used in writing to each other. It is clearly designed to be read to

Annie, and is the kind of straight-faced statement of the absurd that they would all understand.

2. MHS, 27 October 1864.

3. SL, 21 December 1864.

4. To Mr. Stoddard, EI, 20 July 1866.

5. Tryon, *Parnassus*, 290. The second comment is from Van Wyck Brooks, *New England: Indian Summer* (1940; New York: World Publishing, 1946), 50.

6. Letter, 2 November 1864, in *Gail Hamilton's Life in Letters*, ed. H. Augusta Dodge (Boston: Lee and Shepherd, 1901). Hamilton's letters were collected and published (and, I think, censored) by her sister after her death. Hamilton was a witty, intelligent, and fearless woman who never hesitated to say what she thought. She is also accused of being one of the lovesick ladies who supposedly haunted Whittier; Albert Mordell assumes so in spite of Hamilton's clear distaste for marriage and her disgust at what it did to women. She never became Larcom's friend, but was always on the fringe of her life since she was close to both Whittier and Sarah Jane Spalding. Hamilton admired Larcom; I suspect that Larcom felt some jealousy of Hamilton, not because Whittier was so fond of her (Larcom would have had to be jealous of a number of women in that case, many of whom were her close friends) but because Hamilton was free of so many of the conflicts and inhibitions that Larcom had to deal with in herself. Larcom could not approve the other woman's behavior, but I suspect there were times when she envied it.

7. UV, 6 April 1865.

8. EI, 19 June 1865.

9. J. B. Pickard, *Letters*, 13 June 1865, 3:94–95.

10. Robinson, Journal, 21 November 1865.

11. Robinson, Journal, 14 February 1866.

12. EI, 11 September 1866.

13. The book was first published as *Breathings of a Better Life* (Boston: Fields, Osgood, 1866). For the eighth edition the "of a" in the title was changed to "of the." A preface was added to the third edition (1879), which was described as "new and less expensive."

14. SL, January 1867.

15. For further information about Annie Fields and charity work, see Nathan Irwin Huggins, *Protestants against Poverty. Boston Charities, 1870–1900* (Westport, Conn.: Greenwood Press, 1971).

16. Rogers, *Colusa*, 102.

17. Robinson, Journal, 21 June 1869. The letter and the account in Hattie's journal do not quite agree; the letter does not suggest that Frank gave her alternatives. Since she eventually destroyed all his letters, there is no

way of being sure; it is possible, however, that she exaggerated the situation to Hattie because of her friend's insistence on the superior condition of married women.

18. UV, 21 September 1867. This is the last existing letter to Ann Spaulding and Rebecca Danforth, although I doubt very much that the correspondence ended. It had already grown less frequent as Larcom's life became busier, but she would not have chosen to lose these friends. She probably visited them when she went to Alton for the Monticello Anniversary in 1885. Unfortunately for the biographer, no other letters she wrote are as full of detail as these.

19. J. Warren Thyng, *Reminiscences of the Poet Whittier* (Manchester, N.H.: Granite State, 1908). A great many of the visitors to Bearcamp wrote about it, and there are references in Larcom's and Whittier's letters. The West Ossipee railroad station is now Mount Whittier station and is in the center of a ski area. No trace of the Bearcamp Hotel remains. See also S. T. Pickard, *Whittier-Land*.

20. Robinson, Journal, 10 April 1868.

21. Robinson, Journal, 16 December 1867.

22. J. B. Pickard, *Letters*, 22 May 1867, 3:153–54. Larcom's children's poetry was frequently anthologized and often appeared in school readers. It would be pleasant to think that a young boy who moved from California to New Hampshire in 1885 read the poem and shared the experience, then later wrote his own version. Robert Frost's "Birches," admittedly, bears little resemblance to Larcom's verses.

23. The members of the tribunal were James G. Blaine, Charles Storrs, and A. H. Rice.

24. Gail Hamilton, *The Battle of the Books* (Boston: Hurd and Houghton, 1869).

25. J. B. Pickard, *Letters*, 3:239. The date is 1870.

26. Robinson, Journal, 8 November 1868.

27. Robinson, Journal, 6 November 1868.

28. Larcom probably took over in November 1868 and held the position until spring of 1870. Trowbridge's name remains as one of the editors, and letters indicate that Larcom and he worked together during this time. Mrs. Cowles, a friend from Ipswich Academy, wrote her a letter of congratulations and hoped "that you will be paid just as a man who was as capable and faithful and did the work so well would be" (MHS, 13 November 1868). She was not; Howells, as assistant editor of the *Atlantic*, earned one hundred dollars a week.

29. HL, 6 November 1869.

30. Howells, *Literary Friends*, 124.

31. SL, 9 June 1869.

32. Larcom, Journal, 30 January 1860.

33. Mrs. Spalding, who had known Higginson during his brief stay as a minister in Newburyport, was not an admirer. She wrote Larcom, "How do you like Col. Higginson's story? I knew his habit of catching at folly as it flies, in the sense of trying to fasten himself on to it to mount into notice. Fourierism, abolitionism, table tappings and rappings (that 'rat-home revelation'), temperance—when it had a spasm of protest, women's rights, war—no matter what, the last monster out he has always saddled and rode, but I did not expect to see him aping French and fast things. Neither did I expect to see him overcrowd in this vulgar American way, which puts ornaments to nose, wrist, arm, ankle, waist, neck, anywhere to get them all on. It reminds me of a picture I saw lately of a little mill-stream where there were the beclouded sky, the distant hills, the greatest variety of trees, the running stream, the falling water, the mill, and on the banks of the river, regular beds of flowers. Can't these people tell us a bird sings without generalising, as birds usually do so and so and so and so? Don't they expect to live in any other state of existence when there will be plenty of space and time for all their wit without stuffing it in like sausage meat?" (BHS, 9 March 1869).

34. Robinson, Journal, 14 July 1868.

35. Robinson, Journal, 7 July 1871.

36. Robinson, Journal, 21 June 1869.

37. EI, 20 November 1868.

38. See Kelley, Private Woman, 280–84.

39. J. B. Pickard, Letters, 22 August 1868, 3:178. As many of his letters show, Larcom's were not the only poems Whittier "edited." Samuel Pickard tells the story of a poem sent to Our Young Folks about which Larcom asked Whittier's advice. He worked on it, then sent it back with a note, "I send 'Jack' in a new dress. Whose is it? The conception is so fine, some of its verses so good, that I have been tinkering on it, to get it into readable and printable shape" (20 April 1871, in S. T. Pickard, Life, 574).

40. Addison, Life, 68. The excerpt that Addison quotes is undated, and the original is not in any of the collections. I assume that it was written near this time because there are no more "editing letters" about Larcom's poems. She did, however, occasionally ask his advice about submissions to the magazine.

41. Rushlight, 30.

42. Faith Gartney's Girlhood (Boston: Loring, 1863) is listed by Frank Luther Mott, Golden Multitudes (New York: Macmillan, 1947), 307, among best-sellers for 1860–69, when the required sale for that category was three hundred thousand. Whitney published as Mrs. A. D. T. Whitney.

Chapter Ten. In and Out of the City

1. Dow, *Old Days*, 64.
2. SL, 5 December 1870.
3. HN, 23 December 1872.
4. EI, 12 January 1870.
5. EI, 12 April 1870.
6. William R. Alger, *The Friendships of Women* (Boston: Roberts Brothers, 1868). Besides glorifying the friendships of women, the book, in a way that must have shocked many readers, suggests that instead of women trying to be like men, men should try to achieve the womanly virtues rather than publicity and power.
7. The scandal caused by Harriet Beecher Stowe's defense of Lady Byron, in the August 1869 *Atlantic*, may have added to Fields's unhappiness.
8. See Weber, *Osgood*, for more information about the publisher and details of his business transactions.
9. SL, 21 April 1871.
10. EI, 15 Janauary [1869].
11. BL, 26 June 1872.
12. Mrs. A. D. T. Whitney, *The Other Girls* (Boston: Houghton Mifflin, 1873), 295. The disease of the horses was epizoötic distemper, called "the epizootic."
13. SL, 18 November 1872. Whitney uses the fire as a significant part of *The Other Girls* , and her descriptions of it and its effect on people living in the city are excellent. The plight of the sewing girls who lost their places of employment as a result of the fire is also incorporated into the book.
14. MHS, [1869?]. This letter is undated, but internal evidence places it in the autumn of 1869.
15. The letter book is in the Houghton Library.
16. Ballou, *House*, 172.
17. Pattee Library, Penn State University, 9 June 1871. My special thanks to Charles Mann, Jr., Rare Books Librarian, for his kindness.
18. HL, letter book, 6 January 1873. The date of the first letter is not legible.
19. Ballou, *House*, 172. It is quite possible that when Larcom and Fields made their arrangements, they decided that her salary should continue to be one hundred dollars a month, but that she would work at home while Trowbridge handled the office. There is no indication in her letters or her behavior that her income was suddenly cut. The business part of running the magazine never came easily to her; Annie Fields noted that, according to Mrs. Spalding, Larcom even talked in her sleep about the magazine: "'Mr.

Osgood has it I think or if not Mr. Clark one of the two.' I found her the first thing in the morning busied over an article she was correcting in proof" (Annie Fields, Journal, MHS, December 1869).

Trowbridge mentions Larcom only twice in his autobiography, *My Own Story* (Boston: Houghton Mifflin, 1908), and then as briefly as possible: he gives her name as one of the three editors and then says he replaced her. The autobiography, which has certainly colored my attitude toward its author, suggests that he alone was almost totally responsible for the success of the magazine, and that his work was absolutely first-rank literature; it also suggests a fairly inflated ego. Catherine Morris Wright, *Lady of the Silver Skates* (Jamestown, R.I.: Clingstone Press, 1979), in her biography of Mary Mapes Dodge, says Trowbridge answered a request "with customary spleen" (131). Her source is not clear, but I do not doubt it.

Larcom never indicated anything other than goodwill toward Osgood, but she was not a stupid woman and she must have been aware that Trowbridge could not force her out of the magazine unless the publisher was willing. In fairness to Osgood, he was in financial trouble and may not have realized what was happening. Or perhaps he sold the magazine to get rid of both his editors.

20. HN, 7 March 1873.

21. J. B. Pickard, *Letters*, 23 January 1873, 3:286–87.

22. HL, 23 January 1872.

23. Elizabeth Stuart Phelps, *Chapters from a Life* (Boston: Houghton Mifflin, 1896), 182. There are several versions of this story; the one in *Rushlight* (57) has Whittier saying "Lucy, if thee says another word till we get to the bottom of this hill, I'll never speak to thee again as long as I live."

24. *Independent*, 7 December 1871. In the early editions of *Lucy Larcom's Poems* (1884) this one reads "savage hands . . . with desecrating tread" (8–9). I assumed this was one of Larcom's occasional lapses, but a letter from Thomas Wentworth Higginson to Daniel Dulany Addison explains that "hands" was a misprint for "bands," which also went into Higginson's *American Sonnets*. Higginson says he advised Larcom to turn a longer original into this sonnet (MHS, 10 January 1894).

25. MHS, 25 July 1873.

26. HL, 8 October 1873.

27. J. B. Pickard, *Letters*, 8 December 1873, 3:310–11.

28. Jean Pond, *Bradford: A New England Academy* (Bradford, Mass.: Alumnae Association, 1930), 207.

29. S. T. Pickard, *Life*, 575. The letter is dated November 1871.

30. J. B. Pickard, *Letters*, 19 November 1873, 3:307–8.

31. There is no evidence one way or the other. Given the kind of life Larcom was trying to lead and her desire to hold on to what she had gained,

added to her past history of reaction to stress, her behavior can be explained in mental rather than physical terms.

32. I am grateful to Professor Joanne Braxton of William and Mary College for calling to my attention a local belief that Larcom did buy a farm in South Tamworth. A check of the property records of Carroll County, New Hampshire, shows that she never owned property there.

Chapter Eleven. Finding the Way

1. One of the features of the Authors' Room was an autograph book for the habitués. Stowe, Whitney, Whittier, Aldrich, and others wrote characteristic lines. Larcom's illustrates her kind of humor. The entry at the bottom of her page reads, "A woman shall not have the last word. / Samuel A. Drake," but under it Larcom crowded in, "But to me it has just occurred / This last line to take,—" and her signature. See Caroline Ticknor, *Glimpses of Authors* (1922; Freeport, N.Y.: Books for Libraries Press, 1972), 82–83; and Dorothea Mann, *A Century of Book Selling. The Story of the Old Corner Book Store on the Occasion of Its One Hundredth Birthday* (Boston: Old Corner Book Store. Privately printed; reprinted from the *Boston Evening Transcript*).

2. BL, 2 November 1874. I assume she did not write the piece for two reasons. I could not find it in the available copies of the *Daily Graphic* and *Hearth and Home*, although admittedly the runs are incomplete. Second, Larcom never talked or wrote about spiritualism; only faint hints suggest she may have had such an interest. Harriet Robinson's statement, quoted earlier, that Larcom had table-tipping power, is the only definite indication I have seen.

3. SL, 3 January 1875.

4. Stephany Roller, "A Portrait," shares my reaction to this poem.

5. SL, 7 February 1875.

6. It was probably about this time that she wrote "In Vision." "A Whisper of Memory" may have been written at the time of Frank's last letter to her.

7. "Among Lowell Mill-Girls," *Atlantic Monthly* 48 (1881): 593–612.

8. SL, 6 November 1875. Harriet Hanson Robinson's review article (*Independent*, 4 November 1875), while it supported and praised the *Idyl*, did nothing to ease Larcom's annoyance at the paper. It was about six years before she gave a poem to the paper again.

9. RBH, 25 August 1875.

10. J. B. Pickard, *Letters*, 22 September 1875, 3:339. The undated letter is given in the same place. I have assumed the undated letter is the second,

written because the first did not quite work. Neither of the participants in the near quarrel kept a record; my explanation is pieced together from hints and suggestions in Larcom's letters and confirmed by Whittier's.

11. Bushman, *Wife*, 138, says that Harriet completed and sold the book because of her urge for power. That may have been part of her motivation, but so, it seems to me after reading her letters and her journal, was her love and admiration for her husband. After his death there is a ten-year gap in the journal; when she begins writing again, her subjects are chiefly women's clubs and suffrage.

12. Richard P. Zollo, "Oak Knoll—Whittier's Hermitage," *Essex Institute Historical Collections* 117 (1981):37, says that Larcom did not attend the wedding because she was still angry. There is no evidence in her letters either way; her discomfort with Whittier does not seem to have affected her fondness for Lizzie. Later that summer the whole group gathered at Bearcamp as usual. It is quite possible that Larcom was simply too busy and too unwell to take time from her work.

13. S. T. Pickard, *Whittier-Land*, 114. Pickard describes the vacation at length (110–18). The verses quoted are from this text. Whittier's letters covering the same topic are in J. B. Pickard, *Letters*, 3:351–56.

14. Edmund Gosse, "A Visit to Whittier," in *Portraits and Sketches* (New York: Charles Scribner's Sons, 1914), 138–39. See Zollo, "Oak Knoll," for an example of the opposite view.

15. Mordell, *Quaker Militant*, says that Whittier deliberately set the dogs on her. He also classes Hamilton and Larcom as "Pilgrims," a term that Whittier used for admiring but annoying strangers who came uninvited to call on him.

16. EI, 18 April 1877.

17. HL, 19 April 1877.

18. SL, 31 January 1877.

19. Information about Phillips Brooks comes from Raymond W. Albright, *Focus on Infinity. A Life of Phillips Brooks* (New York: Macmillan, 1961); Alexander V. G. Allen, *Life and Letters of Phillips Brooks* (New York: Dutton, 1900); William Lawrence, *Phillips Brooks* (Boston: Houghton Mifflin, 1903).

20. Lawrence, *Brooks*, 23. Lawrence points out to "modern" readers that the public statement of this belief was a startling change, a "dispelling of darkness by the light of the rising sun" that brought hearers "relief, light, and exhilaration."

21. RBH, 26 June 1877. Some accounts written after her death make a pathetic picture of a homeless wanderer, but Larcom's letters do not suggest more than a mild regret and some annoyance at having to find a place for her

belongings. She had seldom stayed in the Farms during the winter and was always away through the autumn.

22. HN, 10 September 1877.

23. William B. Lapham, *History of Bethel, Maine* (Augusta: Press of the Maine Farmer, 1891), 196.

24. *Portland Transcript*, 9 August 1877.

25. To S. J. Spalding, EI, 5 December 1877.

26. Henry Nash Smith, "That Hideous Mistake of Poor Clemens's," *Harvard Library Bulletin* (Spring 1955): 145–80. The *Atlantic* dinners are mentioned in most accounts of James T. Fields as well as in Ballou, *House.* See also Arthur Gilman, "*Atlantic* Dinners and Diners," *Atlantic Monthly* 100 (1907): 646–57.

27. *Landscape in American Poetry*, illus. J. Appleton Brown (New York: D. Appleton, 1879).

28. This lecture is in the Wheaton College Library; others are in the Massachusetts Historical Society. One lecture, called "Woman as a Lyric Poet," avoids dealing with a near contemporary: "Margaret Fuller's verse was perhaps too much weighted with thought to be truly lyrical" (MHS).

29. To Elizabeth Whittier Pickard, HL, 2 February 1879.

30. See M. A. DeWolfe Howe, *The Atlantic Monthly and Its Makers* (Boston: Atlantic Monthly Press, 1919), 21–23.

31. William Winter, *Old Friends* (New York: Moffat, 1909), 122–23.

32. Addison, *Life*, 198. Whittier wrote this passage in a letter to Holmes, who copied it and sent it in a congratulatory letter to Larcom. Larcom and Holmes had been neighbors in Beverly Farms, but she was not especially impressed by the Autocrat, who, she felt, too often sacrificed feeling for wit.

33. HL, 21 May [1881].

Chapter Twelve. Working Close to the Margin

1. At the end of *A New England Girlhood* Larcom wrote, after disclaiming anything remarkable about her life: "In the words of one of our honored elder writers, given in reply to a youthful aspirant who had asked for some points of her 'literary career'—'I never had a career,'" (274).

Another mark of professionalism that developed about this time was her handling of fan mail. She had treated these letters as personal mail; now she answered most with a brief formula. She had pictures taken so that she could answer requests for pictures and autographs with a card giving the direction of the photographer and her signature. Requests for a stanza or a poem in her own handwriting she learned to refuse graciously but firmly.

2. For more details about Osgood's business dealings, see Weber, *Osgood*. His publishing house lasted for about five years.

3. Ballou, *House*, 47. See also Horace Scudder, *Henry Oscar Houghton* (Boston, Houghton Mifflin, 1897).

4. *Boston Transcript*, 14 April 1923.

5. HL, 22 October 1880.

6. HL, 24 September 1879.

7. BPL, 20 November 1879, and 6 October 1880. After the "Ma and Becky" correspondence, these letters provide the most detailed account of Larcom's daily life, although they lack the intimacy of the former. Locke treasured the letters all her life, eventually giving them to the Boston Public Library. Larcom and Brooks were able to interest friends in the child, and eventually she was informally adopted, possibly by the Sparhawk family of Newburyport.

8. To Elsie Locke, BPL, 28 June 1881.

9. HL, 14 August 1881.

10. "Fallow" (in her collected works this poem is titled "Flowers of the Fallow") is one of several poems on a thesis that recurs throughout Larcom's work: the importance in the whole universe of the small, inconspicuous things, whether plants or lives. One of these poems, "Fern-Life," is used by Cheryl Walker in *The Nightingale's Burden* (Bloomington: Indiana University Press, 1982) to support the "composite life" of women poets that she presents. Walker interprets the ferns as "images of women" and the flowers as men, admitting parenthetically that "some attempt is made to deflect this towards the human vs. the divine" (45). I must disagree with Walker's interpretation; the poem is about the place of all living things in God's universe, regardless of who they are or what they look like, and is an extension of Larcom's belief that all created things have God's spirit within them. Another poem, "Flower of Grass," directly compares a woman with the lowly plants; it ends,

> She was the flower of grass, that only stirs
> To soothe the air, and nothing doth require
> But to forget itself in doing good;—
> One of life's lowly, saintly multitude.

Larcom's concern with women and their place in society is consistently overshadowed by her interest in souls in relation to God.

Although generally I agree with what Walker is trying to do, I would be happier if her book were not so full of errors of fact. In the Larcom sections there are many: for example, Larcom's date of birth is wrong; Walker says that her father's death prevented her from attending secondary school (74), but her father died when she was seven, and it was her mother's inability to manage that ended her schooling; the poem that made her famous was "Hannah Binding Shoes," not "A Loyal Woman's No" (77); she did not become involved with the women's rights movement in any capacity (81); I have found no evidence that she felt "feminine betrayals" (85). Perhaps these are small points, but they tend to raise questions about the validity of the book and its conclusions. Part of the problem, of course, is the unreliability of the available evidence about Larcom and other women writers; the Addison biography, for example, is slanted to support its thesis.

11. There are even more versions of this story than there are of the one in which Larcom and Whittier are driving together, and there are more variants. The unfortunate speaker may be a naive young man, a pompous clergyman, or a well-meaning but silly elderly lady. In one, Whittier cannot bear to tell the earnest speaker that he is wrong.

12. HL, 17 September 1884; emphasis mine. Somewhere during this time two years disappeared from Larcom's age; many accounts give her birthdate as 1826.

13. WL, undated fragment.

14. BL, 10 February 1882.

15. Mary B. Claflin, *Under the Old Elms* (New York: Crowell, 1895), 55–62, 94–96.

16. Larcom, "American Factory Life—Past, Present and Future," *Journal of Social Science* 16 (1882): 141–46. Harriet Robinson's paper is in the same volume.

17. SL, 22 October 1882.

18. *Our Famous Women* (Hartford: Worthington, 1883). Thirty women were honored in this volume: Catherine Beecher, A. D. T. Whitney, Harriet Beecher Stowe, Harriet Prescott Spofford, Rose Terry Cooke, Clara Louise Kellog, Louise Chandler Moulton, Mary L. Booth, Mary A. Livermore, Clara Barton, Lucy Larcom, Margaret Fuller, Frances E. Willard, Mary Virginia Terhune (Marion Harland), Louisa May Alcott, Lucretia Mott, Anne Whitney, Elizabeth Prentiss, Lydia Maria Child, the Doctors Blackwell, Mary Mapes Dodge, Abby Hopper Gibbons, Maria Mitchell, Susan B. Anthony, Elizabeth Cady Stanton, Mary Clemmer, Charlotte Cushman, Elizabeth Stuart Phelps, Frances Hodgson Burnett, and Julia Ward Howe. Stowe, Cooke, Spofford, Phelps, Larcom, Whitney, Moulton, Clemmer, Livermore, Harland, Howe, and Stanton wrote sketches as well; other contributors were Kate Sanborn, Susan Coolidge, Lucia Gilbert Runkle, Laura Curtis Bullard, Lilian Whiting, Elizabeth T. Spring, Elizabeth Bryant Johnson, and Maud Howe. I would like to thank Roberta Kevelson for giving me a copy of this book.

19. Clarke Historical Library, Central Michigan University, 18 September 1883. The roads through the White Mountains are so good today that it is

difficult to imagine what they must have been like in Larcom's time. Even with good roads, the Notches, particularly Crawford's, can seem forbidding, and the road to the top of Mount Washington still needs careful driving.

20. HL, 2 November 1883.

21. Details of this financial arrangement are not clear, and are frequently confused with Whittier's successful securing of a pension of one hundred dollars a year for Larcom in 1887. Apparently he originally envisioned an annuity, then gave that idea up; Pitman questions him about the annuity that will "increase with time" (HL, 13 October 1883), and Larcom's letter of thanks suggests that she received a lump sum. The quotation marks around the word annuity in the letter directly thanking Whittier as well as her other comments make it clear that she was referring to the royalties from *Songs of Three Centuries*.

22. EI, 26 October 1883.

23. EI, 7 November [1883].

24. Samuel Eliot Morison, *One Boy's Boston* (Boston: Houghton Mifflin, 1962), p. 64, remembers his grandfather saying "that if ever a statue were erected to 'that rascal Butler' in the State House grounds, he would sell 44 Brimmer Street and move out of the Commonwealth."

25. *Portland Transcript*, 30 January 1884.

26. HL, 28 January 1884.

27. HL, 10 March 1884.

28. WL, 11 May 1884. The play was probably *Captain Mary Miller*, about a woman who became a riverboat captain.

29. HL, 25 June 1884.

30. BPL, 13 July 1884.

31. HL, 13 November 1884.

32. HL, 11 November 1884.

33. There is little information about Ellen M. Carpenter beyond what can be found in various references on American women artists and biographical encyclopedias, but she apparently was highly regarded. Larcom's interest in painting never faded; in fact, she added many artists to her list of friends during the last ten years of her life, and she continued her own pleasant if undistinguished painting. Wheaton College Library has several examples of her work.

34. To S. J. Spalding, HL, 7 October 1885.

35. EI, 13 April 1886.

36. HL, 22 March 1886.

37. Larcom's letters to her publishers are addressed to Frank Garrison, Azariah Smith, Horace Scudder, and Henry O. Houghton; they are politely determined and show her real interest in the whole book. They are also

rather amusing; she knew what she was doing. Most of these letters are in the Houghton Library.

38. HL, 29 June [1886].

39. HL, 4 September 1886.

40. HL, 8 September 1886.

Chapter Thirteen. "A Delight to Live in this World"

1. BL, 20 March 1892.

2. Richard Harmond, "The Time They Tried to Divide Beverly," *Essex Institute Historical Collections* 104 (1968): 19–33, is my chief source of information. There are newspaper clippings, broadsides, and handouts for public meetings in the Beverly Historical Society, as well as records of the testimony from many hearings. John Larcom's testimony comes from one of the handouts.

3. In talking about this annuity, Addison quotes the conversation in which Whittier persuaded Larcom to accept the money (*Life*, 234). Since he does not say how he happened to overhear their words, I do not give his report much credence.

4. HL, 22 April 1887.

5. To Miss Rantoul, BHS, 23 April 1887.

6. Much has been written about the decline of Boston toward the end of the century. See Martin Green, *The Problem of Boston* (New York: Norton, 1966); Henry Steele Commager, *The American Mind* (New Haven: Yale University Press, 1950); Van Wyck Brooks, *New England: Indian Summer* (New York: Dutton, 1940). For literary people the move of William Dean Howells from Boston to New York in 1889 seems to indicate the end of Boston's dominance.

7. SL, 20 December 1889.

8. SL, 8 March 1861.

9. Journal, 20 January 1861; quoted on p. 167.

10. The letter is quoted by Addison (*Life*, 283–85) who gives the date as 14 March 1893. By that date, however, Larcom was too ill to write this kind of letter. She could have seen either Dickinson's *Poems* (1890) or *Poems: Second Series* (1891), both edited by Mabel Todd Loomis and Thomas Wentworth Higginson (Boston: Roberts Brothers). A few poems had been published in magazines earlier, but internal evidence in the letter suggests that it was written in 1891.

11. SL, 4 May 1891.

12. See note 10; this passage is from the same letter.

13. James L. Onderdonk, *History of American Verse* (Chicago: McClurg, 1901), 203. Van Wyck Brooks calls her "one of the glowing moons of this mild planet" (the mild planet is Whittier) (*New England: Indian Summer*, 52).

14. J. B. Pickard, *Letters*, 17 December 1879, 3:413–14.

15. For a discussion of the pervasive influence of the older writers, see Leonard Lutwack, "The New England Hierarchy," *New England Quarterly* 28 (1955): 164–85. Lutwack points out that even critics and editors like Howells or Stedman, whose work was so different from the "greats," did not ever challenge their importance.

16. EI, 12 March 1888.

17. *Rushlight*, 107–10.

18. The comparison with Tennyson appears in James Grant Wilson, *Bryant and His Friends* (New York: Fords, Howard and Hulbert, 1886), 279, in a letter from Fitz-Greene Halleck to Bryant. He compares the "lady" and the "laureate."

19. A. D. T. Whitney, *Bonnyborough* (Boston: Houghton Mifflin, 1886).

20. E. C. Stedman, *The Poets of America* (Boston: Houghton Mifflin, 1885), 445.

21. EI, 26 January 1888.

22. I have not seen this work. A letter from Frances E. Willard to Larcom requesting her to write something for the temperance cause is in Wheaton College Library, dated 4 February 1886.

23. BPL, 27 December 1887.

24. To Elsie Locke, BPL, 4 December 1887.

25. To S. J. Spalding, BL, 20 August 1887.

26. WL, 5 January 1888.

27. Columbus Avenue and most of the South End areas in which Larcom lived are very different today. Nevertheless, it is still possible to see the handsome architecture under dirt, debris, and boarded-up windows.

28. Henry O. Houghton to Larcom, BL, 15 March 1888.

29. There are several letters from this correspondence; one, in the Beverly Public Library, held the leaves secured with a blob of sealing wax. Herbert Ward later married Elizabeth Stuart Phelps.

30. According to an account, probably from Ann Spaulding's granddaughter (undated fragment in the Beverly Public Library), Larcom had to sell her Monticello poem to get money to make the trip. I suspect the memory is confused; the poem she sold was probably "The Beckoning West." That Monticello had indeed changed is suggested from another source; the heroine of the popular novel *The Crisis*, by Winston Churchill (New York: Macmillan, 1901), attends Monticello. She is more given to flashing eyes and heaving bosom than intellect.

31. To Susan Hayes Ward, BHS, 30 June 1888.
32. EI, John Greenleaf Whittier Papers, 14 September 1888.
33. BPL, 9 January 1884.
34. HL, 5 August 1889.
35. HL, 21 November 1889.
36. *A New England Girlhood, Outlined from Memory* (Boston: Houghton Mifflin, 1889). The book has twice been reprinted: New York: Corinth Books, 1961, with an introduction by Charles T. Davis, as part of the American Experience Series; and Boston: Northeastern University Press, 1986, with an excellent foreword by Nancy F. Cott.
37. HL, 17 September 1884; quoted on p. 250.
38. From the draft of the autobiography in the Beverly Historical Society.
39. Larcom, *NEG*, 33.
40. The quoted passage from the *Atlantic* is part of an article called "Two New England Women"; the other section of the article reviews Ednah Dow Cheney's *Louisa May Alcott: Her Life, Letters, and Journals* (Boston: Roberts Brothers, 1889). There is no indication that Alcott and Larcom knew each other, although they undoubtedly did, but there is a signed photograph of Alcott among the Larcom papers in the Addison Collection, Massachusetts Historical Society.
41. SL, 10 February 1891.

Chapter Fourteen. Last Years

1. BL, 20 March 1892.
2. WL, 30 January 1892.
3. HL, 24 February 1892.
4. HL, 15 December 1891.
5. Addison (*Life*, 252–53), quotes the relevant passages from her journal at length.
6. SL, 10 November 1892.
7. SL, 28 August 1892.
8. Elizabeth Stuart Phelps, "The Bearer Falls," *Independent*, 4 May 1893. This is Larcom's obituary, but it begins by describing Whittier's funeral, and in presenting Larcom as the "bearer," again makes her an adjunct.
9. HL, 20 September 1892.
10. HL, 16 October 1892. She had written to Whittier's cousins at Oak Knoll, telling them of his promise that the mountain picture she had given him long ago was to be returned to her and the painting of Elizabeth was to remain in Amesbury as long as the house stayed in the family. At the time she wrote the quoted letter to Lizzie (October) she had received no answer.

11. HL, 11 November 1892.

12. HL, 21 November 1892.

13. HL, 5 January 1893.

14. SL, 10 November 1892.

15. SL, 12 January 1893.

16. Letter from Lucy Larcom Spaulding Clark to Daniel Dulany Addison (MHS, 16 May 1894). Addison wrote most of Larcom's close friends for information and letters; he does not seem to have asked Harriet Hanson Robinson. Another letter, whose date is not clear, indicates that George Spaulding objected to a description of him and that Addison changed the passage.

17. Lucy Spaulding to Elsie Locke, BPL, 11 April 1893.

18. Phillips Brooks, *Perfect Freedom* (Boston: Charles E. Brown, 1893).

19. Mount Larcom, a small and rather bosomy mountain, lies along Route 25 west of Mount Whittier in South Tamworth, New Hampshire.

20. MHS, 11 November 1893.

21. Justin Henry Shaw, "The Centenary of a New England Poet," *Boston Evening Transcript*, 8 March 1924.

Works by Lucy Larcom

"American Factory Life—Past, Present and Future." *Journal of Social Science* 16 (1882): 141–46.
"Among Lowell Mill-Girls." *Atlantic Monthly* 48 (1881): 593–612.
As It Is in Heaven. Boston: Houghton Mifflin, 1891.
At the Beautiful Gate. Boston: Houghton Mifflin, 1892.
Beckonings for Every Day. Boston: Houghton Mifflin, 1886.
Breathings of a Better Life. Boston: Fields, Osgood, 1866.
Childhood Songs. Boston: Osgood, 1875.
Child-Life. Ed. with J. G. Whittier. Boston: Osgood, 1871.
Child-Life in Prose. Ed. with J. G. Whittier. Boston: Osgood, 1873.
The Crystal Hills. Illus. F. Schuyler Mathews. Boston: Prang, 1889.
Easter Gleams. Boston: Houghton Mifflin, 1890.
Easter Messengers. New York: White, Stokes, and Allen, 1886.
Hillside and Seaside in Poetry. Ed. Boston: Osgood, 1877.
An Idyl of Work. Boston: Osgood, 1875.
"In the Ossipee Glens." *New England Magazine* (October 1892): 192–207.
Landscape in American Poetry. New York: D. Appleton, 1879.
Larcom's Poetical Works [also titled *Lucy Larcom's Poems*]. Boston: Houghton Mifflin, 1884.
Leila among the Mountains. Boston: Hoyt, 1861.
Lottie's Thought-Book. Philadelphia: American Sunday-School Union, 1858.
A New England Girlhood. Boston: Houghton Mifflin, 1889.
Poems. Boston: Fields, Osgood, 1868.
"Recollections of L. L." *Lowell Offering* (1845): 211–16, 220–23.
Roadside Poems for Summer Travellers. Ed. Boston: Osgood, 1876.
Semi-Centennial Sketch of Wheaton Seminary. Cambridge: Riverside Press, 1885.
Ships in the Mist, and Other Stories. Boston: Hoyt, 1860.
Similitudes, from the Ocean and Prairie. Boston: Jewett, 1853.
Songs of Three Centuries. Ed. with J. G. Whittier. Boston: Osgood, 1876.
The Unseen Friend. Boston: Houghton Mifflin, 1892.

Wild Roses of Cape Ann and Other Poems. Boston: Houghton Osgood,
1880.

Works Consulted

Abbot, William F. "The Genealogy of the Larcom Family." *Essex Institute
Historical Collections* 58 (1922): 41–48, 129–50.

Addison, Daniel Dulany. *Lucy Larcom: Life, Letters, and Diary.* Boston:
Houghton Mifflin, 1894.

Albright, Raymond W. *Focus on Infinity. A Life of Phillips Brooks.* New
York: Macmillan, 1961.

Alcott, Louisa May. *Rose in Bloom.* 1876. Reprint. New York: Grosset and
Dunlap, 1918.

Alger, William R. *The Friendships of Women.* Boston: Roberts Brothers,
1868.

Allen, Alexander V. G. *Life and Letters of Phillips Brooks.* New York: Dutton, 1900.

Allen, Gay Wilson. *American Prosody.* New York: American Book Company, 1935.

Altick, Richard D. *Lives and Letters.* New York: Knopf, 1965.

Amory, Cleveland. *The Proper Bostonians.* New York: Dutton, 1947.

Anderson, John, and Stearns Morse. *The Book of the White Mountains.* New
York: Minton, Balch, 1930.

Ardener, Shirley, ed. *Perceiving Women.* New York: Halstead Press, 1978.

"A $2.5 Million Find." *Newsweek,* 5 November 1979, 115–16.

Austin, James C. *Fields of the Atlantic Monthly.* San Marino, Calif.: Huntington Library Press, 1953.

Bacon, Edwin M. *Literary Pilgrimages in New England.* New York: Silver,
Burdett, 1902.

Bailey, Philip James. *Festus, A Poem.* London: Pickering, 1839. Reprint.
Boston: Mussey, 1845.

Ballou, Ellen B. *The Building of the House: Houghton, Mifflin's Formative
Years.* Boston: Houghton Mifflin, 1970.

Banner, Lois W. *American Beauty.* New York: Knopf, 1983.

———. "On Writing Women's History." *Journal of Interdisciplinary History*
2 (1971): 347–58.

Battis, Edward C. "The Brig *Mexican* of Salem, Captured by Pirates, and Her
Escape." *Essex Institute Historical Collections* 34 (1898): 41–63.

Baym, Nina. "Melodramas of Beset Manhood: How Theories of American
Fiction Exclude Women Authors." *American Quarterly* 33 (1981): 123–
39.

———. "Portrayal of Women in American Literature, 1790–1870." In *What*

Manner of Woman. Ed. Marlene Springer, 211–34. New York: New York University Press, 1977.

Beatty, Richmond Cromm. *Bayard Taylor, Laureate of the Gilded Age.* Norman: University of Oklahoma Press, 1936.

Beebe, Lucius. *Boston and the Boston Legend.* New York: Appleton-Century, 1935.

Bender, Thomas. *Toward an Urban Vision: Ideas and Institutions in Nineteenth Century America.* Lexington: University of Kentucky Press, 1975.

Bennett, Whitman. *Whittier, Bard of Freedom.* Chapel Hill: University of North Carolina Press, 1941.

Berg, Barbara. *The Remembered Gate: Origins of American Feminism.* New York: Oxford University Press, 1978.

Billington, Ray Allen. *Westward Expansion.* New York: Macmillan, 1967.

Birley, Robert. *Sunk without Trace. Some Forgotten Masterpieces Reconsidered.* London: Hart-Davis, 1962.

Blewett, Mary H. "'I am Doom to Disappointment': The Diaries of a Beverly, Massachusetts, Shoebinder, Sarah E. Trask, 1849–51." *Essex Institute Historical Collections* 117 (1981): 192–212.

Bode, Carl. *Anatomy of American Popular Culture.* Berkeley: University of California Press, 1959.

Bowen, Catherine Drinker. *Adventures of a Biographer.* Boston: Little, Brown, 1959.

––––––. *Yankee from Olympus.* Boston: Little, Brown, 1944.

Branch, E. Douglas. *The Sentimental Years. 1836–1860.* New York: Hill and Wang, 1934.

Brooks, George E., Jr. "A Salem Merchant at Cape Palmas, Liberia, in 1840." *Essex Institute Historical Collections* 98 (1962): 168–74.

Brooks, Phillips. *Perfect Freedom.* Boston: Brown, [1893].

Brooks, Van Wyck. *The Flowering of New England.* New York: World, 1946.

––––––. *New England: Indian Summer.* New York: World, 1946.

Burt, Helen. "Reminiscences of the Poet Whittier." *Bookman* 1 (1895): 230–34, 309–12.

Bushman, Claudia. *A Good Poor Man's Wife.* Hanover, N.H.: University Press of New England, 1981.

Cady, Edwin Harrison, and Harry Hayden Clark, eds. *Whittier on Writers and Writing.* Syracuse: Syracuse University Press, 1950.

"California Letters of William Goodridge of Beverly," *Essex Institute Historical Collections* 78 (1942): 376–86.

Carlson, Eric W., ed. *Emerson's Literary Criticism.* Lincoln: University of Nebraska Press, 1976.

Carpenter, George Rice. *John Greenleaf Whittier.* Boston: Houghton Mifflin, 1903.

Carrico, Joseph. "Log of the Barque *San Francisco.*" Beverly Historical Society.

Chambers-Schiller, Lee Virginia. *Liberty. A Better Husband.* New Haven: Yale University Press, 1984.

Cheney, Ednah Dow. *Reminiscences.* Boston: Lee and Shepard, 1902.

Chubb, Edwin Watts. *Stories of Authors.* New York: Macmillan, 1926.

Claflin, Mary B. *Personal Recollections of John Greenleaf Whittier.* New York: Crowell, 1893.

——. *Under the Old Elms.* New York: Crowell, 1895.

Clifford, James L. *Biography as an Art.* New York: Oxford University Press, 1962.

Commager, Henry Steele. *The American Mind.* New Haven: Yale University Press, 1950.

Congregational Year-Book. Boston: Congregational Sunday School and Publishing Society, 1897.

Coolidge, John. *Mill and Mansion. Architecture and Society in Lowell, Massachusetts, 1820–1865.* New York: Columbia University Press, 1942.

Cott, Nancy. *The Bonds of Womanhood.* New Haven: Yale University Press, 1977.

Crawford, Lucy. *Lucy Crawford's History of the White Mountains.* Ed. Stearns Morse. 1845, 1860, 1966. Reprint. Boston: Appalachian Mountain Club, 1978.

Crocker, George Glover. *From the Stagecoach to the Railroad Train and the Streetcar.* Boston: Clarke, 1900.

Currier, John J. *History of Newburyport, Mass., 1764–1905.* Newburyport, Mass.: Library of American Civilization, 1906.

Currier, Thomas F. *A Bibliography of John Greenleaf Whittier.* Cambridge: Harvard University Press, 1937.

Curtis, Harriot, and Harriet Farley, eds. *The Lowell Offering.* 5 vols. Lowell, Mass.: Powers and Bagley; Boston: Saxon and Peirce, and Jordan and Company, 1840–45. Reprint. Westport, Conn.: Greenwood Press, 1970.

Davis, David B. "Some Recent Directions in American Cultural History." *American Historical Review* (1968): 696–707.

Davis, Rebecca I. *Gleanings from Merrimac Valley.* Haverhill, Mass.: Chase Brothers, 1887.

Degler, Carl N. "What Ought to Be and What Was: Women's Sexuality in the Nineteenth Century." *American Historical Review* 79 (1974): 1467–90.

Diaz, Abby Morton. *A Domestic Problem. Work and Culture in the Household.* Boston: Osgood, 1875.

Dillon, Merton L. *The Abolitionists. The Growth of a Dissenting Minority.* New York: Norton, 1977.

Dodge, H. Augusta, ed. *Gail Hamilton's Life in Letters*. Boston: Lee and Shepherd, 1901.

Dolbee, Cora. "Kansas and 'The Prairied West' of John G. Whittier." *Essex Institute Historical Collections* 81 (1945): 306–47.

Douglas, Ann. *The Feminization of American Culture*. New York: Knopf, 1977.

————. "The 'Scribbling Women' and Fanny Fern: Why Women Wrote." *American Quarterly* 23 (1971): 3–24.

Dow, Mary Larcom. "Lucy Larcom—A Memory." Unpublished talk; copy in Beverly Historical Society.

————. *Old Days at Beverly Farms*. Beverly, Mass.: North Shore, 1921.

Dublin, Thomas. *Women at Work: The Transformation of Work and Community in Lowell, Massachusetts, 1826–1860*. New York: Columbia University Press, 1979.

Dubos, Rene, and Jean Dubos. *The White Plague: Tuberculosis, Man and Society*. Boston: Little, Brown, 1952.

Eisler, Benita. *The Lowell Offering*. New York: Lippincott, 1977.

Emerson, Ralph Waldo, ed. *Parnassus*. Boston: Osgood, 1874.

Ernest, Joseph M. "Whittier and the 'Feminine Fifties.'" *American Literature* 28 (1956–57): 184–96.

Farley, Harriet, ed. *The New England Offering*. 3 vols. Lowell, Mass.: Harris, 1848–50. Reprint. Westport, Conn.: Greenwood Press, 1970.

Farnham, Elizabeth. *Life in Prairie Land*. New York: Harper and Brothers, 1846.

Fields, Annie Adams. *Authors and Friends*. Boston: Houghton Mifflin, 1896.

————. Journal. Massachusetts Historical Society.

————. *Memoirs and Correspondence of James T. Fields*. London: Sampson Low, Marston, Searle and Rivington, 1881.

————. *Whittier: Notes of His Life and of His Friendships*. New York: Harpers, 1893.

Fields, James T. *Yesterdays with Authors*. Boston: Osgood, 1872.

Foner, Philip S. *The Factory Girls*. Chicago: University of Illinois Press, 1977.

Forbes, J. D. *Israel Thorndike, Federalist Financier*. New York: Exposition Press, 1953.

Fuller, Wayne E. *The Old Country School: The Story of Rural Education in the Middle West*. Chicago: University of Chicago Press, 1982.

Gilman, Arthur. "*Atlantic* Dinners and Diners." *Atlantic Monthly* 100 (1907): 646–57.

Goodrich, Carter, and Sol Davidson. "The Wage-Earner in the Western Movement." *Political Science Quarterly* 51 (1936): 61–116.

Gosse, Edmund. *Portraits and Sketches.* New York: Charles Scribner's Sons, 1914.

Green, Harvey. *The Light of the Home.* New York: Pantheon, 1983.

Green, Martin. *The Problem with Boston.* New York: Norton, 1966.

Griswold, Rufus W., ed. *Female Poets of America.* Philadelphia: Moss Brothers, 1850.

Grizzell, Emit Duncan. *Origin and Development of the High School in New England before 1865.* New York: Macmillan, 1932.

Guild, Curtis. *A Chat about Celebrities.* Lee and Shepard, 1897.

Hamilton, Gail [Mary Abigail Dodge]. *The Battle of the Books.* Boston: Hurd and Houghton, 1869.

————. *Country Living and Country Thinking.* Boston: Ticknor and Fields, 1862.

————. *A New Atmosphere.* Boston: Ticknor and Fields, 1863.

Harmond, Richard. "The Time They Tried to Divide Beverly." *Essex Institute Historical Collections* 104 (1968): 19–33.

Harrington, Edward. "The Letter-Book of Edward Harrington." *Essex Institute Collections.*

Hart, James D. *The Popular Book.* New York: Oxford University Press, 1950.

Higginson, Thomas Wentworth. *Cheerful Yesterdays.* Boston: Houghton Mifflin, 1899.

————. "Old Corner Bookstore." *Independent,* 10 September 1903.

————, and E. H. Bigelow, eds. *American Sonnets.* Boston: Houghton Mifflin, 1890.

History of Madison County, Illinois. Edwardsville, Ill.: Brink, 1882.

Hogeland, Ronald W. "'The Female Appendage': Feminine Life-Styles in America, 1820–1860." *Civil War History* 17 (1971): 101–14.

Holzman, Robert S. *Stormy Ben Butler.* New York: Macmillan, 1954.

Howard, Bret. *Boston: A Social History.* New York: Hawthorn, 1976.

Howe, M. A. DeWolfe. *The Atlantic Monthly and Its Makers.* Boston: Atlantic Monthly Press, 1919.

————. *Memories of a Hostess.* Boston: Atlantic Monthly Press, 1922.

Howe, Octavius Thorndike. *Argonauts of '49. History and Adventures of the Emigrant Companies from Massachusetts, 1849–1850.* Cambridge: Harvard University Press, 1923.

Howells, William Dean. *Literary Friends and Acquaintance.* New York: Harper and Brothers, 1900.

Huggins, Nathan Irwin. *Protestants against Poverty. Boston Charities, 1870–1900.* Westport, Conn.: Greenwood Press, 1971.

Humphrey, Frances A. *Stories about Favorite Authors.* Boston: Lothrop, 1885.

Hurd, D. Hamilton, ed. *History of Essex County.* 2 vols. Philadelphia: Lewis, 1882.

Jackson, Joseph. *Anybody's Gold.* San Francisco: Chronicle Books, 1970.

Jeffrey, Kirk. "Marriage, Career, and Feminine Ideology in Nineteenth-Century America: Reconstructing the Career of Lydia Maria Child, 1828–1874." *Feminist Studies* 2 (1975): 113–30.

Jones, Howard Mumford. "Literature and Orthodoxy in Boston after the Civil War." *American Quarterly* 1 (1949): 149–65.

Jones, Jacqueline. *Soldiers of Light and Love. Northern Teachers and Georgia Blacks, 1865–1873.* Chapel Hill: University of North Carolina Press, 1980.

Josephson, Hannah. *The Golden Threads.* New York: Duell, Sloan and Pearce, 1949.

Kaufman, Polly Welts. *Women Teachers on the Frontier.* New Haven: Yale University Press, 1984.

Kelley, Mary. *Private Woman, Public Stage.* New York: Oxford University Press, 1984.

Kessler, Carol Farley. *Elizabeth Stuart Phelps.* Boston: Twayne, 1982.

King, Thomas Starr. *The White Hills: Their Legends, Landscape, and Poetry.* Boston: Crosby, Nichols, 1860.

King's Handbook of Boston. 7th ed. Cambridge: King, 1885.

Kirkland, Caroline. *A New Home: Who'll Follow?* New York: Francis, 1839.

Kirkland, Edward Chase. *Men, Cities and Transportation: A Study in New England History, 1820–1900.* Cambridge: Harvard University Press, 1948.

Kribbs, Jayne K., ed. *Critical Essays on John Greenleaf Whittier.* Boston: Hall, 1980.

Laighton, Oscar. *Ninety Years at the Isles of Shoals.* Boston: Beacon Press, 1930.

Lapham, William B. *History of Bethel, Maine.* Augusta: Press of the *Maine Farmer*, 1891.

Lawrence, William. *Phillips Brooks.* Boston: Houghton Mifflin, 1903.

Layer, Robert G. *Earnings of Cotton Mill Operatives, 1825–1914.* Cambridge: Harvard University Press, 1955.

Longfellow, Henry Wadsworth, ed. *Poems of Places.* 31 vols. Boston: J. R. Osgood, 1876–79.

Loring, Katherine. *The Earliest Summer Residents of the North Shore and Their Houses.* Salem, Mass.: Essex Institute, 1932.

Lowell: A City of Spindles. Trades and Labor Council of Lowell. Lowell, Mass.: Lawler, 1900.

MacGill, Caroline E. *History of Transportation in the United States before*

1860. Carnegie Institute of Washington, Publication no. 215C. Washington, D.C.: Smith, 1948.

Mann, Dorothea. *A Century of Book Selling. The Story of the Old Corner Book Store on the Occasion of Its One Hundredth Birthday.* Boston: Old Corner Book Store. Privately printed. Reprinted from the *Boston Evening Transcript.*

Marble, Annie Russell. "Elizabeth Whittier and the Amesbury Home." *Outlook* 77 (1907): 29–35.

Marchalonis, Shirley, ed. *Patrons and Protégées: Gender, Friendship and Writing in Nineteenth-Century America.* New Brunswick, N.J.: Rutgers University Press, 1988.

Miles, Henry A. *Lowell, as It Was and as It Is.* Lowell: Dayton, Merriel and Heywood, 1846.

Minnigerode, Meade. *The Fabulous Forties, 1840–1850.* New York: Garden City, 1924.

Moore, Isabel. *Talks in a Library with Lawrence Hutton.* New York: Putnam's, 1905.

Mordell, Albert. *Quaker Militant: John Greenleaf Whittier.* Boston: Houghton Mifflin, 1933.

Morison, Samuel Eliot. *One Boy's Boston.* Boston: Houghton Mifflin, 1962.

Mott, Frank Luther. *Golden Multitudes.* New York: Macmillan, 1947.

——. *History of American Magazines.* 4 vols. Cambridge: Harvard University Press, Belknap Press, 1957.

Nash, Howard P., Jr. *Stormy Petrel: The Life and Times of General Benjamin F. Butler.* Rutherford, N.J.: Fairleigh Dickinson University Press, 1969.

Onderdonk, James L. *History of American Verse.* Chicago: McClurg, 1901.

Our Famous Women. Hartford: A. Worthington, 1883.

Palmer, George Herbert. *The Life of Alice Freeman Palmer.* Boston: Houghton Mifflin, 1908.

Pattee, Fred Lewis. *The Feminine Fifties.* New York: D. Appleton-Century, 1940.

Pearce, Roy Harvey. *The Continuity of American Poetry.* Princeton: Princeton University Press, 1961.

Penny, Anne Judith [Brown]. *The Afternoon of Unmarried Life.* New York: Rudd and Carleton, 1859.

Perry, Bliss. *Park Street Papers.* Boston: Houghton Mifflin, 1908.

Phelps, Elizabeth Stuart. "The Bearer Falls." *Independent,* 4 May 1893.

——. *Chapters from a Life.* Boston: Houghton Mifflin, 1896.

——. *Doctor Zay.* Boston: Houghton Mifflin, 1882.

Pickard, John B., ed. *The Letters of John Greenleaf Whittier.* 3 vols. Cambridge: Harvard University Press, 1975.

Pickard, Samuel T. *Life and Letters of John Greenleaf Whittier.* 2 vols. Boston: Houghton Mifflin, 1895.

_____. *Whittier-Land.* Boston: Houghton Mifflin, 1904.

Pollard, John A. *John Greenleaf Whittier, Friend of Man.* Boston: Houghton Mifflin, 1949.

Pond, Jean. *Bradford: A New England Academy.* Bradford, Mass.: Alumnae Association, 1930.

Pulsifer, Janice Goldsmith. "Gail Hamilton." *Essex Institute Historical Collections* 104 (1968): 165–216.

Rantoul, Robert [1778–1858]. "Autobiography." Beverly Historical Society.

Rantoul, Robert E., "Some Personal Reminiscences of the Poet Whittier." *Essex Institute Historical Collections* 37 (1901): 129–44.

Richardson, Joe M. *Christian Reconstruction. The American Missionary Association and Southern Blacks, 1861–1890.* Athens: University of Georgia Press, 1986.

Robertson, Frederick W. *Sermons.* Ed. Stopford A. Brooke. New York: Harper and Brothers, 1863.

Robinson, Harriet Hanson. *Captain Mary Miller.* Boston: Baker, 1887.

_____. Journal. Schlesinger Library, Radcliffe College.

_____. *Loom and Spindle.* New York: Crowell, 1898.

Rogers, Justus H. *Colusa County. Its History and Resources.* Orland, Calif., 1891.

Roller, Stephany. "Lucy Larcom. A Portrait of Nineteenth-Century America." Senior thesis, Wheaton College, 1962.

Rosenberg, Rosalind. *Beyond Separate Spheres.* New Haven: Yale University Press, 1982.

Rugoff, Milton. *The Beechers.* New York: Harper and Row, 1981.

Sanborn, Franklin B. *Recollections of Seventy Years.* Boston: Gorham Press, 1909.

Scudder, Horace. *Henry Oscar Houghton.* Boston: Houghton Mifflin, 1897.

Shackford, Martha H. *Whittier and the Cartlands: Letters and Comments.* Wakefield, Mass.: Montrose Press, 1950.

Shade, William G. "A Mental Passion: Female Sexuality in Victorian America." *International Journal of Women's Studies* 1 (1978): 13–29.

Shaw, Justin Henry. "Centenary of a New England Poet: Lucy Larcom." *Boston Evening Transcript,* 8 March 1924.

Sheehan, Donald Henry. *This Was Publishing. A Chronicle of the Book Trade in the Gilded Age.* Bloomington: Indiana University Press, 1952.

Shepard, Grace F. "Letters of Lucy Larcom to the Whittiers." *New England Quarterly* 3 (1930): 501–18.

Showalter, Elaine. *A Literature of Their Own.* Princeton: Princeton University Press, 1977.

———. "Feminist Criticism in the Wilderness." *Critical Inquiry* 8 (Winter 1981).

Smith, Emily Binney. *Whittier.* Amesbury: Whittier Press, 1935.

Smith, Henry Nash. "That Hideous Mistake of Poor Clemens's." *Harvard Library Bulletin* (Spring 1955): 145–80.

Smith-Rosenberg, Carroll. "The Female World of Love and Ritual: Relations between Women in Nineteenth-Century America." *Signs* 1 (1975): 1–29.

Spalding, Samuel J., ed. *The Spalding Memorial.* 2 vols. Boston: Mudge, 1872.

Sparhawk, Frances Campbell. *Whittier at Close Range.* Boston: Riverdale Press, 1925.

Spofford, Harriet Prescott. *A Little Book of Friends.* Boston: Little, Brown, 1916.

Stedman, E. C. *The Poets of America.* Boston: Houghton Mifflin, 1885.

Stillman, William J. *The Autobiography of a Journalist.* Boston: Houghton Mifflin, 1901.

Stone, Edwin M. *History of Beverly.* Boston: Munroe, 1843. Reprint. Salem, Mass.: Deschamps, for the Friends of the Beverly Public Library, 1975.

Strong, Helen P. *Memory's Sketchbook.* New York: Worthington, 1892.

Tassin, Algernon. *The Magazine in America.* New York: Dodd, Mead, 1916.

Taylor, William R., and Christopher Lasch. "Two Kindred Spirits: Sorority and Family in New England, 1839–1846." *New England Quarterly* 36 (1963): 23–41.

Thaxter, Celia. *Among the Isles of Shoals.* Boston: Osgood, 1873.

Thompson, Margaret. "Ben Butler versus the Brahmins: Patronage and Politics in Early Gilded Age Massachusetts." *New England Quarterly* (1982): 163–86.

Thyng, J. Warren. *Reminiscences of the Poet Whittier.* Manchester, N.H.: Granite State, 1908.

Ticknor, Caroline. *Glimpses of Authors.* 1922. Reprint. Freeport, N.Y.: Books for Libraries Press, 1972.

Trowbridge, John Townsend. *My Own Story.* Boston: Houghton Mifflin, 1903.

Tryon, Warren S. *Parnassus Corner. A Life of James T. Fields.* Boston: Houghton Mifflin, 1963.

———. and William Charvat. *The Cost Books of Ticknor and Fields.* New York: Bibliographical Society of America, 1949.

Vallier, Jane E. *Poet on Demand.* Camden: Down East Books, 1952.

Valuation and Assessments of the Town of Beverly for the Year 1886. Beverly, Mass.: Bates, 1886.

Wagenknecht, Edward. *Longfellow: A Full-Length Portrait.* New York: Longmans, Green, 1955.

———. *John Greenleaf Whittier: A Portrait in Paradox.* New York: Oxford University Press, 1967.

Waggoner, Hyatt H. *American Poets from the Puritans to the Present.* Boston: Houghton Mifflin, 1967.

Walker, Cheryl. *The Nightingale's Burden.* Bloomington: University of Indiana Press, 1982.

Walsh, Henry L. *Hallowed Were the Gold Dust Trails.* Santa Clara, Calif.: University of Santa Clara Press, 1946.

Ward, Susan Hayes, ed. *The Rushlight: Special Number in Memory of Lucy Larcom.* Trustees of Wheaton Seminary. Boston: Ellis, 1894.

Ware, Edith Ellen. "Political Opinion in Massachusetts during Civil War and Reconstruction." *Columbia Studies on History, Economics, and Public Law* 24, no. 2 (1916).

Warren, Robert Penn. *John Greenleaf Whittier's Poetry.* Minneapolis: University of Minnesota Press, 1971.

Weber, Carl. *The Rise and Fall of James Ripley Osgood.* Colby College Monograph no. 22. Waterville, Maine: Colby College Press, 1959.

Wells, Anna Mary. *Dear Preceptor: The Life and Times of Thomas Wentworth Higginson.* Boston: Houghton Mifflin, 1963.

Welter, Barbara. "Anti-Intellectualism and the American Woman." *Mid-America* 48 (1966): 258–70.

———. "The Cult of True Womanhood, 1820–1860." *American Quarterly* 18 (1966): 151–74.

———. *Dimity Convictions.* Athens: Ohio University Press, 1976.

Westbrook, Perry D. *Acres of Flint: Sarah Orne Jewett and Her Contemporaries.* Washington, D.C.: Scarecrow, 1951. Revised ed. 1981.

Whipple, Edwin. *American Literature and Other Papers.* Boston: Ticknor, 1887.

Whitehill, Walter Muir. *Boston: A Topographical History.* Cambridge: Harvard University Press, 1979.

Whitney, Adeline Dutton Train. *Bonnyborough.* Boston: Houghton Mifflin, 1886.

———. *The Other Girls.* Boston: Osgood, 1872.

———. *A Summer in Leslie Goldthwaite's Life.* Boston: Fields, Osgood, 1866. Reprint. Boston: Houghton Mifflin, 1894.

———. *White Memories.* Boston: Houghton Mifflin, 1894.

Whittier, John Greenleaf. *Legends of New England.* Boston: Carter, Hendee and Babcock, 1831.

———. *A Stranger in Lowell.* Boston: Waite, Peirce, 1845.

———. *Whittier's Complete Poetical Works.* Boston: Houghton Mifflin, 1894.

Wilson, James Grant. *Bryant and His Friends.* New York: Fords, Howard and Hulbert, 1886.

Winter, William. *Old Friends.* New York: Moffat, 1909.

Wolfe, Allis Rosenberg. "Letters of a Lowell Mill Girl and Friends: 1845–1846." *Labor History* 17 (June 1972): 96–102.

Woodwell, Roland H. "William Ashby of Newburyport and His Laurel Parties." *Essex Institute Historical Collections* 84 (1948): 15–28.

Wright, Carroll D. *The Working Girls of Boston.* Boston: Massachusetts Bureau of Statistics, 1889.

Wright, Catherine Morris. *Lady of the Silver Skates.* Jamestown, R.I.: Clingstone Press, 1979.

Zollo, Richard. "Oak Knoll—Whittier's Hermitage." *Essex Institute Historical Collections* 117 (1981): 27–42.

Robinson's, 190; Beverly Farms controversy, 236–38
Popularity: Larcom's, 3, 4–5, 117–18
Portland Transcript, 4, 186, 211, 213, 221, 237, 248
Powers, Hiram, 177
"Prairie Nest, A," 216
"Prairie Pastoral, A," (1849), 49
Prang, Louis, 197, 244
"Preacher, The" (Whittier), 125
Prescott, Harriet, 2, 170, 174–75, 215
Presidential mountain range, 206. *See also* White Mountains
Professor at the Breakfast Table, The (Holmes), 130
Progress of Religious Ideas, The (Child), 174
Prose poems, 86–87, 113, 130, 132
Pseudonymity: women writers', 4, 83; Larcom's, 49, 83, 87
Psyche Literary Society, 95, 243
Psychosomatic illness, 98, 99
Public Gardens (Boston), 197, 231
Public speaking: Larcom and, 196, 214
Publishers. *See* Fields, James T.; Osgood, James R.; *and names of specific publishers and publications*

Quebec, 238

"Real Folks" books (Whitney), 175
"Recollections of L. L." (1845), 266 (n. 1)
"Red Schoolhouse, The" (1876), 164
"Re-Enlisted" (1864), 151
Religion and religious beliefs, 6–7, 16, 66, 74–75, 97, 110–12, 166, 209–10; in Larcom's writings, 2, 87, 110, 216, 242; afterlife, 71; God, 85, 111–12, 129. *See also* Church attendance; Trinity Church
Religious poems, 110, 216, 242

Remmonds, Thomas, 58
Renaud, Alphonse, 124
Republican party, 89, 103
Rheumatism, 158, 161, 167
Richardson, C. A., 109
Richardson, Henry Hobson, 209
Richter, Jean Paul, 87
Riverside Library for Young People, The, 246–47
Riverside Press, 219. *See also* Hurd and Houghton
Roadside Poems for Summer Travellers (1876), 204
Roberts Bros., 254
Robinson, Harriet Jane Hanson, 130, 181, 224, 262; friendship with Larcom, 6, 84, 90, 105, 150, 170, 177; writings on mills, 26–27, 226, 257; feminist activities, 9, 179–80, 249; on *Lowell Offering*, 34–35; marriage, 84, 158, 190; Larcom's letters to, 122; death of son, 130; widowed, 203; memorial to husband, 211; verse play, 230–31
Robinson, Hattie. *See* Robinson, Harriet Jane Hanson
Robinson, William S., 137, 185, 190, 210, 211; editor, 83, 90, 168; and Larcom, 83–84, 90, 144, 177; marriage, 84, 158, 190; "Warrington" articles, 109, 134, 190; and women's rights, 180; death, 203
"Rose Enthroned, The" (1861), 137, 138–39, 168, 244
Round Table, 168
"Rover, Ruth," 49, 83
Royalties: for anthologies, 188, 195, 203, 229; for poetry collection, 166
"Rumors of Peace" (1848), 50
Rushlight, The, 95, 243, 262–63, 270 (n. 1)

St. Nicholas, 188, 204, 213, 226
Salem Register, 47, 49